To Bob,

Much Love.
Happy Birthday

Marina

Mapplethorpe

A Biography

Mapplethorpe

A Biography

PATRICIA MORRISROE

MACMILLAN

First published 1995 by Random House Inc., and simultaneously
in Canada by Random House of Canada Limited, Toronto.

First published in Great Britain 1995 by Macmillan
an imprint of Macmillan General Books
25 Eccleston Place London SW1W 9NF and Basingstoke

Associated companies throughout the world

ISBN 0 333 57220 X

Grateful acknowledgement is made to the following for permission to reprint previously
published material:

W.W. Norton & Company Inc., and Patti Smith: Excerpts from "jeanne d'arc","babelogue", "piss factory" and "oath" from *Early Work: 1970–1979* by Patti Smith. Copyright ©
1994 by Patti Smith. Reprinted by permission of W.W. Norton & Company Inc., and Patti
Smith.

Screw Magazine: Brief excerpts from "Review of Sex in the News" by Gil Reavill (April
18, 1983). Copyright © Milky Way Productions Inc., *Screw Magazine*. Reprinted by
permission.

Patti Smith: Excerpt from "Land", by Patti Smith. Copyright © Linda Music. Excerpts from
"Sister Morphine" and "Female" by Patti Smith. Copyright © 1978 by Patti Smith.
Reprinted by permission of Patti Smith.

Tickson Music: Three lines from "So You Want to Be a Rock 'n' Roll Star" by Jim McGuinn
and Chris Hillman. Copyright © 1966, 1967 by Tickson Music (BMI). International copyright secured. All rights reserved. Reprinted by permission.

The Village Voice: Excerpt from "Pretty Poison: The Selling of Sexual Warfare" by Karen
Durbin (May 9, 1977). Reprinted by permission of the author and *The Village Voice*.

Edmund White: Excerpt from the Introduction by Edmund White to the catalogue for the
"Black Males" exhibit at Galerie Jurka. Copyright © 1980 by Edmund White. Reprinted by
permission.

1 3 5 7 9 8 6 4 2

A CIP catalogue record for this book is available from the British Library

Printed and bound in Great Britain by Mackays of Chatham plc, Chatham, Kent

For Lee

Contents

List of Illustrations

Author's Note

I first met Robert Mapplethorpe in 1983, when I received an unexpected call from photography dealer James Danziger, who was then picture editor of the London *Sunday Times Magazine*. Danziger was editing a special issue on photography and wanted someone to write a profile of Mapplethorpe to coincide with the opening of the photographer's retrospective at the Institute of Contemporary Art. I confessed I'd never heard of Robert Mapplethorpe, but Danziger was on a tight deadline and persuaded me to write the piece.

The following day I took a cab to Mapplethorpe's loft at 24 Bond Street in Manhattan, where a junkie was sprawled on the sidewalk, a needle dangling from his arm. I had to step over the man to reach the front door of Mapplethorpe's building, as if crossing a boundary to a place I wasn't sure I wanted to go. A creaking freight elevator took me up to the photographer's loft, which was decorated with Arts and Crafts pottery and devil statues. In the center of the living room was a huge chicken-wire cage that contained a mattress covered in black satin sheets. Opposite the cage, Mapplethorpe was sitting in a black-leather-upholstered chair, his legs drawn up around him. He was handsome in a dissolute way, with piercing green eyes and white skin tinged with blue. He spoke in a soft voice and seemed intent on creating an aura of mystery that precluded any discussion of his early family life in Floral Park, Queens. His relationship with the poet-performer Patti Smith was off-limits, too. Instead, he handed me a portfolio of graphic sex pictures, and watched as I flipped through them.

I knew Mapplethorpe was waiting for a reaction, but what was the appropriate response? The situations were so alien to me that the images barely registered on my brain. Yet something about the photographs triggered memories of crucifixion scenes, and I asked him, "Did you grow up Catholic?" Mapplethorpe warmed up immediately and showed me one of his latest pictures, of a black man wearing a metal crown of thorns. "I guess you could say I have a certain Catholic aesthetic," he explained. I was relieved to discover some common ground, although I realized it would take more than two hours to understand how a middle-class Catholic boy from the borough of Queens became the documentarian of the gay S&M scene. "My life," he promised, "is even more interesting than my photographs."

Mapplethorpe was then only thirty-six—too young, in some ways, for a biography—and I didn't think much about him for the next several years. Then AIDS wreaked havoc with the notion of the "average" life span; people were dying at the peak of their careers, and the illness tragically mimicked the deterioration of old age. I'd heard rumors that Mapplethorpe had AIDS, but I didn't approach him about writing his biography until August 1988. By then he had been acclaimed as the greatest studio photographer of his generation, and a pivotal figure in elevating photography's status in the art world. A controversial retrospective of his work at the Whitney Museum of American Art had opened two months earlier, and the exhibit would become one of the most highly attended events in the museum's history.

Sadly, Mapplethorpe faced the painful realization that he was finally achieving everything he had ever wanted at a time when he was

most likely going to die. He had already set up the Robert Mapplethorpe Foundation to ensure his posthumous fame, and he was
eager for someone to start working on a book about him while he
still had the energy to tell his story.

Mapplethorpe had moved to a more elegant loft since our first
encounter, and despite his illness he usually dressed up for our meetings, in black velvet pants and matching cashmere sweater. His
green eyes were still vibrant, but he looked like a man in his eighties,
and he punctuated his sentences with an agonizing cough. I interviewed him a total of sixteen times until a month before his death on
March 9, 1989; I never knew from one interview to the next
whether I'd see him again. Mapplethorpe didn't enjoy talking about
himself, yet he was extremely candid about things most people keep
secret. One afternoon, after smoking a joint, he began outlining his
sexual life in vivid detail; he didn't stop even after his nurse placed
him in bed and hooked him up to an intravenous tube. The situation reminded me of Anne Rice's *Interview with the Vampire,* for
Mapplethorpe painted himself as a creature of the night—"a sex
demon"—who had no control over his voracious appetite.

The photographer wasn't apologetic about his sexual obsessions;
in fact, his biggest regret was that he wouldn't reap the benefits of
his celebrity. Ironically, he would become even more famous after
his death, when the Corcoran Gallery of Art in Washington, D.C.,
abruptly canceled a retrospective of his work. Mapplethorpe's "The
Perfect Moment" exhibit had been partly funded by the National
Endowment for the Arts, and the Corcoran's decision to cancel the
show in June 1989 ignited a fierce debate over federal financing of
sexually explicit art. U.S. Senator Jesse Helms of North Carolina
accused him of "promoting homosexuality" and described his
wife's reaction at seeing "The Perfect Moment" catalogue as "Lord
have mercy, Jesse, I'm not believing this. . . ." A year later, when the
exhibit arrived at the Contemporary Arts Center in Cincinnati, director Dennis Barrie was charged with pandering obscenity and misuse of a minor in pornography. The Cincinnati trial became a test
case for current standards of obscenity, and Mapplethorpe would go
down in history as a symbol of artistic freedom or, depending upon
one's viewpoint, "deviant art."

While Mapplethorpe's name was on the front pages of newspapers across the country, I was tracing his life backward in time. I'd supposed that gathering information about a contemporary figure would be easier than tackling a biography of someone long deceased, but Mapplethorpe's world had already receded into the past. AIDS had silenced many of the witnesses, and his pictures of the gay S&M subculture had become relics of a lost civilization.

Eventually I found several hundred people who knew Robert Mapplethorpe in all his various incarnations—Catholic schoolboy; ROTC cadet; hippie; sexual explorer; celebrated artist; and famous AIDS victim. Their stories helped animate his pictures and bring his visual diary to life. What I discovered wasn't one "Perfect Moment" but a series of moments—some pure, some blemished, but all emblematic of the paradoxical times in which he lived.

Mapplethorpe was obsessed by male beauty, but his most enduring relationship was with the female rocker Patti Smith. He worshiped black men, but he denigrated them with racial epithets. He became famous for the liberating frankness of his gay S&M pictures, but he was petrified that his parents would discover he was homosexual. He was a master of black-and-white photography, but ultimately there wasn't anything black and white about him at all. His life was all dusky and gray and morally ambiguous, and his death signaled the twilight of an era.

Mapplethorpe

A Biography

PROLOGUE

A pair of black limousines traveled thirteen miles east from Manhattan on Union Turnpike, past fur salons selling fluffy rabbit coats, past Chinese restaurants, Irish bars, bagel shops, and beauty parlors with the Breck Girl still featured in the window. The cars turned right at a Woolworth's in Floral Park, Queens, and headed down 258th Street toward an ugly orange-brick building emblazoned with the words COME WORSHIP WITH US. Robert Mapplethorpe's former assistant, Brian English, whipped off his sunglasses to get a better look at the church where Mapplethorpe's family worshiped, and where the artist's funeral was about to begin. "This," he said, "is very weird."

Our Lady of the Snows had been conceived originally as a gymnasium, but with the addition of an altar and pews it had been transformed into a Catholic church. Except for the chrome cross and the faux stained-glass windows, its all-purpose architecture was reminiscent of a Howard Johnson's. It seemed the last place that Mapplethorpe, whose *New York Times* obituary portrayed him as an aesthete of rare and exquisite taste, might want his funeral to be held.

Mapplethorpe had given his friends and colleagues virtually no clues to his past. It wasn't until they arrived in Floral Park that they began to understand where he had come from, and why he had left. Mapplethorpe's artistic credo had always been to "see things like they've never been seen before," but there was nothing about this church, or its surroundings, that would lend itself to creative alchemy. "Robert deserved a cathedral, with beautiful spires and real stained glass," said his friend Amy Sullivan, who had traveled to Queens for the funeral. So had his lawyer Michael Stout, stylist Dimitri Levas, editor and writer Ingrid Sischy, photographer Lynn Davis, and several Mapplethorpe employees.

The previous evening, a memorial service had been held for Mapplethorpe at Da Silvano, an Italian restaurant in Greenwich Village. Ingrid Sischy, who was seated at a table with the artists Brice Marden and Francesco Clemente, had praised Mapplethorpe for his "incredible honesty," reiterating a theme from an earlier essay in which she had commended him for creating "work that is ultimately about no coverup, no censorship, no shameful secrets." It was difficult for Mapplethorpe's friends to think of Floral Park as anything but a land of shameful secrets, for the landscape confirmed every cliché of middle-class narrow-mindedness. "Wherever Robert is," said Brian English, "it's got to be better than this."

The Manhattan contingent waited outside the church until the organist struck up the first chord of what would be several hymns, along with "Morning Has Broken," a song written by the seventies pop star Cat Stevens, now a radical Muslim who would soon be calling for Salman Rushdie's death. A few minutes later the priest, a gray-haired man in his late fifties, stepped in front of a simple white altar. A swath of purple fabric hung on the wall to commemorate Lent, the season of penitence and spiritual preparation for the death and resurrection of Christ. Midway through the Mass, the priest moved to the lectern to say a few words about the deceased photographer, and Mapplethorpe's friends steeled themselves for the worst.

"There is a dark side to the human soul that is filled with conflict and torment. It is a side of the human soul that few people are brave enough to explore. Some poets, like Baudelaire, Mallarmé, and Blake, have tried. The novelist Joseph Conrad in *Heart of Darkness* presented Marlowe and Mr. Kurtz looking around at the chaos and devastation they saw and exclaiming four words, 'The horror, the horror!' "

Harry Mapplethorpe, Robert's father, had loaded a wheelchair and oxygen tank into his Buick Skylark, then smoked the third cigarette of the morning as he waited for his wife, Joan, to finish dressing for the funeral. He had once been a handsome man, but the family's recent misfortunes had taken a toll on him, and his face had hardened into an expressionless mask. Until his retirement at Underwriters Laboratories in 1980, he had spent his career examining the insides of electrical appliances to see if they passed safety regulations. He applied the same cautious standards to his own life: he was the first person on 259th Street to equip his home with fire and burglar alarms, and for nearly half a century he had succeeded in creating a safe haven for himself. Then, in 1985, Joan spent five months in intensive care battling emphysema; in 1986 his favorite son, Richard, suddenly died of lung and brain cancer; and three years later Robert was dead of AIDS.

Harry helped Joan into the car, and they drove up the block to Our Lady of the Snows, where they saw two black limousines conspicuously parked in front of the church. The Mapplethorpes wondered who was inside, for they had never met any of Robert's friends, and they were almost afraid to. Their son had been a complete mystery to them, and the more they knew about him, the more enigmatic he became. For years Joan had mistakenly thought Robert had been married to the punk rock singer and poet Patti Smith; she had only recently learned of his homosexuality. She still didn't completely believe it, even after she saw a retrospective of his work at the Whitney Museum of American Art, where photographs of the gay S&M subculture provided a salient clue. She had wanted to ask her son if the pictures reflected his own sexuality, and why he had felt the need to photograph himself with a whip inserted in a private place; but some things, Joan thought, were perhaps better left unsaid.

Harry wheeled Joan into the church, which was painted a Santa Fe peach color and decorated with homemade religious art. They took their seats in the front pew next to their four remaining children and eight grandchildren. Joan was pleased that so many of her friends from the Rosary Society and her bowling league had made the effort to attend, but most of all she was happy that Father George Stack had agreed to officiate at the Mass. Several months before Robert's death, she had sent the priest to see Robert in case her son needed spiritual guidance. Her own faith in God had helped her through difficult times, but what of Robert? What of his soul?

> "The last time I spoke with Robert he said he tried to present what he saw as beautiful in the most truthful way possible. He also believed in trying to be a good person, compassionate and generous. Later on, I realized that these qualities of which Robert spoke were traditionally attributes that the philosophers and theologians apply to God. In a very real sense, I believe that Robert was in his own way searching for God. . . ."

Father George Stack drove from Brooklyn to Our Lady of the Snows Church in Floral Park, Queens, where, twenty-five years earlier, he had first served as a parish priest. He was returning to "Snows," as the locals called it, as a favor to Joan Mapplethorpe. Robert had once been a member of the Catholic youth group he supervised, and the priest remembered him as a shy adolescent whose passion for art had set him apart from the other teenage boys. Robert would often drop by the rectory to show the priest his drawings—portraits of the Madonna mostly, sometimes with the baby Jesus in her arms. Over the years, Father Stack had lost touch with Robert, and from the little he knew of his homoerotic photographs, he suspected they wouldn't have had much in common. But then, in November 1988, Joan Mapplethorpe asked him if he would visit her son. "Father, he has AIDS," she confided, "and I want him to die in a state of grace."

The two men spent an afternoon talking to each other, after which Robert had asked the priest to come back one day; but then the photographer died on March 9, and the priest now found himself wondering what he could possibly say about him. *"No one who comes to me will I ever reject.*" These words of Jesus in the Gospels had always been a special comfort to Father Stack, and he usually included the phrase in his funeral homily. Yet the standard homily didn't apply in this case, for Mapplethorpe wasn't an upstanding member of the community, a responsible family man, or a good Catholic. In fact, by all the traditional standards of the Catholic Church he was a paragon of sinfulness.

Father Stack dressed for the Mass by layering his silk and linen vestments over his chest, until he was covered in luminous white. The priest kept thinking about Conrad's *Heart of Darkness,* and "the fascination of the abomination." He knew Mapplethorpe took pictures of gay sadomasochistic acts, but that the photographer off-set these by also photographing exquisitely beautiful flowers. Weren't Mapplethorpe's lilies, then, a symbol of resurrection?

> "We need to believe in a God who is good and gracious and merciful, especially in the dark moments of life. 'No one who comes to me will I ever reject.' Because of that promise we trust that when Robert went through the gates of death and stood before the judgment seat of God, Jesus opened His arms and welcomed Robert home."

Harry and Joan had invited everyone back to their house for coffee and donuts, and a line of American-made cars, plus two limousines, formed a procession down 258th Street. Traditionally, a burial service followed a Catholic funeral, but in accordance with Robert's wishes he had been cremated. A perfectionist about every detail of his life except the last one, he hadn't specified where he wanted his ashes scattered, with the result that Michael Stout, the executor of his estate, had no idea what to do with them. Joan hoped her son's remains would be returned to Queens so that at least in death he wouldn't be lost to his family. But now that he was finally gone, she still didn't know how to get him back.

PART ONE

Dark Secrets

CHAPTER ONE

"I got that feeling in my stomach, it's not a directly sexual
one, it's something more potent than that. I thought that if I
could somehow bring that element into art, if I could
somehow retain that feeling, I would be doing something
that was uniquely my own."

—*Robert Mapplethorpe*

Harry Mapplethorpe craved the ordinary the way others
lust for the strange and exotic. He wanted a life without any emotional highs or lows and never imagined that his biography would
warrant more than a line or two on the obituary page of the local
newspaper. "Nothing much happened," Harry said, without a trace
of regret. "It was perfectly normal." He grew up in Hollis, Queens,
the only child of a middle-level bank executive whose name was also
Harry, and whose parents came to New York from England. The
elder Harry hated his job at National City Bank, but nevertheless
stayed there for fifty years because he cherished the routine—he
worked from nine to five Mondays through Fridays, then spent
every weekend attending to his coin and stamp collections.

The younger Harry remembered his German mother, Adelphine
Zang, as someone who never read a newspaper without donning
gloves and draping a tea towel over her lap. "She was an immaculate

housekeeper," he said. There were no other Mapplethorpe children, so Harry, taking a cue from his father, devoted his free time to his own hobbies—target shooting and photography. The description under Harry's picture in the 1937 Jamaica High School yearbook provides a concise summary of his personality: "A straight shooter." His son Robert would turn out to be a straight shooter, too; perhaps not as sexually straight as Harry would have liked, but rigorous in his photographic technique. He was his father's boy in more ways than either of them cared to admit, but where Robert would transgress boundaries, Harry derived comfort from them.

By the time Harry was sixteen he had already met his future bride at a neighbor's graduation party. Joan Maxey was perfect for him: she lived only a few blocks away; she, too, was Catholic, of Irish and English descent; and her father, an engineer for Bell Telephone Laboratories, had raised her solidly middle-class. The young couple even looked alike: they both had brown wavy hair, fair skin, light eyes, and slight builds, and people sometimes mistook them for brother and sister.

In 1937 Harry enrolled in the engineering school at Pratt Institute in Brooklyn, where he commuted from home every day and saw Joan nearly every night. They were married on June 20, 1942, six months after the Japanese bombed Pearl Harbor, and moved from their parents' homes into a three-room apartment in nearby Jamaica Estates. Harry was deferred from active duty because of his job as a field engineer for a naval architecture firm, and unlike many of their young married friends, they weren't separated during the early years of the war. They had two children in quick succession: first Nancy in April 1943, then Richard in March 1945, after which Harry was transferred to Washington, D.C.—a situation he described as a living nightmare. Without Joan to anchor him, he felt lost in Washington, and every day after work he returned to his rooming house lonely and depressed. The minute the war was officially declared over—VJ Day, August 25, 1945—Harry submitted his resignation to the Defense Department and packed his bags for Queens. He considered it the most reckless move of his life, for he didn't have another job lined up and had little savings. But within days of his homecoming he had procured a position at Underwriters Laboratories. He knew with the certainty of a man who valued continuity over change that it was truly the job of a lifetime.

Robert Michael Mapplethorpe was born on November 4, 1946, at Irwin Sanitarium in Hollis. Harry had few memories of his son's birth and toddler years, but Joan felt an immediate attraction to her third child, who, from the moment he came into the world, expressed his dissatisfaction with it by screaming louder than any baby she had ever heard. He soon developed a reputation as "the fussy Mapplethorpe." Joan understood that mothers weren't supposed to prefer one child over the others, but Robert was her favorite. What she remembered about him, however, was colored with an Addams Family ghoulishness, such as the time he killed his turtle, Greenie, by impaling the pet on his index finger. She didn't know what it meant, nor did she know why, among the hundreds of other possible stories, she chose to define her son's early years by that one. But whenever she thought about two-year-old Robert, she thought about Greenie.

Joan's fourth child, Susan, was delivered in August 1949, and several months later the Mapplethorpes purchased their first and only home, at 83-12 259th Street in Floral Park, Queens. The World War II community had been built almost overnight to accommodate the housing demands of returning veterans, and acres of potato fields began sprouting nearly identical Cape Cod bungalows. The Mapplethorpes' white house looked like every other white house on the street; it had four small bedrooms and a bay window overlooking a single tree. Harry and Joan didn't have to worry about the grass being greener on somebody else's lawn, because everyone on the block moved in at the same time and watched the grass grow together; they shared lawn equipment and garden tools; warned one another's children to keep off the virgin turf; and later celebrated the greening of 259th Street with barbecues and plastic-pool parties. The neighborhood was so saturated in 1950s conformity that when one family painted the cupola of their house green instead of the standard white, they were chastised for breaking protocol.

There was one aspect of Floral Park, however, that made it truly unique; it was a place that didn't exist—at least in the eyes of New York City officials, whose vision turned myopic when it came to confronting the problems of a neighborhood on the city's eastern border. Residents nicknamed Floral Park the "Lost Community," and banded together to petition the appropriate city agencies for better sanitation services, police protection, and storm sewers; but for years no one paid attention to them. Garbage piled up in towering heaps; sewers overflowed when it rained; the poorly paved roads grew more pitted and bumpy. In addition to the abuse it received from the city, the area had to endure the humiliation of being constantly compared to its more affluent next-door neighbor—Floral Park, Long Island. That Floral Park didn't have to rely on the city for its services, so it had all the amenities the other one lacked, and since it was established in 1920, it was considered the legitimate one as opposed to its lost relative on the other side of the "tracks."

Robert's parents were oblivious to the implications of living in the "Lost Community," for, having paid $11,490 for their house, they were more concerned with meeting the mortgage. Harry was one of the few white-collar professionals in a blue-collar neighborhood and the only person among their clique of local friends to have an advanced degree. Yet even as a "college man" he didn't earn substantially more than the other husbands, and after putting the down payment on the house, he couldn't afford a car and commuted an hour and twenty minutes each way by bus and subway to Underwriters Laboratories in Manhattan. When Harry got home at night he wanted to eat dinner, maybe watch *Dragnet* or *The Jackie Gleason Show,* and retire to bed. Weekends were reserved for hobbies, and Harry had a wide variety of them, from collecting stamps and coins to building cuckoo clocks and raising tropical fish. The unifying thread that ran through all of Harry's endeavors was that he could do them alone and maintain complete control. Even when he took pictures of his family he derived the greatest pleasure not from interacting with his subjects, but from developing the prints himself. It was the technical challenge he enjoyed, not the so-called "creative" part.

People in the neighborhood admired Harry for his ability to fix broken vacuum cleaners and Mix-Masters, but they adored Joan for her warm, outgoing personality. She loved to play cards, to go bowling with her Tuesday night league, and to get together for "club meetings" with several female friends. The meetings were the 1950s version of consciousness-raising sessions, and over coffee and pastries the women would make little jokes about their husbands' annoying habits, or complain about the mess the children had created. No one ever delved too deeply, but it was a congenial way for them to air their domestic frustrations. Joan always seemed perfectly content, however, and while she had a biting sense of humor, it was rarely aimed at her husband. Pat Farre, who lived two doors away from the Mapplethorpes and was a member of the "club," never heard Joan utter a bad word about Harry in forty years.

"The first time I went over to Joan's house," Farre said, "I was so impressed. She had these four little tots, and they were all washed, their faces scrubbed shiny clean, and they were sitting nicely on the couch. She had an apron on, and she was preparing dinner, and it was just so perfect. Joan was the heart of that family. Harry was very reliable, but Joan was the creative one; she'd write little poems and always had clever things to say. People really loved her."

Yet there was a more complicated side to Joan that wasn't immediately apparent because it manifested itself in the one area for which she earned the highest marks. She was a fanatical housekeeper and often cleaned to the point of exhaustion. Certainly Harry liked a tidy house—he had been raised by a fastidious woman and was so orderly himself that he arranged each item in the refrigerator according to shape and size—but Joan surpassed even his expectations. "It was like someone had pressed a panic button," Joan explained. "I didn't care what time it was. If the floors needed to be scrubbed, I'd do it, even if it was two in the morning." Several decades later, Joan would seek psychiatric help after suffering a serious bout of depression, and it was only then, according to her daughter Nancy, that she was diagnosed as a manic-depressive. At the time, however, Joan was an inspiration to the other women in the neighborhood. "At Christmas, I never saw anything like it," Pat Farre said. "Joan raced around baking cookies, and she'd make two different kinds of fruitcakes because her mother and mother-in-law had given her recipes and she didn't want to alienate either of them. Then she'd be rushing around wrapping all the presents and putting them under the tree. She really kept a beautiful house, though I did notice that Joan always had a little tremble; you could see it in her hands." Joan's penchant for chain-smoking cigarettes made the nervous flutter even more obvious. Both she and Harry were heavy smokers—he often smoked two cigarettes at once—but since Joan suffered from asthma, and later emphysema, the consequences of her habit were more significant. "I think she was an addictive personality," Farre observed. "She quit smoking for a while, but then went right back to it. Sometimes she would have such a fit of coughing you'd think she was going to choke to death. The kids reeked of nicotine."

In 1954 Joan's mother died of lung cancer at the age of fifty-five, and although the Mapplethorpes' small house could barely accommodate their current family, Joan invited her diabetic father, James Maxey, to live with them. Reluctantly, he moved upstairs to the Mapplethorpes' attic, where he paid for the renovation of a fourth bedroom next to the one eight-year-old Robert shared with ten-year-old Richard. (The two girls, Nancy and Susan, occupied a bedroom downstairs opposite their parents.) James Maxey was not a doting grandfather; having lost his wife and his privacy, he was often cranky and irritable, and his grandchildren resented the demands he placed on their mother's scattered attention. Joan was always worried about him, for he was dependent on insulin and needed to eat special meals to stabilize the level of glucose in his system. "A couple of times her father went into shock," Pat Farre recalled, "and that really scared her. Once he came to live with them, Joan couldn't just give him a TV dinner; she had to cook special foods, and everything became so overwhelming to her."

Daily life was such a challenge for Joan that she couldn't provide her favorite child, Robert, with the individual attention he craved. Intuitively she understood that Robert was unique, and of all her children she thought he would be the one to distinguish himself, yet he was never singled out for extra encouragement or praise. Robert grew up in the shadow of his older brother, Richard, who spent so much time playing outdoors he seemed to have a permanent suntan. Pat Farre considered Richard one of the handsomest children she had ever seen, as opposed to Robert, who had been a cute toddler—"pretty enough to be a girl," said Farre—but who had matured into a gawky young boy. He was much smaller and scrawnier than Richard, and while he had inherited the Mapplethorpes' most striking physical trait—beautiful eyes, which, in his case, were a dusky green color—he had big ears, unruly brown hair, and legs so thin that Joan had to take in all his pants on her sewing machine. She called him her "skinny willy," and indeed he showed no interest in food except as a weapon of war. The dinner table became the battleground on which Robert and Harry waged their most bitter fights.

Both father and son had extremely poor appetites, and Harry could not wait for the day science developed a pill to do away with food entirely. Nevertheless, he felt duty-bound to clean his plate and he expected his children to follow his example. Sometimes Robert would dispose of his meals by initiating food fights; he would load peas onto his knife and flick the green pellets at his siblings until an exasperated Harry would come as close as he ever did to swearing by shouting, "Jingo Netties! That's enough!" Usually Robert would be sent to his room, where in one instance he kicked the bedroom door with the heels of his shoes for two hours before Joan finally went upstairs to calm him down. Richard had a healthy appetite, so he was not affected by the clean-plate edict, but Robert was ordered to eat everything, and if he procrastinated he had to sit at the table until he finished. Such scenes were, and are, regularly acted out in homes across America, but the way in which Harry used food to dominate his son was profoundly disturbing to Robert, and he later complained to his friend Dimitri Levas that his father once forced him to eat burned eggs while he sat on the toilet seat.

Robert's experience growing up in a rigid household was compounded by his early Catholic training, which sensitized him to the concept of guilt and sin. There was no Catholic school in Floral Park, so Robert attended Christian Doctrine classes every Wednesday while the other students at P.S. 191 were taking arts and crafts. He memorized the Baltimore Catechism and learned the hierarchy of the afterlife: Heaven, Limbo, Purgatory, and Hell. He discovered which sins were mortal, which were venial, and how to cleanse his soul through the sacrament of Confession. Yet in addition to the Church's rigorous dictates, he was also exposed to a liberating spirituality that celebrated the miracle of Christ's resurrection after the pain and torture of his crucifixion. Each time he went to Mass, he could watch the priest transform bread and wine into the body and blood of Christ. "A church has a certain magic and mystery for a child," Mapplethorpe told Ingrid Sischy. "It still shows in how I arrange things. It's always little altars. It's always been this way—whenever I'd put something together I'd notice it was symmetrical."

But even as Robert derived a sense of order and harmony from Catholicism, he bridled at its constraints. "Robert didn't take his religion lightly," said his neighbor Bill Cassidy, who was the same age as Richard Mapplethorpe. "He seemed to believe in all that devil stuff, and once he told me, 'There's this clock in Hell that chimes every hour, 'You will never get out . . . you will never get out . . . you will never get out.' "

Escape came once a year when Harry's mother took her grandchildren to the amusement park at Coney Island, and that is where Robert caught his first glimpse of the world beyond Floral Park. He was overwhelmed by the sparkling lights, leering clowns, boisterous carnival barkers, and the Wonder Wheel and Cyclone. It was such an exhilarating experience that the sights and smells stayed with him forever, and for years afterward the whiff of a sizzling hot dog could reawaken his memories of having lunch with his grandmother at Nathan's—"Home of the Frankfurter."

What Robert liked best, however, was the freak displays, where "ape girls," bearded women, tattooed men, snake charmers, and dwarves were hidden away in dark booths. His older sister, Nancy, was terrified of them, but Robert always wanted to peek inside and was frustrated by his grandmother's efforts to keep him away. "There's nothing worse than wanting to see something and having someone stop you," he said. The freaks became symbols to him of all things strange and forbidden, and while he would not pursue them as vigilantly as Diane Arbus did in her photographs, they would crop up in different guises in Mapplethorpe's pictures. By identifying the Catholic Church and Coney Island as the two most vivid memories of his childhood, he was touching upon the essential drama of his photographs—the push-pull between the sacred and the profane that was to give his work what he called an "edge."

Nancy was closer in age to Richard, yet she admired Robert's individuality and viewed him as the more interesting of the two brothers. Whenever the four children played together, she and Robert would pair up against Richard and Susan—the rebels versus the conformists. Richard and Susan never questioned their parents' authority, while Robert and Nancy were not as inclined to accept the traditional roles imposed upon them. Nancy was the neighborhood tomboy; instead of playing with dolls, she climbed trees with such abandon that she was frequently covered with bruises and scrapes. Robert eschewed toy guns and war games for more feminine activities; one Christmas he asked for a jewelry-making kit, and it was the first time he discovered what he called "the magical feeling in my fingers." He directed his talent at providing his mother with baked-enamel pins and earrings. Yet Joan was continually besieged by problems that pulled her focus away from Robert, and in 1957, when he was ten years old, she learned that she was pregnant again.

She had serious misgivings about starting what she called a "second family" at the age of thirty-six. The bedrooms were already filled to capacity, and since every house in Floral Park was the same size, they couldn't move to a larger house unless they left the neighborhood.

Joan anguished about the decision for months, but finally she asked her father to move out to a nearby apartment building. A few weeks before her fifth child was delivered, in February 1958, James Maxey died of a stroke at the age of sixty-nine. Joan had not been able to reach her father on the telephone, and she dispatched Harry to the apartment building, where he discovered the dead body.

Joan named her son James, in memory of her father, but even the new baby did not erase her guilt over his death. She fell into a depression, which was compounded by another pregnancy that ended in a miscarriage.

It was during this rocky period in the family's history that Robert became more involved in art, and he moved from making jewelry to executing pencil sketches. Linda Bahr, a student in his sixth-grade class at P.S. 191, was the recipient of one of his earliest drawings—a portrait of an angelic young girl smelling a flower. Bahr was struck by the tenderness of the image, and how it represented such a departure from the rough-and-tumble world of sixth-grade boys. "Robert wasn't handsome like his brother—all the girls loved Richard," Bahr said. "But Robert was sweet and gentle, and he had beautiful hands—artist's hands, I always thought."

Robert's creativity gave him a sense of purpose, but it alienated him from the other boys in the neighborhood. Tom Farre considered Robert's artistic pursuits "unmasculine," and even though the two boys were the same age, he preferred to play with the older and more athletic Richard. "Whenever I think about Robert," Farre said, "I see this snot-nosed kid whose pants were always hanging off him, and who walked around like Howdy Doody." Robert was not adept at sports, but to please his father, who expected his sons to be good athletes, he joined the local baseball team. Yet Robert was poorly coordinated, and he was not comfortable throwing or hitting a ball; Harry had never played catch with him. Robert spent most of the time sitting on the bench, waiting for his name to be called.

Brian Pronger, in his book *The Arena of Masculinity,* explores the gay experience of athletics and gives numerous examples of homosexual boys who, through lack of interest or unwillingness to embrace an orthodox masculinity, failed miserably at team sports. Since sports are viewed as a boy's initiation into manhood, this failure to perform can be devastating. Twenty-five years later, Robert would still describe his experience on the baseball team as one of the most humiliating ordeals of his life.

There was one athletic activity, however, at which Robert excelled, and that was jumping on a pogo stick. He had already won the title "Pogo Stick Champion of 259th Street," so one Saturday afternoon he set out to break the Guinness world record in pogo stick jumping. He positioned himself in full view of the living room bay window, surely hoping his father would see him, and began jumping up and down while calling out the numbers . . . 404 . . . 405 . . . 406. He knew his father was inside, so he kept jumping and shouting until finally he felt dizzy and collapsed on the lawn. He didn't break the world record, but it amounted to his personal best. He understood that it wasn't like hitting a home run, but he couldn't wait for his father's reaction. When Robert went inside, however, he found Harry sound asleep on the living room couch.

In September 1958, when Robert reached seventh grade, his parents pronounced him old enough to ride the subway into Manhattan, and taking full advantage of his new freedom, he began spending Saturdays in the city. He was usually accompanied by his best friend, Jim Cassidy, who lived on the same block and who also attended seventh grade at P.S. 172. Both boys had been admitted to the school's accelerated program, which compressed junior high school into two years. It was nicknamed "SP" for Special Progress, but Robert liked to think the initials stood for Special People, and by the standards of the neighborhood the two boys were certainly unique. Jim's father was a fireman with a passion for opera, and he occasionally took his son to see performances at the Metropolitan Opera House. "I saw *Carmen* last night from the fourth-row orchestra!" Jim would later boast to the other boys, who, being more interested in the Brooklyn Dodgers, dismissed him as weird. Jim's grandfather had been a graphic artist and his mother painted as a hobby, so Jim didn't consider Robert's artistic leanings bizarre or effeminate. (It was the Cassidys, in fact, who had outraged the neighbors by painting the cupola of their house green.) Like Robert, Jim was small for his age, and next to his older brother, Bill, he gave the impression of being a weakling. But Jim made up in verbal skills what he lacked in athletic ability, and while his loquaciousness was off-putting to many of his peers, Robert was starved for stimulation; his relationship with Jim became the first of many alliances with mentor figures who would help him in his career.

Jim was not artistic himself, but he recognized Robert's creativity, and the two boys would occasionally spend Saturdays at the Metropolitan Museum of Art and the Museum of Modern Art. Afterward Jim enjoyed talking about the various artists whose work they had seen, but Robert wasn't a verbal person and could not put the experience of viewing art into words. Instead, it came out in his drawings. "Robert had an excellent reproductive style," Cassidy recalled. "If he had just seen a Salvador Dalí, for example, he'd incorporate certain Daliesque touches into his drawings. But ultimately I think Robert was most influenced by Picasso." Up until now, Robert's vision of art had been limited to the iconography of the Catholic Church—the madonnas and Christ figures to whom he directed his prayers. His trips to the museums added another dimension, and he began drawing Cubist madonnas, inspired by Picasso. "These were not beautiful Botticelli-type madonnas," said Cassidy, "but grotesque creatures with split profiles. I guess they were religious in that they were madonnas, but there was something disturbing about the way he had broken up their faces."

These Cubist madonnas became a staple of Robert's early work, and while he may not have been consciously alluding to his relationship with his mother, he kept returning to the image of a fragmented mother figure. Toward the end of Robert's second year at P.S. 172, Joan gave birth to her sixth child, Edward, who was delivered in April 1960. She joked to Pat Farre that she could become pregnant just by having someone look at her, but to Robert there was nothing amusing about it. "My mother's just a baby producer," he complained bitterly to Jim Cassidy.

Joan had another miscarriage after Edward, and when she began to hemorrhage she was admitted to the hospital for a hysterectomy. With his mother increasingly unavailable to him, Robert made periodic stabs at forging a bond with his father, but even when he took up photography as a hobby he still failed to penetrate Harry's indifference. Both Robert and Jim had received Brownie cameras for Christmas, and some of the first pictures Robert ever took were of his baby brother James. "He wasn't into artistic composition then," said Cassidy. "It was mostly getting the baby to be quiet, then taking the picture. We had these photography developing kits so we'd develop the negatives at his house."

Yet Robert's father could not recall that his son had ever picked up a camera. "With all that equipment in the house," Harry remarked, "you'd think he would have shown some interest in photography, but he never did."

Robert graduated from P.S. 172 in June 1960, and that fall he entered Martin Van Buren High School, an unsightly beige-brick building on Hillside Avenue that accommodated five thousand students. The "SP" program had allowed Robert to skip a grade, so he was a year younger than the majority of incoming sophomores; since he was already small for his age, he felt he suffered from a social disadvantage with the girls in his class. In addition, he was a Catholic in a school where the student population was predominantly Jewish, and he perceived himself as an outsider. "Almost all the fraternities were closed to us," explained Jim Cassidy, who was raised a Protestant, "and the one that accepted Christians rejected Robert and me."

Robert looked to Our Lady of the Snows for his social opportunities, and he joined the Columbian Squires, a Catholic fraternal organization to which his brother Richard belonged. The Squires had a reputation for attracting the most macho teenagers in the parish, and Robert wore the group's uniform—a navy blue jacket decorated with a white Maltese cross—as a badge of masculinity. He began telling friends to call him "Bob," and he slowly drifted away from Jim Cassidy, whose cultural interests had branded him as effeminate. Yet no matter what actions Robert took to bolster his shaky self-esteem, he was still a misfit. "Here was this gentle, creative person surrounded by all these gung-ho macho types," said Father George Stack, who presided at the Squires' meetings. "He was like a fawn, and it was obvious to me he didn't belong with the other boys."

Robert was torn between a desire to emulate his brother Richard, and thus to please his father, and a creative drive that led him in the opposite direction. He regularly appeared at the rectory door to show Father Stack his Cubist madonnas, and while the priest thought Robert's rendering of the subject was unconventional, he always made a point of praising the young artist because he seemed so hungry for recognition. Terry Gray, Robert's best friend in the Squires, was a down-to-earth, no-nonsense type whose idea of a good time was taking people for a ride on his tandem bicycle. He paid little attention to Robert's art, but Robert nevertheless would always take his drawings over to the Grays' house to show Terry's mother, Dotty. She invariably offered the same bleak assessment of them. "They're weird, and you're weird," she would tell him, despite Robert's frustrated demands of "Can't you see the beauty in them?" But she could not see the beauty of madonnas with eyes in the middle of their foreheads. Attempting to push Robert in a more traditional direction, she asked him to paint an American eagle over the electric meter in the family's basement, so the Con Edison man would have something to look at. Robert obliged Dotty Gray, but later ranted to Terry, "I'll never do that again! I'm going to be a real artist . . . a famous one."

Robert told Terry that he intended to change his name from Robert Mapplethorpe to the heartier, more masculine "Bob Thorpe," which may have been Robert's way of forging his identity as an artist without forfeiting his virility. He was perhaps struggling with sexual feelings he did not understand, and there was no one in whom he could confide. The priests at Our Lady of the Snows were vigilant in their efforts to purge "impure thoughts" from the adolescent mind; they cautioned the parish teenagers to avoid occasions for sin, which included seeing "condemned" movies, such as *Splendor in the Grass,* Elia Kazan's drama of teenage repression. Robert learned that sexual activity outside the holy sacrament of matrimony was considered immoral, and that the ultimate goal of sexual intercourse was to create human life. Anything less was regarded as an abuse of the body-spirit unity of the individual.

Robert's parents did not discuss sex at all, so he was shocked when he discovered a copy of *Lady Chatterley's Lover* hidden in their closet. The unexpurgated version of D. H. Lawrence's novel had not been available in the United States until 1959, when a New York judge ruled that banning the book from the mails was in violation of the First Amendment. Robert was familiar with the censorship trial in that *Lady Chatterley's Lover* was known to him as a "dirty book," and he skimmed the pages for the sex scenes between Lady Chatterley and the gamekeeper. It was the first time Robert had ever masturbated, and while he felt guilty about it, he kept returning to the dark closet and to the previously censored book. It was not long afterward that he discovered several nudist magazines that had also been stashed away in the closet, and while he enjoyed staring at pictures of naked women, he realized he was also attracted to men. He felt guilty enough about masturbating but the idea that he might be homosexual was frightening beyond belief. The people he grew up with had nothing but contempt for homosexuals— "queers," "fags," "fairies." Robert had gone so far as to take Spanish as a second language because French was regarded as "only for the faggots." He wasn't about to embarrass himself, and worse, commit a mortal sin. "I knew homosexuality was wrong," he said, "and that it wasn't something you were supposed to be."

It certainly wasn't anything he would ever discuss with Richard, whom he had increasingly grown to despise, and although the two brothers shared a room they were barely on speaking terms. An invisible line was drawn down the center of their bedroom, and neither was allowed to cross into the other's territory. Richard didn't understand the root of Robert's anger and tended to dismiss him as the family oddball. Besides, he was preoccupied by his teenage love affair with a neighborhood girl named Marylynn Celano, whom he intended to marry one day. "It was like a fairy-tale romance," Jim Cassidy recalled. "They were both really good-looking, and when you'd see them at the bus stop together, they'd take your breath away." Robert, who was already resentful of Richard's relationship with their father, was now consumed with envy over his brother's courtship of Marylynn, and he set about to win her over himself. He frequently called Marylynn on the telephone and showed up at her house with his latest drawings; he confided his dreams of being an artist and offered to do her portrait. Marylynn was not romantically interested in Robert, but she respected him more than she did Richard, whom she believed was too much in Harry's sway. "It was clear Harry favored Richard," she said. "He was the fair-haired boy, but Robert was his own man somehow."

Yet Robert was still unsure of what it meant to be a man, and the pressures of having to live up to a stereotypical image finally reached an exploding point. The incident was a relatively minor one in the life of a teenage boy, but it shook up the Mapplethorpe household so badly that Robert's parents and siblings later recounted the story as the defining episode of his adolescence. Robert and Terry Gray had attended a neighborhood party where Robert, who had previously never touched alcohol, suddenly chugged an entire bottle of whiskey, then promptly passed out on the living room rug. Unable to revive him through the usual methods of caffeine and a cold shower, Terry slung him over his shoulder and deposited him on the Mapplethorpes' doorstep a little after midnight. Fearing that Robert had lapsed into a diabetic coma, Joan telephoned the family doctor, who rushed over to the house and quickly diagnosed the boy's condition. He forced Robert to walk around the living room by kicking him in the pants, but the alcohol had unleashed a swarm of furies; Robert beat the floor with his hands and began hurling obscenities and insults at his parents until his voice went hoarse. Afterward no one could remember anything he said.

Robert graduated from Martin Van Buren High School in June 1963, and although he had wanted to go away to college, Harry had convinced him to attend Pratt Institute, his alma mater, and to commute to school in Brooklyn from home. Robert was miserable about having to remain in Floral Park, for he was now the oldest sibling in the house; Nancy had married her high school boyfriend and was living in another town, and Richard had followed his father's advice and had enrolled at the State Maritime Academy at Fort Schuyler, where he was studying to be an engineer. That left Robert at the dinner table with fourteen-year-old Susan and two rambunctious toddlers. "I felt really sorry for Robert," said Jim Cassidy, who was planning to attend college in Buffalo. "He was more desperate to escape from Floral Park than anyone I knew."

That summer Robert worked as a messenger at National City Bank, where his grandfather had started his own career a half century before. Robert's job consisted of riding the subway to deliver packages between the bank's midtown Manhattan office and Wall Street. His lunch hours were spent at Times Square, where, after a hot dog at Nathan's, he would go to Hubert's Freak Museum to feast his eyes on such human curiosities as Sealo the Seal Boy, whose hands grew out of his shoulders; a hermaphrodite named Alberto Alberta; and Congo the Jungle Creep, a Haitian in a fright wig who performed voodoo rituals. Diane Arbus found many of her subjects at Hubert's, but Robert lost interest in the freaks after he spotted a gay pornographic magazine in a store on Forty-second Street.

The magazine was wrapped in cellophane and the model's genitals were covered by slashes of black tape. Robert was under eighteen, so he couldn't buy the magazine, but he became obsessed with trying to see what was inside. "[The magazines] were all sealed, which made them even sexier somehow, because you couldn't get to see them," he told Ingrid Sischy. "A kid gets a certain kind of reaction, which of course once you've been exposed to everything you don't get. I got that feeling in my stomach, it's not a directly sexual one, it's something more potent than that. I thought if I could somehow bring that element into art, if I could somehow retain that feeling, I would be doing something that was uniquely my own."

Over the years Robert would always recount this story whenever he was asked to explain why he had incorporated the pornographic into his work, yet he rarely elaborated on his emotions beyond the phrase "that feeling in my stomach." But for someone whose previous exposure to pictures of nude men had been limited to nature magazines, it must have been an overwhelming experience to see well-built, attractive men posing for the pleasure of other men, for it meant Robert wasn't alone in desiring members of his own sex.

He kept returning to the store, hoping to slip a copy under his jacket, but he was eventually thrown out. He then found a blind newsdealer who also sold gay pornography, and after watching him for several days to make sure he was really sightless, Robert snatched a magazine. What he uncovered when he ripped open the cellophane and tore off the black tape was so exciting to him that later in the week he returned to the newsstand to steal another one. This time, however, the blind newsdealer had alerted two friends to watch out for anyone taking magazines, and they both pounced on Robert, grabbing him from behind. "Get the cops!" the blind newsdealer began screaming. "Get the cops!" Robert managed to break free and took off down the street. He couldn't imagine what would have happened to him if the police had called his father with the news that his son had been arrested for stealing gay pornography. He vowed to end his flirtation with homosexuality.

For weeks afterward Robert had nightmares of the blind newsdealer, and he would wake up, sweating, in the middle of the night.

CHAPTER TWO

"Robert was a little too intense and conservative for me. He
was almost the stereotypic 'good boy.' "

—*Nancy Nemeth, ROTC Military Ball Queen, 1964*

Mapplethorpe arrived at Pratt Institute in September
1963, and immediately signed up with the campus ROTC unit,
where his father had been a cadet twenty-four years earlier. Robert's
experience with gay pornography had left him feeling so guilty that
he was determined to lead a "normal" life. Pratt, like most American colleges, was then steeped in fifties traditionalism, and a survey
of the school's yearbooks showed the class of '63 to look nearly
identical to the class of '58. The men had neatly clipped hair and
wore button-down shirts, while the women favored bubble cuts and
preppy sweaters and skirts. Campus social activities were dominated
by fraternities and sororities, and the fall semester commenced with
a raucous beer bash known as the "Boola-Boola," succeeded by the
Rush Rallies, a series of smokers and teas.

There were signs, however, that the complacent fifties ethos was
about to expire. Three weeks before Mapplethorpe enrolled at Pratt,

Martin Luther King, Jr., delivered his impassioned "I have a dream" speech to a crowd of 250,000 in Washington, D.C., and before the end of the year, 14,000 people would be arrested in seventy-five Southern cities during civil rights demonstrations. Then, in November, John F. Kennedy was assassinated, shattering America's idealistic view of itself. But no single incident triggered the sixties; instead, it was a steady buildup of events that converged, then exploded.

Mapplethorpe, meanwhile, confronted an educational tradition steeped in common sense and practicality. Pratt was founded in 1887 by industrialist Charles Pratt, who designed the school as a shoe factory in case his efforts at creating a vocational and technical institute failed. From its earliest courses in millinery, forging, and leather tanning, Pratt eventually expanded its curriculum to include architecture, engineering, library science, and art and design. Nevertheless, the school's focus remained on providing students with a sensible education, and its pragmatic approach appealed to lower-to-middle-class parents who expected their children to learn a lucrative trade.

Harry wasn't at all happy with his son's decision to enroll in the art school—he wanted him to study engineering—and pressured him to major in advertising design, so he could learn illustration and typography. Robert's heart belonged to fine arts, or what Pratt called Graphic Arts and Design, but he was afraid his father wouldn't pay his tuition if he studied painting, sculpture, and drawing—subjects Harry considered frivolous.

Harry's influence on his son was so persuasive that Robert even pledged the Pershing Rifles, ROTC's military honor society, of which his brother Richard was a member. The society was named after General John "Black Jack" Pershing, who led the American Expeditionary Forces against the Germans in World War I, and its members were known for their choreographed bayonet-twirling routines. At Pratt the "PRs," as they were called, were the rowdiest, most right-wing students on campus. "We were the tough guys, the Fascists, the ones most likely to become Green Berets," said Tom Logan, who was the company's trick drill commander. Each year twenty-five ROTC cadets pledged the society, but less than half made it through the six-week hazing process that ended in the torturous "Hell Night." Robert was determined to become a Pershing

Rifle for the same reason he had joined the Columbian Squires. Both groups proffered an image of unadulterated masculinity, and their uniforms served as a walking billboard for heterosexuality. "The Pershing Rifles had all the right ribbons and all the right braids," Mapplethorpe said, "and I was obsessed with being with the special people."

Tom Logan was in charge of the hazing procedure, and when he first took a look at Mapplethorpe he dismissed him as someone who would "burst out crying the minute I screamed at him." Mapplethorpe was only sixteen and had yet to grow into his body, with the result that his ill-fitting ROTC uniform gave him the appearance of Charlie Chaplin's Little Tramp. In comparison, Logan was a beefy hulk whose father was an Irish policeman; he had grown up in a tough Brooklyn neighborhood, where his membership in a local street gang had provided a crash course in physical and mental intimidation, and he relished his role as the Pershing Rifles' chief tormentor. Mapplethorpe was petrified of Logan, and he walked around campus with his fingers tightly wrapped around the polished BB pellet he was instructed to carry with him at all times. Invariably, Logan would swoop down from nowhere and force Mapplethorpe to brace against the wall; he would position his face an inch away from Mapplethorpe's and shout, "You're worthless! You're nothing but scum!" Other times, Mapplethorpe was forced to drop to the ground to do a series of push-ups, sit-ups, and squats.

By December, Logan had managed to frighten off more than half of the potential pledges, but to his amazement Robert Mapplethorpe was not among them. The rookie cadet still had to face Hell Night, however, which took place during winter intersession at a local army barracks.

While the other fraternities were transforming the school cafeteria into an ice palace for Winter Weekend, Mapplethorpe packed his duffel bag and traveled to Fort Dix, New Jersey. From the moment he arrived, he was in such a state of nervous anxiety that when Logan placed a half-eaten pear on his pillow one morning, he mistakenly interpreted it as a sign that he had been rejected. Near hysteria, he confronted a Pershing Rifle named Peter Hetzel and demanded to know what he had done wrong. "You've got to tell me," he begged the older cadet. "Where did I fail?" Mapplethorpe suffered an even greater anxiety attack the next evening while waiting for Logan and the other Pershing Rifles to officially begin Hell Night. "I can't go through with it," he confided to Victor Pope, one of the seven remaining pledges. "I'm getting out of here." He grabbed his clothes and was about to run out of the bunk; but, unwilling to face his father with the news that he hadn't been man enough for Hell Night, he stood his ground.

Minutes later, Mapplethorpe heard the rhythmic pounding of heels on the concrete floor, and the Pershing Rifles marched into the barracks. They led the overwrought pledges into another room, where they had devised a variety of different tests, many of which evoked the rituals of gay sadomasochistic sex. The Pershing Rifles were regarded as an elite military unit, and their stylish uniforms played into the fantasy of the master-slave scenario. In this case the "masters" stripped the pledges naked, blinded them with sanitary napkins, and commanded them to perform close-order drill with their bayonets. Subsequently they bound the pledges' penises with one end of a rope, then attached bricks to the other end and ordered them to hurl the brick across the room. Next the pledges were ordered to crawl into a bathroom on their hands and knees; they were told to eat excrement from a toilet bowl—it turned out to be mashed bananas and chunky peanut butter. Mapplethorpe later confided to Patti Smith that someone had also inserted the tip of a rifle into his rectum.

The various tests lasted until dawn, when the pledges finally received news of their acceptance into the military society. Mapplethorpe was thrilled to learn that he had made the cut, for he viewed membership in the Pershing Rifles as positive proof that he had entered the magic circle of "Special People."

Mapplethorpe had expended so much energy on the pledging process that he had ignored his studies, and he received only mediocre grades. He rationalized his marks by telling his parents that his teachers were biased against commuting students. More likely, they were not overly impressed with Mapplethorpe, whose talent, when measured against other Pratt students, was average. In addition, many of the teachers and students favored abstract expressionism, and Robert was not comfortable using paint and canvas as a creative outlet, nor did he care to dredge his psyche for repressed emotions. He preferred the art of self-presentation to self-analysis, and in this regard he was in perfect sync with the emerging pop-art movement. If the abstract expressionists turned inward for inspiration, the pop artists appropriated images from billboards, comic strips, and movie magazines. In 1962, for example, the year that pop art was "born," James Rosenquist exhibited his billboard paintings at the Green Gallery; Roy Lichtenstein showed paintings of comic strips and household appliances at the Leo Castelli Gallery; and Andy Warhol had his first New York show at the Stable Gallery, where he presented his paintings of Marilyn Monroe, Elvis Presley, and Coca-Cola bottles. Pop art was labeled "cool art" by critic Irving Sandler, and nobody was cooler than Warhol, whose emotional detachment appealed to Mapplethorpe.

In the summer of 1964 Mapplethorpe worked at the World's Fair in Flushing, Queens, where he operated the games of chance at the Belgian Pavilion. Coincidentally, Warhol had been commissioned to produce an artwork for the New York State Pavilion; when he delivered the politically charged *Thirteen Most Wanted Men,* which was based on mug shots of criminals, it was ordered removed by Fair officials who thought it might offend the city's Italian constituents—a majority of the "most wanted men" were Italian. Mapplethorpe was aware of Warhol's growing reputation as a pop provocateur, and he had already targeted the elusive artist as "someone who knew what he was doing." Mapplethorpe's attraction both to Warhol and to the Pershing Rifles was an early indication of how he would later take a "cool" approach to his militaristic S&M imagery, but at Pratt he was still too intimidated by his own instincts to allow his creativity free rein.

Living at home further restricted Robert's freedom, and while he was doing everything he could to please his father, in comparison to Richard it was not enough. Richard felt equally pressured by Harry; his constant need to appease his father had rendered him weak and ineffectual in the eyes of his girlfriend, Marylynn Celano. She wanted to break off their relationship, but whenever she broached the subject with him, he became hysterical and threatened to quit the Maritime Academy. "And if I do that," Richard warned, "it will kill my father!" That Richard would hold out Harry's destruction as the ultimate threat made Marylynn even more convinced that his father held too much sway over him. And given that Richard believed he might "kill" his father over a relatively mundane breakup, it's not difficult to understand why Robert struggled so hard to keep his homosexuality a secret.

In September 1964 Mapplethorpe escaped from home by renting a five-room apartment near the Pratt campus, at 160 Willoughby Avenue. He managed, however, to duplicate the strained atmosphere of his family life by selecting as his roommates two men who were virtual stand-ins for Richard and Harry—Tom Logan, his Pershing Rifles nemesis, and an army sergeant in his mid-forties, who derided his younger roommates as sissy college boys. Mapplethorpe and Logan shared a room; once again Mapplethorpe was pitted against an older "brother" whose masculinity was beyond reproach. "We all envied Tom," said Stan Mitchell, a member of Pratt's Pershing Rifles. "He was handsome and strong, with this great booming voice. Women just loved him. Of course those were the days when women loved men in uniforms, but they loved Tom in or out of uniform."

Mapplethorpe was beginning to feel burdened by his virginity; perhaps he hoped he might learn something from Logan, who documented his numerous conquests by stamping a cherry on the kitchen calendar. Several times a week the Pershing Rifles gathered together at a campus bar called Erik's, where Mapplethorpe was often the butt of their jokes. They called him "Maypo" and teased him about his nonexistent love life. Years later, Tom Logan and other Pershing Rifles maintained that it was harmless jesting, but several female observers described their behavior as sadistic. "Poor Bob wanted to fit in so badly, but he just didn't belong with a bunch of macho engineers," recalled Pratt student Bonnie Lester. "Maybe it made them feel better, more masculine to make fun of him, but I remember thinking how hurt he must have been inside."

For Mapplethorpe's eighteenth birthday, Logan decided he would finally put an end to his roommate's virginity by surprising him with a black prostitute who worked on Flatbush Avenue. "There was a group of these women and most of them were drug addicts," Logan said. "It was a very sleazy situation." Nevertheless,

Logan gave the woman twenty dollars, and after having sex with her himself, he passed her along to Mapplethorpe, whose failure to perform was a humiliating cap to his birthday celebration. The story quickly made the rounds at Erik's, where it was used as yet another example of "Maypo's" sexual ineptitude.

No matter what Mapplethorpe did he was still the outsider, and, conscious of his alien status, he began to socialize with three black women who were among the small percentage of minority students at Pratt. "Bob told me his parents rejected him because he was different," explained Rosita Cruz, who along with her twin sister, Violetta, and Fern Urquhart were his main allies. "But how different could he have been? To me, he was a normal gifted kid. But Bob could not get this 'different' thing out of his head. I think he felt comfortable with us because we could understand the idea of not being accepted." He frequently served as Rosita's escort to campus parties, and while he wasn't romantically interested in her, he liked to pretend that she was his girlfriend. Rosita didn't understand the extent to which Robert was deluding himself until he overheard another man asking her out on a date one evening. "Bob threw a temper tantrum right in the middle of the party," Rosita said, "and he began yelling, 'What are you trying to do to me? Make me into a fool? Now you've ruined me. I feel like nothing!' "

Mapplethorpe similarly embarrassed himself in front of Fern Urquhart, who had been voted the Pershing Rifles' company queen, and who also happened to be Tom Logan's girlfriend, and later became his wife. In a replay of his infatuation with his brother's girlfriend, Robert was now enamored of Fern, whom he called on the telephone so often that she complained to the Cruz sisters that he had become a nuisance. He was always asking Fern, "Why am I still a virgin?" One night after too many beers he refused to leave her apartment until she agreed to have sex with him. Pushing him out the door, Fern advised him to "go home and get some sleep," but Robert insisted that he only wanted to sleep with her. When it became clear that Fern wasn't going to open the door, Robert banged on it with his fists, shouting, "Why can't I go to bed with you?! Tell me . . . *why?*" He kept up the assault until he finally collapsed in exhaustion on the front stoop, where he spent the rest of the night crouched in front of Fern's door.

The next day Mapplethorpe ran into Rosita Cruz, who innocently asked, "So, Bob, what did you do last night?" Undaunted, he told her that he had wanted to sleep with Fern, but she wouldn't open her door. Rosita stared at him, amazed. "So you spent the night on her *stoop?*" she said. "What are you—a little dog?"

Black women were exotic to Mapplethorpe, and perhaps, even then, it was the forbidden aspect of interracial sex that excited him. Curiously, his intemperate behavior toward Fern Urquhart and Rosita Cruz stood in stark contrast to the bland and passive personality he presented to Caucasian women. Linda Lee, a Pratt freshman whom he dated for six months, regarded him as a model of deportment. Whenever they went out together, he always dressed in a navy blazer and pressed pants and was perfectly content holding her hand while watching *Soupy Sales* in the dorm lounge. "Bob was one of the nicest people I had ever met," Lee recalled. "He was so sweet, and not at all self-serving. He was very submissive, though. If I'd proposed marriage, I think he would have accepted." Mapplethorpe didn't seem to care that Lee went out with other men, and once when he ran into her on campus with a rival he was so cordial he told them both to have a good time. For Christmas that year, he presented her with a pair of gold earrings and a card illustrated with one of his drawings of the Blessed Virgin.

Mapplethorpe had staked his identity on membership in the Pershing Rifles but had never given any thought to fighting in a war. In February 1965, however, President Lyndon Johnson authorized the bombing of North Vietnam and tens of thousands of U.S. combat troops began flooding into the South. Mapplethorpe's comrades in the Pershing Rifles were yearning for real action, and over beer and roast beef sandwiches at Erik's they plotted revenge against the Vietcong. Mapplethorpe, meanwhile, had barely recovered from a five-day bivouac trip to Fort Dix, where he nearly developed frostbite by marching nine miles in the freezing cold. He was further disheartened when his bid for membership in the Pershing Rifles' trick drill team was rejected. Bob Jacob was in charge of auditioning the candidates, and while he admired Mapplethorpe's tenacity, he also recognized his lack of coordination. "He simply wasn't as good as the rest of the guys," Jacob recalled. "He was gangly, like a puppy or a colt." The trick drill team was the Pershing Rifles' most elite clique, and Mapplethorpe's failure to penetrate the inner circle depressed him.

If his classes had been more engaging, perhaps he might have focused more of his attention on school, but as part of the sophomore-year curriculum he was required to take courses that related to his advertising design major, such as lettering and typography. He found them tedious and resented his father for pushing him in that direction. He enrolled in a photography course but hated that, too. When it came time to produce a portfolio for the final project, he lied, and submitted a collection of his father's prints; the gesture reflected his budding awareness that he was leading his father's life. Yet he directed his frustration not at Harry Mapplethorpe but at Tom Logan, whom he now professed to loathe for reasons he couldn't articulate.

One evening, at the Cruz sisters' apartment, he began to rail against Logan, shouting "I hate him!" while tears streamed down his cheeks. "If you hate him so much," Rosita Cruz asked, "then why are you living with him?" But Mapplethorpe could only shake his head and whimper, "I just wish he were dead." In a contiguous drama, the army sergeant who roomed with them had also grown to despise Logan, and frustrated by his undistinguished military career and a failed marriage, he resented the younger man's youth and bravado. Returning home drunk one night, he pinned Logan against the kitchen wall, held a knife to his stomach, and began screaming that he was going to kill him. When Mapplethorpe walked into the kitchen, the terrifying scene must have represented the culmination of his own murderous rage. "My God!" he shouted. "You can't *kill* him!" Instinctively, he wedged himself between the two men and pleaded with the sergeant to drop the knife. Finally the older man stormed down the hallway into his bedroom, and Logan was left to thank "Maypo" for saving his life. "I'd never really thought of Robert as a brave person," Logan said, "but after that night, I realized that maybe I'd been wrong."

Mapplethorpe's heroics, though, didn't solve the pressing problem of finding a date for the Military Ball, the most important event on the Pershing Rifles' social calendar. He had invited Linda Lee, but she was going with someone else, so he asked Nancy Nemeth, a high school student and aspiring model from Floral Park, whom he occasionally accompanied to Our Lady of the Snows. She agreed to be his date, but after accepting she wrote in her diary: "I don't know if I want to go." She found him to be sensitive and gentle, but too passive and timid for her. "Nothing about him really stands out in my mind," Nemeth said. "There was something almost pathetic about him."

Every year the ROTC cadets elected a Military Ball Queen, and Mapplethorpe submitted the requisite five-by-seven-inch portrait of Nancy Nemeth, which he had taken himself in Floral Park. She won the competition, and several weeks later, at Manhattan's Statler-Hilton, his date was crowned the fourteenth annual Military Ball Queen. It was later noted in the school newspaper that she was escorted by Staff Sergeant Robert Mapplethorpe. "She was one good-looking woman," Bob Jacob recalled. "After that, Mapplethorpe was more accepted as a man."

CHAPTER THREE

"Robert's transformation was remarkable. One day he was in
an ROTC uniform, the next day he was walking around
campus in a sheepskin vest and love beads."

—*Kenny Tisa, Pratt Institute, class of '68*

W hen Mapplethorpe returned to Pratt in the fall of
1965, the most popular song in America was "Eve of Destruction"
performed by Barry McGuire. It had become a hit despite its
doomsday lyrics about "the Eastern world . . . explodin' " and soldiers "old enough to kill but not for votin'." Countering the song's
leftist philosophy, Staff Sergeant Barry Sadler later recorded the pa-
triotic "Ballad of the Green Berets." Todd Gitlin, in *The Sixties:
Years of Hope, Days of Rage,* wrote that one radio station even sponsored a "battle of the Barrys," in which listeners were encouraged to
vote for their favorite song. "Green Berets" won the contest, but,
according to Gitlin, " 'Eve of Destruction' seemed to certify that a
mass movement of American young was upon us."

At the time, Mapplethorpe was fighting his own private battle, for
the political climate on campus was shifting to the left, and the
graphic-arts majors, who already had a bohemian reputation, were

fully embracing the counterculture. "We were the hip ones, the drug takers," said then Pratt student Kenny Tisa. "Since Robert really wanted to be part of the elite, he had to switch gears, or else he'd be a total outcast."

Mapplethorpe understood that it was no longer socially expedient to be a member of ROTC, but he couldn't quit without sacrificing his honor and the forty-dollar stipend he received from the army each month. He did, however, change his major from advertising design to graphic arts, but he kept the news a secret from his father until midway through the semester. "You did this without telling me?" Harry demanded during a Sunday dinner in Floral Park. "Who do you think's paying the tuition?" Robert attempted to explain his reasons for switching majors. "Dad," he pleaded, "I want to be a real artist, not an illustrator or a typographer." But Harry was so enraged by Robert's disobedience that he bore down even harder on his son. "An *artist*," he sneered. "How do you think you're going to earn a living as an artist?" Robert's answer was drowned out by his father's insistent bellowing, and he dissolved into tears. Embarrassed, he fled the house and ran down 259th Street, past the tidy row of white bungalows and identical patches of green lawn. He didn't know where he was going, he just kept running until he heard his father's piercing shouts. "Come back!" Harry yelled. "You've upset your mother." Robert returned home, but the incident was never forgotten. Though Harry continued to pay his son's tuition, he harbored a grudge for years.

In his efforts to radicalize himself, Mapplethorpe stopped socializing with the Pershing Rifles and struck up a friendship with another graphic-arts major named Harry McCue, who eased Mapplethorpe's passage into the counterculture the same way Jim Cassidy had once served as his guide to Manhattan. Harry McCue was an ideal transition figure, for while he was a free-spirited painter, he had a sensible, conservative streak that kept his reckless instincts in check. Like Mapplethorpe, McCue had been raised in a lower-middle-class Catholic home with parents who discouraged him from becoming an artist. His father, a service manager for Mack Trucks, had thrown his son's application to Pratt into the garbage. McCue nonetheless persisted in applying to Pratt and even maintained a positive relationship with his parents, whom he visited regularly at their modest home in Bedford, New York. Mapplethorpe teased him about "living in the sticks," but he never refused an invitation to the McCues' house. He envied Harry for being able to keep ties to his parents without sacrificing his identity, and he constantly lamented his own familial predicament. "My father wants me to be like my brother," he complained, "but I can't be."

Harry McCue paraded his eccentricity by dressing in a confederate officer's uniform, and soon Mapplethorpe was strolling around campus in a magician's cape and bowler hat. One teacher sarcastically labeled them the "Bobbsey Twins" and accused Mapplethorpe of investing more time in his costumes than in his schoolwork. Certainly he was not a campus art star, and the possibility that he might be second-rate depressed him. "You don't think I'm any good, do you?" he asked McCue after his friend had slighted him by rejecting his overture to trade paintings. "Robert was an excellent draftsman," McCue said. "He had a real sense of line, but he could not paint at all. Color eluded him completely."

The two friends were the same age, but Mapplethorpe struck McCue as immature and disorganized—"a total ditz brain." He couldn't handle the simplest tasks, from buying food to going to the bank, and he frequently sent shirts to the laundry with dollar bills protruding from the front pockets. Both men, however, had an equally poor track record with women, and after Tom Logan's sexual showmanship, Mapplethorpe may have felt more comfortable with someone who wouldn't outshine him. He had finally lost his virginity, but the episode was not memorable, and even though he subsequently slept with several other Pratt women, sex was not the exhilarating experience he had hoped it would be. Yet he was determined to keep his homosexual desires buried, and as close as he was to Harry McCue—they later shared a room together—he never indicated that he was attracted to men. "To my knowledge," McCue said, "he wasn't gay at all." But the strain Mapplethorpe felt was noticeable to at least one Pratt student: David Palladini described Robert's face as appearing strangely divided. "One side was boldly feminine," he said, "while the other looked masculine and scared."

At the beginning of the semester Mapplethorpe had moved from the apartment on Willoughby Avenue to a ground-floor studio on

DeKalb Avenue, which he shared with a pet monkey named Scratch. Of all the stories connected to the photographer, the monkey saga remains one of the strangest. He had purchased the animal from a Brooklyn pet store, where the owner had given him a discount because the monkey was already an adult. The owner failed to tell Mapplethorpe that Scratch wasn't housebroken, and while Mapplethorpe made a few feeble attempts at training Scratch, he pronounced the monkey "uncontrollable" and gave it the run of the apartment. The studio was soon covered in urine and feces, and when friends first came to visit they were rendered speechless by the squalor and by Scratch's habit of entertaining Mapplethorpe by masturbating in front of him. Some members of the Pershing Rifles were convinced Mapplethorpe was having a nervous breakdown, for not only was he dressing in weird clothing and smoking marijuana, but he also began to take the monkey everywhere with him. "Whenever I'd see him, my heart would sink," said Stan Mitchell. "I thought he was going right down the gutter."

If Mapplethorpe's homosexuality was the monkey on his back, then Scratch was the living embodiment of his fears about sexual deviancy and loss of control. He half-jokingly described the animal as being possessed by the devil—"Scratch" is a nickname for Satan—but instead of returning it to the pet store, he kept "forgetting" to feed it, and when he returned to his apartment after a weekend away, he found Scratch's body stretched out on the floor. "Scratch is dead!" he shouted hysterically over the phone to Harry McCue, who, after offering a few words of sympathy, inquired if Mapplethorpe had completed the project for his Nature Structure class due the next day.

The assignment was to create a musical instrument from a bone, but it was Sunday night and all the butchers' shops were closed. "Where can I get a bone at this hour?" Mapplethorpe demanded. At two A.M. he called McCue again and informed him that he couldn't return to his apartment because the stench was unbearable. "Scratch is boiling in a pot," he announced. Mapplethorpe had beheaded Scratch with a kitchen knife, and after boiling away the flesh, he transformed the skull into a musical instrument of such beauty that it was one of the few times at Pratt that he received an A for his work. His demons had paid off, but soon the Scratch story took on a life of its own. Some Pratt students believed he had beheaded the monkey while it was still alive, while others hinted that he had eaten the animal's flesh in a voodoo cult ritual. Mapplethorpe fanned the rumors by keeping Scratch's skull in his pocket, then dramatically holding it aloft, like Hamlet contemplating Yorick. The tale became such an integral part of Mapplethorpe's college history that numerous Pratt alumnae were convinced that his later photographs of skulls were, in fact, pictures of Scratch.

Scratch's brief and bizarre history encapsulated many of the major themes of Mapplethorpe's adult life—his preoccupation with images of death and violence; his fascination with the devil; his desire to transform the ugly, or freakish, into works of beauty. It also pointed to a darker side of his nature, which would later emerge in his sexual relationships with other men—a need to break all the rules and transgress taboos.

Mapplethorpe took his first LSD trip while he was working as a counselor at St. Vincent's Boys Camp in Delaware during the summer of 1966. Returning to Pratt in September, he spoke excitedly of the drug to Rosita Cruz, who listened as he described how ordinary flowers had suddenly been transformed into "adorable cartoon figures, with cute faces and pudgy cheeks." In contrast to Mapplethorpe's later decadent floral studies, his LSD flowers have more in common with Walt Disney's *Fantasia,* but his benign, giddy view of nature was perhaps reflective of his own belief that LSD had provided him with the ability to lose himself in a guilt-free sensory experience. And since he felt guilty about so many aspects of his life, drugs temporarily solved his moral dilemma.

For the next twenty years Mapplethorpe would use drugs almost daily—marijuana, amphetamines, Quaaludes, acid, MDA, cocaine, and amyl nitrite; they became an integral part of his sexual experimentation, for they helped blur the distinction between pleasure and pain and allowed him to silence his internal censors. He found that drugs enhanced his creativity, too, and from that time on, he would never put pencil to paper—or later take a picture—without first getting stoned.

Timothy Leary's *Psychedelic Reader* became Mapplethorpe's new bible, and instead of going to church he attended Leary's "Celebrations" of the League for Spiritual Discovery (LSD) at the Village Theater on Second Avenue in Manhattan, which featured multi-media light shows and guest speakers such as LeRoi Jones and Allen Ginsberg.

From living at home, to sharing an apartment with two army men and a studio with a monkey, Mapplethorpe settled into a brownstone on St. James Place, which was described by one occupant as a "psychedelic Animal House." The parquet floors were strewn with mattresses and drug paraphernalia, and hanging from the top of the mahogany staircase was an upside-down Christmas tree decorated with rubber chickens. "Everybody was doing so many drugs that the place had a real hallucinatory quality," said Claude Alverson, an interior-design major who lived on the top floor. The tenants devised a grotesque game called "Creative Kill," for which they were obliged to record on a kitchen clipboard the dates and "creative" ways they exterminated the resident cockroaches. Visitors recalled seeing bugs impaled on safety pins and dangling from tiny nooses made of dental floss.

Acid-inspired art was becoming so common at Pratt that teachers could often tell the exact moment a student had discovered drugs. Mapplethorpe's drawings, for example, became more obsessive and detailed, and after taking LSD he would retreat to the brownstone's garden, where he would spend five or six hours drawing a single leaf, or covering a piece of paper with his signature or thousands of colored dots. He shared a bedroom with Harry McCue, and although McCue refrained from taking drugs, he, too, was enthusiastic about the idea of being a "psychedelic artist." They searched for inspiration in the dreamlike eroticism of Hieronymus Bosch and Egon Schiele, and in photographs by the German surrealist Hans Bellmer, known for his unnerving images of dismembered dolls. They came to the conclusion that they would never be able to produce such graphically disturbing work unless they rid themselves of their traditional Catholic morality and embraced life at its most extreme.

Mapplethorpe picked Andy Warhol to be his role model; the artist had created an antichurch within the Factory, his silver-walled studio on West Forty-seventh Street, where his followers—many of whom, like Warhol, had been raised Catholic—were involved in exploitative sexual games that hinged on a need to confess their sins and seek absolution for them. Their outlandish and pathetic antics had recently been documented in Warhol's *Chelsea Girls,* which Mapplethorpe had found "terrifying" in the way its stars willingly descended into drug-induced paranoia and self-hatred. Clearly, Warhol was more Satan than saint, and after seeing the movie Mapplethorpe was further convinced that exploring the dark side would incite his imagination. He vowed that when he moved to Manhattan after graduation he would find Warhol, and perhaps befriend him.

"We wanted the power of Satan," McCue said, "so we tried to seek out people and situations through which we could get in touch with him." Some of their efforts were almost laughably juvenile, as in the time they bought a goat's head from a butcher's shop and, encircling it with candles, attempted to raise the devil himself. They targeted blacks and homosexuals as two groups with intimate ties to Satan, and they made a concerted effort to socialize with Violetta and Rosita Cruz, whom Mapplethorpe was convinced knew voodoo witchcraft; they also visited Greenwich Village for the purpose of staring at homosexuals in order to bask in their malevolent aura.

On one occasion McCue purchased a pirate's shirt from a shop that catered to gay men, and although Mapplethorpe teased him about looking like a homosexual, he bought the same shirt the following week. It was all done in the spirit of "exploring the weird," as McCue described it, but given Mapplethorpe's attraction to men, his motivations seem far more complicated. As with the Columbian Squires jacket and the Pershing Rifles uniform, he used clothing to forge an identity for himself, and with the pirate shirt he could play at being gay—for art's sake.

Mapplethorpe's wardrobe at the time revealed a psychologically divided man; switching back and forth between a magician's cape, a "homosexual" shirt, and an ROTC uniform, he was still at war with himself. That spring, the growing tension between Pratt's art students and the engineers—"North Prattnam versus South Prattnam," as the school's newspaper described them—would force Mapplethorpe to choose between the two uniforms.

The engineering students largely comprised ROTC, and as the antiwar sentiment grew at Pratt, the army—and the engineers—

were targeted as the enemy. On April 15, 1967, fifty students from "Pratt Action for Peace" joined 125,000 protesters in Central Park, and roused by the demonstration, they staged a sit-down four days later, to denounce the presence of a visiting army colonel on campus. Trapped inside the athletic hall along with the ROTC cadets, the colonel eventually escaped through the back entrance, leaving Robert and his regiment to face the 150 demonstrators who waved signs that read WAR IS HELL and USE YOUR BRAINS NOT YOUR GUNS. Mapplethorpe was booed and hissed by members of his own art department, and soon afterward he began soliciting advice from friends on how to fail his upcoming army physical. They suggested everything from puncturing an eardrum to mangling a leg, but Mapplethorpe eventually opted to swallow a tab of acid before traveling to the army's induction center on Whitehall Street. By the time he submitted to his physical, he appeared so psychotic the doctor deemed him unfit to serve.

Escaping the army was Mapplethorpe's last hurdle to freedom. No longer obligated to keep his hair clipped short, he let it grow past his collarbone. He had always toned down his outfits before he visited Floral Park, but he could not hide his hair; when his father saw it, he flew into a rage. Fathers across America were engaged in similar battles with their long-haired sons, but in this case Harry's contempt was fueled by his growing suspicion that Robert was homosexual. Why else, Harry wondered, would his son have been rejected from the army? "You look like a girl," he shouted. "You make me sick."

In addition, Harry was infuriated by Robert's latest revelation that he would not be graduating with the class of '67, for, having switched majors, he was now a semester behind. Harry had warned his son that he would pay for only four years of college, and true to his word, he refused to give Robert an extra penny. It was not a totally unreasonable position; Harry still had three children to educate on his modest salary. But Robert had failed to make any contingency plans, and he drifted through the rest of the semester in a druggy haze. Sam Alexander, who had taught Robert typographic design several years earlier, recalled that Mapplethorpe stumbled into one of Alexander's evening workshop classes and passed out on the floor. "He wasn't even enrolled in the class," Alexander said, "but he stood there by the door, then he just fell. I caught him and put him in a chair. He was totally blotto."

Harry McCue was growing increasingly concerned about Mapplethorpe's drug use, and while he had once encouraged his friend to walk on the wild side, he now cautioned him to modify his behavior. "Bob was a caring, sensitive guy," McCue said, "and I watched him turn into a drug zombie." Bingeing on amphetamines, Mapplethorpe would stay awake for five days in a row, then sleep for the next week. He began telling McCue crazy stories about selling his soul to the devil for artistic success, and how he was then going to "destroy all the bullshit people" who had never believed in his talent. McCue still had no idea that his best friend was struggling with his sexual identity, but one of Mapplethorpe's drawings from this period hints at his confusion. It shows a young man with a woman's breasts and a heart flowering into a vagina.

Mapplethorpe and McCue continued to share a room together, but their close friendship was over. The coup de grâce was delivered when Mapplethorpe convinced McCue to smoke a joint, which, unbeknownst to either of them, was laced with a psychedelic drug. "Harry completely freaked out," recalled Pat Kennedy, who also lived in the brownstone on St. James Place. "He ran out of the house and never came back."

Before McCue left for Colorado to attend graduate school, he encountered Mapplethorpe again on the Pratt campus. "He was totally dismissive of me," McCue said. "It was like I hadn't measured up. He told me, 'Go to Colorado. You're a hick anyway.' So that was the end of our friendship. I stepped back from the edge, and I guess Bob was looking for a companion in Hell."

CHAPTER FOUR

"She was the first person to open my eyes."

—*Robert Mapplethorpe, about Patti Smith*

Robert Mapplethorpe first met Patti Smith toward the end of the spring semester of 1967, when he was still living at St. James Place. She was searching for Kenny Tisa, an old friend from New Jersey, and someone had mistakenly given her Mapplethorpe's address. So she wandered into the brownstone, where she found Mapplethorpe asleep in his bed. "I'm lookin' for someone," she said in a thick New Jersey accent. Startled, Mapplethorpe wondered if he was dreaming, for the intruder was one of the most curious-looking women he had ever seen. She had a pale, elongated face out of a Modigliani painting, piercing blue eyes, straggly black hair, and a ninety-pound body so sharp and angular that Salvador Dalí later described her as a "Gothic crow." Mapplethorpe himself thought she resembled a "creature from another planet" and, sleepy-eyed and tongue-tied, he escorted her to Tisa's apartment without saying a word.

Their fairy-tale introduction was followed, several months later, by an equally fanciful encounter in Greenwich Village during the height of the Summer of Love. Smith had accepted a dinner date with a stranger, and was now in the awkward position of rebuffing his sexual advances. The newspapers were increasingly filled with violent accounts of young women being raped or murdered in the East Village, which, like San Francisco's Haight-Ashbury, had recently been transformed into a mecca for hippies, drug addicts, and teenage runaways; it boasted the world's first head shop—the Psychedelicatessen—and countless stores selling candles, beads, incense, and astrology books. Smith didn't want to wind up as an unidentified body, so she was delighted to see Mapplethorpe's familiar face amid the carnival of pot-smoking hippies in Tompkins Square Park. He was tripping on LSD, and in his sheepskin vest and love beads he impressed her as the consummate hippie. Eager to be rid of her date, Smith ran over to Mapplethorpe and whispered "Pretend you're my boyfriend," then she waved good-bye to the other man. "Thanks for the dinner," she said, "but I've found the person I've been looking for."

What Mapplethorpe found in Patti Smith was a doppelgänger, someone whose love and intuitive understanding made him feel complete for the first time in his life. They were exactly the same age—both twenty—and they suffered from many of the same problems concerning their parents and their sexual identities. In comparison to Mapplethorpe, Smith had led a colorful and peripatetic life; she was born in Chicago but had spent her early childhood in Philadelphia, where her father, Grant, worked the night shift as a machinist for the Honeywell Corporation, and her mother, Beverly, cared for Patti and her three younger siblings. At the age of seven Patti developed scarlet fever, and lying in front of the coal stove in the kitchen, she was beset by terrifying visions that plagued her for years afterward. She hallucinated regularly, but since her parents did not seem overly alarmed, she used these recurrent episodes as grist for her creativity; she wove imaginative stories for her siblings. Patti didn't have many friends, for most of her classmates couldn't abide her strange behavior and physical appearance; born with a wandering eye, she already wore a black eye patch, in addition to which the scarlet fever had caused her hair to fall out, and she was partially bald.

When Patti was eight, the Smith family moved once again, to Woodbury Gardens, New Jersey, where they purchased a simple ranch house that was near a swamp and several pig farms. Across the street was a white-washed barn called Hoedown Hall, where the locals went square-dancing on Sunday nights, and where Patti would stare at the field in front of the barn conjuring ghosts in the swirling grass.

The world of make-believe provided Patti with a defense against her family's eccentricity. She adored her father, but whenever he wasn't working he would lose himself in the Bible, or in the UFO literature he studied for hours on end. The Smith children, particularly Patti, found it nearly impossible to attract Grant's attention, for nothing they did could possibly rival the phenomenal events that preoccupied him. The more Grant retreated, the more Patti came to regard him as an unapproachable godlike figure, with whom she yearned to communicate. This theme of the all-knowing yet silent father would reappear in Patti's work, as she enlarged her own experience with Grant to encompass the existential dilemma of praying to a mute God.

Beverly Smith was a more accessible figure than her husband, but like Patti she was prone to flights of fancy, and the children could never be sure if the stories she told were true. She was a deeply religious woman and raised her children to be Jehovah's Witnesses. Patti distributed copies of *Awake* to the neighbors and subscribed to the notion of the sinfulness of organized religions. Unlike Mapplethorpe's rigid upbringing, Smith's childhood and adolescence were a bewildering introduction to a volatile universe of miracles, ghosts, UFOs, and the Witnesses' looming millennium. Furthermore, Patti was uncomfortable with her femininity and longed to be a boy, a problem that she addressed in her 1967 poem "Female":

> female. feel male. Ever since I felt the need to
> choose I'd choose male. I felt boy rythums when I
> was in knee pants. So I stayed in pants.
> I sobbed when I had to use the public ladies

room. My undergarments made me blush.
Every feminine gesture I affected from my mother
humiliated me.

Smith's own personality was so muddled that she constantly searched for role models from whom she could fashion an individual style. It was not unlike Mapplethorpe's own obsession with costumes, but Smith didn't move sequentially from one identity to another, but rather she turned herself into a composite of cultural heroes, from Bob Dylan, Mick Jagger, Anna Magnani, Yves Montand, and Jean-Paul Belmondo to actress Maria Falconetti, who starred in Carl Dreyer's *Passion of Joan of Arc.* It was the French poet Arthur Rimbaud, however, who had the greatest influence on her; she developed a crush on him after seeing his picture on the cover of *Illuminations,* and subsequently referred to him as her "brainiac amour." Smith was far more interested in the mythic drama of Rimbaud's debauched life than she was in his poetry, and she identified with his quest to achieve enlightenment by systematically disordering the senses—in Rimbaud's case, with copious amounts of absinthe and hashish. The poet's doctrine of the *voyant* provided Smith with a creative rationale for her own hallucinations, which were unabetted by chemicals and sometimes descended upon her like a swarm of fireflies. She felt she had no other choice but to become an artist herself, for what other role could a woman with "visions" play?

Smith majored in art education at Glassboro State College, New Jersey, but in her junior year she became pregnant and, after dropping out of school, she lived in seclusion with friends in a remote part of the state until the baby was due. For someone who already felt uncomfortable as a woman, the pregnancy was a devastating blow; she loathed her large stomach and swelling breasts and, as she wrote in "Female," she felt "like a lame dog . . . like a bitch." Distraught, she gave the baby girl up for adoption and decided to move to New York that spring. Without any money, she spent her first two weeks in the city sleeping on the subway and on building stoops. Eventually she found a job at Brentano's bookstore on Fifth Avenue—Mapplethorpe, coincidentally, was working at the Brentano's in the Village—and it was then, on that sultry summer evening in Tompkins Square Park, that she encountered Mapplethorpe again.

Their attraction to one another was instantaneous. Since Smith had no place to live, she followed Mapplethorpe home to Brooklyn, where he was now sharing an apartment on Waverly Avenue with Pat Kennedy and his soon-to-be-wife, Margaret. Pat met Robert's new girlfriend the next morning, when he was sitting in the living room with his parents, who had just arrived from Wisconsin. He heard a door squeak and looked up to see the spectral figure of a naked woman coming toward the living room. "It was a long railroad apartment," Pat Kennedy recalled, "so we watched her for what seemed like an eternity. She looked like a swamp rat, and I kept hoping she'd disappear into the kitchen, but she sauntered into the living room and said, 'Hi!' My parents are really Midwestern, so when my mother saw Patti, she was in shock. 'My God!' she said. 'I was afraid New York was going to be like this.' "

Curiously, for someone who professed to loathe her own body, Smith had no inhibitions about it, and wouldn't think twice about undressing in front of total strangers. Her thoughts and visions were equally unrestrained, and she periodically withdrew into her private sanctuary of voices and images. "Patti was like nobody else I'd ever met before," Mapplethorpe said. "She was on the edge of being psychotic in a schizophrenic way. She told me stories, and I didn't know whether they were fiction or nonfiction. If she hadn't discovered art, she would have wound up in a mental institution. But she had a lot of magic in her." Mapplethorpe was enchanted by her lively mind and powerful creativity; she had a gift for language by which she turned even the most garbled nonsense into poetry, and she possessed a talent for drawing as well. He believed he had stumbled upon a true genius, and he assumed the responsibility of protecting her talent. He always made sure she had enough drawing paper, and whenever she became too manic, he helped refocus the energy onto her work. "I didn't believe in myself until I met Robert," Smith explained. "He gave me confidence as an artist."

She in turn helped bolster his poor self-image, and after years of feeling awkward and unattractive, he was finally happy with his reflection in the mirror. Certainly, his appearance was much improved from his early days at Pratt, and the androgynous hippie style suited him well. Mapplethorpe wasn't classically handsome, but with his curly brown hair and arresting green eyes he had a sensual quality that made him appealing to both men and women. Yet Mapplethorpe interpreted his attraction to Smith as evidence that he wasn't homosexual, and he attributed his previous sexual confusion to not having found the right woman. Smith, however, came to the relationship with gender problems of her own, and perhaps the reason they bonded so quickly was that each viewed the other as their missing half. They began trading clothes; friends were struck by their physical similarity to each other. "It was difficult to tell where Robert began and Patti left off," said Pratt student and photographer Judy Linn. "Together, they exuded all kinds of sexual possibilities."

For the next several months Mapplethorpe and Smith lived in the Waverly Avenue apartment, but Margaret Kennedy found Smith to be an impossible roommate and longed to evict her. There were definitely two sides to Smith's personality, and while she could be sweet and loving, she could also suddenly turn cruel and nasty. "Patti really hated women, particularly attractive ones," Margaret Kennedy said. "She was into power and manipulating people, and tried as hard as she could to intimidate me. I'd cook dinner for everyone, then she'd sit down and needle me about the food. Robert was forever apologizing for her behavior. He'd say, 'I know she's difficult, but she makes me happy.' He was totally infatuated with her, but I always thought Patti was out for herself."

In November Mapplethorpe and Smith moved to a brownstone on Hall Street, where they proceeded to transform the shabby apartment into a sixties version of *La Bohème*. Mapplethorpe covered the windows with strands of beads and draped the walls with batik bedspreads. It was the happiest period of his life, for he was desperately in love with Smith, and they were both dedicated to art, and to each other. Having left Brentano's, they were now working at F.A.O. Schwartz, the Fifth Avenue toy store, where she was a cashier and he a window trimmer. When they returned to Brooklyn at night, she would make grilled cheese sandwiches or spaghetti for dinner, then they would spend the rest of the evening on their various art projects. Smith didn't use drugs herself, but Mapplethorpe couldn't work without getting high on marijuana, amphetamines, or LSD. He approached his art with an almost priestly intensity and would sometimes dress in a monk's robe to put him in the appropriate mood. "When I work, and in my art, I hold hands with God," he once scribbled in Smith's notebook. She sparked his interest in the occult, and he often accompanied her to Samuel Weiser's bookstore on Astor Place to buy manuals on witchcraft and astrology. She read the books while he studied the pictures, and he began to fashion an aesthetic that combined Catholic and occult symbols. His favorite motif was the pentagram, a five-pointed "magical" star that would reappear again and again in his sculptures and photographs.

Mapplethorpe believed his own creativity was magic, and that by some inexplicable wizardry he was able to fuse antithetical images and objects into a piece of art. He mounted a large drawing of a pentagram on his bedroom wall at Hall Street and draped a piece of black cloth over a table to create an altar, decorating it with sacred objects he had purchased from a Hispanic religious shop on the Lower East Side—statues of the Blessed Virgin and pictures of Jesus that glowed in the dark. He then added a group of bronze devils that formed a circle around Scratch's infamous skull. Kenny Tisa, who had a reputation as one of the more talented artists at Pratt, took a dim view of Robert's efforts. "I always thought he had an incredibly refined aesthetic that made everything he did look beautiful," Tisa explained. "But I thought he was wasting his time with the crypto-religious art pieces." Nevertheless, Mapplethorpe constantly invited people over to the apartment to see the altar and would spend hours at a time rearranging the objects.

Smith referred to their apartment as "our little art factory," but Mapplethorpe wasn't as prolific as he would have liked; he complained that his job at F.A.O. Schwartz was depleting his strength, so Smith, whose manic energy was boundless, agreed to support him. She could afford to be generous, for she had recently been hired by Scribner's bookstore on Fifth Avenue, where she supplemented her income by failing to ring up purchases on the cash register and pocketing the money. Mapplethorpe had been involved in a similar scam at Brentano's, but he didn't possess Smith's cunning, and once when he pilfered several expensive lithographs from the store's print department, he was so afraid of being caught he impetuously flushed them down the toilet.

Now that Smith was serving as his patron, Mapplethorpe's life was even more perfect than ever; cloistered together in their "art factory," he would draw to the sound of Motown records while she sat next to him, sketch pad on her lap, creating a series of quirky little characters she described as "bad seed children." These "bad seeds" were usually naked little girls, their genitalia exposed and almost painfully accentuated. Sometimes she would also draw a young boy called Pan, who was conceived as Mapplethorpe's alter ego, and whose name was taken from both Peter Pan and the Greek god of shepherds. Eventually she began to scribble poetry around the edges of her drawings, which she now described as "drawlings."

When the weather grew warmer they would often take the subway to Coney Island, where a street photographer snapped their picture on the boardwalk one afternoon. Afterward Smith improved upon the photograph in a drawing, in which Mapplethorpe is wearing bell-bottoms and a mesh shirt and she is nearly naked in the fashion of the "bad seeds." "We were like two children playing together," Smith recalled, "like the brother and sister in Cocteau's *Enfants Terribles.*"

Janet Hamill, who had moved to Brooklyn from New Jersey, remembers the couple as obsessed with fame. "They were both totally enraptured by the idea of being artists and living outside of society," she said. "But they wanted to be rich and famous, too. Fame was particularly important to Patti, because, after losing the baby, she needed a way to reaffirm herself. Robert and Patti were always telling each other, 'We're going to make it, and we'll do it together!' "

Since leaving Pratt, Mapplethorpe had hardly seen his parents at all, but he decided to take Smith to Floral Park to meet them. His brother James never forgot the startling image of two hippies in floppy Day-Glo hats and tie-dyed T-shirts strolling down 259th Street toward the Mapplethorpe house. "I was with another kid from the neighborhood," James said, "and his mouth just dropped open, like he had seen invaders from another planet." Harry was equally shocked and regarded Patti with a look of total disgust. "She was a mess, a slob," he said. "Her hair didn't look like it had been combed in a month." He could barely conceal his contempt, for Patti's appearance presented a surly challenge to his systematic life.

Harry Mapplethorpe hated the sixties and everything the decade stood for. Even Richard, the good son, had surrendered to the craziness; he had married a Korean woman whom he had met while serving as an engineer aboard a naval vessel in Vietnam. Richard couldn't have made a more powerful statement of rebellion against Harry, for his new wife could speak only a few words of English. So now Harry had a daughter-in-law with whom he literally could not communicate, and even his neighbors felt pity for him.

Robert was so worried that Harry would discover that he and Patti were living in sin that he subsequently sent his parents a belated announcement of their "marriage," which supposedly took place in a strawberry field in California. "I don't think he's really married," Harry said after he read the letter, but Joan immediately went shopping at May's department store to buy Patti a negligee for her trousseau. Robert celebrated their unofficial union by presenting Patti with a small sapphire engagement ring and a gold wedding band. She was everything to him—wife, mother, sister, patron, and best friend. They even referred to their art as "the children." "In a way," Mapplethorpe insisted, "we *were* married."

CHAPTER FIVE

"Please don't go. . . . If you go, I'll become gay."

—*Robert Mapplethorpe, to Patti Smith*

"Nineteen sixty-eight had the vibrations of an earthquake about it," reported *Time* magazine. "America shuddered. History cracked open: bats came flapping out, dark surprises." In early April Martin Luther King was murdered and two months later Robert Kennedy was killed in the pantry of a Los Angeles hotel. Two days before the Kennedy assassination, Valerie Solanas, the founder of S.C.U.M. (Society for Cutting Up Men), had fired an automatic pistol at Andy Warhol, who barely escaped death himself. Even Mapplethorpe's little "art factory" on Hall Street was shaken by unforeseen tremors, for his "marriage" to Patti Smith wasn't as permanent as he had thought.

The world they had created together was not unlike that of *David and Lisa*, a movie about two emotionally disturbed adolescents who helped each other cope with reality; but now Smith was feeling stronger, and her life with Mapplethorpe was too confining. "For

Patti, having a boyfriend was as important as art," explained Janet Hamill. "When it came to men, she wanted a pretty conventional relationship. She viewed Jeanne Moreau as a role model, because Moreau was an artist and a sexual woman as well."

Mapplethorpe had never breathed a word about his homosexual inclinations to Smith, who accepted him as a heterosexual. Their own sexual relationship, though, was less than satisfactory, and while she still loved him, she didn't feel passionate about him. Despite the couple's long-range plans to move to Manhattan together, Smith had been secretly wooing another man, a blond abstract painter named Howie Michels, who shared an apartment with Kenny Tisa. "Howie was sweet and beautiful," Janet Hamill recalled. "Everybody worshiped him." Smith bombarded Michels with drawings and poems designed to flatter his ego; sometimes she would slip into his apartment to watch him sleep, and when he woke up in the morning she would be staring at him with a look of rapt devotion. "Patti had a way with boys," Howie Michels said. "She wasn't attractive in a classic way, but she had incredible charisma." Her strange behavior had always intimidated Michels, however, for no matter how crazy his friends acted under the influence of psychedelic drugs, he found Smith to be more "far-out even without drugs"; but against his better judgment, he and Smith decided to share an apartment together.

When Smith told Mapplethorpe she was leaving him, he reacted as though the earth had truly splintered beneath his feet. "Please don't go," he pleaded. "*Please!* If you go, I'll become gay." She didn't take his threat seriously, but when she returned to the apartment to pick up her clothing she found him surrounded by pictures of naked men that he had clipped from gay pornographic magazines. His own dark secret was finally out, and he was literally wallowing in it.

"I was crazed, really crazed, because I was dependent on her at that point," Mapplethorpe told photography critic Carol Squiers. Pershing Rifle Bob Barrett witnessed a traumatic scene in front of the Hall Street apartment. "I'll never forget it," Barrett said. "Mapplethorpe was crying, 'Please don't leave me alone! . . . Please don't leave me alone!' It was really gut-wrenching, because it was like he was losing part of himself."

What Mapplethorpe had lost was his last defense against his homosexuality, and without Smith serving as a "wife," he finally had to grapple with the true nature of his sexual feelings. Yet he was still confused about them, and while he made no effort to pursue other women, he was equally reluctant to seek out men.

In September he returned to Pratt with money from a student loan and moved back in with Pat and Margaret Kennedy on Waverly Avenue. During winter intersession, he left for San Francisco, telling his friend Judy Linn, "I have to find out if I'm gay once and for all." San Francisco had attracted large numbers of homosexuals since World War II, when, according to author Randy Shilts, the massive purges of gay men from the military increased the number of refugees in the Bay Area, which was then the major point of debarkation for the Pacific theater. The stigmatization of homosexuality was so great that while men could congregate in gay bars, they couldn't dance or even touch one another without the police threatening to close the establishment down. Psychiatry regarded homosexuality as a mental disorder, and gays lived in fear of having their "deviant" behavior exposed to their families and employers. Secrecy and a need to "pass" as straight were the cornerstones of their existence.

Throughout the sixties, however, San Francisco's gay population became increasingly visible, as homosexuals renovated the dilapidated Victorian homes in the Castro district and opened up camera shops, bookstores, restaurants, and bars. Meanwhile, thousands of hippies, drawn to the city by the drugs, the Be-Ins, and the rock concerts at the Fillmore and Avalon ballrooms, swarmed into the Haight-Ashbury neighborhood. San Francisco became known as the most sexually tolerant city in America; perhaps Mapplethorpe felt he could finally lose his inhibitions there. He told writer Victor Bockris: "I flew out to San Francisco not knowing anyone and met some boy on the plane who was sort of a hippie and he was going to stay in a commune so I just went with him. It was in the middle of a suburban area where all these kids had taken over this house and it was quite amazing. They were all very sweet and made food for everybody and if some didn't have money, you know . . . it worked at that time. . . . And you know everybody took all kinds of drugs. I wonder what happened to them all. Probably half of them are dead."

The trip to San Francisco represented a turning point for Mapplethorpe, and when he returned home he became involved with a young man named Terry, whom he had met through Judy Linn. Numerous Pratt students were then declaring themselves "bisexual," and the affair with Terry might not have merited much attention except for Mapplethorpe's swift and dramatic embrace of all things homoerotic. "It was like it happened overnight," explained Patti Smith, who, despite living with Howie Michels, continued to see Mapplethorpe nearly every day. "The gay thing wasn't there, and then suddenly it was." His fascination with gay pornography led him to make collages from the pictures in the magazines. Pratt student Tony Jannetti recalled seeing one in which Mapplethorpe had drawn a heart over a picture of two men performing fellatio. "Even by the standards of the sixties," Jannetti recalled, "it was pretty risqué." Mapplethorpe's most-talked-about piece at the time was a sculpture he created by taking a pair of his blue jeans, stuffing the crotch with several socks, and wiring the pants so the groin pulsated.

Mapplethorpe was a work-in-progress himself, and he began to craft another identity. His pendulum had swung to such an extreme that Judy Linn, accompanying him to the beach at Fire Island, was astonished when he slipped off his blue jeans to reveal a studded black leather bikini. "He disappeared the minute he got there," Linn recalled, "and later he told me, 'A limousine brought me home, but the guy was a creep.' It was like suddenly Robert had this secret life that I wasn't going to be part of."

Amazingly, that secret life now involved working as a call boy. Mapplethorpe had been profoundly moved by *Midnight Cowboy*, which won the Oscar for best picture that year, and he identified with Jon Voight's character, Joe Buck, the starry-eyed cowboy who dreams of becoming a fancy gigolo to wealthy Park Avenue ladies. Ultimately Buck winds up plying his trade with gay men in movie theaters and dingy hotel rooms, going so far as to physically abuse an elderly Catholic client, who whimpers pitifully, "I deserve this. . . . I brought this about myself." Joe Buck was hardly an inspirational role model, but Mapplethorpe, nonetheless, began dressing like a cowboy, and he contacted a call-boy service. He was set up with five different men, most of whom were married and lived in the suburbs, and while he described the experience as "interesting," he became physically ill after each encounter. It was almost as if he couldn't accept his homosexuality without associating it with debasement, something he "brought about" himself.

Mapplethorpe was scheduled to graduate from Pratt in June 1969, but he failed his psychology final, and when the teacher gave him an F for the semester, he was short one course for his degree. Despite having attended Pratt for five years, he walked away, then, without a diploma, and he moved to a loft on Delancey Street on Manhattan's Lower East Side. His arrival in the city coincided with the Stonewall riots, the seminal event in gay history that helped to galvanize what had previously been a small-scale movement into a major campaign for social change.

Throughout the sixties gays had been arrested in Greenwich Village bars simply for being gay, but on June 28, when the police raided the Stonewall Inn, riots broke out as two hundred patrons were expelled from the premises. Spurred into action by a handful of drag queens, angry customers fought back, hurling bricks, bottles, garbage cans, and pieces of broken glass. The rioting lasted several days, and within weeks of the event a major social movement began to take root across America. Newly radicalized gays and lesbians sought to remove the stigma of gender deviance from homosexuality, replacing it with the concept that same-sex love was healthy and natural. "Coming out" was promoted as a means of pride and self-affirmation, but in the libertarian atmosphere of the sixties and seventies, gay activists frequently associated "coming out" with the freedom to engage in promiscuous sex. Mapplethorpe's identity as a gay man was focused almost exclusively on erotic activity, and after his friend Terry took him to a gay bar for the first time, he immediately went home to make a collage entitled *Tight Fucking Pants*.

While Mapplethorpe's life was undergoing dramatic changes, Patti Smith was suffering her own growth pains. She was still in love with Howie Michels, but he was having difficulty coping with what he described as her "weird and trippy" personality. She had recently become attached to a wolf skin, which she insisted had magical properties, and she wouldn't go anywhere without it, even taking it to Michels's parents' house in Long Island. She was equally attached to Mapplethorpe, whom Michels pegged as an "untalented artist with an edge of darkness about him." He didn't care for Mapplethorpe's company at all and was annoyed that Smith could not shake herself loose from him. In April she and Michels agreed to live separately, and she moved from Brooklyn to an apartment on West Twelfth Street in Greenwich Village. One afternoon Michels passed a scowling Mapplethorpe on the staircase to Smith's building, and when he entered the living room Michels saw the wolf skin dangling from a noose attached to the ceiling. "Robert and Patti had gotten into a fight," Michels explained, and "Robert had hung the wolf." The next time Michels visited Smith, she sat in a corner muttering an incantation, and as her voice grew louder and the words more jumbled, a strange black cat pounced on the windowsill and entered the room. "It was like a death cat from Hell," Michels said. "I totally freaked." Michels made a swift retreat from Smith, and their relationship ended on that bizarre note.

Smith fell apart once again, but this time she didn't have Mapplethorpe for support. Instead, he cruelly flaunted his relationship with Terry, as if to exact penance for her deserting him. "If I had been going out with another woman, it would have been different," Mapplethorpe explained. "But Patti couldn't compete with a man. It was another thing entirely, and she went crazy." Smith described this period of her life as "unbelievably painful," and according to Janet Hamill, who was then her roommate, she suffered a nervous breakdown and tried to kill herself. "Patti was suicidal," Hamill said. "Seriously suicidal." Smith, however, didn't follow the ordinary route, such as hospitalization and psychiatric intervention. Instead, she took a leave of absence from Scribner's and flew to Paris with her younger sister, Linda, to follow Rimbaud's ghost down the cobblestone streets of Montparnasse.

She and Linda spent nearly three months in Paris, where they joined a troupe of street musicians and fire-eaters, and Patti became expert at playing a toy piano and picking the pockets of passersby. They later followed the troupe to a farm outside Paris, where someone accidentally spilled boiling water on her and she was given morphine and belladonna to ease the pain. The drugs ignited her hallucinations, and for several days she had strange visions that merged Kenneth Anger–like imagery of homosexuals and switchblades with dreams of Brian Jones, the Rolling Stones' guitarist, who drowned in a swimming pool several days later. She described the vision to *Rolling Stone:* "I was crawling in the grass. And there was a whirlpool, rocks and river and ocean and whirlpool, and we were slipping, it was me and Brian, he had my ankle and he was holding on . . ."

She returned to New York on July 21, the day after Neil Armstrong's moon walk, and showed up on Mapplethorpe's doorstep, frightened and disoriented. Mapplethorpe wasn't in much better shape himself, as he had long neglected his dental hygiene and had ulcerative sores on his gums, and the infection had spread to his lymph nodes. They needed each other badly, and to appease Smith, Mapplethorpe ended his affair with Terry. "It was sexually successful," he explained, "but it wasn't going anywhere. He wasn't any replacement for Patti." She moved into the loft on Delancey Street where Mapplethorpe had temporarily taken up residence as a house sitter; the ensuing events were as strange as Smith's dreams.

A neighbor was murdered across the hallway; when Mapplethorpe and Smith saw the chalk marks outlining the dead body, they envisioned the murderer coming back to kill them. They panicked and fled the loft, taking only their art portfolios with them. They checked into the Allerton, a run-down hotel on West Twenty-second Street that attracted derelicts and drug addicts. Mapplethorpe's infection had worsened and his temperature had climbed to 105 degrees. While Smith gave him sponge baths, he lay shivering and sweating on a small rusted cot in their seedy room. His temperature remained dangerously high for several days, but neither of them had any money for a doctor's visit, and she couldn't take him to an emergency ward because if she left the hotel she might be denied reentry, having been unable to pay the bill. Trapped, she whiled away the hours sitting on the fire escape outside their room, listening to the screams of the ambulances as they raced down Seventh Avenue toward St. Vincent's Hospital. She later wrote about the incident in her poem "Sister Morphine": "i imagined my friend dying. i flash blood all over the place."

Finally, after five days in the hotel, Smith devised a plan of escape. She couldn't take Mapplethorpe out the front door without encountering the hotel manager, so she lifted him in her arms and carried him down the fire escape to the street. She hailed a cab, and when the driver asked their destination, she named the only place she knew that might be hospitable to a pair of destitute artists. "The Chelsea Hotel," she said.

The Chelsea was only a block away, and when they arrived Smith lifted Mapplethorpe over the threshold of the hotel and placed him in a chair in the lobby. Then she marched into the office of the hotel manager, Stanley Bard, a slightly built man with a mournful face and the bland personality of an accountant; he seemed an unlikely person to be running a hotel filled with artists, but over the years he had amassed a substantial art collection in lieu of rent, and Smith hoped to barter with him for a free room. She found him seated at a large mahogany desk, a frieze of dancing cherubs on the ceiling above him. "Hi," she said. "My name is Patti Smith, and I've got Robert Mapplethorpe outside. You don't know us, but we're going to be big stars one day, only we don't have any money. . . . Robert's sick . . . nothing serious, just trench mouth." She then presented Bard with her portfolio, urging him to use it as "collateral." Smith was determined to keep up the monologue until Bard either gave them a room or threw them out. "Okay, okay," he finally said, handing her the key to one of the smallest rooms in the hotel.

Smith was triumphant. "Mr. Bard," she exclaimed, "you will not regret this." She helped Mapplethorpe into the elevator and up to room 1017, where they both collapsed on the small single bed. The room was almost as decrepit as the one they had left, but they were so relieved to have escaped the nightmarish incidents of the past week that the Chelsea seemed like paradise to them. Huddled together on the bed, watching the cockroaches creep across the ceiling, they made a solemn pact to stay together until they were both strong enough to stand alone.

PART TWO

Patron Saints

CHAPTER SIX

"My life began in the summer of 1969.
Before that I didn't exist."

—*Robert Mapplethorpe*

Mapplethorpe could not have invented a better place for his rebirth than the Chelsea Hotel, a psychedelic Coney Island for creative geniuses and freaks. The hotel's exterior projected a seedy glamour more appropriate to New Orleans than to West Twenty-third Street, its redbrick facade and florid iron balconies enlivening a grim neighborhood of Irish bars, Greek delicatessens, an Automat, and the McBurney YMCA. Like Mapplethorpe, the Chelsea had undergone numerous transformations, and over the years its interior design had been adapted to suit the times. It was built in 1882 as an elegant residential hotel for artists, and appropriate to the Gilded Age, it offered sprawling ten-room apartments with thirteen-foot ceilings, wood-burning fireplaces, elaborate mahogany cupboards, and stained-glass windows. During the Depression, however, the hotel was stripped of many of its opulent Victorian details, and the grand suites were destroyed to make smaller rooms for transients.

These were later occupied by World War II refugees who had fled Europe. In the mid-sixties, Andy Warhol shot portions of *Chelsea Girls* there, establishing the hotel's reputation as a breeding ground of depravity. Pimps in gold-lamé suits, transvestites in see-through lingerie, and junkies strolled the hallways; rock musicians such as Jimi Hendrix, Janis Joplin, the Allman Brothers, and the Jefferson Airplane crowded the lobby downstairs. By the time Mapplethorpe and Smith arrived at the Chelsea in July 1969, creative chaos reigned supreme. While not all of the Chelsea's occupants were as famous as composer Virgil Thomson, or as eccentric as George Kleinsinger, who kept several monkeys and a thirteen-foot python in his apartment, most were dedicated to the real or imagined life of Art.

No sooner had Mapplethorpe recovered from his infection than he and Patti Smith were networking furiously in the lobby. "Gaining connections" became their primary goal. Smith had returned to her job at Scribner's and resumed supporting Mapplethorpe by skimming money from the cash register. The couple soon developed a reputation for their eye-catching costumes, which, at the Chelsea, was no mean accomplishment. Mapplethorpe had recently purchased a sailor uniform at an Army & Navy store in the Village, and he swaggered around the hotel in tight bell-bottom trousers, a white cap seductively slanted on his forehead. Smith had become enamored of the can-can dancers in Toulouse-Lautrec's paintings and had taken to wearing a purple skirt and bright green tights. She added a personal touch by winding delicate silk ribbons and pieces of antique lace around her wrists and ankles. "Both Robert and Patti came across as stylish and brilliant," recalled Stanley Amos, who had been part of New York's bohemian life for years and now operated an art gallery from his room at the Chelsea. "Of course, Patti could be surrealistically rude, but it was part of the times to be arrogant. And Robert and Patti were terribly of-the-moment people. A lot of us fell madly in love with them."

The Chelsea resident most infatuated with the pair was a filmmaker and photographer named Sandy Daley, who rented an apartment on the tenth floor that had once been occupied by Jackson Pollock. "I knew Robert and Patti were brilliant right off the bat," Daley said, "and I thought it would be a real tragedy if somebody didn't help them. Patti was afraid she was schizophrenic, which was the wonderful link between us. We were both psychotic, we were both suicidal, but we had the most brilliant conversations together." Since Smith worked full-time at Scribner's, however, it was Mapplethorpe who derived the benefits of Daley's tutelage, and she became his guide to the Chelsea and downtown New York.

A tall, elegant woman in her mid-thirties, Daley had long golden hair and a penchant for wearing long chiffon dresses ornamented with half moons and stars. Her personality was equally ethereal, and after graduating from Oberlin College she and her lover Nicholas Quennell moved to a windmill in Oakland, California, where they worked on a series of life-size photographic "paintings." Liquid photo emulsion wasn't then available to the general public, so Daley experimented with different formulas herself, cooking the brew in huge vats on the stove; she and Quennell later projected negatives on the emulsion-soaked canvases for eighteen hours, but the resulting images quickly faded. After years of work, Daley had only two photographs to show for her efforts, although these were later exhibited at the Dwan Gallery in Los Angeles with Warhol's diptych of Marilyn Monroe's lips. It was the high point of Daley's career; she moved to New York hoping to make films, but lacking the money for more than a few eight-millimeter shorts, she spent most of her time conceiving projects that never materialized.

Mapplethorpe's arrival at the Chelsea gave Daley a focus for her creative energy; recognizing in him the determination she lacked, he became yet another project for her. And no one was more receptive to having a mentor than Robert Mapplethorpe. Every morning at eleven-thirty he and Daley had breakfast together in her apartment, then, after smoking some hash, they would look through her photography books. Mapplethorpe held the popular notion that photography was not an art form and had no desire to pursue it seriously, but Daley was a persuasive teacher. She had written her college thesis on the Victorian photographer Julia Margaret Cameron, and in her previous efforts to make life-size images permanent on canvas, she had studied the technical processes invented by William Henry Fox Talbot and Louis Daguerre. "We talked about every aspect of the photographs," Daley said. "I pointed out differences in lighting, and the use of negative and positive space." In addition, she offered her own philosophy of beauty, which was based on austerity and minimalism. Her apartment was painted white from floor to ceiling and furnished with nothing except a mattress, some of Warhol's silver helium-filled pillows, and a vase of long-stemmed tulips or lilies. She had impulsively given away her Hasselblad camera to a "pretty boy on the King's Road" in London the year before, but she still had a Polaroid, which she used to take pictures of her flowers. She urged Mapplethorpe to pick up the camera himself, and influenced by her refined aesthetic, he shot his first flower photographs in her stark white apartment.

Daley was a regular at Max's Kansas City, and soon Mapplethorpe and Smith were heading to Mickey Ruskin's celebrated bar-restaurant at Park Avenue South and Seventeenth Street. "Max's was the place where Pop art met Pop life. . . . everybody went to Max's and everything got homogenized there," Andy Warhol wrote in *POPism*. And indeed the restaurant's location between uptown and downtown helped attract an amazingly diverse clientele—celebrities, such as Mick Jagger, Jane Fonda, Bob Dylan, Jim Morrison, and Warren Beatty, as well as politicians, Park Avenue socialites, photographers, models, hairdressers, Hell's Angels, drag queens, and drug addicts. Yet it was the artists who comprised Max's most faithful customers, and from the time Ruskin opened the bar in 1965 he numbered among his patrons John Chamberlain, Robert Rauschenberg, Neil Williams, Larry Rivers, and Frosty Meyers. Ruskin allowed the artists to trade art for food and liquor, and it was the only restaurant in town that also displayed paintings and sculptures by the very people who were running up astronomical bills at the bar. Like the Cedar Tavern, the macho watering hole of the abstract expressionists, Max's was the scene of numerous drunken brawls. Unlike the fifties, though, when one art style dominated, the sixties witnessed a proliferation of radical new movements—Pop Art, Op Art, Minimal Art, Process Art, Color-Field Painting, Conceptual Art, Earth Art—and the artists at Max's verbally, and sometimes physically, trashed one another's efforts.

Nevertheless, they were nearly all united in their disdain for the habitués of Max's back room, where the social behavior was in shocking contrast to their own aggressively heterosexual attitude. The back room had once been dominated by Andy Warhol and his entourage; but since the 1968 assassination attempt on Warhol by Valerie Solanas, the artist had begun to disassociate himself from "the cultural space debris," as art critic Robert Hughes once described Warhol's followers. To Mapplethorpe's disappointment—he still hoped he and Warhol might become friends—Warhol didn't go to Max's much anymore, but even without the pop artist the scene was distinctly Warholian. In the hellish red glow of Dan Flavin's light sculpture, transvestites glided from table to table, mascara dripping down their cheeks. At the stroke of midnight, a young Warhol acolyte named Andrea Feldman would routinely jump on a table top, rip open her shirt, and start singing "Give My Regards to Broadway" while jiggling her breasts.

Sometimes Mapplethorpe and Smith accompanied Daley to Max's, but more often they went by themselves, spending several hours getting dressed beforehand so they could pass muster at the door. Ruskin and his formidable bouncer, Dorothy Dean, a black woman with a Harvard degree who referred to herself as the "Spade of Queens," were scrupulous about keeping undesirables off the premises and rejected anybody who was too bland or blatantly middle-class. Mapplethorpe and Smith usually had no problem at the door but confronted resistance when they attempted to break into the clique of Warhol groupies and rock musicians in the back room. Night after night, week after week, they occupied a table by themselves and ordered a green salad and a Coke to share. Returning to the Chelsea in the early morning hours, they would then analyze their progress in "gaining connections."

A major breakthrough occurred when rock promoter and writer Danny Fields invited them to join his table, and while he later barely remembered the incident, both Mapplethorpe and Smith hailed it as a triumph of networking. Fields, who was a popular figure at Max's, managed Iggy Pop and Detroit's MC5, whose guitarist Fred (Sonic) Smith would later become Patti's husband. Fields compared Robert and Patti to a "leather version of Sigmunde and Sieglinde," the incestuous twins of Wagner's *Ring* cycle. No one could figure out whether they were lovers, siblings, or best friends, and in the spirit of the times, no one cared if they were straight, gay, or bisexual. "One of the essential ingredients of Max's was the sexual revolution," wrote Ronald Sukenick in *Down and In*. "Some people claimed they were getting laid three times a night out of Max's. Some of the inner circle would use Mickey's office upstairs. Some people would use the phone booths. Some would use the bathroom floors. Even the arabesque bar was not unknown as a place for hard-core sex. . . . It was like Wilhelm Reich a-go-go." The back room attracted a gay population, and Mapplethorpe, in his white sailor suit, exuded sex appeal. "Everybody wanted to know, 'Who's that cute boy with the girl who looks like him?' " Fields recalled. "Do you think anybody was interested in Robert as an artist? They wanted to sleep with him. It was all about sex."

Yet Mapplethorpe was not so eager to risk his relationship with Smith by taking up with a man again, and since they were sharing a small bed at the Chelsea, it was easier to fall back into their childlike "marriage." He had scavenged a children's phonograph from the garbage outside the hotel and repeatedly played Tim Hardin's "Hang On to a Dream." Mapplethorpe's dream was to be rich and famous, and to somehow hang on to Smith without sacrificing his sexuality. Certainly, they were as devoted as any married couple could be and shared everything on a fifty-fifty basis. To stretch Smith's salary, they devised a scheme nicknamed "One Day, Two Day": if she went to the Guggenheim Museum one day, for exam-ple, he could go the next day; if he used paints and paper one day, she could use them the following day. The strategy even extended to drug and alcohol consumption, and if he tripped on acid, she had to make sure she was sober enough to care for him. For Christmas that year, she presented him with four bronze skulls that she had purchased on a layaway plan, and he made a necklace by hanging them on a leather cord. His gift to her was a book he had designed based on a child's advent calendar, where each day is marked by a little door that flips open to reveal a Christmas surprise—a bell, an angel, or a shooting star. Underneath the doors of his calendar were little pictures of Patti.

Mapplethorpe's exposure to the Dionysian atmosphere of Max's had made him even more determined to use gay pornography in his art, and he began searching through Times Square bookstores for old copies of gay magazines in order to understand the conventions of homosexual erotica. In the late forties, muscle and fitness publica-tions such as *Grecian Guild Pictorial* and *Physique Pictorial* had begun to include photographs and drawings aimed at a growing gay readership, and the models, posed in bathing suits and loincloths, personified the idealized man. George Quaintance, an American illustrator and painter, contributed to *Physique Pictorial,* and before his death in 1957 he produced a series of pictures of naked cowboys and sailors who projected the all-American athleticism of Johnny Weissmuller. It was the Finnish-born artist Tom of Finland, however, who pointed to a new homoeroticism that was more overtly sexual. Aroused by his memories of German soldiers during World War II, he created drawings of men in black leather jackets, motorcycle caps, and knee-high leather boots that centered on the "butch" male. It was an image that would become more and more visible as the growing gay rights movement helped erase the prevailing "camp" behavioral style, by which some men adopted feminine mannerisms. Instead, gay activists advanced the notion that a man could be both gay and virile, which served to focus attention on the previously hidden S&M subculture, where men in leather bars enacted complicated master-slave scenarios that tested one's masculinity.

Like the figures in Tom of Finland's drawings, the devotees of the leather cult had a predilection for boots, motorcycle caps, handcuffs, and sometimes Nazi symbols. It was the ultimate in "butch," and for someone like Mapplethorpe who had spent his adolescence attempting to escape the sissy stereotype by joining macho fraternities, the outward trappings of the S&M subculture held great appeal. He was too nervous to go to one of the leather bars alone, however, so he invited Sandy Daley, who disguised herself as a man by donning a leather jacket and piling her long hair in a motorcycle cap. Once inside one of the West Village bars, they sat down at a table and watched various men being physically and verbally abused. "It was like we were on a date," Daley recalled. "Robert kept asking me, 'Are you comfortable . . . do you want something to drink?' He was so polite and attentive that it was hard to believe that men in dog collars and chains were crawling around at our feet."

It isn't known how often Mapplethorpe returned to the bar, or if he actually engaged in any S&M activities at this time, but if his previous behavior is any indication, he probably first approached the situation as a "reporter in search of the weird." What is clear, though, is that the S&M scene immediately captured his imagination and spoke to his darker sexual urges. Mapplethorpe's sexual identity was already so entangled with his feelings of guilt and retribution that by adopting the role of the sadist, he could become the punitive priest—or parent—in any "forbidden" relationships with other men. "There was no going back," he said. "I had found my form of sex." He had found his subject matter, too. The uniforms and sexual paraphernalia provided him with a whole new range of images that he could use in his artwork. Pictures of men in Harley-Davidson motorcycle caps and leather pants began appearing in his collages, as if Mapplethorpe first needed to "play" with them as he had done with the cutouts of male models in gay magazines two years earlier at Pratt. Soon, his art and his sexuality would become so thoroughly entwined that no one, least of all Robert, could untangle the Gordian knot.

Mapplethorpe and Smith's room at the Chelsea was too small to serve as anything more than a crash pad, so they rented the front part of a loft in a building several doors away from the hotel. At first they slept at the Chelsea and worked in their new "art factory," but when the entire loft became available in the spring of 1970 they lived there full-time. It was located at 206 West Twenty-third Street in a five-story building above the Oasis bar, and at night, an electric sign flashed the letters O-A-S-I-S outside their window. The loft served as a sanctuary for Mapplethorpe, and to block out the intrusive sunlight he blackened the windows. The previous tenant had already constructed a thin plasterboard partition to divide the loft into two separate spaces, and Mapplethorpe took the back, Smith the front. When they weren't networking at Max's, they concentrated on their artwork, often in a frenzied, helter-skelter manner. Mapplethorpe had yet to find the best medium for his self-expression, and his art was literally all over the place. In addition to the collages, he began creating more ambitious pieces that owed a debt to Marcel Duchamp, who, in 1917, had signed his name to a urinal and presented it as a piece of "ready-made" art. Scouring the garbage for usable objects, Mapplethorpe made large-scale assemblages from discarded night tables, rolls of chicken wire, lamp shades, and motorcycle parts. At Pratt, he had transformed his bedroom into a psychedelic church; now he was adding S&M totems to religious ones, and the effect was as sinister and creepy as Dr. Caligari's cabinet. Jockstraps dangled like spiderwebs from a chinning bar; a devil's head poked out from the crotch of a pair of blue jeans; pictures of naked men hung on a clothing rack. He had even converted his bed into a piece of art by covering his mattress in black fabric and creating with steel tacks the silhouette of a man's body.

Mapplethorpe had been existing for a while on a diet of amphetamines—in addition to the ten cups of coffee he drank every day—and he had so much nervous energy he could barely contain himself. Unable to determine when a piece was finished, he kept adding more and more elements to it—a statue here, a spool of black thread there. A firm believer in the adage that "clothes make the man," he saw no reason clothes could not also make art, and taking the T-shirts off his back, he hung them, one on top of the other, on wooden frames that served as minimalist grids. A similar technique was used with his bikini underwear; in one case, he simply stretched a pair of pale blue briefs over a white frame; in a more elaborate version, he first placed a picture from a pornographic magazine inside mesh bikini briefs, which he then framed in wood and cellophane. When he wasn't raiding his closet for his art, he was raiding his art for his clothes, and the black T-shirts, which had rarely been washed, were forever being pulled down from the wall to be worn at Max's. Even Smith's apparel was not safe from Mapplethorpe; preparing to dress for Scribner's, she would discover that shirts, pants, and shoes had been sucked into the vortex of her roommate's creations. Frustrated by his constant invasions, she began posing the sarcastic question "Can I wear this? Or is it art?"

That spring, one of Mapplethorpe's denim jackets, embossed with a death's-head and a pair of dice, was part of a group show titled "Clothing as Art" that was organized by Stanley Amos in his room at the Chelsea. The exhibit was mainly targeted at residents of the hotel, and while it was not significant to Mapplethorpe's career, it helped move him into position, from Chelsea outsider to insider. His nightly appearances at Max's were beginning to pay off as well, and once when he wore a piece of jewelry he had designed—a fetish necklace made of dice, skulls, rabbit's feet, feathers, beads, and ivory claws—someone purchased it on the spot. The fetish necklaces became an instant trend among Max's fashionable clientele, and Mapplethorpe began selling so many pieces that a wealthy backer offered to give him seed money to start his own jewelry company. But he declined the proposition because he did not want to be known as a jewelry designer, with its negative arts-and-crafts connotation. Stringing beads and trinkets was a form of meditation, a way to soothe the nerves after a day of taking speed and making art, and he was loath to turn it into a business.

Instead, he persuaded every influential person he met to view his artwork at the loft. Intent on creating the right atmosphere, he carefully choreographed these studio visits so that even the right music—usually a blues record—was playing in the background. Despite his determination, he was shy with strangers and tried to make sure Smith was available to play hostess. Unlike Mapplethorpe, she was never at a loss for words, but social skills were not her strong suit, and sometimes she would not even bother to look up from whatever book she was reading, informing the intruder, "Don't bother me now, I'm learning to speak in tongues," or "Sorry, I'm studying alchemy." Actress Sylvia Miles recalled hearing a series of blood-curdling screams coming from Smith's side of the loft, and when Mapplethorpe continued to show his artwork as though nothing was happening, Miles finally interrupted him. "I think someone's being killed," she announced. Miles then heard Smith yell from the other side of the partition, "Shut up! I'm practicing scream therapy."

No one who visited the loft came away unaffected by it, and the word most frequently used to describe it was "shocking." Sam Green, who had curated Warhol's 1966 retrospective at the Institute of Contemporary Art in Philadelphia, was repulsed by its "creepy" aura. "Robert and Patti played off each other like a sinister George Burns and Gracie Allen," he said. "I certainly couldn't bring important collectors like the Tremaines or the Sculls down there." Fredericka Hunter, who would later exhibit Mapplethorpe's photographs at the Texas Gallery, was working as an assistant at the Richard Feigen Gallery when she first visited the loft and was taken aback by the sexual explicitness of Mapplethorpe's pornographic collages. "I presume I said a lot of stupid things," Hunter recalled, "because my mouth was hanging open the whole time." Clearly, it was not the type of work that made for an easy sale, and whenever anyone actually purchased a piece, it was cause for celebration. In the spring of 1970, critic and curator Mario Amaya, who organized a 1976 exhibit of Mapplethorpe photographs at the Chrysler Museum, bought a leather suitcase that contained a stuffed squirrel wrapped in bandages and a net. But Mapplethorpe's pièce de résistance was purchased by Charles Cowles, who was then the publisher of *Artforum,* and who claimed to have been "mystified" by the loft. "I came from a prep school background and mixed with Park Avenue and Fifth Avenue," he explained. "Here was Robert, this night crawler, who surrounded himself with demonic sculptures." One, in particular, caught Cowles's eye—an assemblage that addressed Mapplethorpe's major themes of religion, homosexuality, and guilt. It was an altarpiece fashioned from a nightstand that rested upon Smith's magic wolf skin; a statue of the Sacred Heart, with black tape covering its eyes, was displayed on the altar, along with two votive candles. To the right of the altar was a portrait of the Sacred Heart, and once again, the eyes were masked out. A fringed lamp hung from the ceiling to illuminate the central image: emerging from the drawer of the night table was a hammer bound in bloodred string. At this stage in Mapplethorpe's career, he occasionally substituted real tools for male genitalia, and in another work from 1970 he presaged one of his most disturbing photographs—of a bloodied, mutilated penis—when he trussed a corkscrew in red thread and attached it to a piece of canvas upon which he had splattered red paint. The "sightless" eyes, the bound genitals, and the contrast between light and dark would all become familiar motifs in Mapplethorpe's photographs. But Charles Cowles was hard pressed to figure out what to do with his unwieldy assemblage; it wasn't anything he wanted to display in his apartment, so he placed it in storage, where the night table/altar remained in the dark for the next twenty years.

Mapplethorpe was disheartened whenever anybody failed to appreciate his art, yet he never questioned his talent. The positive feelings he had as a child—the "certain magic" running through his fingers—sustained him as an adult. "I always thought I was good," he said. "That's why it was so frustrating when other people didn't agree." Certain prominent art dealers, such as Leo Castelli, provided artists with monthly stipends to be applied against sales of their work, and Mapplethorpe frequently discussed with Smith his desire to find "patronage." Accompanied by Sandy Daley, he made the rounds of dealers along Fifty-seventh Street, at that time the heart of the art market, but he usually received a chilly reception. "An assistant at the front desk would take his slides and never bother to return them," Daley recalled. "Dealers would set up appointments to visit the loft and never show up." Mapplethorpe complained to Smith that dealers were loath to exhibit his work because of its homosexual content, and that several privately advised him that if he wanted to become successful, he had to soften the gay themes. Smith herself had similar conversations with gay dealers, who confided their reluctance to support Mapplethorpe for fear that it might draw attention to their own homosexuality. "Several of them told me, 'I think the work is really interesting, but how can I exhibit it without making a statement about who I am?'" Smith said. "Robert was really hurt by that."

Emmanuel Cooper in *The Sexual Perspective* describes the difficulties faced by homosexual artists over the past hundred years, and how their self-expression was restrained by law, church, and society. Gay artists were forced to tone down their work to make it less threatening to the status quo, and an elaborate code developed to help them express homoerotic feelings. The male nude was often placed within an acceptable context, such as a gymnasium, boxing ring, or swimming hole, or else it was elevated beyond contemporary morality by the use of classical and religious themes. "The nakedness of St. Sebastian, for example, has been used not to show the humiliation of the saint," Cooper writes, "but as an excuse for a display of the male naked body." The social changes of the sixties allowed gay and lesbian artists greater freedom of expression. David Hockney produced a series of etchings illustrating the writings of the homosexual Greek poet Constantine Cavafy, then progressed to autobiographical paintings of his friends and lovers. But Hockney's world of beautiful gay men lounging by elegant swimming pools was far removed from Mapplethorpe's collages of oral sex, and leather men with their faces obscured by bloodied gauze pads. "My sexuality was interesting to me," Mapplethorpe explained, "and it was something I wanted to explore." But perhaps because his sexuality was still incomprehensible to him, his art was often criticized as unfocused and incomplete. Fredericka Hunter outlined what she believed to be his biggest problem: "I was having dinner with Charlie Cowles and Klaus Kertess [who then owned the Bykert Gallery] and we had all just seen Robert's work, and he was really pressing hard for someone to give him a gallery show. We all said, 'What is there to show?' More than anything, it was the atmosphere of his loft that was so unique, and unless you moved the entire thing into a gallery, there wasn't anything really tangible."

Robert's life couldn't have been more different from that of Harry Mapplethorpe's, yet his loft owed a debt to his father's almost fanatical rigidity. Robert, too, despised slovenliness, and while he went for days without bathing—the loft was equipped with only a toilet and sink—he made sure that each object in his dark garret had its rightful place. His decorating style may have impressed visitors as insanely disordered, but he knew where everything was, and why it was put there. Conversely, Patti's room not only looked chaotic but also lacked an underlying logic of neatness. Month-old doughnuts, dirty laundry, soda cans, chopsticks, charcoal pencils, and satin ribbon were strewn across the floor. Unlike Robert, who carefully preserved his work, she seemed to court the destruction of her own art by flinging her "drawlings" around the room, where people frequently mistook them for worthless scraps of paper and trampled on them. When she lost one notebook that contained a year's worth of sketches, Mapplethorpe was nearly apoplectic. "How could you let something like this happen?" he lectured her. Ann Powell, who worked at Scribner's with Smith and became a close friend, found Mapplethorpe to be "extraordinary" in his unwavering support of his roommate's career. "There was no doubt that Patti was much smarter than Robert," she said, "but I never saw them be competitive with one another. In fact, I think Robert was the only man in Patti's life who never tried to stifle her creativity."

Even with Mapplethorpe's encouragement, Smith had a restless imagination that kept pushing her in different directions at once. She had a talent for drawing and writing, but anyone who listened to her hold forth on such diverse subjects as masturbation, hemorrhoids, and God recognized that her personality was the greatest gift of all. She was a brilliant performer. Still grappling with her own gender issues, she sometimes dressed as a boy in straight-legged pants, white shirt, and black jacket—her "Charles Baudelaire look" —and sometimes patterned herself after a sexy Jeanne Moreau, in high heels, silk stockings, and garter belt. Complaining that she felt "burdened" by her pencils and sketch pad, she had recently given up drawing to concentrate on poetry, and the question of sexual identification underscored much of her writing. She began spending her lunch hours at the Gotham Book Mart on West Forty-seventh Street, where members of the literary avant-garde had been going to buy books or give readings since 1923. Surrounded by photographs of Gertrude Stein, Dylan Thomas, Jean Cocteau, and Marianne Moore, Smith would sit cross-legged in the aisle and study poetry by the French Symbolists. "Patti always looked bizarre and ema-ciated," recalled Gotham owner Andreas Brown. "I felt sorry for her." When she returned to the loft at night, she tapped her creative impulses with a technique she borrowed from the French writer Jean Genet. "I'd sit at the typewriter and type until I felt sexy," Smith later confided to *The New York Times Magazine,* "then I'd go and masturbate to get high, and then I'd come back in that higher place and write some more." In that "higher place," she spun out a series of vivid poems that formed the basis of her first book, *Seventh Heaven,* published in 1972.

Smith's writing was marked by a slapdash quality—she used low-ercase typeface and crude punctuation—but it had a raw power that derived from its disturbing subject matter. Many of her poems were about women who were seduced, raped, and otherwise victimized by men, and it was Patti herself who sometimes adopted a male voice. Smith's male characters were often barbaric, but her women were frequently portrayed as pathetic slaves to biology, destined to be "bloated" bitches or "kitten pick-ups like Brigette [*sic*] Bardot." Eve was blamed for original sin because she allowed "the stud" Satan to snake between her legs; even heroines such as Joan of Arc are stripped of all dignity—waiting to be burned at the stake, she fantasizes about having a brutal sexual encounter with a guard:

> I dont want to die
> I feel like a freak

dont let me cut out
I wasnt cut out
to go out virgin
I want my cherry
squashed man
hammer amour

The violence of this scene and others is clearly related to Smith's drawings, in which, consciously or not, she evokes the horror of sexual abuse in her pictures of naked little girls. In fact, she illustrated her poem "A Useless Death" with a horrifying drawing of a female figure hurtling toward a phallic-shaped household plunger aimed directly at her genitals.

Yet Smith was extremely comfortable around men and drew support and inspiration from them. One of her first contacts at the Chelsea was Bob Neuwirth, a prominent downtown figure who was friendly with Smith's idol Bob Dylan. He introduced her to Janis Joplin and to minimalist painter Brice Marden, with whom she had a brief affair; he created a painting for her titled *Patti Smith, Star.*

She then met poet Jim Carroll, who, at sixteen, had become a literary cult figure when *The Paris Review* published an excerpt of his book, *The Basketball Diaries.* It was an account of his high school days at New York's exclusive Trinity School, where he played basketball and hustled homosexuals to subsidize his heroin habit. He called it "perversion for profit." He later served time at Riker's Island Juvenile Reformatory for possession of heroin, and after his release he checked into the Chelsea to write the poems that would eventually be included in *Living at the Movies,* which was nominated for a Pulitzer Prize. Carroll, who was then nineteen, was handsome in an ethereal, drug-addicted way, and it didn't take Smith long to realize that he was an archetypal Rimbaud figure. She met him at a poetry reading in the early spring of 1970, and even though he was then dating a fashion model, she employed the same vigorous courtship style she had used to win Howie Michels. Before going to Scribner's every morning, she stopped at the Chelsea to take Carroll his favorite breakfast—two light and sweet coffees, several chocolate doughnuts, and a pint of chocolate Italian ice from a local pizza shop. More important, she gave him money to buy heroin. "Patti was one of the few women I met who actively encouraged my addiction," Carroll said. "I think she would have been disappointed if I had *stopped*." Ultimately Smith's strategy worked, and Carroll moved his belongings into the front part of the loft. "Robert was living in the weirdest space I'd ever seen," Carroll recalled. "It was as if some Hell's Angels had sailed through Miss Havisham's room and landed in her bridal suite. The only thing missing was the cake with the cobwebs."

Mapplethorpe reacted with surprising equanimity to Carroll's invasion of their privacy and displayed no outward signs of jealousy. He and Smith had grown accustomed to leading separate sexual lives, and he did not perceive Carroll as a threat. In fact, he enjoyed his company, and the trio of roommates spent spring evenings strolling around Times Square, where they reveled in the whistles and catcalls from men who mistakenly took them for male prostitutes. During one such outing, Mapplethorpe suddenly disappeared into a dilapidated building on Forty-second Street, and Smith and Carroll reluctantly followed him up a narrow flight of stairs. At the top of the landing a heavyset man in a seersucker jacket inquired, "Are you here for the exhibition?" Smith and Carroll paid the entrance fee and, walking into a gloomy room, were confronted with two dozen life-size mannequins of the type one might find in medical school; their inner organs were visible to the eye, and in this case, the organs were supposedly ravaged by cancerous tumors. Carroll wrote about the incident in *Forced Entries:* "The stout man ran all this down for us, caressing the fiberglass images, even removing, with a frightful snap, the various diseased sections. He petted them as if they were ill canaries . . ." Smith and Carroll were so repulsed by the exhibit they rushed for the door, but Mapplethorpe was mesmerized by the grim display and stayed behind.

For the next several weeks Mapplethorpe kept returning to the "Cancer Hall of Fame," as Carroll called it, and his artwork reflected a renewed interest in freaks. In addition to gay pornography, he was now making collages from pictures of Siamese twins, bearded ladies, and encephalitic men. He had always been drawn to the unusual, but his fascination with cancerous organs was extreme even for him. What would prompt someone, day after day, to stare at replicas of hideous tumors? Smith labeled this phase of

Mapplethorpe's life the "Freak Period," and brushed off his trips to the "Cancer Hall of Fame" as "something a young artist goes through."

Mapplethorpe, however, lived in a culture where homosexuals were viewed as sexual curiosities—the families of homosexuals had a legal right to commit them to mental institutions. Vito Russo in *The Celluloid Closet* demonstrates Hollywood's reluctance to portray gays as anything but sadists, psychopathic killers, or pitiful sissies. Nineteen-seventy was the year Mart Crowley's play *The Boys in the Band* came to the screen, and while it was considered revolutionary for Hollywood even to make a film about homosexuality, the men, or "boys," reinforced the prevailing notion that gays were sad and pathetic creatures. The character of Michael, the guilt-ridden Roman Catholic, expressed the self-hatred internalized by many homosexuals in American society when he recited the film's most celebrated line: "You show me a happy homosexual, and I'll show you a gay corpse."

Mapplethorpe was still preoccupied with the issue of whether he was gay, bisexual, or straight; going to the leather bars with Sandy Daley had opened his mind to the mysteries of human sexuality, but the experience hadn't clarified his own status. Even though Jim Carroll was four years younger, Mapplethorpe viewed him as more sophisticated and continually solicited his advice on sexual and social matters. From Carroll's unique perspective of being both a student at the Trinity School and a street hustler, he was comfortable with Upper East Side debutantes as well as junkies. "I knew how to make class transitions," Carroll said, "and Robert wanted me to teach him how to move from one society to another. You could see the same thing in his work, a tension between two extremes. He always had an intuitive understanding of counterpoint." One night Carroll went with Mapplethorpe to a gay bar, and later Mapplethorpe asked him if he ever wondered whether he was gay himself since he had once hustled homosexuals. "No matter how beautiful the guy was, I always asked for the money," Carroll said. "That's how I knew I was straight."

"I wish," Mapplethorpe replied, "that I could be that sure."

CHAPTER SEVEN

"If it doesn't make you horny, it's not art."

—*The Holy Modal Rounders' motto*

"When Robert took pictures, it was like he owned the subject. He dominated them completely. He didn't see you as a person, but as an art object."

—*David Croland, about Robert Mapplethorpe*

Mapplethorpe's "coming out" was a gradual process of dramatic advances and muddled retreats. Within a year he had had an affair with Terry, worked as a hustler, resumed his relationship with Patti, and embraced, at least visually, the culture of the leather bars.

Mapplethorpe believed he couldn't freely explore his sexuality if he stayed in contact with his family, so from the time he moved to Manhattan, he had withdrawn from them; he would hardly see his parents for the next several decades. "I would never have done what I'd done," he explained, "if I'd considered my father as somebody I wanted to please." He also attempted to keep his expeditions to the leather bars a secret from Smith, who, despite her freethinking ways, was close-minded about homosexuality. "Robert and Patti had gone through a lot of formidable times together," Jim Carroll explained, "but the idea that he could be a homosexual was distressing to her. She had a strong Puritanical streak."

Aspects of Mapplethorpe's life had much in common with J. M. Barrie's Peter Pan. Smith, in fact, called him "Pan," and certainly she played the role of Wendy, who, by providing him with a more positive self-image, became an integral part of his identity—his shadow, as it were. Together they had created a Neverland in their various "art factories," where he frequently confided his fear of growing old to a permissive mother who indulged his homosexual fantasies as long as they did not cross over into real life. Smith maintained that she never thought of Mapplethorpe as either gay or straight, but rather "as an artist." Artists, as Smith frequently pointed out, were "beyond gender," which gave her the freedom to live with Mapplethorpe in a land of polymorphic sexuality. It was fitting, then, that of all the people who had an impact on Mapplethorpe, the one who finally "outed" him went by the name of Tinkerbelle.

Tinkerbelle was the ultimate seventies creature, an elfin beauty whose caustic wit made her a star on the disco circuit before she later committed suicide by jumping from a window. Tinkerbelle, prone to acts of petty cruelty, was jealous of Patti and made a point of introducing Robert to a young model named David Croland, who had just moved back to New York from London and was temporarily sharing her room at the Chelsea. Croland was over six feet tall and had thick brown hair, dark eyes, and an aquiline nose that gave his face a slightly haughty air. He had been raised in New Jersey, the son of a textile executive, and while still a teenager had become a regular fixture on the New York club scene, where his stature as "a beauty" granted him easy access to Warhol's inner circle. He dated Susan Bottomly, a Factory superstar known as International Velvet, and they spent evenings together at such clubs as Ondine, Il Mio, Arthur, and the Scene. In the late sixties Croland moved to London and worked as a fashion model, a profession to which he was ideally suited, for even when he wasn't in front of a camera he loved to pose. "David was completely image conscious," recalled Richard Bernstein, who designed the covers for Warhol's *Interview*. "He always had to surround himself with the most beautiful models. I think he wasn't only in love with Robert but loved the idea of being seen with him." Mapplethorpe's appearance served as a counterpoint to Croland's aristocratic good looks. "Robert was a real Cocteau beauty," Croland recalled. "His hair was wild and curly, and he had a wide, sensuous face and piercing green eyes. But it wasn't a refined face. There was something rough trade about it."

Croland had been planning on returning to London, but when he met Mapplethorpe on Memorial Day, 1970, he abruptly changed his plans and moved from the Chelsea to an apartment on East Fifteenth Street. "The relationship just took off like a rocket," he explained. They began to see each other every day, but Mapplethorpe managed to keep the affair from Smith for fear that it might precipitate a breakdown or suicide attempt. The memory of how badly she had reacted when she learned about Terry was still fresh in his mind. Tinkerbelle, however, telephoned Smith at her parents' house and, in a singsong voice, announced, "Robert has a boyfriend." Smith became hysterical and bitterly confronted Mapplethorpe about his deceitful behavior, and they did not speak to each other for days afterward. But once the initial shock had worn off, she begrudgingly accepted the relationship as an attraction between two men who loved to look at themselves in a mirror. "I saw it as a mutually narcissistic thing," she said. "David had nothing to do with the relationship I shared with Robert." It was Mapplethorpe, in fact, who was most upset with Tinkerbelle and held the indiscretion against her for the rest of his life. "Tinkerbelle," he lamented, "spilled the beans."

That being the case, Mapplethorpe decided to mark the occasion with a personalized rite of passage, and he proposed to Sandy Daley that she make the film *Robert Having His Nipple Pierced*. He then enlisted the aid of Dr. Herb Krohn, the Chelsea's resident physician, who, after warning him that he felt uncomfortable puncturing "cancer-prone" tissue, reluctantly agreed to perform the procedure. "It was an unusual request," Krohn said, "but I'd lived at the Chelsea long enough so that nothing really surprised me." Daley had conceived the event as a Happening and had invited friends from the Chelsea to watch her shoot the movie. There was no script and the minimal props consisted of several roses, a plate of strawberries, a single black feather, and a vase of carnations. Daley did not want anything to distract from the central "work of art"—Mapplethorpe himself, who had taken a hallucinogenic drug and, bare-chested and glassy-eyed, swooned in Croland's arms, like Michelangelo's "dying slave." Dr. Krohn swabbed Mapplethorpe's chest, which was littered with rose petals, with bloodred antiseptic; then, after piercing his skin, he covered the wound with a piece of gauze and a strip of black tape in the shape of a cross. For the remainder of the thirty-three-minute film, Mapplethorpe and Croland rolled around on Daley's all-white floor in their black leather pants. Afterward, when Mapplethorpe removed the bandages, he discovered that his gold earring was not dangling from his nipple after all, but from the skin underneath. "You missed it by about an inch!" he admonished Krohn, who assured him it was healthier that way. But while Mapplethorpe may not have had much experience with S&M, he knew that a "tit ring" had only one logical place, and he did not wear it again.

More important than the actual ritual, though, was the liberating effect Tinkerbelle's disclosure had on Mapplethorpe's work. After years of using pictures appropriated from gay porn magazines, he now borrowed Daley's Polaroid camera and began taking his own photographs. "It was," he said, "more honest, somehow."

In his new spirit of candor, he first turned the camera on himself, as if he had become the literal representation of the models in the porn magazines. Adorned in a cock ring, nipple clips, and a leather harness, he was curious to discover which sensations were pleasing to him, and these Polaroids serve as a document of his sexual education. David Croland became Mapplethorpe's first male model, and Robert took pictures of David wearing black leather pants and a leather vest, a bandana tied around his eyes. Mapplethorpe's photographing men whom he physically desired would become a lifelong pursuit for him, and his photographs would serve as a diary of his sexual adventures.

At first Croland enjoyed modeling for Mapplethorpe but he soon grew to dislike the latter's coercive tactics. Croland was always being pushed to wear more suggestive outfits or to pose in compromising positions. "When Robert took pictures," Croland explained, "it was like he owned the subject. He dominated them completely. He didn't see you as a person, but as an art object."

Mapplethorpe had little or no power over Smith, and consequently of all the people he photographed over the years she was the
only one to elude his manipulative grasp. A comparison between his
Polaroids of Croland and those of Smith reveal the photographer's
strikingly different approach to his two subjects: Croland is a lifeless
mannequin, while Smith's quirky personality dominates the picture,
whether she is posing in a black bra and panties or wrapped in a
Chelsea Hotel towel. Unlike bodybuilder Lisa Lyon, who later
epitomized the "Mapplethorpe female," Smith did not possess a
physique of Olympian proportions. Small and narrow-hipped, she
had large breasts that drooped so low on her chest she sometimes
appeared flat-chested; a cesarean scar bisected her lower stomach,
and silver stretch marks flecked her pale skin. Hers was a body that
was eminently human, yet Mapplethorpe found beauty in it nonetheless, and he often remarked that something magical happened
whenever he looked at her through the lens. "I just couldn't miss
with her," he said. As Mapplethorpe had once raided Smith's closet
for "clothing as art," he now pursued her with his camera; he
photographed her in the bathroom, reading a book, going to sleep
at night, dressing for work. It got to the point where she felt she
could not make a move without seeing an instant frozen replay a few
minutes later.

Nothing, however, was safe from art that summer, as people encircled one another like vampires. Sandy Daley even made a movie
about Smith's menstrual period and filmed Mapplethorpe changing
her sanitary napkin. Smith relentlessly picked Jim Carroll's brain
about writing poetry, and when she began to develop a reputation as
a poet herself, she split up with him. Carroll then wrote a thinly
veiled account of his life with Smith in *Forced Entries* that included
details of her affliction with "crabs," and how she would preserve
the tiny parasites in a specimen jar. Mapplethorpe and Smith had
developed such a reputation for their strange brand of creative wizardry that when a fifteen-year-old hustler named Jesse Michael
Turner moved into the loft with them, Chelsea resident Stanley
Amos wondered if perhaps he was only "a figment of their madness." Turner, who as of this writing is in prison for bank robbery,
had been living on the street for five years when he arrived at the loft
with an art dealer. Mapplethorpe and Smith decided to temporarily

"adopt" him, and he moved into the loft about the same time as Patti's sister, Linda, who was so frightened by Mapplethorpe's sinister assemblages that every time she went into his room she drew crosses on her forehead with eyebrow pencil. At first, Turner was also intimidated by Mapplethorpe's skulls and devil's heads, but he came to regard him as a "truly caring person not out to exploit." In an effort to convince Turner that even he could transform his life into art, Mapplethorpe donated wall space in his loft so the young hustler could create something special on it. Inspired by Mapplethorpe's collages, Turner covered the wall with aluminum foil and thousands of pictures of the Rolling Stones. Later, when Turner was incarcerated at Lewisburg State Penitentiary in Pennsylvania, he began writing poetry "on the pleasure of crimes against the establishment."

Turner left the loft at the end of the summer, but not before witnessing a strange incident. Mapplethorpe had been taking LSD when he suddenly began screaming, "I'm the devil! I'm the devil!" Turner ran to the Chelsea to "get some Thorazine from a guy named Crazy Matthew so Robert could crash," but Mapplethorpe, meanwhile, stripped off his clothes and began sprinting down Twenty-third Street stark naked while still shouting, "I'm the devil!" Croland, who had been at the loft, took him back upstairs, but when he tried to calm him down, Mapplethorpe insisted that Croland was the devil, too. "How can I be the devil?" Croland asked him, to which Mapplethorpe replied, "You're beautiful, and beauty and the devil are the same thing."

Yet Mapplethorpe was not about to turn his back on Croland, who served as a junior patron of sorts. Croland didn't have a lot of money, but he and Mapplethorpe often rode uptown in his Corvair convertible to Bloomingdale's, where they ordered tuna sandwiches and a chocolate malt at the lunch counter; afterward, Croland would charge the bill to his mother's store credit card. Unfailingly, the two young men caused a stir at Bloomingdale's, for while Croland dressed in simple clothes so as not to distract from his own beauty, Mapplethorpe was a leather-plumed peacock. The "S&M look" was not then widely seen on the streets of New York, and certainly not on the Upper East Side at high noon, but Mapplethorpe, oblivious to the weather, often wore a black mesh T-shirt under a black leather jacket; black leather pants, over which he had strapped a codpiece; studded leather wristbands; Smith's skull necklace and several skull rings; dangling earrings; and layers of fetish necklaces. Watching as Croland dressed in a black blazer and black turtleneck, Mapplethorpe once mused, "I wish I could be elegant like you." Croland told him, "You'll never be elegant, but you have other qualities."

Chelsea resident Arnon Vered described Mapplethorpe as someone who "intuitively knew how to move in the world of public people." Specifically, he knew how to make contact with the people who could help him move in that world. Croland frequently took him to Halston's East Side apartment, where the fashion designer surrounded himself with some of the world's most stylish women, such as Marisa and Berry Berenson; the model Verushka; jewelry designer Elsa Peretti; and Loulou de La Falaise, who worked for Yves Saint Laurent. Loulou de La Falaise and Berry Berenson were then sharing an apartment and sometimes double-dated with Mapplethorpe and Croland. "I thought Robert was just divine," exclaimed Berenson, the widow of actor Anthony Perkins, who died of AIDS. "Of course there was that dark side to him. I had no idea he was gay at the time, or what activities he was involved in. You've got to remember that in those days people didn't spend hours analyzing things. We were just out to have fun." Returning home from one of their double dates, Mapplethorpe, who was totally in awe of both Berenson and de La Falaise, excitedly told Smith, "I think I'm being accepted by the fashion crowd." Smith did not like Croland's social clique at all and dismissed them as petty and "snidey." She worried that Mapplethorpe's education had taken a superficial turn, and that he was now judging people based on whether or not "they looked like *Vogue*."

Throughout the summer Smith had been giving impromptu poetry readings at the Chelsea, and using her raspy voice to accentuate the rhythm of the words, she was unconsciously edging her way toward a career in music. Certainly she could not have failed to notice the sudden prominence of rock and roll at Max's Kansas City, where the Velvet Underground performed five nights a week, thereby paving the way for the emergence of a local New York band scene. Encouraged by the success of the Velvet Underground,

Mickey Ruskin opened a cabaret on the second floor and helped launch the careers of Billy Joel and Bruce Springsteen. Eventually the musicians began to outnumber the artists, as Max's evolved from an art scene to a music scene.

On Saturday nights Smith could be found at Village Oldies, a record store on Bleecker Street, where she first met Lenny Kaye, who would become a member of the Patti Smith Group. He was writing rock criticism and earning extra money by working part-time as a sales clerk. Having been infatuated with Smith from the time he first spotted her at Max's months earlier, he was thrilled whenever she stopped by the store, and they would drink beer and dance to their favorite oldies, such as the "Bristol Stomp" by the Douvells. That fall, Kaye and Smith began experimenting with the idea of adding musical accompaniment to her poetry readings, and even though Kaye knew only a few basic guitar chords, they settled into a comfortable rhythm together. "At the time we didn't have any big plans to do anything," he explained, "but looking back, the seedlings of some of our songs were in those poems."

Robert Mapplethorpe celebrated his twenty-fourth birthday on November 4, 1970, with his first one-person show, at Stanley Amos's gallery in the Chelsea. He designed the invitations himself by taking gay pornographic playing cards, masking out the models' eyes, and printing the details of the show on the back. The main focus of the exhibit, however, was not gay pornography but twelve "freak collages" that he had been working on for the past several months. These were interesting for the way Mapplethorpe had positioned his pictures of fat women, Siamese twins, and rubber men next to pieces of Mylar that simulated mirrors. He would later return to this theme by creating multipanel pieces in which an actual mirror is juxtaposed to a sex picture, thereby drawing the unwitting observer directly into the scene. In the most effective of his freak collages, a master of ceremonies beckons the viewer into an open coffin, the top of which is covered in Mylar. "Welcome to the cabaret," the MC might be saying, for the image suggests Joel Grey in the musical *Cabaret*, inviting his guests to enjoy the garish and macabre pleasures of Berlin's Kit Kat Klub.

Cabaret was loosely based on Christopher Isherwood's *Berlin*

Stories, which had also inspired John Van Druten's play *I Am a Camera*—a perfect title for Mapplethorpe and Smith's life together. Everything was still being recorded for art's sake, and when Smith became involved with Sam Shepard, he served as yet another camera.

She met the playwright at the Village Gate, where he was playing drums with the Holy Modal Rounders, a cult band from Vermont. Shepard was only twenty-six, but he had already written twenty plays, including *La Turista* and *The Unseen Hand,* and he had won six Obie Awards from *The Village Voice.* Physically, he was a blend of Mapplethorpe and Jim Carroll; he had narrow blue eyes, straight brown hair, a lean, rangy build, and, even then, a movie star's magnetism. In his early plays Shepard often dealt with the difficulties of achieving the right balance between independence and enslavement in relationships, and his characters usually wound up fleeing for their lives. In real life, while Shepard had been married to his wife, O-Lan Johnson, for only a year and had a six-month-old son, he became involved with Patti Smith. "Me and his wife still even liked each other," Smith explained. "I mean, it wasn't like committing adultery in the suburbs or something." In fact, Shepard and Smith regarded themselves as partners in crime, and often when they went to Max's they would drink too much and start fights. "Everything you heard about us in those days is true," Smith admitted. "We'd have a lot of rum and get into trouble. We were hell-raisers."

Smith fell deeply in love with Shepard, and although Mapplethorpe was still involved with Croland, he was jealous of their relationship. Shepard represented more of a threat than Jim Carroll or any of the other men with whom Smith had had affairs, and Mapplethorpe never lost an opportunity to criticize him. Even though he had never read a word Shepard had written—Mapplethorpe's reading consisted mostly of gay porn—he pronounced him "overrated." Furthermore, he warned Smith that if Shepard had left his wife and baby, wouldn't he leave her, too? But she was so infatuated with the playwright that she even staged her own public *rite d'amour* by having an Italian gypsy named Vali give them both tattoos (hers was a lightning bolt, his a hawk moon) while Sandy Daley made a film of it. Even Mapplethorpe temporarily put his reservations aside to take Polaroids of Smith showing off the dainty zigzag on her knee.

At each stage of her life Smith managed to align herself with a man whose interests reflected her own. Now that she was attempting to combine music and writing, Shepard was an ideal partner, for not only did he dream of being a rock and roll star himself, he also approached his plays almost as improvisational jazz; he was less interested in plot and characterization than in convulsive bursts of imagery. He encouraged Smith to do lyrics for his play *The Mad Dog Blues,* while she urged him to write the prose poems that later appeared in *Hawk Moon,* which he dedicated to her. "Sam loved my writing more than anybody I ever knew," Smith explained. "He wasn't so supportive of some of the other things I was doing, like my singing and stuff, but he made me value myself as a writer."

Shepard was in the audience, along with Smith's other "favorite guys"—Robert Mapplethorpe and Brice Marden—when she made her public debut as a poet at St. Mark's Church on February 12, 1971. St. Mark's in-the-Bowery had a long tradition of hosting avant-garde events, and several of Shepard's early plays had been staged there. It was Mapplethorpe, however, who indirectly pushed Smith into the spotlight, when he pressured poet and photographer Gerard Malanga to submit her name to the church's Poetry Project. Malanga had been scheduled to give a reading himself, and he requested Smith as his opening act. "She wasn't known at all," Malanga recalled, "and when I brought up her name, everybody said, 'Who?' Then, after I helped her out, she later berated me for making her go on first. Patti was talented but not very humble."

Smith had asked Lenny Kaye to accompany her on guitar, and after giggling nervously and temporarily losing her train of thought, she launched into her own version of Bertolt Brecht's "Mack the Knife." For the next twenty minutes Patti mesmerized the audience as she chanted her poems in a tough, working-class New Jersey accent that seemed at odds with her frail, Edith Piaf appearance. She delighted in being outrageously sacrilegious, and in one poem she described Jesus Christ as "the great faggot in history having twelve men to lick his feet," and expressed her overall disdain for Christianity in "Oath," which was later incorporated into the rock song "Gloria":

> So Christ
> I'm giving you the good-bye . . .

I can make my own light shine
and darkness too is equally fine
you got strung up for my brother
but with me I draw the line
you died for somebody's sins
but not mine.

Smith had spent her life entertaining people with her wild, meandering monologues, but this was the first time she had used her "special
powers" to captivate a large audience. She was an exuberant and
obscene Sally Bowles for the 1970s, truly a Blue Angel, and those
who saw her first performance at St. Mark's realized they had witnessed something unique.

Smith had no time to savor her success, for the relationship with
Shepard had reached new heights of hysteria. Sometimes they lived
in his room at the Chelsea, other times they stayed at the loft, but no
matter where they were, their activities and conversations were
marked by a theatrical frenzy that was too intense for real life. "I
think Sam was terribly jealous of her talent," explained Ann Powell,
Smith's friend from Scribner's. "I remember a terrible scene when
he destroyed some of her drawings, and she was absolutely crushed
about it." Fittingly, the most accurate picture of their relationship is
Cowboy Mouth, a play they wrote together in two nights by shoving
an old typewriter back and forth between them. Smith's character,
Cavale, is a deranged woman who kidnaps Slim from his wife and
baby and attempts to turn him into a "rock-n'-roll Jesus with a cowboy mouth." Slim accuses Cavale of ruining his life by continually
tempting him with seductive dreams of stardom. "You're twisting
me up," he screams. "You're tearing me inside out!" In between
shouting matches, Slim and Cavale order food from the Lobster
Man, who eventually sheds his shell to become the rock-n'-roll savior himself. The play ends as Cavale sits at the edge of the stage
delivering another monologue, and the Lobster Man points a gun
to his head and pulls the trigger.

When Cowboy Mouth opened at the American Place Theater on
April 29, Smith and Shepard starred in the play. Only a month previ-
ously he had appeared at the same theater with his wife, O-Lan, in
The Mad Dog Blues, in which she had played a character based partly

on Smith. But the merry-go-round of life imitating art was becoming too much for Shepard, and he left the show after a few performances to join the Holy Modal Rounders in Vermont. "It didn't work out because the thing was too emotionally packed," he told his biographer Don Shewey. "I suddenly realized I didn't want to exhibit myself like that, playing my life onstage. It was like being in an aquarium." Not long afterward, Shepard took his wife and son with him to London, where he gave up drugs and happily distanced himself from the chaotic life he had known in New York.

"Patti was devastated by Sam's departure," said Ann Powell. "It completely ripped her apart." Helen Marden, who suspected an affair had taken place between her own husband and Patti Smith, recalled the night a drunken Smith was carried out of Max's screaming Shepard's name. During the weeks Smith mourned Shepard's departure, Mapplethorpe made a point of curtailing his activities to keep her company, but he still pursued her with his camera. One day she became so exasperated by his picture-taking that she fled the loft and ran upstairs to the roof of the building, where he followed with his Polaroid. Pedestrians on Twenty-third Street heard a female voice seemingly from out of the sky shout, "I hate art. . . . I hate art."

CHAPTER EIGHT

"No one wanted to be normal in the seventies.
We all wanted to be wild and fabulous."

—*Maxime de La Falaise McKendry*

"I woke up pretty quick. It was like, now I get it. . . .
Robert will do anything for his career."

—*David Croland*

On July 3, 1971, David Croland unwittingly introduced Robert Mapplethorpe to his next patron, at a medieval feast hosted by Maxime and John McKendry in their apartment at 190 Riverside Drive.

Maxime, the food editor of *Vogue,* was in the process of writing *Seven Hundred Years of English Cooking,* and she regularly gave dinner parties to test out such exotic recipes as roast peacock, fifteenth-century hare pies, gilded bird, and jellied veal hocks. Guests often joked about her culinary peculiarities and wondered if she spiced her food with eye of newt and toe of frog, for one infamous dinner ended with everybody suddenly falling asleep at the table. But despite the unconventional and occasionally hypnotic fare, the McKendrys' parties were a magnet for a stylish crowd that included Diana Vreeland, the former doyenne of *Vogue;* Mick Jagger; Andy

Warhol; Metropolitan Museum curator Henry Geldzahler; art historian John Richardson; costume jewelry designer Kenneth Jay Lane; socialites Dru Heinz, Nan Kempner, D. D. Ryan, and Mica Ertegun; and a host of British bluebloods, including the Tennants, the Lambtons, the Guinnesses, and the Ormsby-Gores.

John McKendry presided over these dinners like Lewis Carroll's Mad Hatter. With his slight build, wispy brown hair, and freckled skin, he had a fairy-book quality that friends attributed to a personality that was "lighter than air." At thirty-eight, he held the prestigious position of curator of prints and photographs at the Metropolitan Museum of Art, but his primary vocation was fabricating the myth of John McKendry. He dressed in silk shirts, harem pants, and a long velvet coat that he cinched at the waist with a heavy Moroccan belt studded with antique coins, and he wore silver rings on every finger. For the past several years he had been working on a book of eighteenth- and nineteenth-century fireworks engravings that he intended to be his major contribution to the print field. Fireworks, as numerous friends pointed out, were "pure John."

Mapplethorpe sensed a kindred spirit in McKendry and wasted no time striking up a friendship with him; he telephoned the next day to thank him for the dinner, then eagerly accepted an invitation to visit the apartment that evening. McKendry had been on medical leave from the museum since February, when he was hospitalized for a condition doctors would later diagnose as cirrhosis of the liver. He also suffered from manic-depression, and since Maxime had just left for a trip to Europe, he was in the blackest of moods. Yet he was temporarily cheered by Mapplethorpe's arrival and took him on a tour of the apartment—a whimsical bohemian lair decorated with faded Geoffrey Bennison–type fabrics and fanciful flea market objects. Afterward they smoked hashish and watched the Fourth of July fireworks display over the Hudson River. Two days later, McKendry traveled downtown to see Mapplethorpe's latest work, which included a nude self-portrait encased inside a spray-painted paper bag. The picture was visible through a "peephole" covered by a piece of mesh screen that resembled the partition separating the priest from the penitent in the confessional booth. "I liked it but hate feeling so shy about expressing myself," McKendry confided to his diary. "We got stoned . . . then I took a cab home and left him on 23rd Street. Wish that all my friendships were far more intimate. Feel lonely right now."

During the following week, Mapplethorpe and McKendry spent nearly every day together; they went to Palisades Park in New Jersey and rode the Cyclone; they had lunch at Quo Vadis and dinner at Elaine's. Often they wouldn't return home until four A.M., and then they would sleep until late morning and start the day with wake-up calls to each other. By mid-July the curator was not only temporarily cured of his loneliness, but he was also totally infatuated with Robert. It hardly mattered to him that Mapplethorpe might not share his passionate feelings, for McKendry thrived on the concept of unrequited love. Anything less romantic might bear the burden of reality and provide an aching reminder of his dreary Canadian childhood.

John McKendry had spent his youth in Calgary, where he fell asleep each night listening to the noise of locomotives as they rumbled past his family's small house. He liked to imagine what it was like to sit inside one of the train compartments and watch the landscape flash by the window. His Irish-born father was a Catholic Communist who earned a dollar a day as a gardener. Photographs of Stalin and the pope decorated the McKendrys' living room wall, and dinner conversations centered on strikes and labor disputes. John worked his way through the University of Alberta, then moved to New York in 1958 to attend New York University's Institute of Fine Arts. Fellow student Allen Rosenbaum, now the director of the Princeton Museum, compared McKendry to the main character in Willa Cather's "Paul's Case," the story of a young man who, repulsed by the "flavourless, colourless mass of every-day existence," comes to New York and indulges in the glamour of the city. McKendry's eyes, like those of Cather's Paul, burned with a "certain hysterical brilliancy," and he, too, became intoxicated by New York's riches. He would stand outside the Plaza Hotel for hours just to watch the women in furs and diamonds descend the red-carpeted steps. "My father believes in Labour and the Catholic Church," he told *Interview*. "I believe in neither. I believe in the very rich."

With a group of high-spirited students who dubbed themselves

"The Gang," McKendry went to art openings and spent the nights drinking himself into a stupor. Allen Rosenbaum recalled a trip to Philadelphia during which McKendry impulsively jumped into an icy stream. "John turned blue and became totally stiff," he said. "Somebody had to give him mouth-to-mouth resuscitation. But he was always searching for ecstacy."

In 1961 McKendry joined the staff of the department of prints and photographs at the Metropolitan Museum, and six years later was named curator of the department when his mentor, A. Hyatt Mayor, retired from the job. The same year he married Maxime de La Falaise, daughter of the English portraitist Sir Oswald Birley, and the former wife of Comte Alain de La Falaise, with whom she had two grown children, Loulou and Alexis. Maxime, whose ancestry was Irish, possessed the kind of remarkable beauty that was once attributed to Maud Gonne, the muse of William Butler Yeats. Certainly, John's love was capable of reaching poetic heights, and although Maxime was eleven years his senior, he was enthralled by her "noble face" and high-born social connections. "I married the Met," Maxime was fond of saying, "and John married an aristocrat."

McKendry's role at the Met, however, was approaching the farcical, for while he was a brilliant and talented man—colleagues described the curator's eye as "exquisite"—he was bored by the day-to-day administrative details of running a department and had even less patience for doing research and planning exhibits. What he liked best was to travel around the world purchasing illustrated books, photographs, and architectural drawings for the museum. When he was in New York he presided over champagne lunches in his office as though he were a trustee instead of a curator. His assistant Andrea Stillman would set the table with Maxime's china, crystal, and silver, then wash everything in the ladies' bathroom sink afterward. "It was too bizarre for words," Stillman recalled. "If you wrote my job description down nobody would have believed it. I paid his bills. I had to fend off his creditors because he was wildly extravagant and generous." He spent afternoons poring over Christie's and Sotheby's catalogues for upcoming jewelry auctions, and although his curator's salary was barely more than $25,000 a year, he would circle descriptions of sapphire rings and emerald necklaces that he intended to buy for Maxime. Sometimes he would contact the jewelers directly and Stillman would watch in horror as they delivered the gems to McKendry's office, where he would hold them up to the light and marvel at their brilliance—only to return the pieces a day or two later. "Once John came into the Met with this beautiful ring—I think it was a pink sapphire," Stillman said. "I thought to myself, 'God, how is he going to manage that?' Of course the ring went back several weeks later, but maybe it mattered to John that he owned it for just a little while."

At another time in history, or perhaps at another museum, McKendry's behavior might not have been tolerated, but the Met under the leadership of the city's former Parks commissioner Thomas Hoving had so thoroughly adapted itself to the "swinging" sixties and seventies that McKendry felt perfectly comfortable snorting cocaine with Henry Geldzahler in his office. McKendry consumed nearly every drug under the sun, and while his health was deteriorating—he suffered memory lapses and confusion—he refused to curb his excessive conduct. "John was playing a game of Russian roulette," Maxime explained, "and when he finally decided to live, it was too late. For a while he was absolutely obsessed by the moon. I never knew why, and I never asked. He would spend hours just staring at it. He was a mad, mad romantic."

When Maxime returned from Europe at the end of the summer, she discovered that her husband was madly in love with Robert Mapplethorpe. True to her upper-class European heritage, she was not overly concerned, for she knew John had had affairs with people of both sexes. To Maxime, a marriage filled with high drama was infinitely preferable to a boring one, and John's crushes rarely amounted to anything; at different times, he had been enamored of Jackie Onassis, Diane Von Furstenberg, Maria Callas, Rudolf Nureyev, and the Japanese novelist Yukio Mishima. Maxime was even tolerant of the incest fantasies John harbored toward her own son, Alexis. It was well known among the curator's friends that he had fallen in love with Alexis, and John even spoke openly to Allen Rosenbaum of how he had once desired his own brothers and sisters. "John was fascinated by the forbidden," Rosenbaum said. "He loved the idea of being a bad Catholic." Maxime believed that John was not so much in love with her son as in love with the *idea* of him. "He was fascinated by our whole family," she said. "He wanted to *be* us."

Mapplethorpe was equally fascinated by the McKendry–de La Falaise clan. He had dinner at their apartment two or three times a week. Occasionally he took Patti Smith with him, but although John found her personality delightful, Maxime dismissed her as a "prima donna," and a "dirty" one at that. "I think people were rather horrified by Patti because she always seemed to have creepy-crawly things running up and down her legs," Maxime said. "I remember visiting Robert at his loft, and Patti was in bed complaining that her feet were stuck in her typewriter." Smith had recently met the rock musician Allen Lanier, who was in the band that was to become Blue Öyster Cult. While Smith was still in love with Sam Shepard, with whom she regularly corresponded, she would soon begin a seven-year relationship with Lanier.

Smith didn't care whether or not she was accepted by the McKendrys, but their approval was critical to Mapplethorpe. Many of Maxime's longstanding friends, however, regarded him as uncouth and low-class. "I thought Robert was rather weird," said Boaz Mazor, an assistant to Oscar de la Renta. "He was clearly someone on the make. He wanted to be accepted, and he was not acceptable in the uptown world. John McKendry opened the door for him. He saw the potential in Robert Mapplethorpe when none of us saw it."

Mapplethorpe took full advantage of the social opportunities John provided, and after meeting Mazor at the McKendrys', he followed up the introduction with an offer to take his picture. "He came to my apartment and asked me to crouch on the floor like a runner about to take off on a race," Mazor recalled. "I don't like the pictures at all. But Robert didn't select me to pose because he thought I was a great model. He wanted to get to know me better, and maybe through me he'd meet people in the art world like John Richardson. The camera was a social tool for Robert." Mapplethorpe met Henry Geldzahler at the McKendrys', and Geldzahler then introduced him to David Hockney, who did a drawing of Mapplethorpe in exchange for a Polaroid photograph of a male nude. Mapplethorpe was introduced to the photographer Francesco Scavullo, who invited him to his house on Fire Island and later bought from him a portrait of a young Frenchman, which Scavullo hung in his apartment. "I knew that socializing was beneficial to my career," Mapplethorpe explained. "But it was all very subtle. I wasn't an aggressive socializer. It was subtle aggressiveness. Subconsciously calculating, I guess."

In September, John McKendry left for a monthlong trip to London, and he offered to take Mapplethorpe with him. David Croland had no idea his introduction had sparked such an intense relationship, and Mapplethorpe, before leaving for London, broke the news to Croland over hamburgers at David's Potbelly on Christopher Street. "I'm meeting John in Europe at the end of the week," he casually announced.

Croland was stunned. "You're crazy!" he replied. "You hardly know John." With a nervous catch in his throat, Mapplethorpe explained that over the past few months he and McKendry had become "very good friends." Croland was so upset he could not even touch his food. He had been seeing Mapplethorpe steadily for over a year now, and they even had a little business together—they bought Art Deco bakelite jewelry at junk shows, then doubled the price and sold it to Halston, who then quadrupled the price and sold it retail to his customers. How could Mapplethorpe suddenly go off with John McKendry, who was married to his friend Loulou de La Falaise's *mother*? "I was very hurt and surprised," Croland said. "Robert had always been emotionally withholding, but I never expected anything like this. But then I woke up pretty quick. It was like, now I get it. . . . Robert will do anything for his career."

McKendry was already ensconced at the Ritz Hotel when Mapplethorpe arrived in London on September 20. Although the curator could not afford the hotel's regular rates, it was so important to him to keep up appearances that he opted for one of the tiny maids' rooms on the top floor just to utter the golden words, "I'm staying at the Ritz." McKendry was a charming and erudite guide to London; he knew "everyone" in the city, and in addition to his own art world contacts, he drew on Maxime's friends and family, including her brother Mark Birley, who owned the fashionable club Annabel's. McKendry introduced Mapplethorpe as a "brilliant young artist and photographer" and arranged for him to stay with a friend,

Catherine Tennant, at her flat on the King's Road. Catherine was a member of a wealthy and eccentric family that included her half-brother Colin Tennant, who owned the island of Mustique, and great-uncle Stephen Tennant, a flamboyant homosexual who wore makeup and decorated his house with seashells and fishnets. Mapplethorpe soon discovered that among British aristocrats being eccentric and homosexual was not regarded as an impediment to social success. "Nobody was shocked by anything," he explained. "A lot of the people I met came from these really decadent families where the married men were gay and nobody thought anything about it. I became the toast of London."

Mapplethorpe was overstating the case, but he did find immediate acceptance among McKendry's circle of friends. "I think Robert felt very at home in England, much more than in New York," Maxime said. "Americans think of themselves as having no class distinctions, but money in itself is a class distinction. There's an aristocracy of money here, and if you don't have it, you're somehow lower-class. In London, Robert was immediately accepted as a hippie aristocrat. Don't forget that whole London group were trying to pretend they were Cockneys at the time. That was like the sons and daughters of Park Avenue trying to speak with Brooklyn accents. It was ridiculous, but everybody was doing drugs and trying to be daring and outré."

Mapplethorpe had planned to stay in London only a week, but he was enjoying himself so much he kept postponing his departure. He had no money of his own, so he supplemented his small allowance from McKendry by making and selling jewelry. He had recently begun sporting a swastika pin on his jacket—Nazi regalia was growing increasingly popular in the gay S&M subculture—and before leaving for London he had been evicted from a local delicatessen by its Jewish owner, who was appalled by Mapplethorpe's callous indifference to the significance of the symbol. Nevertheless, Mapplethorpe toyed with the idea of creating a whole line of "Nazi jewelry," and the swastika became yet another amulet in his fetishistic necklaces. While in London he met painter, theater designer, and filmmaker Derek Jarman, who died of AIDS in 1994, and whose own controversial career included the movie *Sebastiane*, which incurred the censor's wrath for its portrait of homosexuality.

They spent several days together rummaging through junk markets for pieces to use in Mapplethorpe's jewelry. Jarman later described Mapplethorpe as a "sharp art hustler" and his story as "the story of Faust."

Certainly Mapplethorpe used McKendry, but then McKendry allowed himself to be used, for he was so enraptured by the young artist that he would have done anything for him. He believed Mapplethorpe had a unique opportunity to take portraits of the new generation of British aristocrats, much as Cecil Beaton had photographed the society figures of the thirties and forties, and he encouraged Robert to make Polaroids of everyone he met. But Mapplethorpe was too busy arranging sexual liaisons, and he did not take many pictures during his three-week visit. He did, however, photograph McKendry in the bathtub of Alexis de La Falaise's farmhouse in Wales. When word filtered back to Maxime, who was in the process of planning a commemorative feast honoring Henry IV's coronation, she was livid that John had had the nerve to take Mapplethorpe to her son's house while her son and his family were there. "I mean, *really*," Maxime said.

Despite appearances, Mapplethorpe and McKendry's relationship was not a sexual one, mainly because Mapplethorpe was not attracted to the curator, whose poor health and high-flown notions of romantic love prevented him from being the aggressor. One night, though, when they were both very stoned, Mapplethorpe made the mistake of having sex with McKendry, and repelled by the curator's soft, almost womanly body, he could barely face him the next day. He liked McKendry and did not want to hurt him, nor did he wish to ruin his own opportunities for advancement. When McKendry returned to New York at the end of October, Mapplethorpe was relieved to see him go, and instead of flying home with him, he left for Paris, where once again he proclaimed himself "the toast of the town."

Mapplethorpe stayed with fashion designer Fernando Sanchez, McKendry's friend, at his apartment on Place Furstemberg, where the two men spent lazy autumn afternoons drinking champagne together in the bathtub. "Robert was one of those people I desperately wanted to be like," Sanchez explained. "I thought he was a hero. How do you say it in English? . . . A fallen angel, that was

Robert. Whenever we would get together, he would push and provoke me. We had an attraction, which wasn't sexual. It was more like playing with the devil." They spent evenings together with Loulou de la Falaise and Yves Saint Laurent, for whom Loulou worked. Since people rarely spoke English, Mapplethorpe was usually excluded from the dinner conversations and served more as an exotic centerpiece—a pretty boy in fetish jewels—than a scintillating companion. "It was hard to sit through dinner for three or four hours and not say a word," he recalled. "I kept thinking that if I listened hard enough I could understand, but of course I couldn't. Then I felt stupid. . . . Yves didn't speak any English, and he would just giggle. I was wearing my crazy jewelry, which he copied for his own collection. I was furious because I didn't have any money. He invited me to the show and the models came out with my dice jewelry and domino cuffs."

Mapplethorpe turned twenty-five in Paris on November 4, 1971, and to mark the occasion he carefully drew the number 25 on a piece of paper, with an arrow pointing downward. He feared that his career was losing momentum. When John McKendry called to wish him happy birthday, he told the curator he was determined not to return to New York until he had taken more pictures. He wasn't telling the whole truth, however, for while he was unhappy about his lack of career progress, he really wanted to stay in Paris because he was having an affair with a handsome, dark-haired Frenchman named François, whom he would photograph several times over the next five years. Colta Ives, McKendry's assistant curator, had recently given him a photograph of Mapplethorpe that had appeared as part of an article on the Chelsea Hotel, in which the artist had been described as a "fallen Burne-Jones angel." McKendry kept the picture tucked away in his diary and impatiently waited for Robert to come home.

Mapplethorpe arrived in New York on November 20, and no sooner had he checked through customs than he called McKendry, who immediately invited him to dinner that evening. Without even bothering to drop off his bags at the loft, Mapplethorpe took a taxi straight to the McKendrys' where, during the dinner conversation, he revealed that he had written him some "nice" letters from Paris, but that he had mistakenly mailed them to 190 West Ninety-first Street instead of 190 Riverside Drive. The next morning McKendry raced out to collect the letters from the Ninety-first Street address and was heartsick when he discovered a vacant lot instead of an apartment building. The incident summed up his relationship with Robert; McKendry, as usual, was left grasping at thin air. "John believed Robert was a divine creature," explained Gary Farmer, who later worked for McKendry at the Metropolitan Museum. "I think he was more fascinated by him than by his work. Of course John was the type of man who could also fall madly in love with a pair of shoes or a silk shirt."

On November 24 *Robert Having His Nipple Pierced* had its premiere at the Museum of Modern Art—a triumph for Sandy Daley, who, through sheer determination, had managed to convince MOMA of the film's merits. Even more interesting than the movie was the fact that John McKendry, Maxime de La Falaise, and David Croland were all sitting together in the audience to watch Mapplethorpe, whom John adored and Maxime detested, make love to ex-boyfriend Croland. Patti Smith added another twist to the real-life subplot by providing the voice-over to the film: while Mapplethorpe and Croland tenderly kissed, Smith blamed Mapplethorpe for giving her a venereal disease, expressed her discomfort toward homosexuals because she didn't like "asshole stuff," then offered a rambling and bizarre account of how her father saved her pubic hair after it had been shaved off by the nurses before she gave birth.

At the end of the movie the audience gave Daley a standing ovation, but just as she was about to acknowledge the applause, a man shouted, "You people need psychiatrists!" Daley was so distraught that she sank back down in her seat, and although Bob Colacello, reviewing the movie in *The Village Voice,* later described both her and Patti as "highly talented verbal and visual originals," she considered the entire night a failure; whatever fragile confidence she had disappeared. Daley subsequently developed hepatitis and eventually left the Chelsea for an apartment in Brooklyn, where she lives today surrounded by twenty-five boxes that she refuses to open because they contain too many souvenirs of the past. "I helped launch

Robert and Patti," she said. "I got them into the Museum of Modern Art, then they went on without me."

By the end of 1971, Allen Lanier was living with Patti Smith in the loft, and Mapplethorpe did not seem to mind the intrusion, perhaps because he was not intimidated by him the way he had been by Sam Shepard. Unlike Smith's previous "hero/boyfriends," Lanier was almost ordinary, and while he was a talented musician, he was neither famous nor handsome. Yet he had a pleasant face framed by long brown hair, a soft speaking voice, and he was more intelligent and well read than many of the musicians who gravitated toward heavy metal. "I learned later that he had a dark side," Smith explained, "but I had no sense of that then. To me, he lived a quiet, almost virtuous life, and after Sam, I needed that."

Tension was building between Mapplethorpe and Smith, however, due to the poor living conditions in the loft. They had grown accustomed to taking showers at the Chelsea, but there was no heat either, and during the winter months they had to sleep with their coats on. In addition, Patti was tired of having to go through Robert's room in order to use the bathroom, and she complained about the lack of privacy, the last vestige of which was destroyed when a city building inspector tore a hole through the partition dividing the rooms because it violated the fire code. Mapplethorpe woke up one morning to see a power saw coming toward him, and realizing his pictures were hanging on the plasterboard, he began screaming, "My art! My art!" His pictures were saved, but a gaping hole now existed in the wall, through which Smith continually had to hop to get to the other side. "She was like a creature out of Beatrix Potter's 'The Rats in the Wainscot,' " recalled Maxime, who, with John McKendry, made several late-night runs down to the loft to lend Mapplethorpe twenty dollars for food.

Except for borrowing money and occasionally selling jewelry, Mapplethorpe had no idea how to support himself, and while McKendry helped out whenever he could, the curator was already heavily in debt to his drug dealer. Nevertheless, McKendry surprised Mapplethorpe by giving him a Polaroid camera for Christmas. Up until now he had been making do with Sandy Daley's Polaroid, and while he had recently purchased a secondhand one, it had fallen apart. Now Mapplethorpe, finally, had a working camera of his own.

Several days after Christmas, he wrote John a letter in which he acknowledged the generosity of both McKendrys toward him: "I hope that one day I will be able to show the two of you in one way or another my appreciation for helping me to somehow struggle through this period. . . . I'm real happy with my work right now and convinced more than ever that it will develope [sic] into something that will in some way influence the course of one thing or another."

Mapplethorpe still had not committed himself exclusively to photography, and he spent an equal amount of time on his collages and assemblages. From his student days at Pratt, he had been intrigued by Joseph Cornell's boxes, and he created two Cornell-inspired pieces for the McKendrys. The larger one, composed of two separate boxes, contained such typical Mapplethorpe totems as a statue of the Sacred Heart, a crucifix, and a skull. The smaller one, however, was the more revealing, for he had placed two small baby dolls inside the stomach of a larger doll, which was then attached to the bellows of a camera, as if the camera itself was giving birth to the babies. Certainly John nurtured Robert's nascent photography career by providing access to the Metropolitan's private collection, where Robert had the opportunity to see photographs that had never been exhibited before. "John taught Robert about photography in the best possible way," explained Henry Geldzahler, who was then curator of contemporary paintings at the museum, and who died in 1994. "He showed him a wide range of pictures. Thomas Eakins's photographs of nude boys weren't seen very much at that time; the same was true of Stieglitz's photographs of Georgia O'Keeffe nude. All these things weren't readily available to the public and I think it helped to stretch the boundaries of what was possible for Robert."

Mapplethorpe's previous experience of looking at photographs had largely been confined to reproductions in books, but by actually holding prints by Alfred Stieglitz or Edward Steichen in his hands and by studying the remarkable range of tones in a black-and-white picture, he began to view the medium differently. "Looking at those photographs made me think photography maybe could be art," he said. "I had never thought about that before, but now I found myself getting excited about the possibilities."

He realized he had a powerful ally in McKendry, and he encouraged him to take a more active role in making photography more visible at the Met; but McKendry was the wrong curator at the wrong museum. While the Metropolitan owned the Alfred Stieglitz collection, which consisted of works by the photographer himself, as well as by other Photo-Secessionists such as Steichen and Clarence White, the museum had always treated photography as an illegitimate child. It did not warrant a separate department, and exhibition space was in short supply; moreover, despite the wealth of material in the Stieglitz collection, the museum had ignored the efforts of many other important photographers of the nineteenth and early twentieth centuries, and had virtually turned its back on contemporary work. In late 1967 McKendry had organized an important show, "Four Victorian Photographers," which featured the work of Julia Margaret Cameron, David Octavius Hill, Adolphe Braun, and Thomas Eakins, and he was currently in the early stages of preparation for a Paul Strand retrospective. But whether due to manic-depression, liver disease, or drug and alcohol abuse, he had great difficulty concentrating for long periods of time. "John was trying to hold it together, but he was really falling apart," explained Allen Rosenbaum. "He was giving a presentation during an important acquisitions meeting and his Moroccan belt suddenly crashed to the ground. He lived in fear of physical offense and gracelessness, and he was mortified."

Throughout the spring of 1972, McKendry's diary entries indicate a man on the verge of despair. "Robert just left after coming here on our way from dinner at the Veau d'Or," he wrote on March 14. "I just gave him that velvet jacket from my English suit. . . . I feel as unhappy as I've ever felt and there seems no way out. . . . I wish I had some sleeping pills as I'd just like to go to bed and go immediately to sleep without thinking or feeling anything." Yet he was still determined to help Mapplethorpe, and a month later took him to Boston to meet with executives at the Polaroid Corporation, which had recently initiated a program that provided free film for artists. Several days afterward, McKendry invited Mapplethorpe to dinner at the Ginger Man near Lincoln Center, where McKendry had just seen a performance of one of his favorite operas, Leoš Janáček's *Makropoulos Case*. It is the story of an opera singer who, having imbibed an elixir of eternal youth, now finds herself questioning whether life loses its value if it is lived too long. When McKendry returned home that evening he recorded a line from one of the arias in his diary: "There is no joy in goodness, no joy in evil, just a vast eternal loneliness."

McKendry's loneliness was so deep and profound that even if Mapplethorpe had returned his affection it would have provided only temporary relief; still, the physical rebuffs pained him, and at the end of an evening he would wait for a good-night kiss like a teenage boy, then endure the humiliation of having the door shut in his face. "What am I going to do about John?" Mapplethorpe constantly asked Smith, for the curator's behavior unnerved him. McKendry would drop by the loft uninvited and, holding his head in his hands, would begin to weep; at other times he would be deliriously happy about buying a new Tiffany watch, or listening to a Maria Callas record. No matter how beneficial McKendry was to Mapplethorpe's career, Robert could not handle his mood swings, and he began to withdraw from him. He did not visit the McKendrys' apartment nearly as often, and whenever John called, he made up excuses not to see him. They still remained friends, but by the early summer of 1972 Mapplethorpe had replaced him with a more powerful patron.

CHAPTER NINE

"If Sam hadn't had the money, I might not have been
involved with him. He was a package, so to speak."

—*Robert Mapplethorpe, about Sam Wagstaff*

It was well known among gay men in the art world that Sam
Wagstaff was searching for "someone to spoil," preferably a young
artist toward whom he could play out his Pygmalion fantasies. Wagstaff was a brilliant curator with an eye for extraordinary objects, and
a recent inheritance from his stepfather had given him extra spending money. Moreover, at fifty years old, he was so good-looking that
anyone who met him, no matter what gender, invariably described
him as the handsomest man on earth. "[Beauty] makes princes of
those who have it," Oscar Wilde wrote in *The Picture of Dorian
Gray,* and indeed Wagstaff had a regal self-confidence that came
from knowing that few men, at least physically, were his equal.

Wagstaff resembled Gary Cooper, and like the actor, he projected
an idealized version of American manhood; he was over six feet tall,
with sandy-colored hair, large gray-blue eyes, sensuous lips, a strong
nose and jaw, and dimpled cheeks. "Sam was remarkable-looking,"

said art dealer Klaus Kertess. "I watched him swim once and I never saw such grace. You could not look at him without desire."

Wagstaff had recently left his job at the Detroit Institute of Art and was temporarily at loose ends. That spring, he enrolled in a three-month training course organized by the Arica Institute, an East Coast version of Esalen, the California sensitivity spa, and in between practicing meditation and yoga and doing his Arica exercises, he pursued his interest in psychic phenomena by visiting astrologers, numerologists, and gypsy fortune tellers. Wagstaff was seeking to find himself, as well as someone to indulge, and what better way to accomplish both than to acquire a young man whose career—and perhaps even his horoscope—blended perfectly with his?

Ironically, David Croland, who had still not forgiven Mapplethorpe for his relationship with John McKendry, helped introduce him to Sam Wagstaff. Croland had met Wagstaff through art curator Sam Green and photographer Peter Hujar, at Green's beach house in Oakleyville, a remote part of Fire Island. When Wagstaff learned that Croland was an aspiring artist, he went to Croland's apartment to view his work and paid him one thousand dollars for two drawings. Before Wagstaff left he spotted a Polaroid of Mapplethorpe in a French sailor hat that Croland kept in his living room, and when he asked who it was, Croland experienced a sense of déjà vu. "It was like I gave them to each other," he explained. "When Sam walked out the door, I said to myself, 'This is it.' "

Wagstaff immediately telephoned Mapplethorpe and opened the conversation by asking "Is this the shy pornographer?" in a voice so well bred that it immediately elevated the status of "pornographer" to a privileged profession. Mapplethorpe, who already knew of Wagstaff's reputation and his desire to provide patronage to the right young man, was so happy to hear from him that when he hung up the telephone he immediately leaped through the hole in the plasterboard to tell Smith the good news. "Yippee!" she shouted, jumping up and down on the floor and sending cans and bottles rattling across the room. "You've been saved!"

Several days later, Wagstaff visited Mapplethorpe's loft, where he was greeted by the unmistakable sounds of people engaged in sexual activity. When he walked into the room, he realized the noise was actually coming from an audio tape of a pornographic movie, which was playing on a tape recorder hidden inside the pocket of a black motorcycle jacket. The jacket was hanging on a clothing rack next to a pair of leather pants with a loaf of French bread protruding from the crotch. Mapplethorpe had wanted to impress Wagstaff with his versatility, so, in addition to the constructions, he showed him the collages, jewelry, and Polaroids. He had recently completed a series of photo transfers by taking images from magazines and newspapers, such as an advertisement for briefs by a company called Skinwear by Ah Men. By using a special solvent he transferred the pictures to a piece of stretched canvas and framed them. In the pop-art tradition of Jasper Johns, who cast two Ballantine ale cans in bronze, he also transferred a magazine photograph of a penis onto a Miller beer can, as though the penis itself was a thumb capable of hoisting the beer to an unseen mouth.

Initially Wagstaff was embarrassed by the explicit nature of the work, for while he had achieved a reputation as a champion of renegade art, he still maintained a proper Yankee reserve about sexual matters and referred to pornography as "naughty pictures." Yet he also found Mapplethorpe's sexual candor surprisingly exhilarating, and after years of being cast in the role of the handsome bachelor, he had grown weary of leading a double life. "Sam really respected the way I was honest about being gay," Mapplethorpe explained. "He had lived his life trying to hide it. He came from a social background where everybody always questioned whether he was gay or not, but he never let it out of the bag. I helped Sam be more open about his sexuality." Wagstaff was physically attracted to Mapplethorpe, and the psychological fit was obvious—he was looking for someone to spoil, and Mapplethorpe wanted nothing more than to be spoiled—yet there was another element that sealed their unspoken contract. Wagstaff asked Mapplethorpe what sign he was born under, and when he discovered they were both Scorpios, with the same birthdate, he trusted their mutual stars would cast a favorable light upon their relationship.

Wagstaff invited Mapplethorpe back to his apartment, which was located in a loft building on the corner of Bond Street and the Bowery. Mapplethorpe was shocked by Wagstaff's spartan living quarters, for the loft was no better than the one he shared with Patti

Smith, and gave no indication that its owner had any money at all. Wagstaff's only furniture was an old sofa and a rattan mat that he used as a bed; hundreds of books lined the perimeter of the room, and in one corner stood an eight-foot prism that reflected light from the window onto his prized avocado trees. Strangely enough for someone who had spent his life collecting art, he did not surround himself with it and, in fact, kept many of his paintings and sculptures stashed in the closet. Smith recalled discovering a Vuillard painting, wrapped in rags, that Wagstaff had absentmindedly misplaced, and when she pulled the piece from the closet he muttered, "Ah, yes, the Vuillard . . . goody."

Wagstaff made it clear to Mapplethorpe that his loft was not an indication of his bank account and that he was willing to help him. They spent the night together, and by the next morning Mapplethorpe was thoroughly smitten; for years he had wondered if he would ever find someone to love as much as he had loved Smith, and in Wagstaff, he had finally found the right man. "He swept me off my feet," he said. "It was love at first sight. After that, everything turned around for me."

Samuel Jones Wagstaff, Jr., was a member of an old New York family whose American roots could be traced back to 1790, and whose ancestors had once owned the southern portion of Central Park. His father attended Harvard and Columbia Law School, but although he later worked as a lawyer he seemed happiest when collecting objects that struck his fancy, from tobacco tins to pieces of opalescent beach glass. Sam's uncle, David Wagstaff, was a collector, too, and he eventually amassed one of the largest libraries of sports books in the world. Clearly Sam inherited his acquisitive instincts from the Wagstaff side of the family, and even as a small child he saved news photos, postcards, and tea tags. From his mother, Olga Piorkowska, he acquired a love of art, for she had worked as an illustrator for *Vogue* before she met Sam's father. She doted on her son, who, unlike her younger daughter, Judith, was an extraordinarily beautiful child; she dressed him accordingly in white ruffled shirts and short velvet pants, and each week she doled out his allowance, penny by penny, from a silk purse. Her marriage to Sam's father was an extremely unhappy one, and when Sam was ten years old and a student at St. Bernard's, she divorced his father and married a wealthy artist, Donald Newhall. Newhall's family had established ties to California during the gold rush, when his ancestors founded the community of Newhall in Santa Clarita.

Olga and Donald Newhall immediately embarked on a two-year trip to Europe, and while they left five-year-old Judith in the care of Samuel Wagstaff, Sr., they took young Sam everywhere with them.

When Sam returned home he attended Hotchkiss and distinguished himself as one of the most eligible escorts at the debutante balls. "Every girl would swoon the minute he walked into the room," recalled writer Dominick Dunne. "He looked like those pictures of young British aristocrats who were killed during World War One. He was unbelievably dashing."

Wagstaff did everything that was expected of him: he went to Yale, where he majored in English and joined the exclusive Wolf's Head Society; then, upon graduating in 1944, he enlisted in the navy and fought at Omaha Beach. After the war he worked on Madison Avenue and, as one of the city's premier bachelors, continued to squire numerous young women around town. By the mid-fifties, however, he was close to a nervous breakdown; he hated advertising because he felt the business was built on deception, and his personal life, too, was based on a lie. He was not an eligible bachelor at all, he was a homosexual with no intention of marrying.

When Wagstaff fell ill with hepatitis he took it as a sign that his current life was so poisonous to him that he had to make a change. Immediately upon his recovery he quit the advertising business and, borrowing money from his mother, enrolled at New York University's Institute of Fine Arts. It was a courageous move, for he was already thirty-six years old and an art career was not regarded as a particularly manly profession; but Wagstaff later confided to Mapplethorpe that he would have killed himself if he had remained in advertising.

In 1959 the National Gallery of Art awarded Wagstaff a David Finley fellowship, and he spent several years in Europe studying the old masters and Paul Gauguin. Two years later he was named curator of painting, prints, and drawing at the Wadsworth Athenaeum, a museum in Hartford, Connecticut. While he came to an art career relatively late in life, he possessed a quirky brilliance and a supreme confidence in his own aesthetic judgment. He told *The New York Times Magazine* in 1985: "I've always been visually acclimatized to the world. The great poet Wallace Stevens said something about most people are interested in people, I'm interested in places. I say: Most people are interested in people—not that I'm not also—but I'm overly interested in things." His self-assurance was based, in part, on his birthright as a Wagstaff. Secure in his social status, he did not feel obliged to conform to the established orders of taste, and in fact, he enjoyed tweaking convention. If he liked something, however curious it might be, he expected others to fall in line behind him, and if anybody questioned his opinion he often gave them a withering look and a long lecture. "Sam could be unbearable," said Sam Green, who was then curator at the Institute of Contemporary Art in Philadelphia. "Sometimes he'd go on so long that you just wanted to kick him in the shins and run away."

From the moment Wagstaff arrived in Hartford he was resolved to enliven "the damn dull town," and during his tenure at the Wadsworth he curated the first minimalist exhibit; showed Andy Warhol, Robert Motherwell, Frank Stella, and Ad Reinhardt before they were well known; inaugurated sculptor Tony Smith's debut exhibit; and sponsored a dance performance by choreographer Merce Cunningham, with costumes and sets by Jasper Johns and Robert Rauschenberg. Wagstaff's enthusiasm for the avant-garde was greeted with skepticism by the museum's conservative board of trustees, who were already antagonized by the curator's independent personality. "Hartford was consumed with Edwardian stuffiness," explained Jim Elliott, who later became the museum's director. "There were a lot of gay bachelors in Hartford, but they were heavily closeted. They were accepted as long as they led a 'bachelor's' life, which meant escorting widows and unmarried daughters to social events." Wagstaff did not want to fall into that trap again, so instead of spending his weekends at dinner parties with members of the community, he went to New York, where he kept a loft, and spent his time visiting galleries. "It was certainly a reasonable thing for a curator to do," said Elliott, "but people were scandalized."

It was in Hartford that Wagstaff first established the pattern of using his curator's clout as a tool for seduction, and he fell in love with a young artist whose career he promised to nourish. To fend off any potential gossip, he simultaneously struck up a close friendship with a divorced woman in her mid-fifties named Mary Palmer, who fell in love with him. He never once mentioned to her that he was gay, though she was well aware of it. "What Sam did for Robert Mapplethorpe wasn't peculiar to Mapplethorpe," Palmer explained. "Sam was absolutely ga-ga over young artists. He found them to be the most fascinating people in the world, and he wanted to know what made them tick. I think he secretly harbored a wish to be an artist himself, but since he didn't have the talent, he wanted to go down in history as the patron of someone famous. The young kid Sam got involved with in Hartford was a pretty good painter, but he also had a girlfriend. The four of us would have dinner together, and we all shared a real camaraderie, except, of course, it was a bit strained at times. But there was real pressure on Sam to conform, and not to let people know he was gay."

The young painter eventually ended his relationship with Wagstaff whose disappointment at being passed over for the director's job at the museum—it was awarded to Jim Elliott—was now compounded by a broken heart. He accepted an offer from the Detroit Institute of Art to become curator of contemporary paintings, and in September 1968 he made his entrance into Motor City in a dilapidated Volkswagen beetle. The atmosphere he confronted in Detroit was the exact opposite of staid Hartford, for Detroit had barely recovered from the fire bombing and looting of the '67 race riots.

One of the neighborhoods ravaged by the riots was the Cass Corridor, which still managed to distinguish itself as the epicenter of Detroit's most vibrant art scene. Among the derelicts, drug addicts, and prostitutes, a group of artists was intent on creating tough, spontaneous art that mirrored the gritty landscape. Many of the artists were in their mid-twenties and had been influenced by the poet and musician John Sinclair, who helped found the Artists' Workshop, Detroit's first avant-garde art collective, and the rock group the MC5, whose song "Kick Out the Jams" became a rallying cry for the city's counterculture. Within weeks of his arrival in Detroit, Wagstaff had kicked out the jams himself, and while the museum had hired a forty-three-year-old curator in Brooks Brothers clothing, it now had to contend with a middle-aged hippie who smoked pot, wore blue jeans and Indian tunics, attended rock concerts at the Grande Ballroom, and hung protective charms, including chicken feet, on his office door.

The Cass Corridor artists were ecstatic, for they finally had a curator to whom they could relate. "The important thing Sam did in Detroit was that he asked, 'So, where are the artists?' " said painter Ellen Phelan. "Nobody else had ever thought of asking that question before, and Sam went out looking for them. Now this could have been about cruising, too, because the first people he picked up on were handsome young blond boys, but that's all right. A lot of people get driven around by their sexual interests, and there are worse bases for aesthetic judgments."

Wagstaff became totally enamored of several artists, most notably twenty-one-year-old Gordon Newton, whose reputation he enhanced by convincing local collectors to buy his work. In addition to helping bridge the gap between the rebellious Cass Corridor artists and the sedate collectors in wealthy suburbs such as Grosse Pointe, Wagstaff gave Detroit a taste of the New York avant-garde by showing at the museum Carl Andre, Richard Tuttle, Lynda Benglis, Walter de Maria, and Robert Morris. But while Wagstaff would eventually be acknowledged as one of the most innovative curators in Detroit's history, the trustees could not fathom such orderly chaos as the Robert Morris installation, which consisted of scattered metal scraps, mirrors, and pieces of asphalt.

"Sam was a visionary," said art dealer Susanne Hilberry, who then worked in the museum's education department, "but he could also be a brat. If he liked you, he would be generous with his time, but if he didn't, he was totally dismissive. He absolutely refused to play up to the trustees, and when anybody asked him to explain anything, he'd scornfully tell them, 'Great art needs no defense.' " Wagstaff's main ally was twenty-five-year-old Anne Manoogian, who was married to a member of one of Detroit's wealthiest families, and who had been arrested in an antiwar protest in Washington the weekend she was named to the museum's board of trustees. "Detroit was in the dark ages when it came to art," she explained, "and Sam was doing things that were considered revolutionary. It was great for someone like me, but the sixty-year-old trustees found it very threatening."

Wagstaff sealed his fate in March 1971 when he arranged for Michael Heizer to create an earthwork on the museum's north lawn. He raised the money for the project himself, mainly because he believed in Heizer's work, but also because he had a crush on the twenty-eight-year-old artist, whose birthday, significantly, coincided with his own. For Wagstaff, Heizer's earthwork was the next logical step after the Morris show, for Morris's seemingly haphazard mounds of junk not only evoked the physicality of the landscape but also illustrated the notion that art can be the act of creation itself. Heizer created *Dragged Mass* by literally dragging a thirty-five-pound granite slab across the museum's frozen lawn with the help of four bulldozers, a crane, and a crew of twenty men. Trustees and the media failed to grasp the underlying significance of the piece, however, and *Dragged Mass* was likened to an act of vandalism. Wagstaff was ordered to remove it from the museum, and when he was interviewed by the local press he sarcastically described the edict as "a victory for manicured grass over fine art." He stayed in Detroit until October, but he was miserable at the museum and probably would have been fired had he not submitted his own resignation.

Donald Newhall had recently died, and while Wagstaff's modest inheritance hardly made him a wealthy man, he no longer had to work for anybody else. Before he left town, Anne Manoogian gave him a black-tie farewell party, where, according to Manoogian, he took his revenge by purposely getting one of the trustees wives so stoned she had to be carried out the door, while he howled with laughter.

Wagstaff's experience in Detroit had left him frustrated and bitter, and when he returned to New York he had no idea what to do. He had always been a visually insatiable man, and among his many collections were those of African tribal sculpture, American Indian artifacts, Greek coins, stamps, and, most recently, contemporary paintings and minimalist art. But now that he had more time to devote to collecting, he pronounced himself "bored" with the contemporary art scene. He wanted to collect something new, but what? Meanwhile, he continued his search for a young artist to shape and nurture, and it was only when he found Robert Mapplethorpe that he found his purpose.

Wagstaff immediately arranged for one of Mapplethorpe's photographs to be included in a show at the Willis Gallery in Detroit's Cass Corridor, and when he returned to the city in August 1972 for the dedication of Tony Smith's *Gracehoper* at the museum, he took Mapplethorpe with him. "I looked at this young man standing next to Sam," Susanne Hilberry said, referring to Mapplethorpe, "and all I could think of was, here we go again."

Mapplethorpe hoped Wagstaff would buy him a place to live, for Patti Smith had made it clear that she and Allen Lanier wanted to move to an apartment in Greenwich Village; since Mapplethorpe could not afford to rent the loft on his own, he was in a panic about it. The phone had been disconnected because Smith had stopped paying the bills, and he could not imagine another winter without heat. Unbeknownst to Mapplethorpe, Wagstaff had confided to Smith that he actually intended to buy Mapplethorpe a loft, but that he enjoyed seeing him "sweat a bit." Smith and Wagstaff had struck up an immediate rapport, and with their love of literature and art they had more to talk about than they did with Mapplethorpe, whose interests were narrowly focused on himself and his career. Yet their main link was a concern for Mapplethorpe—"our boy," Wagstaff called him—and not long after they first met, Smith told Mapplethorpe she had a "feeling" Wagstaff would make him truly happy.

A predominant theme in Smith's own romantic life continued to be the ongoing struggle to balance the aggressive part of her personality, which she interpreted as male, with the passive, or "female," side. To complement Sam Shepard, she had become an outlaw, a "hell-raiser," but now with Allen Lanier she assumed the subordinate role of his "mistress" and concocted a submissive identity that was based on the numerous artists' biographies she had read, most notably that of Amedeo Modigliani. His mistress, Jeanne Hébuterne, nine months pregnant with his second child, lived on tinned sardines while attending the artist's deathbed in their freezing cold studio, then threw herself out of a window when he died. Smith loved that story and later dedicated a song on her album *Wave* to Hébuterne and "to all women who sacrifice themselves for men."

At least publicly, Smith played the sacrificial "rock wife" to Lanier and extolled the virtues of doing his laundry and washing out his socks. She compared herself to Stella Kowalski, the submissive wife in Tennessee Williams's *Streetcar Named Desire,* in a piece for *Interview,* and she spoke of the pleasures of subjugation. "It was the first time I considered that a woman's true position was on her back. The first time I assumed a completely passive role. . . . I'm different now, I don't mind getting knocked around a little."

Smith nevertheless was all "masculine" defiance when it came to her career, and after her striking debut performance at St. Mark's Church a year earlier, she had kindled the interest of Steve Paul, who managed the careers of Edgar and Johnny Winter; he was eager to work with her, but only if she dropped the poetry from her act. "He wanted me to be a sort of leather Liza Minnelli," Smith complained to *Rolling Stone.* "But the whole thing that Steve did for me, he made me fight for what I believed in. Because he was so adamant, I got adamant. We parted with me saying, 'I ain't never gonna do this shit, I ain't never gonna do a record unless they let me do exactly what I want to do.'" Smith, meanwhile, wrote rock reviews for publications such as *Creem,* appeared in an off-off-Broadway production of Anthony Ingrassia's *Island,* in which she played a methedrine addict, and completed two volumes of poetry, *Seventh Heaven* and *Kodak.* Glenn O'Brien, who reviewed *Seventh Heaven* for *Interview,* admitted that he did not understand Smith's poetry but nonetheless admired her personal style. Accompanying the review was a Mapplethorpe photograph of Smith dressed in a diaper holding a dishtowel to her breasts.

In October Wagstaff gave Mapplethorpe fifteen thousand dollars for a loft on Bond Street, a dozen yards away from his own. Mapplethorpe's contemporaries viewed his good fortune with a mixture of envy and disdain, for there was something about being "kept" that ran contrary to the spirit of the times. "A lot of people had those kinds of offers," said writer Fran Lebowitz, "but Robert was one of the few people I knew who actually took somebody up on it. Nobody had any money in those days. I drove a cab. Robert certainly wouldn't have done that—not that taking money from Sam Wagstaff was the only alternative to being a cab driver, but I can't imagine what kind of job Robert Mapplethorpe would have been suited for." Kenny Tisa, who had observed Mapplethorpe since their days together at Pratt, was not surprised by this latest development:

"Robert had worked hard trying to get to know the gay elite of New York, and Sam was gay, wealthy, and an art collector. Sam collected things, and Robert knew his value as a collectible."

Several weeks before his twenty-sixth birthday, Mapplethorpe and Smith moved from the loft. They had lived together since their arrival in Manhattan three years earlier, when, penniless and frightened, they had made a promise to take care of each other until better days came along. Now those days had arrived, and without a glance backward, they embraced the present.

PART THREE

Sex and Magic

CHAPTER TEN

"Sex is the only thing worth living for."

—*Robert Mapplethorpe*

"I don't think any collector knows his true motivation. An obsession—like any sort of love—is blinding."

—*Sam Wagstaff*

Robert's new loft at 24 Bond Street was close to SoHo, a twenty-six-block area in Lower Manhattan that was rapidly being transformed into New York's contemporary art center. A decade earlier SoHo had been a dreary ghost town, its ornate cast-iron factory buildings relics of the post–Civil War industrial age. One by one, the companies that produced lace, silk, dolls, hats, and pinking shears went out of business; landlords had difficulty finding replacement tenants, and many of the floors in the buildings remained empty. Attracted by the low rents and large spaces, artists began moving to the area in the late 1950s, but since it was illegal then to live in the manufacturing lofts, they were constantly on the lookout for policemen and building inspectors. That changed in 1971, when the city's new zoning regulations granted them the right to live full-time in the lofts. Simultaneously, Madison Avenue art dealers such as Leo Castelli, Andre Emmerich, and Ileana Sonnabend recognized the benefits of displaying large pieces of contemporary art in the bright and airy spaces of the factory buildings, and they opened galleries in a renovated paper warehouse on West Broadway. Novice collectors who had been intimidated by the somber atmosphere of the uptown galleries began spending Saturday afternoons in SoHo, where they could "collaborate" with artist Vito Acconci by walking into the Sonnabend Gallery, where Acconci masturbated under a wedge-shaped ramp. He called the piece *Seedbed*, and his sexual fantasies were incited by the presence of the gallery-goers.

In contrast to SoHo, which exemplified the spirit of the avant-garde, Bond Street remained stubbornly industrial. Mapplethorpe's neighborhood was home to D & D Salvage Company, Etna Tool & Die Corporation, a truck garage, and a gas station; a half-dozen derelicts from the nearby men's shelter routinely dozed on the sidewalk. The interior of his building was equally uninviting, and except for a flickering fluorescent ceiling light and a small wooden bench usually littered with Chinese menus, the lobby was dingy and bare; at the far end, a creaking wrought-iron elevator carried visitors to his loft on the fifth floor.

"The whole point is to try to integrate your life into your work if you're an artist," Mapplethorpe later told *House & Garden*, and to this end, his earliest efforts at decorating were aimed at turning his bedroom into a sculptural environment. Mapplethorpe had always remained physically close to his work, living in an "art factory" and sleeping on a mattress that often doubled as a piece of art. He now transformed his bedroom into a cage by taking pieces of chicken wire and framing them in symmetrical square grids; the effect was similar to the screens he had used in his pornographic collages to separate the observer from the observed. This time, however, he had literally climbed behind the screen to become the central player in his own pornographic drama. Near the bed hung a "masturbation machine," which he had designed by surrounding a mirror with dozens of white lights that blinked off and on, like a carnival roulette wheel. The mirror served the same function as the Polaroid self-portraits; Mapplethorpe, like Narcissus, was infatuated with his own reflection, and he still maintained a juvenile curiosity about his body. The cage was a playpen of sorts, and Robert the insatiable child.

Early in their relationship, Mapplethorpe wrote to Wagstaff: "Thank you for giving me some of the happiest months of my life. I love you." While the two men looked nothing alike, they personified an idealized father and son. Certainly Wagstaff functioned as a surrogate father to Mapplethorpe; he loved and supported him in ways Harry Mapplethorpe was incapable of doing, and with his urbane manner, he was the antithesis of Floral Park. Furthermore, while Harry was often cold and remote, Sam loved to cuddle Robert and talk baby talk to him. He called Robert his "little monkey," while Robert referred to him as "Grampa." Yet there was one area in which Sam and Harry were alike: both used money to control Robert.

Despite his willingness to play patron, Wagstaff was notoriously stingy in other areas of his life; he would drive miles out of his way to save fifty cents on a toll and rarely picked up a restaurant check. He wore the same shirts he had purchased at Brooks Brothers several decades earlier, and the same green blazer. On the rare occasions he paid for a cab himself, he was known to tip the driver with pennies. Wagstaff's frugality was learned from his mother, who parceled out money to her son as though he were still dressed in knickers. Anne (Manoogian) MacDonald recalled: "Once Sam needed ten dollars, so his mother instructed him to go into her bedroom, open the third drawer of her bureau, and get a little change purse that was hidden under her sachet. Sam waited by her side while she slowly unfolded her money and counted out the exact amount, then he hid the purse in the bureau drawer again." Wagstaff would reenact this little ceremony with Mapplethorpe, who was often reduced to whimpering for money like a five-year-old. "Whenever I wanted anything, I'd ask him, 'Sammi, can I please have a present?' " he explained. "I guess it *was* kind of a father-son relationship."

For at least the first six months, Mapplethorpe and Wagstaff remained more or less monogamous; they had brunch together nearly every day and dinner most nights, and since their lofts were only five minutes apart, they were used to dropping by unannounced. A few weeks after Mapplethorpe moved to Bond Street, however, Wagstaff was startled to find him in bed with a young Parisian, and when he lost his temper he received the following lecture from his protégé: "This is the way I live, and sex is the only thing worth living

for." Mapplethorpe drew upon his sexual relationships for inspiration. He wanted to bring pornography into the realm of art, so he felt he needed not only to understand pornographic conventions, but also to continue to explore his own sexuality. Nevertheless, he was careful to keep his liaisons to a minimum because he couldn't afford to lose Wagstaff and everything he represented.

Although Wagstaff didn't share Mapplethorpe's single-minded devotion to sex, he was hardly a prude; his erotic tastes ran to private parties that featured live sex shows, and, on at least one occasion, he photographed the activities himself. In fact, Wagstaff allowed Mapplethorpe to photograph him in a series of explicit poses, even donning a pair of rubber underwear. The bond they shared, however, was ultimately more visual than sexual.

The month of January 1973 marked Mapplethorpe's first photography show and Wagstaff's birth as a photography collector. Independent of Wagstaff, Mapplethorpe had taken his Polaroids to Harold Jones, the director of the Light Gallery, which was located at 1018 Madison Avenue and had been established two years earlier by lawyer Tennyson Shad. Light was the only gallery in New York to focus almost exclusively on contemporary photographs, and Jones, who had previously been a curator at the George Eastman House in Rochester, had set aside time each week to view work by aspiring young photographers. He recalled that a surprising number of pictures were sexually explicit, as the popularity of the Polaroid camera had allowed photographers to document instantly their most intimate gestures. Lucas Samaras, for example, had exhibited four hundred Polaroids at the Pace Gallery in 1971 that dealt with his autoerotic fantasies.

Mapplethorpe's Polaroids impressed Jones as different from the rest, however, for while Mapplethorpe was dealing with sexually charged material, he treated it in the detached manner Andy Warhol brought to his own work. Despite Robert's libidinous subject matter, his photographs were resolutely "cool." Jones agreed to feature the work in the gallery's "experimental" back room, and Mapplethorpe set about crafting an invitation that would attract maximum attention. "An exhibition doesn't begin when you enter a gallery," he said. "It begins the minute you get an invitation in the mail." When people opened the envelope, they saw a nude self-portrait of Mapplethorpe holding a camera, his penis covered with an adhesive dot.

The show opened on January 6, and when Tennyson Shad found himself face to face with a Polaroid of a penis in a cock ring, he had only one question for Harold Jones: "What the hell is going on here?" Since Shad was not in charge of organizing the exhibits, he paid scant attention to the work being featured in the back room, and not being one of three hundred people to receive Robert's invitation, he was ill prepared for the photographic striptease that ensued. "I was flabbergasted," he recalled. "Maybe I had a 'suburban aesthetic,' but I didn't want my teenage daughters seeing this stuff." Yet Shad was equally astonished by the crowds of people who actually came to the opening, and was impressed by the sheer force of the "Wagstaff-Mapplethorpe machine." In this case, though, Wagstaff's input was negligible, for Mapplethorpe's "gaining connections" strategy had been so successful that between the people he had met at Max's and those he knew through Patti Smith, David Croland, and John McKendry, he already had a substantial following. Certainly they did not comprise the usual Light Gallery audience, to whom photography often meant allegiance to the "straight" image—pictures that mirror external reality, such as those by Aaron Siskind and Harry Callahan. The term "straight" was appropriate in its slang definition as well, for the people who tended to gravitate to the Light Gallery were not, for example, the same "downtown" types that congregated in Max's back room. They were photography students, camera buffs, or those drawn to the medium simply because they liked looking at pictures, not because of its investment potential or because celebrities might appear at the opening.

Mapplethorpe's crowd was another story entirely; Tennyson Shad's recollection was of drag queens and men in black leather descending on the gallery in droves, but the photographer's contacts were wider than that, and he had invited nearly everyone he had ever met at the McKendrys' dinner parties and elsewhere. This diverse mixture of social types—a trademark of Warhol's universe—would subsequently become a major feature of Mapplethorpe's openings as well.

His subject matter, too, would remain unvaried over the years, and at Light he revealed the three motifs that would preoccupy him for the rest of his life—portraits, flowers, and sex pictures. Mapplethorpe had been experimenting with unconventional framing techniques in his collages, by placing the images in paper bags, for example, or encasing them in linoleum. Now he presented his Polaroids in the original plastic cassettes supplied by the manufacturer. In some cases, he painted them different colors, as with the portrait of transvestite Candy Darling, who was framed in candy-colored pastels. For a multiple portrait of Patti Smith, he even included the Polaroid film instructions that provided a concise summary of his protective attitude toward her: "DON'T TOUCH HERE. Handle only by edges." The most ambitious piece in the exhibit was a series of four nude self-portraits juxtaposed against two photographs of classical sculpture. It pointed the way to Mapplethorpe's future obsession with the relationship between sculpture and the human form, and the possibilities of using the camera to chisel the body.

Mapplethorpe's photographs were on sale for approximately one hundred dollars apiece, but there was not a big market for them— nor, for that matter, was there a big market for photographs in general. From the time Alfred Stieglitz established his 291 Gallery in 1905, only a handful of dealers had been willing to stage photography exhibits, and rarely did anyone make money from these ventures. In the thirties, Julien Levy, who specialized in surrealist painting, showed Man Ray, Brassaï, and Atget at his West Fifty-seventh Street gallery, but even at ten dollars apiece the prints went unsold, and the dealer himself purchased the majority of them. Twenty years later, Helen Gee opened the Limelight, a combination gallery and Greenwich Village coffeehouse that sold espresso and pastries in addition to photographs by Edward Weston, Paul Strand, and Elliott Erwitt. The pastries, however, outsold the photographs, and Gee had to rely on profits from the coffeehouse to keep the gallery alive. Lee Witkin, who opened a gallery on East Sixtieth Street in 1969, fared better than his predecessors, for he presented photographs the way book dealers tendered books, and customers were drawn to his gallery for its homey, slightly musty ambience. Witkin exhibited both a mixture of contemporary and historical work—he handled Edward Weston—yet he was not overly concerned with broadening photography's audience beyond the small cadre of people who already collected it. Witkin had dominated the market until the inauguration of the Light Gallery, which promoted the concept that photography was equal in stature to painting and sculpture.

Critic Barbara Rose, in a 1972 article for *New York* magazine entitled "The Triumph of Photography, or: Farewell to Status in the Arts," discussed the age-old prejudice against photography: "Such distinction separating the 'minor' arts of photography, film, graphics, and the various crafts from the 'major' arts of architecture, painting and sculpture are status distinctions imposed at the end of the Middle Ages. . . . Painting was proclaimed the noblest art because it was the cleanest and most spiritual—sculptors still being forced to do the dirty work of actual carving stone and casting bronze." Photography was dirtier still, according to Rose, because "elitist" critics felt it dealt "strictly with found images," and was therefore "less freely imaginative than painting and sculpture."

Sam Wagstaff maintained a similar prejudice, and while he enjoyed taking pictures himself—his favorite subjects, oddly enough, were flowers and cats—he associated photography with the photo essays in *Life* and *Look*. He had always hated them, and the name W. Eugene Smith was enough to send him off on a half-hour tirade about "socially conscious" photographers who subjected viewers to maudlin portraits of valiant midwives and heroic country doctors. "Why?" he intoned, "does a photograph have to carry a message?" Wagstaff had attended the Museum of Modern Art's "Family of Man" exhibit, which was considered the major photographic event of the fifties, and that had further alienated him from the medium. Edward Steichen, who was then the director of photography at the museum, had gathered together 503 images from 68 countries to celebrate the "essential oneness of mankind throughout the world." Wagstaff dismissed the show as vulgar, and regularly cited it as an example of everything that was wrong with photography; as he later told *The New York Times*, "The kiss of death in art is sentimentality."

What changed his mind about photography was "The Painterly Photograph" exhibit at the Metropolitan Museum of Art, which opened several days after Mapplethorpe's debut at the Light Gallery. The show focused on the Photo-Secessionists, a loosely knit group of American pictorialists who were led by Alfred Stieglitz, and whose dreamy, poetic pictures of landscapes, cityscapes, and nudes were influenced by impressionist and symbolist painting. The photographs had been part of the Metropolitan's Stieglitz collection, but many had not been seen since Stieglitz had printed them in *Camera Work* fifty years earlier. They had been assembled and hung by John McKendry's assistant Weston Naef, as the curator himself was too distracted for such a project. Though Wagstaff reluctantly accompanied Mapplethorpe to the show, he had no intention of liking anything until he reached Edward Steichen's *Flatiron Building*. The picture was tinted a foggy green that gave it a lyrical, "painterly" quality. Wagstaff stared at the image and absorbed the details: the silhouette of the horse and buggy driver; the glow of the street lights; the pen-and-ink delicacy of the trees. He could not believe it was photographed by the same Edward Steichen who had created what Wagstaff considered to be the plodding "Family of Man" exhibit. A *New York Times* reporter later compared Wagstaff's reaction to that of Saul of Tarsus blinded on the road to Damascus, for, suddenly and without warning, he became a convert to photography. "I thought this photograph ranked with Eakins, with Whistler, with any painting made by any American at that time," he later told *Newsweek*. "It was magnificent."

Wagstaff could not stop talking about the picture, and he began to ruminate on the benefits of collecting photography. Mapplethorpe urged him to do so, for he was afraid Wagstaff was becoming too involved with the Arica Institute, and he worried that he might suddenly give away all his money to them. Before Wagstaff made any decisions about his life, however, he needed to consult a battery of psychics and astrologers, and one evening he went to Patti Smith for a Tarot card reading, to determine if collecting photography made sense. "The outcome," she concluded, after she read the cards, "is very favorable."

When Wagstaff first began collecting photographs, he had the field largely to himself. His main competitors, other than museums and private institutions, were Chicago lawyer Arnold Crane and Paris book dealer André Jammes, but both men had already completed the bulk of their collections. Crane had cornered the market on Walker Evans, Man Ray, Laszlo Moholy-Nagy, and Hippolyte Bayard, while Jammes's specialty was nineteenth-century French photography. With so few individuals actively involved in buying pictures, Sam spotted an opportunity to make his mark. Photography was one of the last frontiers in art where unknown masterpieces could still be discovered and history rewritten. Wagstaff no longer cared if art historians cast aspersions on photography; he loved a good fight, and, as an art historian himself, who better to enlighten his comrades? "I think Sam had always felt that his life had been a failure," explained Paul Walter, who later amassed a significant photography collection of his own. "Advertising hadn't worked out for him, then he didn't get the director's job at the [Wadsworth] Athenaeum. Sam's experience in Detroit was another disappointment, and after that, he drifted into drugs and became involved with spiritual quacks. Photography saved him."

Over the years it became widely assumed that Mapplethorpe and Wagstaff had entered into some kind of mutual arrangement whereby Mapplethorpe helped Wagstaff with his collection and Wagstaff promoted Mapplethorpe's photography career. But such an obvious quid pro quo deal never happened. Mapplethorpe still had mixed feelings about photography, and if he had demonstrated any talent as a painter, he probably never would have picked up a camera. But his options were limited, besides which he lacked the discipline for working on anything that took more than a few hours. He told curator Janet Kardon in 1988: "It [photography] was the perfect medium, or so it seemed, for the seventies and eighties, when everything was fast. If I were to make something that took two weeks to do, I'd lose my enthusiasm. It would become an act of labor and the love would be gone. With photography, you zero in; you put a lot of energy into short moments, and then you go on to the next thing. It seems to allow you to function in a very contemporary way and still produce the material." Given that Wagstaff saw himself as photography's main disciple, and that Mapplethorpe was dependent on him, emotionally and financially, it was only natural for them to join forces. It was perhaps even more natural that when Wagstaff later set forth his own standards of photography, Mapplethorpe's work would become the centerpiece of the Wagstaff hierarchy.

. . .

Wagstaff was always unfailingly generous in praising Mapplethorpe for stimulating his interest in photography, but in truth, Wagstaff already knew more about the medium than his "mentor." Nevertheless, he liked to tell people that Mapplethorpe was "purely a visual instrument," and that he used him as a divining rod to uncover masterpieces. In February, Mapplethorpe led Wagstaff to a pornography dealer on Staten Island, where he had hoped to buy some Tom of Finland drawings, and was disappointed to find photocopies instead of originals. "Aside from that," Mapplethorpe told the *Print Collector's Newsletter*, "he had mostly chicken porn."

Mapplethorpe and Wagstaff were preparing to leave when the man pulled out some books of photographs, and Mapplethorpe asked if the dealer had ever heard of "some count or baron or something who took photographs of children in Italy?" The man immediately brought out several dozen photographs by Baron Von Gloeden, a homosexual photographer who worked in Taormina, Italy, in the early nineteenth century. Von Gloeden specialized in pictures of dark-skinned Sicilian boys in classical settings that he sold to gay collectors throughout Europe and America. Similar to the way homosexual painters had once used classical and religious themes to justify the male nude, Von Gloeden dressed his models in togas and wreaths and posed them against the picturesque ruins of Taormina. "If you had a classical column somewhere in the photograph," said Allen Ellenzweig, author of *The Homoerotic Photograph*, "the male nude became permissible to look at within that context. It even permitted straight men to look at the image without feeling threatened." Mapplethorpe urged Wagstaff to buy the photographs, and the campy Von Gloeden nudes for twenty-five dollars apiece became the first pictures in the Wagstaff collection. Later, Wagstaff presented Mapplethorpe with several of the Von Gloedens so he, too, could start a photography collection.

In March, Wagstaff made a more substantial purchase when dealer George Rinhart sold him a group of Frederick Evans's platinum prints of Kelmscott Abbey from 1896. A few weeks later, Wagstaff invited Rinhart to dinner at his loft on Bond Street. "I took a taxi down to this terrible street and got out in front of this terrible building," Rinhart recalled. "And *there* was terrible Robert Mapplethorpe." Rinhart had met Mapplethorpe through John McKendry a year earlier, and had dismissed him as a "street punk on the make." That Mapplethorpe had now managed to move beyond McKendry to Sam Wagstaff impressed Rinhart as nothing short of incredible. Over the years Wagstaff became one of Rinhart's best customers, and he frequently took Mapplethorpe to the dealer's apartment on West Eighty-third Street, and later to his home in Connecticut. "They often played this little game," Rinhart recalled, "where Sam would look over and say, 'Robert, would you like this photograph?' And Robert would answer, 'Yes, Sammi,' in a little baby voice. Sam just adored Robert. He would have done anything for him."

Mapplethorpe was not as indulgent of Wagstaff's whims, however, and whenever he saw him picking up a camera, he threw a childish temper tantrum. Wagstaff understood that he was only an amateur, and while he fantasized about becoming an art photographer someday, he had not reached the point where he felt confident enough to stand behind one of his pictures "with a bucket of my own blood." Yet just as Wagstaff fell in love with artists as a way of getting closer to art, he sought to use the camera as a means of establishing a more intimate bond with photography. He attempted to set up a photo session with Patti Smith, but Mapplethorpe effectively foiled his efforts and reproached him for trespassing on his turf. "You're the collector," he reminded him. "*I'm* the artist."

The hard feelings persisted when Mapplethorpe flew to Amsterdam that May for a five-day vacation, while Wagstaff remained in New York to care for his ailing mother. Both men were scheduled to rendezvous later in the week for an upcoming photography auction at Sotheby Parke-Bernet in London. Since none of the New York auction houses held regular photography sales, Wagstaff felt it was important for him to be at the one in London, but he did not want to leave his mother unless her condition stabilized. When Mapplethorpe left Amsterdam he checked into the Constantin Hotel in South Kensington and immediately telephoned Wagstaff. The two men began arguing again over Wagstaff's hobby, with Sam accusing Robert of trying to "inhibit" his activities; he suggested they might benefit from time apart. After Mapplethorpe hung up the telephone, he panicked; Wagstaff was his lifeline, and he depended on him to cover bounced checks and to see that his phone wasn't disconnected when he forgot to pay his bills on time. He could not imagine returning to the hand-to-mouth existence of the pre-Wagstaff era, so he quickly wrote Wagstaff a letter that included a quasi-apology: "I am selfish but then that's an atribute [sic] that all artists possess."

Wagstaff's mother died in mid-May, and one of the first things he did was to take a deathbed portrait of her. Although his actions might seem ghoulish, he was actually following in the tradition of Victorian photographers who took pictures of the dead to serve as mementos for bereaved families. Wagstaff also photographed the room in which she died at the St. Regis Hotel; he wanted to remember all the details—the billowing curtains, an ornate brass doorknob, a stack of lace handkerchiefs. "I feel a little bad about not being with you for your mother's funeral," Mapplethorpe wrote from London, "but those things depress me so." He was nervous about attending the upcoming Sotheby's auction by himself, and on May 24 he wrote to Wagstaff: "Ran up Southerby's [sic]. I've never bidded [sic] on anything before but I imagine one could get off on it. If your [sic] not here I'll try to find a bargain but I can't promise anything as I'm not familiar with the prices of such things."

Mapplethorpe, meanwhile, took his own Polaroids to several art dealers, but as he later wrote to Wagstaff, he was greeted with "the same old nonsense about not being able to show that kind of work." Mapplethorpe concluded that if he was going to be successful, he needed to strike the right balance between the acceptable and the unacceptable, as he detailed in a letter to Wagstaff: "I took some photographs of flowers today—I think I should be a little less concerned with the bizarre aspects of my work if in fact I'm interested in having my work catch on. One must ease the public into it— That's an art in itself. . . .— Sell the public flowers . . . things that they can hang on their walls without being uptight."

Olga Newhall's death left Sam Wagstaff a wealthy man, and both he and his sister, Judith, inherited several millions of dollars worth of stock in the Newhall Land and Farming Company. Contrary to appearances, the Wagstaffs had never been rich, at least by the standards of many of their old-money peers, and while Sam had lived a life of privilege, up until his stepfather's death he had always been dependent on his curator's salary. Now he would never have to work for a living again, and he pursued his dream of collecting with a renewed passion.

"I don't think any collector knows his true motivation," he told *Art & Antiques*. "An obsession—like any sort of love—is blinding." Wagstaff purchased dozens of photographs at a time, but ever the penny-pincher, he refused to spend extra money on taxis, so he traveled on the subway with thousands of dollars' worth of pictures stuffed inside brown paper shopping bags. Mapplethorpe often accompanied him on his scouting trips, but even when he didn't, Wagstaff would stop by the loft on his way home and spill the contents of the bags on the floor. The two men would surround themselves with images of cathedrals, battlefields, movie stars, male nudes, American Indians, Civil War corpses, angels, flowers, and skulls. Like Proust's madeleine, certain pictures unleashed a flood of feelings and sensations; Wagstaff could almost smell his mother's perfume when he stared at Cecil Beaton's 1926 photograph of debutantes, or Irving Penn's portrait of the elegant Mrs. William Rhinelander Stewart. "You've got to crash through the sight barrier and tell the mind to shut up," he advised Mapplethorpe. "Photography is silent talk."

Mapplethorpe had already been tutored in photography by both Sandy Daley and John McKendry, but his experience with Wagstaff was altogether different. "I did learn a lot," Mapplethorpe told Janet Kardon, "and it was a great experience to be able to handle the pictures. Often you see pictures under glass, and it's not the same." Moreover, he had the opportunity to study pictures few Americans had ever seen before. Wagstaff was responsible for bringing into the country the first collection of photographs by the nineteenth-century portraitist Nadar, who took pictures of France's most celebrated personalities. Nadar was a celebrity in his own right: flamboyant and stylish, he stood as an equal to his portrait subjects, and this distinction was an important one for Mapplethorpe, who later cited Nadar as the photographer he most admired.

For the next several years Mapplethorpe would be inundated with photographic imagery, and while he later bristled at the suggestion that Wagstaff's collecting had any influence on his aesthetic—"I already had a way of seeing"—it would have been impossible for him not to have been affected by it. Whenever Wagstaff gave speeches about photography, he always stressed how important it was for young photographers to know the history of the medium: "Then maybe some of the power, some of that magic, some of that excellence, would rub off on them."

Wagstaff's obsession with the past, however, was so powerful that Mapplethorpe had to fight against letting it overwhelm his own career. Wagstaff enjoyed having company when he looked at pictures, and Mapplethorpe was often pressured into traveling with him. At times he resented it, for he wanted to work on his own art. Wagstaff had given him fifty thousand dollars—not an overwhelmingly generous gift in light of Wagstaff's own inheritance, but enough so that Mapplethorpe didn't have to worry about paying the bills. He had recently purchased a 4 × 5 Graphic, to which he attached a Polaroid back, and since the Polaroid Corporation had now produced positive-negative film, he could make bigger pictures from the negative. This precipitated a need for larger frames, so he hired a carpenter named Robert Fosdick, who would collaborate with him for the next several years. "It was a very exciting time for Robert," Fosdick recalled, "because he finally had the resources to fully explore his ideas. Often he would sketch out a design, then expect me to build it. Robert never picked up a tool himself. He was a firm believer in the division between art and craft."

The pieces Mapplethorpe created were far more ambitious than the Polaroids exhibited at the Light Gallery, when he had used flimsy plastic cassettes as frames. In *Self Portrait, 1973,* he took a photograph of himself in a leather vest and nipple clamp, then reinforced the sadomasochistic theme by framing the picture in black leather. In *Made in Canada* he poked fun at the conventional family album, by first shooting a series of sixteen Polaroids of a nude man, probably Wagstaff, trussing his penis with a black cord; he then placed the pictures in a black photo album, and took a picture of the album. Finally, he placed the photograph in a horizontal red frame that Fosdick had constructed for him. The result was that Mapplethorpe had effectively framed the pictures three times—first by placing them in the album, then by taking a picture of the album, and lastly by literally framing the photograph of the pictures in the album. His mixed media piece entitled *Gentlemen* was an attempt to

merge sculpture with photography, but the outcome was almost
laughably juvenile and revealed his worst excesses. He had taken a
wooden barrel, painted it red, trimmed the top with black leather
and metal studs, then placed a crucifix upon it. The barrel itself was
then positioned on a wooden pedestal marked with a plaque that
read GENTLEMEN, the reference to a toilet made abundantly clear by
the self-portrait on the opposite side of the pedestal. It showed a
naked Mapplethorpe crouched over the barrel, as though he were
either defecating on the crucifix or being anally penetrated by it.
Gentlemen was exhibited in early 1974 at the Buecker & Harpsichords gallery as part of a group show entitled "Recent Religious
and Ritual Art." *ARTnews* described the participating artists as "visionaries who stumble at times into the slapstick or insane."

Patti Smith was just such a visionary, and throughout the spring of
1973 she regularly performed at the Mercer Arts Center, where she
read her poetry to the accompaniment of a toy piano and snarled
obscenities at the audience. She drew her inspiration from two unlikely sources: the Russian poet Vladimir Mayakovski, who attempted to "depoetize" poetry through crude language, and
talk-show host Johnny Carson, whom Smith admired for his unruf-
fled delivery and smooth patter. The Mercer Arts Center was the
home of such glitter rock bands as the New York Dolls, direct
descendants of David Bowie in his androgynous Ziggy Stardust
incarnation, and they, too, wore outrageous makeup, sequined costumes, and sky-high platform boots. In comparison to the Dolls,
Patti Smith was downright cerebral, and the bored audience often
greeted her poetry with catcalls and jeers. Picking up a megaphone,
she would taunt them back until, exhausted and hoarse, she had
won them over. Then she would recite her poetry again, sometimes
stopping to tell stories about her own life, flitting, as always, between the real and the imagined. "Here was this skinny little thing
valiantly trying to make art out of her life," said Jane Friedman, who
had recently become Smith's manager. "Patti laid herself emotionally bare. In all the time I listened to her, I never heard her repeat a
story. She was completely spontaneous. Words just flowed from her
mouth." Friedman, who worked at the Wartoke publicity firm, had
been reluctant to manage Smith, for she wasn't sure how to pro-

mote a poet. Smith, however, let it be known that she was "dying of tuberculosis," and Friedman felt so bad that she agreed to meet with her. By the time she discovered the ruse she had been seduced by Smith's personality, and since the Mercer Arts Center was one of Friedman's clients, she was able to book Smith as an opening act.

In May, Friedman obtained another job for Smith at Kenny's Castaways, where she opened for a singer performing "Rag and Roll" music. "Maybe a little filth'll liven this place up," she shouted on the evening a critic for *The Village Voice* attended the show, then she began reciting the poem "Rape," about a "wolf in a lambskin trojan." The *Voice* critic later wrote that she was "in the vanguard of cultural mutation; a cryptic androgynous Keith Richard look-alike poetess-applique."

Smith's career was moving so fast and in so many directions that it was difficult to keep pace with her activities. One week she was traveling to France to do research for a never-completed biography of Rimbaud; the next week she was modeling Revillon furs for Fernando Sanchez in a Saks Fifth Avenue fashion show. In September, Andreas Brown, the owner of the Gotham Book Mart, published her third volume of poetry, *Witt*, and arranged for a simultaneous exhibit of her drawings to be shown at the bookstore. Smith made sure that Mapplethorpe took the photo of her for the cover of *Witt*, and convinced Brown to include Mapplethorpe's photographs in an upcoming group show that also featured Polaroids by Andy Warhol and his associate Brigid Polk.

Over the years Mapplethorpe's attitude toward Warhol had gone from adulation to competitiveness. Mapplethorpe had once hoped to be Warhol's friend, perhaps even his protégé, but he had quickly learned that Warhol wasn't exactly the mentor type—people helped Warhol, not the other way around. Bob Colacello, in *Holy Terror: Andy Warhol Close Up*, recounts a hilarious incident in which both Mapplethorpe and Warhol showed up to photograph Rudolf Nureyev at Lincoln Center and played dueling Polaroids while the temperamental ballet star proceeded to rip up the photos. Warhol later scolded Colacello for inviting the photographer along. "You don't have a crush on Robert Mapplethorpe, do you?" Warhol repeatedly asked Colacello, who was then editor of *Interview* and did indeed have a crush on Mapplethorpe. "He's so dirty," Warhol complained. "His feet smell. He has no money. And that horrible Patti Smith . . ." Mapplethorpe worried that Warhol was going to steal his ideas and viewed him, perhaps rightfully so, as someone who "sucked the life out of people." Certainly Warhol had a reputation for borrowing art concepts from his Factory employees, but he had been taking Polaroids long before Mapplethorpe. And it was Warhol, not Mapplethorpe, who attracted the most attention at the Gotham exhibit; in fact, Andreas Brown could not even remember Mapplethorpe's Polaroids at all. "They must have been good because I included them in the show," he concluded, "but people came to see Andy."

Sam Wagstaff made sure that nothing like that would happen again, and he stepped up his efforts to spread the word on Mapplethorpe. "It was like no other artist existed in the world," Sam Green recalled. "Gauguin, Velázquez, forget it. It was only Robert Mapplethorpe." In October Mapplethorpe and Wagstaff attended the frenzied Scull auction at Sotheby Parke-Bernet, where the record crowds and TV cameras heralded the art boom of the seventies and eighties. Robert Scull, who owned a fleet of taxis, and his wife, "Spike," were the most famous collectors of contemporary art in America, and their rise from "hoi polloi" to "haute monde" had been chronicled by Tom Wolfe, who described them as "the folk heroes of every social climber who ever hit New York." Making his way through the crowds at the auction house, Wagstaff located Bob Scull and introduced him to Mapplethorpe. "You should know his work," Wagstaff confided, one collector to another, "because it is going to become famous."

CHAPTER ELEVEN

"I went into photography because it seemed like the perfect
vehicle for commenting on the madness of today's existence."

—*Robert Mapplethorpe*

Francesco Scavullo took a portrait of Robert Mapplethorpe
and Sam Wagstaff in 1974 that could be called "The Perfect Moment," to borrow the title of Mapplethorpe's 1988 exhibit, for just
as Mapplethorpe photographed flowers at the height of their
bloom, Scavullo captured Robert and Sam at the peak of their love
affair. They would never look so happy, nor as handsome, again.

For a time Mapplethorpe had been satisfied with the arrangement
he'd struck with Wagstaff; they were together several nights a week,
with no questions asked about the nights they spent apart. But Mapplethorpe's desire for adventure increased in direct proportion to
the number of his sexual encounters. If he had once been an S&M
voyeur, he was now a full-fledged participant in the scene, and he
was so obsessive about having sex that it threatened to overwhelm
everything else in his life. It was as if he had suddenly opened Pandora's box and out came a swarm of bewitching young men tempt-

ing him with amyl nitrite "poppers" and MDA, and with sexual accoutrements of all shapes, sizes, and designs. Wagstaff had been indulgent of Mapplethorpe's promiscuity, but he had no idea that this need for sexual gratification would escalate into the compulsive behavior it became. Mapplethorpe complained that he didn't feel alive unless he had sex every day, and he freely admitted that he was a "sex addict."

Certainly Mapplethorpe was addicted to drugs: he started his day with marijuana and cocaine, then later, at night, it was more cocaine, then MDA, Quaaludes, and whatever else he had at his disposal. He rarely drank alcohol, except for an occasional beer or glass of champagne, because he felt it made him "sloppy." Drugs, however, were an integral part of the gay S&M scene, for they enhanced the pleasure of certain physical encounters that would otherwise have been too painful.

He began going to the bars—"disappearing into the night," as he called it—seven nights a week. Sam Wagstaff had recently commissioned an Iowa psychic to do Mapplethorpe's chart, and the psychic noted that Mapplethorpe had "trouble with his sexual sphere," but that it was inextricably tied to his creativity—"the two are somehow one." Wagstaff's obsession with photography matched Mapplethorpe's preoccupation with sex, and during the first six months of 1974 Wagstaff purchased over two hundred pictures from George Rinhart alone. Not content with art photographs, he frequently returned home from his various expeditions loaded down with nineteenth-century cartes de visites, postcards, stereographs, illustrated books, and musty yearbook albums. Mapplethorpe described him as "a total madman," but they were both slightly mad—one sexually voracious, the other visually insatiable; they consumed people and pictures alike.

Mapplethorpe flew to London for the Sotheby's photography auction in February 1974, and wrote Wagstaff a letter as soon as he boarded the BOAC jet: "Sammi—I promise to work real hard this year. Maybe by next year the muffin will be bringing home some of the monies. You've been really good to me. I love you Sammi." Wagstaff met him at the Constantin Hotel a week later, but returned to New York immediately after the auction, while Mapplethorpe remained in London until the end of March. "Maybe it's just the distance," he wrote after one transatlantic phone call. "But I was missing you. And somehow you didn't seem happy to hear from me. It was as though someone was sitting next to you and you couldn't talk." He was even more open about his insecurities in a follow-up letter: "I don't want our relationship to fall apart. I know it's hard with me all sexed up 24 hours. I've got to control myself as it seems to be too much for you. Or maybe you're just tired of me. I don't quite understand it—but somehow it's gotta work. I don't really want to be with anyone else. I really do love you."

Yet when Mapplethorpe returned to New York he immediately fell into the same old pattern of cruising the gay bars every night. Countless other gays were involved in stable domestic partnerships and did not subscribe to prevailing notions of power through promiscuity. However, Christopher and West Streets had become the center of what many young gays believed to be a Brave New World of sexual freedom, and a "clone culture" had developed around the ultramasculine or "butch" male. The clones derived their inspiration from such stereotypical notions of masculinity as policemen, cowboys, construction workers, and bodybuilders, and they outfitted themselves accordingly. In addition to black motorcycle jackets or flannel shirts and work boots, they wore tight T-shirts, and button-fly Levi's with one button undone; they dangled keys and handkerchiefs from their jeans pockets as an indication of which sexual acts they preferred, and which sexual positions. While the clones looked alike, their sexual activities had become so specialized that they now divided themselves into erotic subcategories: "masters" who sought "slaves"; fetishists who eroticized boots, gloves, jockstraps, and even urine and excrement.

Mapplethorpe had grown up despising the homogeneity of Floral Park, where all the homes were identical and where many of the people, he thought, had the same "suburban look." Yet he was now cruising West Street surrounded by men nicknamed "clones," who wore their hair in the same clipped style and who had the same rippling gym bodies encased in the same uniforms. Sociologist Martin P. Levine, in an essay that appears in *Gay Culture in America*, describes the clones as having the look of a "doped-up, sexed-out Marlboro man." In some respects, Christopher Street was not unlike a gay Floral Park; Mapplethorpe had replaced one homogeneous environment with another.

Mapplethorpe was determined to distinguish himself as a master magician of sex. He didn't dangle just one colored handkerchief from his pocket; he had sewn together at least half a dozen so that he advertised a rainbow of sexual preferences. He viewed S&M not as sadism and masochism, but as "sex and magic." He told writer and editor Joe Dolce in a 1982 interview: "Sex *is* magic. If you channel it right, there's more energy in sex than there is in art."

In most of his sexual encounters Mapplethorpe was the dominant partner; he preferred giving pain to receiving it. Except in the visual sense, bondage didn't appeal to him, and he found the idea of tying someone up boring and tedious. He was most interested in the really freakish aspects of a person's sexual behavior, and he would often canvass his friends to find out if they knew anybody who had something "interesting" to offer him, a "sexual schtick" he hadn't seen before. It was almost as if he were revisiting Coney Island, except now the "freaks" wore leather suits and bondage masks. If he found someone who enjoyed "fisting"—the act of inserting a fist into a partner's rectum—he'd then want to find a man who enjoyed two fists, or three. It wasn't enough that someone experience orgasm—he wanted the orgasm to be produced by some "creative" act, such as having a catheter, or a needle, inserted into the penis.

Mapplethorpe's concept of "sex and magic" involved certain rituals that were as rigid as anything he had ever rebelled against in his youth. Before going out at night, he made sure he put on his clothes in exactly the same order; he was careful not to wash beneath his underarms because he believed perspiration odor was vital to his sex appeal. He picked up men at the bars by staring at them to see if he could detect "something" in their eyes; those who passed the eyeball test came home with him, but then he had difficulty maintaining an erection unless his partner stared into his own eyes. Sight, he believed, was the most important of all the five senses. If his partner reached a premature climax, Mapplethorpe considered the evening a failure, and no matter what time it was, he would put on his clothes—jeans or leather pants, sometimes a codpiece, shirt, vest, studded leather cuffs, black leather jacket—and return to the West Village.

Sadomasochism was practiced by only a small percentage of the gay population, yet the uniforms and equipment were everywhere in the West Village. S&M accessories, such as studded cuffs, ropes, chains, and bondage masks, were sold at places like the Marquis de Suede and the Pleasure Chest. Artist Robert Morris, whose work Sam Wagstaff had shown in Detroit, publicized his April exhibit at the Castelli-Sonnabend Gallery by designing a poster that featured him in a Nazi helmet, his hands manacled to a thick chain attached to his neck. Susan Sontag in her 1974 essay "Fascinating Fascism" quotes Morris as saying he considered the picture to be "the only image that still has any power to shock." Six months later, Italian film director Liliana Cavani brought out *The Night Porter,* the story of an SS officer (played by Dirk Bogarde) who carries on an S&M love affair with one of his former concentration camp victims (played by Charlotte Rampling). The following year S&M had so infiltrated American consumer culture that it was being used to sell everything from clothing to records.

The style was described by one feminist critic as "brutality chic," and it was most evident in the work of fashion photographers Helmut Newton and Chris von Wangenheim. Newton was responsible for a controversial *Vogue* spread entitled the "Story of Ohhh," which ended with a man sadistically grabbing a woman by the breast. Von Wangenheim created a shoe advertisement by photographing a Doberman pinscher biting a woman's ankle. Photographer Ara Gallant later took "brutality chic" to the extreme when he devised the Sunset Boulevard advertisement for the Rolling Stones' album *Black and Blue.* Karen Durbin described the image in *The Village Voice:* "The billboard showed a woman looking properly sensual (tumbled hair, pouty mouth) and wearing an artfully torn, minimal garment that once may well have been a dress. She was also bruised and bound, hanging from her wrists with legs wide apart and crotch resting on the record album cover; the copy read 'I'm "Black and Blue" from the Rolling Stones and I *love* it!' "

What was different about Mapplethorpe's work, and consequently more unsettling, was that instead of a woman being tied up in ropes—a standard pose in "straight" pornography—he had the audacity to turn the tables and reveal a whole universe of submissive men. Helmut Newton could photograph a woman tethered to a bed by a chain around her neck, or another crouched on all fours with a saddle on her back, and the images were viewed as kinky and decadent, for they conjured up a privileged world of *Vogue* fashion shoots and jet-set society. In comparison, Mapplethorpe's S&M photographs made no reference to the outside world at all; his men were defined exclusively by their sexual predilections.

Most of the Polaroids were taken in Mapplethorpe's bare studio on Bond Street, usually after a night of sexual games. Philippe Garner, a director of Sotheby's in London, who has been in charge of photography sales since 1971, recalled seeing Mapplethorpe's Polaroids for the first time earlier that year: "Robert and Sam had come to London for the auctions, and in the course of polite conversation I asked Robert, 'And what do you do?' His laconic answer was, 'I make photographs.' I said, 'I'd be curious to see the work,' and the next day Robert came into my office at Sotheby's, and with barely a word, he pushed a portfolio across the table. I started looking at the pictures, and I was stunned and lost for words—not out of prudishness, but out of the sheer bloody strength of the images. To this day, my sight of those Polaroids remains one of the great photographic revelations of my life. Pornography is a tough challenge, but Robert's work managed to be intensely personal yet speak on a broader artistic level. It was totally frank, but with an elegance of eye that made it electric."

The tension between Mapplethorpe's subject matter and his presentation rendered his pictures distinctly "Mapplethorpe," yet he was not immune to borrowing from his photographic predecessors. *Bondage, 1974* shows an unidentified man, bound and blindfolded, in a series of compliant poses that brings to mind F. Holland Day's turn-of-the-century crucifixion series. Day was an influential member of the American pictorialist movement, and also a homosexual, but in keeping with late-nineteenth-century Boston morality he remained discreet about his sexual orientation. Nevertheless, many of his photographs were overtly homoerotic, and none more so than *Study for the Crucifixion*—Boston's first view of frontal male nudity, in which the photographer assumed a pose that, according to writer

Allen Ellenzweig, has now "become almost a cliché for sexual ardor: head slightly thrown back to reveal the throat; torso off-center, hips tilted, and knees bent." Ellenzweig in *The Homoerotic Photograph* quotes Day's biographer, Estelle Jussim, who thought the photograph looked "more like one of Michelangelo's slave sculptures than a medieval saint." Mapplethorpe himself reproduced Michelangelo's *Dying Slave* at the same time he shot *Bondage, 1974,* by photographing the open pages of a book that duplicated the artist's image, then placing the picture in a wooden frame that bore the name MAPPLETHORPE. By quoting Michelangelo, then affixing his name so prominently on the piece, he may have been alluding to his own desire to merge the sculptural with the photographic, and perhaps to remind viewers that he, too, was "working in an art tradition."

"Robert was very insistent that people see him as an artist, and not as 'Robert Mapplethorpe, the photographer,' " recalled Klaus Kertess, who had finally agreed to exhibit two of Mapplethorpe's pieces in a group show at the Bykert Gallery that fall. Even then, the dealer was skittish about displaying a male nude in his gallery. "I was afraid the other artists would feel their space had been preempted by something a little too hot," said Kertess, who hung the nude in the office of his secretary, future art dealer Mary Boone. The piece Kertess presented out front was *Black Shoes,* a photograph of Mapplethorpe's and Patti Smith's shoes, matted in bright red and framed in black. The shoes are unisex, and when positioned side by side function as mirror images of each other.

Although Mapplethorpe and Smith were not living together anymore, they were still intent on helping each other's careers. "Robert and Patti were so intertwined," said Jane Friedman, "it was like they couldn't exist without sucking off each other's energy." In addition to singing at Reno Sweeney's, a nightclub in Greenwich Village, Smith regularly performed "Rock'n'Rimbaud" concerts—"a little rock, a little poetry"—at various hotels and clubs around the city. In June 1974, Mapplethorpe gave her one thousand dollars to record two songs—"Hey Joe" and "Piss Factory"—at Electric Lady Studios.

Smith had now formed a band that included old friend Lenny Kaye and a handsome young piano player named Richard Sohl, whom Smith nicknamed D.N.V., for *Death in Venice,* because he reminded her of the beautiful Tadzio in Thomas Mann's story. Mapplethorpe attended the recording session and, in his official capacity as "executive producer," chain-smoked cigarettes and nervously paced the room. The two songs the band recorded were classic Patti Smith; she opened "Hey Joe" by wondering if Patti Hearst had been "gettin' it every night from a black revolutionary man and his woman," while "Piss Factory" described her days on the assembly line in Philadelphia and her determination to leave that squalid life behind: "And I'm gonna go I'm gonna get out of here I'm gonna get on that train and go to New York City and I'm gonna be somebody . . . I'm gonna be a big star."

During the summer of 1974 Smith played Max's Kansas City, where she attracted the attention of *New York Times* music critic John Rockwell, who compared her to poet-rocker Lou Reed in her "absorption with demonic, romantic excess." That fall, Jane Friedman booked Smith at Bill Graham's Winterland in San Francisco and the Whiskey a Go Go in Los Angeles. "At the Whiskey, there were only about three people in the audience," Lenny Kaye recalled. "But what was exciting about the whole thing was that we were slowly starting to connect with this weird little rock underground. But when we got back from California we realized that the kind of music people wanted to hear was stuff we weren't sophisticated enough to play. So we hired another guitar player—Ivan Kral—to broaden the sound, then in January 1975 we opened for Eric Burdon at the Main Point in Philly. It was then when we started to realize we had a real act. It wasn't a *traditional* act, but we had enough rock references that I thought, you know, maybe we can do something with this."

Over the past year Mapplethorpe and Smith had not seen much of John McKendry, although they kept hearing reports of strange goings-on at the Metropolitan Museum and elsewhere. McKendry had nearly killed himself on a recent trip to Munich, and he later recounted the hair-raising tale to his close friend Gary Farmer.

"John was in his hotel room and had no clothes on," Farmer said. "He had some drugs—a lot of 'white powder,' he told me—and he was afraid to take it out of the country, so he consumed everything.

He was very high and suddenly he looked into the mirror and found himself naked. He broke the mirror and cut himself badly, then he smeared the blood all over his body and smashed the room up. Meanwhile, the hotel staff was pounding on the door. John looked out the window and saw it was a full moon, and he wanted to touch it, so he saw this electric wire on the window ledge and thought he could reach the moon by swinging on the wire. He grabbed for the wire and fell out the window, and there he was on the ground—totally naked and smeared with blood, and all the bones smashed in his foot. I think he found the whole thing terribly amusing." When Maxime confronted John about his latest maniacal escapade, she was treated to an operatic version of the tale. Balancing himself on his crutches, he began acting out the whole scene for her in Italian—"rather bad Italian," Maxime added. By the time John reached the conclusion, he lost his balance and fell to the floor, and Maxime was so angry she left him there for the rest of the day. "When I returned to the apartment," she recalled, "John was still on the floor."

The Munich incident signaled McKendry's decline, and due to the progressive worsening of his cirrhosis of the liver, he suffered from mental confusion and periodic comas. Maxime would sometimes find him taking a bath fully dressed, or frozen like a statue in a catatonic position. She took him to numerous hospitals, where he was usually placed in the psychiatric ward, but either she didn't want him to stay there, or he rebelled, the end result being that he flitted in and out of the museum like a brilliant but deranged guest conductor. At one point he whimsically took off to London to have all his teeth capped courtesy of the National Health Service. Despite his frequent absences from work, the Metropolitan loyally refused to replace him as head of the department of prints and photography. "The Met would never think of getting rid of a curator," said his assistant Andrea Stillman. "You're on the payroll until the day you die. But it made the running of the department impossible. John was never there, but no one could be appointed in his stead. We were like a rudderless ship."

Coincidentally, while time was running short for the man who had given Mapplethorpe his first camera, the latter was experimenting with his new state-of-the-art Hasselblad, a camera Sam Wagstaff had recently bought him. Mapplethorpe tested out the camera by doing a self-portrait, a variation on the slave/crucifixion theme, in which he leans into the frame with his arm outstretched, a giddy, stoned expression on his face. Roland Barthes in *Camera Lucida* cited the photograph as embodying "a kind of blissful eroticism . . . the photographer has caught the boy's hand (the boy is Mapplethorpe himself, I believe) at just the right degree of openness, the right density of abandonment: a few millimeters more or less and the divined body would no longer have been offered with benevolence . . . the photographer has found the *right moment*, the *kairos* of desire."

John McKendry had spent a lifetime searching for that "right moment" himself, but by the spring of 1975 his health was in serious decline. Even as poisonous toxins due to the cirrhosis destroyed his brain, he derived a perverse pleasure in defying the advice of friends and medical experts; he kept drinking and taking drugs. "This is crazy! You've got to stop all this!" his friend Allen Rosenbaum admonished him. But McKendry remained true to his own myth. "Why should I stop?" he replied. "All my dreams have come true so far." He had indeed come far from the little house near the railroad tracks in Calgary, but he could never possibly be satisfied, because his dreams were as unrealistic as those of Jay Gatsby; he, too, would always be chasing after the green light at the end of the dock, or, in his case, the fireworks in the sky. He lived life as if it were an opera, and he thrived on the grand passion and delirium of it; and since that intensity was impossible for him to sustain, he inevitably collapsed into a state of despair. It was ultimately kinder, perhaps, that McKendry's final days were spent in total delusion.

In May he was admitted to St. Clare's Hospital on West Fifty-first Street, where he thought the psychiatric ward was the Metropolitan Museum of Art. He hired and fired fellow patients and carried on animated discussions with them about future exhibits. He presented his new assistant, who had replaced Andrea Stillman, with his dirty linens, which he believed were archival materials from the museum. "John had read somewhere that you could affect your personality by altering your handwriting," recalled Gary Farmer, "so he practiced changing his signature. Then he started drawing all these mysterious charts with circles and arrows. Of course he was still doing drugs; people were smuggling them into his hospital room."

Mapplethorpe hated being around anyone who was sick, and he was nearly phobic when it came to hospitals, but in mid-June he went to St. Clare's with Patti Smith to see McKendry. Afterward he was so disturbed by the visit that all he could do was stand on the sidewalk outside the hospital and shake his head at the unfairness of it all. Certainly McKendry had been guilty of overindulgence, but who hadn't? He was only forty-two years old, too young to be dying in a hospital. "It's just so stupid," Mapplethorpe kept muttering. "It's just so stupid."

McKendry had asked Mapplethorpe to bring his camera on the next visit, but when he returned to the hospital, he wasn't sure if the curator even recognized him; he was busy slathering a layer of Royal Jelly moisturizer on his cheeks. When McKendry was finished, however, he looked up at Mapplethorpe and whispered, "I'm ready for my picture now."

McKendry had always believed in the camera's magical properties, and years earlier, during a terrorist raid at the Rome airport, he had escaped injury by hiding in a photo booth and taking pictures of himself in his new sunglasses. Perhaps he thought the camera could save him again. For the next ten minutes he drifted in and out of awareness while Mapplethorpe quickly shot his portrait. The scene was too intense for the photographer, and he left the room soon afterward. He liked to keep a distance between himself and his subject, and that was impossible when confronting the searing image of a dying man. Consequently, the picture is uncharacteristically intimate and revealing. Mapplethorpe cropped it so that only half of McKendry's face is visible, thereby reducing him to the sum of his being—the "exquisite eye" that had helped to turn a gardener's son into a curator. He looks beatific, yet Mapplethorpe telegraphed the sense of impending tragedy by aligning the eye with a light socket on the wall, as if someone is about to pull the plug on McKendry's picture-making machine.

When Mapplethorpe later presented the portrait to Maxime, she angrily accused him of exploiting her husband's confused mental state. "I was shattered by the picture," she said. "To me, John had changed inch by inch, day by day, and one always carries the hope that someone they love will get better. When I saw that photograph

I realized how wrong I had been. John *was* dying, and Robert had captured him in his tiny room, in his little corner of Hell."

John McKendry finally succumbed to complications of liver disease on June 23, and at his memorial service at St. Thomas More's Roman Catholic Church, Henry Geldzahler delivered a suitably romantic eulogy: "John was a Rabelaisian butterfly, a being interested in states of ecstasy without the constitution to support his appetites. . . . We cherish his memory because the life he chose had an enchanting perfection and an aesthetic completeness."

Mapplethorpe could not attend the funeral because he was in London photographing the archbishop of Canterbury, a triumph of networking John McKendry had been indirectly responsible for. McKendry had introduced Mapplethorpe to Catherine Tennant, who later introduced him to Guy Nevill, who rented a floor in Tennant's house off the King's Road. Nevill's father had been a friend and secretary to Prince Philip, and Nevill himself had been a former page of honor to the queen. Nevill now collected and sold sporting art and was writing a biography of his cousin, Lady Dorothy Nevill, who had been a confidante of Disraeli and Darwin. Mapplethorpe stayed with Nevill for several weeks that June, and during one of the numerous dinners they attended he found himself seated next to the bishop of Suffolk. One supposes the conversation would have been limited, for Mapplethorpe was hardly a raconteur, and what he enjoyed talking about most—his voracious sexual appetite—was not a topic he would have been likely to broach with a cleric. The bishop was obviously so intrigued by Mapplethorpe, however, that he invited him to his residence for a portrait sitting. When Mapplethorpe arrived there several days later, he found the archbishop of Canterbury to be a houseguest as well. Mapplethorpe persuaded the two men to pose outdoors in their ceremonial robes, and recognizing the impact of the liturgical purple against the velvety green lawn, he put color film in the camera, and later created one of his first dye-transfer images.

Mapplethorpe's signature colors, in his art, were red (blood), purple (the Church), and black (Satanism and the leather culture), and he returned to those colors again and again. The bishops in their purple robes were perfect for his aesthetic, and they enhanced his social reputation as well. "Robert had much more of a society success in England than he did in New York," Bob Colacello explained. "And he was snobby enough to let you know that while *you* might be impressed by Pat Buckley or Mercedes Kellogg, he was in a much higher society because it was *English* society."

Patti Smith's success was the antithesis of Mapplethorpe's; it revolved around CBGB, the seedy Bowery bar that nurtured punk rock in New York. She had not been happy with Allen Lanier for some time now, and reports of his frequent infidelities while on the road with Blue Öyster Cult may have prompted her to have an affair with Tom Verlaine (né Miller), a symbolist soulmate, and a founder, with Richard Hell, of the group Television. It was Verlaine, in fact, who had helped transform CBGB into a rock club by convincing Hilly Kristal, the bar's owner, to let Television play there on Sunday nights. English entrepreneur Malcolm McLaren was so taken by Richard Hell's physical appearance, which Craig Bromberg, in *The Wicked Ways of Malcolm McLaren,* described as an "otherworldly version of amphetaminized beefcake," that he returned to London and began to manage the Sex Pistols. The punk style was stridently antistyle, and it was constructed on bad manners, bad taste, and, very often, bad music; indeed, bands like the Sex Pistols derived their creative identity from being as outrageously "bad" as possible. The Sex Pistols had barely cut their first record before their subversive antics caused them to be banned from BBC radio, and numerous municipalities in Britain prohibited their appearance onstage. The punk style reached its apotheosis on the King's Road, where the "Swinging London" of the sixties had given way to the subversive spectacle of young men and women in luridly colored mohawk hairdos, their clothes and bodies pierced with safety pins.

At the beginning, though, punk didn't have such an extreme connotation; in fact, when Patti Smith and her band played an eight-week engagement at CBGB in the spring of 1975, the term "punk rock" wasn't even being used to define the emerging sound. "I think all the groups had one similarity in that we wanted to elevate the idea of rock while still trying to keep it simple," Smith said. "It was a real reaction against disco music and the glitter-rock thing. Our lyrics were much more sophisticated, and we weren't into artifice at all. The whole punk phenomenon in England was much more reactionary and more 'high style.' We didn't comb our hair not because we were making a political statement, but because we just didn't comb our hair." Smith has often been credited with initiating the trend for ripped or shredded clothing, as she mutilated her T-shirts because she often felt "claustrophobic" in them. Other performers embellished the "ripped" style by piecing their clothing together again with safety pins, and later borrowing the accessories of the S&M subculture, to which punk owed a debt in its outlaw mentality and fascination with extremes. Such was the connection between music and sex that Malcolm McLaren even owned a shop in London called SEX, which sold leather and bondage gear to both hardcore enthusiasts and artists alike. The shop was co-owned by fashion designer Vivienne Westwood, who summed up the prevailing ethos: "We're totally committed to what we're doing and our message is simple. We want you to live out your wildest fantasies to the hilt."

Rock and roll provided Patti Smith with a way of doing that, and in few other professions would she have been allowed to battle her demons in such a public way. In truth, she had always been a punk phenomenon, only now she had found an audience, and they loved her. "I remember walking to CBGB's," she said, "and it was never dark, always twilight, and you'd have these old guys warming their hands over trash bins. Hilly Kristal had this great dog, which later got hit, and I remember thinking maybe we could cure the dog just with our energy alone. The place was always so packed, and the feeling so intense. It was like a revival meeting." Yet while Smith's version of "Gloria" was subtitled "in excelsis deo," it began with the unorthodox sentiment "Jesus died for somebody's sins but not mine," which she then followed up with a rowdy chorus of "G-l-o-r-i-a" from the old Van Morrison song. "Land" was another recreated rock oldie, in which Smith merged a violent William Burroughs–esque fantasy about an adolescent boy named Johnny with Fats Domino's "Land of a Thousand Dances":

> And suddenly Johnny
> gets the feelin'
> he's bein' surrounded by

horses horses horses
comin' in all directions,
with their noses in flames . . .
Do you know how to pony?
like boney maroney

CBGB was only a block away from Mapplethorpe's loft, so he frequently dropped by to hear Smith perform, on his way to the leather bars at night. Quietly slipping into the back of the room, he would give her a smile and a little wave. "Sometimes I'd be singing about Johnny in his leather jacket," Smith recalled, "and then I'd see Robert in *his* leather jacket, and he was like he had just stepped out of the song."

Smith's appearances at CBGB sparked enormous interest among record company A & R people who began traveling down to the Bowery to hear the woman people were describing as a combination Rimbaud and Keith Richards. Stephen Holden, who was then at RCA, thought Smith was the best new solo artist since Bruce Springsteen, and later, in a review for *Rolling Stone,* he wrote that "she seems destined to be the queen of rock & roll for the Seventies." It was Clive Davis at Arista, however, who eventually signed Smith to his label, and even though the band was still short a drummer, he awarded them a seven-record deal worth $750,000. At one of her first meetings with Davis, Smith was eerily prescient about her career. "I'm not getting any younger," she told him. "I have to be in a rush—I don't have the strength to take too long becoming a star."

CHAPTER TWELVE

"The rock-n'-roll star in his highest state of grace will be the
new savior . . . rocking to Bethlehem to be born."

—*Patti Smith and Sam Shepard*, Cowboy Mouth

"I wouldn't have touched Robert without Sam. And there
were others like me who felt the same way."

—*art dealer Holly Solomon*

In May 1975 Patti Smith played the Other End, and her idol
Bob Dylan paid a symbolic and widely photographed visit to hear
her—the music-world equivalent of being blessed by the pope.
Whether Smith would ever become as famous as Dylan, or prema-
turely self-destruct like Jim Morrison, was still a big question mark,
but her transition from cultdom to stardom was already being
closely tracked by the press. With a new drummer named Jay Dee
Daugherty, Smith and her four-piece band spent much of the late
summer recording *Horses*, which was produced by musician John
Cale, one of the founders of the Velvet Underground. In addition
to the surreal imagery of "Land," about the leather-jacketed
Johnny—Greil Marcus in *The Village Voice* compared the song's
"terminal violence" to Buñuel's film *Un Chien Andalou*—Smith's
other lyrics touched upon lesbianism, suicide, UFOs, and Wilhelm
Reich. Smith had devised the band's catchy slogan herself—"three-

chord rock merged with the power of the word"—and certainly few rock singers would think of shouting "Go Rimbaud" and "Do the Watusi" in the same breath. James Wolcott in *New York* described Smith as a "phenomenal anomaly."

What Smith needed, then, for the cover of *Horses* was a photograph that captured her intriguing ambiguity, and while she could have selected almost any photographer for the job, she asked Robert Mapplethorpe to take the picture. "Robert and Patti talked about the cover endlessly," Janet Hamill recalled. "They'd just go on and on about it. . . . Should it project a *Vogue–Harper's Bazaar* quality? Or was that too glamorous? Then they'd argue about what 'glamour' was. He had much more conventional ideas than she did, and ultimately I don't think she paid a lot of attention to him." Mapplethorpe was far from being a professional photographer, and unlike his mechanically minded father, he was intimidated by technical equipment. He didn't do any of his own printing and his black-and-white negatives were developed for him at a local photo lab. He didn't even have supplemental lighting, so he was confined to shooting his pictures in daylight; and as a result, he was always looking for interesting light and shadow effects.

Sam Wagstaff had purchased a new penthouse at One Fifth Avenue in the Village, a block from Washington Square Park, and since the apartment was bare and painted white, Mapplethorpe occasionally used it as a photography studio. He had recently noticed that midway through the afternoon the sun formed a perfect triangle on the wall, and whenever he thought of the *Horses* cover, he kept envisioning that triangle.

On the day of the shoot Mapplethorpe and Smith spent several hours drinking coffee at the Pink Teacup on Bleecker Street. Then Mapplethorpe suddenly looked at his watch and panicked. "Let's get out of here," he told Smith, throwing change on the table and running from the café. Smith had no idea what was happening but she followed him as he sprinted down the street. "The light," he called out. "We can't lose the light."

When they reached Wagstaff's penthouse the triangle of light was still on the wall, but Mapplethorpe spotted an ominous patch of clouds in the distance. He was so agitated he had difficulty setting up his tripod, and it kept collapsing on the floor. Meanwhile, Wagstaff was busy in the kitchen making hot chocolate for Smith, and when Mapplethorpe saw her drinking a huge cup of it, he threw up his hands. "Great," he groaned. "Now your teeth are going to be all brown for the picture." Smith told him she wasn't smiling anyway, so it didn't matter. She already had a mental image of the portrait, in which she would blend together Rimbaud, Baudelaire, Frank Sinatra, and Jean-Luc Godard to create a French Symbolist–Las Vegas–*Nouvelle Vague* persona—but she knew better than to explain any of this to Mapplethorpe. He had finally fixed the tripod and was pacing up and down the living room waiting for Wagstaff to leave the apartment so he could be alone with Smith. Finally Wagstaff said good-bye, and Mapplethorpe motioned Smith to stand in front of the wall. The afternoon had turned partly cloudy, and the triangle kept fading from view. "Don't you even want to use a comb?" he asked, staring at Smith's unruly black hair, but she refused to touch it. Instead she flung an old secondhand jacket over one shoulder in a Frank Sinatra pose and imagined that she was the French actress Anna Karina being filmed by Godard. Mapplethorpe made sure to line up her body so that the tip of the triangle jutted out from her collarbone, like an angel's wing. He knew he had taken a good picture even before he saw the contact sheets.

Clive Davis did not share Mapplethorpe's enthusiasm for the image, and in fact, he was quite appalled by it. One of the unwritten rules of the record business was that "girl singers" were supposed to look sexy and pretty, or at the very least like girls; not only was Smith wearing a man's tie, but she hadn't even bothered to put on makeup or run a comb through her hair. Davis understood that Smith's music might not be for everyone, but while it was one thing to write a reggae song about suicide on a lesbian beach, it was commercial suicide to place a black-and-white photo of a sexually androgynous woman on an album cover. Furthermore, Smith even had a trace of dark facial hair on her upper lip.

Davis wanted to scrap the image entirely, but when Smith had signed her deal with Arista she had been given artistic control of her albums, and she refused to change the cover, even ignoring Davis's advice to allow the art department to airbrush the mustache. "I felt it would be like having plastic surgery or something," she said. "I remember the art department also wanted to change my hair into a bouffant. I told them 'Robert Mapplethorpe is an artist, and he doesn't let anyone touch his pictures.' I didn't know that for sure—maybe he wouldn't have minded—but *I* would have.''

Years later, when *Rolling Stone* composed a list of "The 100 Greatest Album Covers of All Time," *Horses* ranked twenty-sixth. The stark black-and-white imagery provided a dramatic contrast to the psychedelic palette of most seventies rock albums, and Smith's swaggering unisex pose radically altered the prevailing feminine stereotype of "girl singers." "I saw *Horses* in a record store in Australia," said art critic Paul Taylor, who died of AIDS in 1992, "and immediately fell in love with the picture. I didn't know anything about Patti Smith or about punk, but I bought the album on the strength of the photograph. It was elegant and totally modern, and I remember looking at the photo credit and wondering, 'Who is Robert Mapplethorpe?' "

Mapplethorpe's pictures had never received national exposure before, but when *Horses* was released in November, his photographs of Smith were in nearly every major magazine. "We had always dreamed about becoming successful together," Smith said. "It was all part of our grand scheme." Certainly she could not have expected more from a first album, and *Horses* was trumpeted in the press as a bona fide musical event. John Rockwell in the *Times* described it as an "extraordinary disc, every minute of which is worth repeated hearings. . . . *Horses* may be an eccentricity, but in a way that anything strikingly new is eccentric. It will annoy some people and be dismissed by others. But if you are responsive to the mystical energy, it will shake you and move you as little else can."

Patti Smith had always been a favorite of rock critics, in part because both she and Lenny Kaye had been rock writers themselves, but also because she was rock's version of Sylvia Plath; she made a good story because there was something almost tragically predetermined about her career. A few years later, Gilda Radner on *Saturday Night Live* would do a takeoff on Smith as "Candy Slice," a befuddled rock singer who belches and spits her way through a number about Mick Jagger before collapsing on the stage. Yet Smith's highs and lows were generally more exhilarating and terrifying than Candy Slice's stoned antics, and during the four-month national tour that followed the release of *Horses,* she dominated the stage one minute, then seemingly wilted under the pressure the next. She sneered, spat, and pranced around the stage like Muhammad Ali, punching her fists in the air and revving up the audience with a jubilant "We're gonna have a real good time together!" Her ragged voice could move from being soft and feminine to a full-throated wail. Her stage persona was an extension of the voice she often used in her poetry, and she ricocheted between girlish vulnerability—"the kitten pick-up"—to a swaggering masculinity. In between, she occasionally lapsed into incoherence; she would lose her train of thought, giggle, then stare into space.

At the Bottom Line in December, John Rockwell, after watching her slump to the floor and bang her head against the pipe organ, wrote a review for the *Times* in which he described the incident as a " 'performance' terrifying in its intensity, like some cosmic, moral struggle between demons and angels." He pinpointed the performer's personality as her greatest liability: "She has always walked the line between genius and eccentricity, between the compelling and the merely odd, between art and insanity. The word 'insanity' may seem a little strong; this listener hasn't been inside Miss Smith's head. But she acts crazy sometimes, and if it's an act, it's an act that she plays so intensely that it's become its own kind of reality." The real question in Rockwell's mind was whether Smith could keep her art exciting without veering off into madness. In her poem "pinwheels" she wrote about a girl with "eyes like pinwheels," who was "waltzing on the edge of a stick." Clearly, the girl was Patti Smith, and every day she was dancing faster and more feverishly.

Despite the success of the *Horses* cover, Mapplethorpe could not afford to sit in his studio and wait for the phone to ring. His portfolio was slim, and since people weren't clamoring to have their pictures taken by him, he had to actively seek them out.

Sam Wagstaff was still helping him pay the bills, but Mapplethorpe couldn't be sure how long that would last. Technically, they were no longer a "couple" and didn't have a sexual relationship anymore. Wagstaff had grown to accept Mapplethorpe's promiscuity, and ultimately, perhaps, he was even titillated by it. Mapplethorpe often telephoned Wagstaff the morning after his latest debauch to describe his experiences. Sex, however, had never been their primary bond; Wagstaff was a surrogate father to Mapple-thorpe the way Smith was a sister. In fact, Mapplethorpe's relationship with Wagstaff had come to mirror the relationship he shared with Smith; he was once again being supported by a permissive ex-lover, who allowed him to act out his fantasies.

In March 1976 Mapplethorpe traveled to Mustique, where Colin Tennant, the island's owner, was celebrating his fiftieth birthday with a lavish "Gold on Gold Ball." Mapplethorpe had received an assignment from *Interview* editor Bob Colacello to shoot the party, but since the magazine wasn't paying his travel expenses, Wagstaff subsidized the trip. Tennant was in the process of building a miniature Taj Mahal for himself on the island, and he had imported an eighteenth-century marble pavilion from Delhi, which arrived in 180 different packing crates. An equally fastidious party-giver, he had festooned the palm trees with gold streamers for the ball, and had instructed his guests to wear gold costumes. They arrived on the tropical island with suitcases filled with clothing more appropriate to a Diaghilev-produced ballet—gold turbans and harem pants, heavy brocade vests, metallic slippers, iridescent jackets, billowing scarves.

Another person might have been intimidated by the opulent scene, but Mapplethorpe made an unforgettable impression himself. His concept of beachwear was a leather bikini topped with a denim vest, and he wore silver and ivory bangles up to his elbows. The sun had given a rosy tint to his normally sickly pallor, and his green eyes matched the color of the Caribbean. "He's very beautiful, isn't he?" fashion designer Carolina Herrera whispered to her husband, Reinaldo, when they first caught sight of him. "My wife is a very aesthetic person," Reinaldo Herrera explained, "and she was immediately drawn to him. Robert had this innate taste which was nothing to do with one's parents, or how one is brought up. It enabled him to move gracefully in every social circle."

"The whole experience is definitely extraordinary," Mapplethorpe wrote in a letter to Wagstaff. "Colin's made himself a kingdom over here. . . . Everyone changes their clothes here at least 3 times a day— It's the perfect place to wear your jewels. The whole thing is completely mad.—I went snorkeling yesterday and ended up too close to the reef with sea urchins in my toes. . . . I should try to get some sleep as one doesn't know what tomorrow may bring—

Thank you Sammi for helping me to be able to do things like this—
I miss the old thing, Love, Robert."

The sybaritic pleasures of the island were so overwhelming, in
fact, that Mapplethorpe wished he had never agreed to take on the
Interview assignment; he was an invited guest and didn't want the
others to perceive him as a common paparazzi, yet he couldn't afford to return home empty-handed if he expected more assignments. With a marked lack of enthusiasm, he carried his camera and
tripod to the beach one afternoon while the other guests were enjoying a lavish barbecue. For the next several hours, he trudged up
and down the shore in his leather bikini attempting to take formal
portraits in a swirl of servants balancing trays of mangoes and pa-
payas, calypso singers, and dancing girls adorned in gold garlands.
The previous afternoon he had been introduced to Princess Margaret, who owned property on the island that was reportedly given to
her by Colin Tennant as a wedding gift upon her 1960 marriage to
Anthony Armstrong-Jones. She was currently in the throes of a love
affair with Roddy Llewellyn, a former landscape gardener and aspiring rock singer, whom the British press had labeled "The Singing
Gardener." When Robert spotted Princess Margaret on a lounge
chair next to Llewellyn he asked if he could take their picture, but
sensitive to press criticism of their affair, she made sure her lover was
out of camera range. She neglected to remove the half-empty bottle
of Beefeater gin, however, and this figured prominently in the photograph. Mapplethorpe wound up with a severe burn from his day at
the beach—"the Princess insisted on moving the tables into the
sun," he wrote to Sam—and he was determined never to mix business and pleasure again.

Photojournalism struck him as being a dishonest profession because he didn't like intruding on people's privacy. "The best picture
I got was Bianca Jagger whispering in Mick's ear," he said. "I
caught them telling a secret, which is sort of rude. That's what that
kind of photographer is . . . it's stealing secrets. If I'm at a party, I
want to be *at* the party. Too many photographers use the camera to
avoid participating in things. They become professional observers,
which is something I never wanted to be."

A month or so after his ten-day trip to Mustique, Mapplethorpe
left for San Francisco, where he hoped to build up a sex network.

From his observations at the leather bars, he realized he was in a position to become the documentarian of the 1970s' gay S&M scene, but unlike photojournalism, this was a niche that allowed his own sexual compulsions to flourish. He did not approach it as a voyeur, but as an active participant. "The brilliant aspect of Robert's career was that he permitted his neuroses to work to his advantage," said George Stambolian, a prominent gay writer and art historian who died of AIDS in 1991. "Other people might have been overwhelmed by such a powerful sexual drive, but Robert found a way to make art from it." Like any other form of social networking, though, he could not barge into a leather bar and begin shooting pictures; he first had to acquire the right introductions. So he made an appointment to see Jack Fritscher, the editor of *Drummer,* a magazine for leather enthusiasts that features beefcake shots of men in leather harnesses and interviews with such masters of the pain-pleasure principle as Fakir Musafar, whose ritualized body piercings were simulated by Richard Harris in the movie *A Man Called Horse.*

Fritscher was a former Catholic seminarian who now wrote pornographic short stories with titles such as "I'm a Sucker for Uncut Meat" and "Tit Torture Blues"; he preached a religion based on the priapic energy of male sexual bonding. He believed the essence of gay style owed too large a debt to the "great ladies of the silver screen," and he postulated the idea of the "homomasculine man" as someone for whom S&M was a celebration of masculinity and a second "coming out." Mapplethorpe had always been drawn to people with highly developed verbal skills, and Fritscher, the "Master of Sleaze," as he was known to *Drummer* readers, was effusive on the subject of S&M. The two men had dinner together after their first meeting, then immediately went to bed; by the end of the evening, the ex-seminarian in Fritscher had become totally infatuated with the man he called "the serpent in Eden." He was eager to elevate the amateurish photography in the magazine, so he gave Mapplethorpe an assignment to shoot an S&M call boy named Elliot for the cover.

Elliot lived in New York, but while Mapplethorpe was in San Francisco, he took advantage of his *Drummer* affiliation. "Robert figured if he could get a cover of *Drummer,*" Fritscher said, "men would give in quicker and allow him to photograph them." His color photograph of Elliot, a fierce, stocky man with a dagger tattoo and a cigar, appeared on the cover of issue number twenty-four. It was the only time Mapplethorpe worked for *Drummer,* but Elliot was instrumental in introducing him to other S&M contacts, and later modeled for the photographer standing next to a man named "Dominick," who is suspended upside down in a chain-and-pulley contraption. "There's a sex network like any other kind of network," Robert explained. "It wasn't just about having sex, although I had plenty of that. It was about talking to people and gaining their trust. You also had to be adaptable." He was so adaptable, in fact, that Fritscher recalled an incident when the photographer had mistakenly walked into a "lumber bar" in full leather and, realizing his error, immediately switched into a Pendleton shirt and logger boots.

Mapplethorpe further demonstrated his talent for being a quick-change artist when he flew to London at the beginning of June to do more portraits of his English friends. From S&M call boys, he was now photographing Isabel and Rose Lambton, the daughters of a former cabinet minister; Guy Nevill in his riding gear; Lady Astor's granddaughter, Stella; Colin Tennant's son, Charlie; John Paul Getty III; and beer heiress Catherine Guinness. "This might indicate some schizoid nature in his work, a meretricious split in approach and interest," Mario Amaya wrote in the catalogue to Mapplethorpe's 1978 Chrysler Museum exhibit. "In fact, although these subjects come from a universe of extravagant contrasts, Mapplethorpe casts them from the same mold. The polished world of high fashion and country-house living seems as hard and brittle as the underworld of burnished chains and studded leather."

Sometimes the two worlds overlapped, as was the case with Catherine Guinness, who publicly proclaimed her fascination with two gay clubs, the Anvil and the Toilet, in a piece Steven M.L. Aronson wrote for *Interview* on the occasion of his visit to Stanway, the country house Guinness shared with her then husband, Lord Neidpath: "I remember my father writing me a wonderful letter saying, 'Cacky, I hear you're the queen of the New York Toilet. How *clever* of you.' Well, I went to all those sort of bars. I spent a *lot* of time there, because it was just such fun. And they were the only sort of bars where you could go by yourself because no one's going to pick you up, 'cause you're a girl, and so, like three o'clock in the morning sometimes, I'd just sort of get dressed and go down there, have a couple of beers, and sit and chat to people and have a really *lovely* time."

Not surprisingly, a conspicuous ambiguity is evident in many of Mapplethorpe's portraits of his English friends; Guy Nevill, as Patti Smith once pointed out, could be a coachman or a prince, while Rose Lambton smoking a cigarette on a park bench might easily be mistaken for a London streetwalker. It is almost as if he was purposely telegraphing a message to the viewer that all is not what it seems, and just as a bondage mask might conceal a politician or a priest, the inhabitants of grand country homes might, in fact, prefer the Toilet.

It was during this trip to London that Mapplethorpe took one of the photographs that would lead to the 1990 prosecution of Dennis Barrie, director of Cincinnati's Contemporary Arts Center, on charges of "pandering obscenity" and exhibiting child pornography. Robert photographed four-year-old Rosie, a member of one of England's most distinguished families, on a stone garden bench, the child's genitalia visible beneath a plaid cotton dress. The photograph, which is sometimes mistakenly titled "Honey," was singled out by Judith Reisman, who appeared as a witness for the prosecution, in an article for the *Washington Times:* "Honey is roughly 6 years old, dirty and unkempt, her stringy hair hanging limply about her thin little face as she crouches on the cold steps of an old building. Mr. Mapplethorpe's eye, and camera, peep under the child's skirt to expose her hairless genitalia provocatively to the world—just as thousands of other child molesters/pornographers before and after him." Reisman, who listed her credentials as the "associate director in charge of research" at the American Family Association, a conservative watchdog group organized by the Reverend Donald Wildmon, had wrongly transformed Rosie into Dickens's Little Nell, yet given Mapplethorpe's visual doublespeak, the child could have been a princess or a pauper, and the photographer's intentions guileless or lewd. Art critic Arthur C. Danto expressed his own discomfort with the image in his introduction to *Mapplethorpe:*

> I am not certain of how the expression on Rosie's face is to be read. It could be childish abstractness, or it could be uncertainty with a hint of

fear. In any case, one cannot avoid feeling uncomfortable with the photograph. Rosie is not proud of her sexuality—she does not know her body the way the body-builder Lisa Lyon knows *her* body, to take an extreme example. And there is the question of whether Mapplethorpe saw her in that pose and decided to shoot her, or whether he put her in the pose for the sake of getting the shot of a child's sex.

It is unlikely that Mapplethorpe set up the picture of Rosie to reveal her genitalia, as it was not in his nature to coerce children to do things against their will. Photographer Gilles Larrain, who met Mapplethorpe in the early 1980s, recalled showing him a picture of three children, in which a small boy is laughing with near maniacal abandon. Mapplethorpe complimented Larrain on capturing the boy in such a spontaneous pose, and told him that he found children to be the most difficult subjects of all. "You can't control them," he complained. "They never do what you want them to do." Indeed, in comparison to his rigid pictures of adults, his photographs of children are rarely fixed and stationary. Melia Marden is exposing her buttocks in one picture because she had voluntarily taken off her own clothes, and while Robert was photographing her older sister, Mirabelle, she kept running in front of him. Jesse McBride is posed on a chair without his clothes because, according to his mother, Clarissa Dalrymple, he had been dashing around their apartment that way and wouldn't sit still. "It was all done in a spirit of fun and innocence," she recalled. "I don't know how anyone could describe it as 'child pornography.' " Mapplethorpe certainly wasn't above selecting the most provocative image from the contact sheets. "Children are sexual beings," he told the Norfolk *Ledger-Star,* "but it's an area that makes most people feel uncomfortable." In most cases Mapplethorpe's pictures of children were as innocent as the "bathtub" shots in family photo albums, but the way in which they were often juxtaposed with his S&M images begged the child-pornography issue.

Mapplethorpe remained in London for three weeks, then flew to Paris, where he engaged in an endless round of club-going and sex. He later confided to Victor Bockris in *New York Rocker* that he had been a nymphomaniac in Paris and blamed his promiscuity on the copious amounts of cocaine he had used: "[It] makes me think of sex a lot more than I would otherwise." Yet despite his debilitating social schedule, he was still intent on building up his portfolio, and among the people who had agreed to sit for his camera was actor Dennis Hopper, who was then living with fashion editor Caterine Milinaire, the daughter of the duchess of Bedford. Mapplethorpe knew Milinaire from New York, and the evening before he was scheduled to shoot Hopper, Milinaire invited him to accompany them to Club Sept, where they remained until three A.M., dancing and drinking. "Caterine and Dennis were really affectionate toward each other," Mapplethorpe recalled, "and it was nice being around them." The next morning at ten o'clock he arrived at their apartment, and noticing the door ajar, he buzzed several times before letting himself in. He was shocked by the state of the apartment: furniture was smashed; paintings were ripped from the wall; mirrors and lamps were splintered into dozens of pieces. Hopper was sitting in the middle of the room, his head resting on his hands, a leg thrown over the side of the chair. "Where's Caterine?" Mapplethorpe demanded, but Hopper didn't answer him. Mapplethorpe was about to call the police when he heard a low whimpering from the direction of the bathroom, where he found Milinaire, her beautiful face bruised and swollen. "Get me out of here!" she pleaded with him. On the way to her uncle's apartment, she explained that Hopper had beaten her in a drunken rage.

Mapplethorpe had always considered Milinaire to have the most perfect features of any woman he had ever met, but now that her face was a bloody mess, he found her even more extraordinary looking than ever. He saw not a "battered" face, but one exquisitely transformed by a series of bruises that fell like shadows across her cheekbones. He had brought his camera with him, and when they reached the other apartment, he asked if he could take her portrait. She reluctantly agreed because she felt it was important to have a document of the incident if only to illustrate the fact that battered women cut across all socioeconomic borders. Moreover, she felt it served as a valuable record of the era. "In the mid-seventies, people were going to such extremes in their behavior," she explained. "There were so many drugs and so much sex that everybody was pushed to the limit. It seemed fitting that Robert would be there when Dennis and I collided. I can't think of any other photographer who would have captured that moment better."

In Mapplethorpe's absence, Sam Wagstaff spent the summer in Oakleyville, a section of Fire Island that was so isolated and remote that Greta Garbo could occasionally be spotted walking in the woods on the way to her friend Sam Green's house. Wagstaff had previously rented a house in the Pines, a fashionable gay ghetto of white sandy beaches, all-night discos, and the "Meat Rack," a woodsy area of trees and dunes where hundreds of men communed with nature by engaging in outdoor sex. But this year he was content having a "floppy summer," and he amused himself by scavenging the woods for huckleberries and beach plums, clamming and swimming in the bay, and reading Jean Rhys novels. Sam always had a soft spot for "sweeters," the term he used for good-looking young men long on ambition and short of cash, and he had recently become infatuated with an eighteen-year-old architecture student named Mark whom he had reportedly picked up on the subway. It was the first time since meeting Mapplethorpe that Wagstaff had become enamored of another young man, and when Mapplethorpe learned of the affair, he immediately called Wagstaff collect from Paris to assess the potential damage. Wagstaff assured him in a letter dated July 21 that Mark didn't "begin to replace or substitute for my muffin." Three days later Wagstaff confessed to Mapplethorpe, "I'm never really lonely when I have you to think about. I don't know why you're still fond of me, but I'm very very pleased that you do [sic]. There aren't that many people to connect with in life, is [sic] there?" Despite Mapplethorpe's unhappiness over the architect, he had to agree that Wagstaff was right. "We have something together that neither of us will ever have with anyone else," he replied. "I love the old thing and I always will."

Wagstaff remained a stalwart champion of Mapplethorpe's career, and he cajoled numerous friends into having Mapplethorpe shoot their portraits. Robert photographed Paul Walter, who had recently started to collect photography himself, and Harry Lunn, who had once been a CIA agent before he opened an art gallery in Washington, D.C., and cornered the market on Ansel Adams's prints. The

Lunn connection would prove to be an important one for Mapplethorpe, as the influential dealer was openly enthusiastic about his
work, and would later copublish his "X," "Y," and "Z" portfolios.
Both Mapplethorpe and Wagstaff were frequently seen at the
Greenwich Village apartment of Norman Fisher, an upscale drug
dealer who often traded cocaine for art. Mapplethorpe took a portrait of Fisher, who was then dying of cancer, and the drug dealer
later donated his Mapplethorpe photograph to the Jacksonville Art
Museum in Florida, where the "Norman Fisher Collection" in-
cludes work by David Bowie, Robert Indiana, Malcolm Morley,
Richard Serra, Ellsworth Kelly, and William Wegman. Mapplethorpe met other artists at Fisher's apartment, which functioned as a
salon of sorts, and in addition to those he already knew, he began to
photograph members of New York's avant-garde—choreographer
Lucinda Childs, composer Philip Glass, director Robert Wilson, and
Brice Marden.

   Toward the end of the summer Mapplethorpe's biggest career
break resulted from a fleeting sexual liaison with a young man who
worked at the Holly Solomon Gallery; the man convinced the dealer
to look at Mapplethorpe's work, and she made an appointment to
visit the Bond Street loft. In personality and style, Holly Solomon
did not seem a likely match for Mapplethorpe; she had once been an
actress, and everything about her was staged and mannered; she
seemed to enunciate as though playing to the back balcony and was
extremely conscious of the effect she created with her expensive
avant-garde clothing and white-blond hair. She lived on Park Avenue with her husband, Horace, a manufacturer of ladies' hair orna-
ments, and with his financial backing, in 1975, she opened a gallery
in SoHo. Solomon quickly gained a reputation for showing the
work of such "pattern-and-decoration" artists as Robert Kushner,
Kim MacConnel, and Robert Zakanitch, who experimented with
decorative techniques and materials to produce large paintings and
sewn works on stretched fabric that suggested wallpaper designs or
Oriental carpets. Mapplethorpe considered the work gaudy and
overwrought and privately denounced Solomon's aesthetic as "vulgar," but she was one of the few art dealers willing to show photography.

   When Solomon first visited Bond Street, Mapplethorpe pulled

out his sex pictures to test her shock quotient, but the dealer wasn't so much shocked as disinterested. "I never thought the 'dirty pictures' were his best work," she said. "What the hell is giving dignity to porno? What kind of bullshit is that?" She admired his portraits, however, and decided to "audition" him, as she had done with Roy Lichtenstein, Andy Warhol, Robert Kushner, and Richard Artschwager, all of whom had created Holly Solomon portraits. Warhol, in fact, created nine Holly Solomons as part of his 1966 silkscreen portrait of the dealer. Mapplethorpe realized he was up against stiff competition—Solomon described the Lichtenstein portrait as "like the Mona Lisa . . . an archetype of our time"—and when he arrived at her Park Avenue apartment he played up Solomon's unfulfilled dreams of movie stardom by photographing the dealer reclining on her bed, head thrown back in profile. He positioned her against a backdrop of swirling wallpaper that cleverly suggested the pattern-and-decoration movement with which she had made her name, then later presented her with a framed triptych—Holly Solomon three times. "When I looked at the Mapplethorpe portrait," Solomon explained, "I saw a woman who's very comfortable with who she is—someone who's accepted the theatricality about herself. She's not a young woman anymore, but she's accepting of that, too. I thought Robert handled me very well. Unlike painters, photographers must have one great quality, which is the ability to deal with people. Robert understood his 'customer.' He was gentle, perceptive, and very smooth. I figured if he worked well with me, he'd work well with other people. I said, 'Would you like a show?' And he said, 'Yes.' "

One reason Solomon agreed to represent Mapplethorpe was his understanding of contemporary painting and sculpture as well as photography. "Most photographers only know the specific worlds in which they work—the fashion world, for example. Robert had a context in art, and I appreciated what he was trying to do with his frames. Up until that point, most people who collected photographs would keep them in drawers, stored away in plastic envelopes. By making excessive frames, Robert was saying that a photograph has just as much prestige as a painting, and that it is okay to hang it on the living room wall. He gave the photograph honor."

Solomon knew that Mapplethorpe carried Sam Wagstaff's imprimatur, and that considerably enhanced her admiration for him. "Sam was considered the great photography collector," she explained. "He had many people who believed in him, especially me. I knew he and Robert had been lovers, but Sam was a man of real intelligence and ability. I wouldn't have touched Robert without Sam. And there were others like me who felt the same way." No matter how Mapplethorpe managed to secure a dealer, having one gave him the credibility he needed as an artist, and that November a Mapplethorpe photograph of a dalmatian was part of a group show, "Animals," that also included work by Susan Rothenberg and William Wegman. Solomon promised Mapplethorpe a one-person exhibit early in 1977. "I didn't expect to get money right away," she said. "What could I get for one of his photographs—a hundred and fifty dollars? I earned much more by selling a painting. But I was committed to Robert. I told him, 'You're good, and you deserve my support, but this is probably going to kill me.' "

Exactly a year after Patti Smith recorded *Horses,* she was back in the studio again with *Radio Ethiopia;* she and her band spent the month of July with producer Jack Douglas working on the album. Having traveled the country on a promotional tour for *Horses,* Smith had emerged with an even stronger dedication to playing rock and roll music, and to deflect attention away from herself as "the poet-performer," she changed the name of the band from "Patti Smith" to the "Patti Smith Group." She had always had a self-sacrificial streak, and it is no coincidence that she considered *Radio Ethiopia* a "feminine" album as opposed to the "masculine" *Horses,* in which she was dominant instead of submissive. She described Jack Douglas as treating her like a "chick singer," and *Radio Ethiopia* as a "sexy album for the girls." But Smith's vocals were mixed so far back that her lyrics were unintelligible, and Jane Friedman, the band's manager, felt she was destroying her main asset—"the power of the word." Smith, however, was intent on creating raw animal noises that mimicked the sounds of a woman in labor, and she infused the song "Radio Ethiopia" with guttural howls and screeching guitar sounds that consisted of her playing one note over and over again. Charles M. Young in *Rolling Stone* characterized the album as "an interminable Sixties freak-out."

Smith insisted it was "High Art" and backed up her contention with a cryptic philosophy about rock and roll music having the power to transport its listeners to a pre–Tower of Babel period when everyone spoke the universal language of the "lost tongue." She spilled forth some of her blurry ideas in the album's liner notes: "an animal howl says it all . . . notes pour into the caste of freedom . . . the freedom to be intense . . . to defy social order and break the slow kill monotony of censorship . . ." Smith claimed she was attempting to communicate with God through her music, and in the song "Ain't It Strange" she pleaded with Him to show Himself: "Come on, God, make a move." Her urgent appeals to a distant God had been a theme since childhood, and her various attempts at communication echoed the young Patti's efforts to break through to her own unapproachable father who spent his time reading the Bible.

Radio Ethiopia failed to communicate its message to Arista president Clive Davis, who, while being respectful of his artist's creativity, must have suspected he had a disaster on his hands. This time Smith had asked her longtime friend Judy Linn to take the cover photo; she felt Mapplethorpe's career was doing nicely without her, and she wanted to give Linn a boost. Linn's picture showed Smith sitting on the floor of an apartment, telephone wires running along the wall behind her; it lacked the visual excitement of Mapplethorpe's *Horses* cover and reflected the album's defiantly uncommercial tone. Smith had insisted on including a song entitled "Pissing in a River," even though the mild obscenity was enough to keep it off the radio. Arista executives implored her to change it to "Sipping in a River," but Smith refused, as the whole idea behind *Radio Ethiopia* was to liberate the airwaves.

Smith's personality had always been a mass of contradictions, and she took the same scattershot approach to her career. She compared her band to the Rolling Stones and longed to reach a mass audience, yet she refused to compromise and offered up *Radio Ethiopia* instead. It was evident that she saw herself as the "rock-n'-roll savior" she had written about in *Cowboy Mouth*, and began referring to herself as the "field marshal of rock and roll." She compared her performances to war and showed reporters the bruises and scrapes she suffered in combat. "Physically I have to be like one of those Israeli women," she told *Melody Maker*. "The only difference is that my guitar is my machine gun. By the end of a performance I feel so nuts, so crazy, so filled with the last spurts of adrenaline—there's sweat in my eyes and I've been crawling across the floor in the dirt—that I feel just like I'm in a foxhole. I feel like my guitar is my machine gun and I just short-circuit out." Yet beneath her daredevil facade was a frightened and fragile woman whose art had always been drenched in images of sexual violence and death, and whose primal howling on "Radio Ethiopia" summoned all the rage and anger of her early life.

That fall Mapplethorpe took a portrait of Smith in which he captured her precarious state of mind. She had moved into the loft with him because the lease had expired on her apartment and she was having a difficult time deciding what to do with Allen Lanier. Somehow her relationship with him had survived her affair with rock guitarist Tom Verlaine, and while she and Lanier would soon purchase an apartment together in Sam Wagstaff's building at One Fifth Avenue, she was unhappy with him. Mapplethorpe photographed her one morning as she crouched naked in front of a radiator, knees under her chin, bony ribs painfully obvious beneath the skin. Patti resembled a baby bird emerging from a cracked shell.

The Patti Smith Group spent part of October in Europe, where Smith's "field marshal" rhetoric became even more heated after the band performed in England. The Sex Pistols had just released their first single, "Anarchy in the U.K.," and while Smith didn't identify with the band's loutish behavior, she was in sympathy with the punk movement's goal of rousing a complacent society. When she returned from Europe she was banned from the radio station WNEW for injecting a four-letter word during a live interview, and she began passing out pamphlets at her concerts that read: "We believe in the total freedom of communication and we will not be compromised. . . . We Want the Radio and We Want it Now." At the end of November, when the band played a week at the Bottom Line, she was "in full confrontational mode," according to Lenny Kaye, and her performances were insanely self-destructive. "I remember each show getting crazier and crazier," Kaye said. "At one point during 'Ain't It Strange' I remember running out into the audience, and Patti chased me and dragged me back, and we were walking on tables. It was just a lot of this adolescent energy and anarchy, and there was something very liberating about it because we were pushing the edge of the envelope."

In late January 1977 Smith's convulsive energy reached a climax when she opened for Bob Seger and the Silver Bullet Band at Curtis Hixen Hall in Tampa, Florida. She was performing "Ain't It Strange," spitting out the lyrics and miming X-rated sexual acts with Lenny Kaye before she began spinning like a top. "Go, go on, go like a dervish," she shouted. "Come on, God, make a move." She twirled faster and faster, whipping herself into an orgiastic frenzy; then she tripped over a monitor, and, like Icarus, suddenly fell to earth.

"When I fell off that stage," Smith explained, "it was like God said, 'If you keep bugging me, this is what's going to happen.' I began to realize that maybe I was mortal after all."

CHAPTER THIRTEEN

"When these pictures first appeared, there were shivers and
most often people turned away, myself included. But no one
who knew about them forgot these scenes . . ."

—*Ingrid Sischy, about Mapplethorpe's "Erotic Pictures"*

"I am an American artist and I have no guilt."

—*Patti Smith*

Patti Smith landed on the concrete floor, fourteen feet
below the stage, and was immediately taken by ambulance to the
emergency room of Tampa General Hospital. Blood spurted from a
large gash in her head, and she had broken several vertebrae in her
neck.

The accident was a sobering fall from grace for the "rock-n'-roll
savior," and when she returned to New York she began experiencing
paralysis in her legs and double vision. Doctors worried that she
might never be able to perform again. In addition to her devastating
physical condition, *Radio Ethiopia* had been a commercial and critical flop, and she could not help boost the album's sales by touring
with the band. Moreover, since she had recently spent most of her
money on the new one-bedroom apartment she had purchased with
Allen Lanier, she was broke and didn't even have health insurance to
cover the doctors' bills.

Harry and Joan Mapplethorpe on their wedding day in 1942. They wanted nothing more than to lead an "ordinary" life together.

Robert Mapplethorpe revolted against everything his parents represented. Here he poses for Harry's camera—one of the few times father and son ever saw eye to eye.

Joan Mapplethorpe had three children in quick succession: Nancy, Richard, and Robert—her favorite.

Mapplethorpe's Catholic upbringing sensitized him to the concept of guilt and sin. He is shown here with his mother on the day of his first Holy Communion.

Mapplethorpe (*bottom right*) with his brother Richard (*standing at left*) and their friends from Floral Park. For Halloween one year Mapplethorpe (*below, second from left*) dressed up as Pinocchio.

One Christmas Mapplethorpe asked Santa for a jewelry-making kit and discovered what he called "the magical feeling in my fingers."

On a visit to the graves of his maternal relatives, Mapplethorpe stole an American flag off a nearby plot and asked his sister Nancy to take a picture of him lying in front of the Maxey tombstone.

Joan Mapplethorpe had misgivings about starting what she called a "second family" at the age of thirty-six. Here the "two families" pose for Harry (*from left*): Robert; Nancy and baby James; Susan; Richard and Edward.

Robert and Richard grew to despise each other, and although the two brothers shared a room, they drew an invisible line down the center.

Richard (posed here with his parents) enrolled at the State Maritime
Academy at Fort Schuyler, where he followed his father's lead
by studying to be an engineer.

Mapplethorpe tried to please his father by attending Pratt Institute,
Harry's alma mater, and by joining the Pershing Rifles,
an elite military fraternity.

Mapplethorpe in transition: At Pratt he climbs atop a pedestal and presents himself as an art object. At the Chelsea Hotel several years later,
he adorns himself with his own fetish necklaces.

Mapplethorpe and Patti Smith lived together at the Chelsea Hotel, and later in a loft on West 23rd Street. He gave her a wedding ring and told his parents they were married.

Mapplethorpe moved to Manhattan hoping to befriend Andy Warhol,
but he was disappointed by the artist's vacuous personality.
In Mapplethorpe's portrait of him, Warhol is
part saint, part Wizard of Oz.

Pictures of men in Harley-Davidson motorcycle caps and leather pants suddenly began appearing in Mapplethorpe's collages.

Mapplethorpe took the T-shirts off his back and framed them. "Can I wear this?" Patti Smith joked. "Or is it art?"

Mapplethorpe and Smith were regulars at Max's Kansas City, Mickey Ruskin's celebrated bar-restaurant, where "Pop art met Pop life."

Top row, left to right: Mickey Ruskin, Tally Brown, Fran Lebowitz. *Second row, left to right:* Donald Lyons, Danny Fields, Robert Mapplethorpe. *Third row, left to right:* Candy Darling, Mick Jagger, Andrea Feldman. *Bottom:* Taylor Mead (*far right*) cavorts in the back room.

"I knew Robert and Patti were brilliant right off the bat," said filmmaker Sandy Daley, who is shown here in her Chelsea Hotel apartment.

"I think he wasn't only in love with Robert," said Richard Bernstein about David Croland, "but loved the idea of being seen with him."

Patti Smith viewed poet and songwriter Jim Carroll
as an archetypal Rimbaud figure.

Patti Smith and Sam Shepard cowrote *Cowboy Mouth* and appeared
together for one performance at the American Place Theater in 1971.
The autobiographical play reflected their own domestic turbulence.

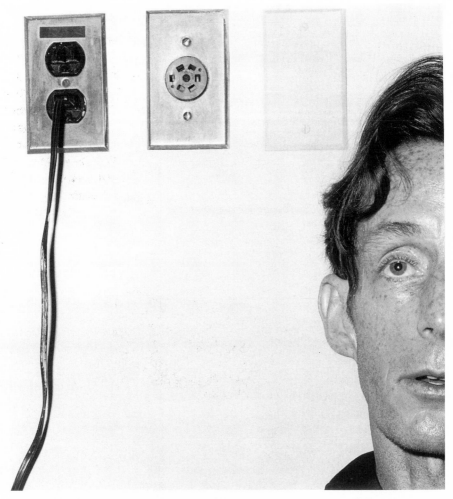

John McKendry, a curator at the Metropolitan Museum of Art,
was one of Mapplethorpe's earliest "connections."
Mapplethorpe took this haunting photograph of McKendry
a few days before his death in 1975.

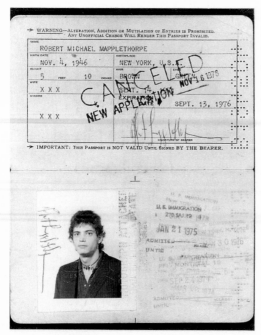

McKendry helped place Robert on the international scene by escorting him to London in the fall of 1971.

Mapplethorpe took this photo of Princess Margaret and Reinaldo Herrera during a 1977 trip to Mustique to photograph Colin Tennant's Gold on Gold Ball for *Interview*. Afterward he vowed never to do photojournalism again—"stealing secrets," he called it.

Mapplethorpe's dramatic black-and-white photograph of Patti Smith appeared on the cover of her first album, *Horses*.

It was well known among gay men in the art world that Sam Wagstaff was searching for "someone to spoil." This 1974 portrait of the couple by Francesco Scavullo captures Wagstaff and Mapplethorpe at the peak of their love affair.

Mapplethorpe had watched Smith's career surge ahead of his, and while he had never expressed any jealousy, he often teased her about her becoming famous first. Now she was temporarily sidelined, and he was about to score his first major success with a show of portraits at the Holly Solomon Gallery.

Mapplethorpe, realizing Solomon didn't fully appreciate his "dirty pictures," at the same time arranged to exhibit those pictures at the Kitchen, an alternative space in SoHo. Consequently, Robert Mapplethorpe had two openings on February 4, 1977—"Portraits" at Solomon and "Erotic Pictures" at the Kitchen.

The strategy of splitting up his work was born of necessity, but it later become a staple of his career; the X-rated material gave him the notoriety, but it was the "PG" pictures that made money, and by separating them he could reach both a gay and a straight audience. Mapplethorpe's invitations to his two February openings revealed his uncanny awareness of how to market himself. He had taken two photographs of his hand writing the word "Pictures" on a piece of paper, but for the Solomon announcement he wore a conventional striped shirt and Cartier tank watch, while the Kitchen invitation showed him in a black leather glove and studded wrist band.

Before Mapplethorpe went downtown for the openings, he stopped by One Fifth Avenue to pick up Sam Wagstaff and to see if Patti Smith felt well enough to accompany them, but she did not. Considering she couldn't walk and had blurred vision, it was another example of how stunningly narcissistic he could be, but Smith excused his behavior because she understood how important the shows were to him. "It was almost like he couldn't enjoy something unless I was there, too," she explained. "He needed me to verify the event."

An ophthalmologist had reassured Smith that she would regain her full vision, but her legs were still partially paralyzed. Doctors had recommended a spinal operation, but she was afraid of undergoing general anesthesia. Instead of having the operation, she had decided to follow the advice of a sports-medicine doctor whose remedy would ultimately include a rigorous Nautilus regime to strengthen her legs. In the meantime, he had prescribed total bed rest for three months, and so even though Mapplethorpe persisted in trying to convince her to rent a wheelchair for the openings—"Sam will pay for it"—she declined the offer and resumed reading the large-print Bible she now kept by her side.

Wagstaff had devoted the past month to making sure the openings were a success, but his doting behavior was beginning to wear thin on Holly Solomon. "Sam was a very sweet and elegant man," Solomon said, "but he was like a Jewish mother. I think he must have called me every ten minutes when we were hanging the show." Wagstaff had planned a black-tie party at One Fifth, the Art Deco restaurant on the main floor of his apartment building, to take place after the openings and had made sure to send congratulatory telegrams to Mapplethorpe at both galleries, offering his protégé "monkey hugs" and "lots of love always." Prior to the openings, he had presented Mapplethorpe with a gold signet ring bearing the Wagstaff crest and the family motto: *Perseverantia et Integritas*.

Mapplethorpe's opening at the Solomon Gallery was not as subdued as his conservative invitation might have suggested, just as the portraits on the walls were not only of princesses and art dealers, but of hustlers and drug dealers as well. The picture of Princess Margaret and her bottle of Beefeater gin was paired with a portrait of beefy-looking Harry Lunn; Arnold Schwarzenegger flexing his muscles was a few feet away from a preening transsexual. The eclectic mix of portraits and gallery-goers had remained unchanged since Mapplethorpe's Light Gallery opening three years earlier, but his work had matured from the playful Polaroids with their multicolored cassette frames. He was well versed in the history of photography, and a sense of youthful experimentation had given way to a slicker, more stylized technique that was influenced by the glamour portraiture of Horst and George Platt Lynes. Mapplethorpe still didn't have any studio lights, but many of his portraits at Holly Solomon were dramatically enhanced by natural lighting, most notably *Dennis Walsh, 1976,* in which the model's erotic "Dying Slave" pose is brought into sharp relief by having his face and upper torso illuminated while leaving the rest of his body in shadows. David Bourdon in a review for *Arts Magazine* complimented Mapplethorpe on his "Vermeer-type sidelighting" and noted that he "has a knack for making light palpable in a refreshing, resourceful way that invigorates his compositions."

The exhibit at Solomon's gallery helped establish Mapplethorpe's reputation as a promising new portrait photographer, but "Erotic Pictures" at the Kitchen laid the groundwork for his controversial career.

The impact of the sex pictures at the Light Gallery had been lessened somewhat by the small Polaroid format, but the photographs at the Kitchen were sixteen by twenty inches and had been so elaborately packaged that men in handcuffs and blindfolds were surrounded by luxurious silk mats and exotic wood frames made of violet, ash, and purple heart. Mapplethorpe had once joked to Maria Morris Hambourg, who later became curator of the Met's photography department, that he was just a "fag decorator," and he had spent hours at Bark Frameworks on Grand Street examining swatches of colored silk for the mats. He told owner Jared Bark that he wanted to use only three sides of the mat so that he could leave the bottom bare. He never explained anything further, but Bark realized that Robert was aiming to create a proscenium arch, and that his silk mats functioned as theatrical drapes. "When you discuss frames," Bark said, "it's always the obvious questions about their relationship to architecture and to art. Are frames like furniture? Are they like architectural details? Robert's frames were really more theatrical than anything else, but the mats also functioned as a door—a door to his inner life more than a window on the world."

"Erotic Pictures" lacked the terrifying authenticity of some of Mapplethorpe's later work, but the photographs of men gagged, blindfolded, and hog-tied were still a revelation to viewers unfamiliar with the S&M milieu. "When these pictures first appeared there were shivers and most often people turned away, myself included," Ingrid Sischy wrote in the 1988 Whitney catalogue of the Mapplethorpe retrospective. "But no one who knew about them forgot these scenes, even if the knowledge was only by rumor." Unlike the subjects in his portrait show, the men featured in "Erotic Pictures" were usually identified by their first names only, except for porn stars Peter Berlin and Marc ("Mr. 10½") Stevens, whose private parts were already familiar to viewers of X-rated movies. Mapplethorpe revealed his sly sense of humor in his picture of Stevens by placing the porn star's famous organ on a butcher block, as if it were literally a piece of meat awaiting the cleaver.

After making an appearance at both openings, Mapplethorpe returned to Wagstaff's apartment to change into a velvet dinner jacket, then took the elevator down to greet the first of the two hundred guests arriving at the restaurant for the party. Sandy Daley had been invited, as had David Croland, Fran Lebowitz, Bob Colacello, Danny Fields, Charles Cowles, Klaus Kertess, Mario Amaya, Halston, Elsa Peretti, Diana Vreeland, Caterine Milinaire, Catherine Guinness, Harry Lunn, Paul Walter, Fernando Sanchez, and others who had been directly or indirectly helpful to Mapplethorpe's career. He was so excited by the impressive turnout that he took the elevator back up to Patti Smith's apartment to share the good news. "I'm a success!" he exulted, bursting into the room.

Smith was in bed eating a bowl of couscous, a gray sombrero covering the twenty-two stitches in her head. The bed was littered with an Abyssinian hair shirt, the complete works of Rimbaud and William Burroughs, and a punk Raggedy Ann doll dressed like Smith herself. A cat named Ashley, which Smith had found in the garbage, was picking its way through the clutter. "Everybody in New York is here," Mapplethorpe continued. "You've got to see it for yourself." Smith sent him away, but he was back almost every half hour with another progress report. "I'm the toast of the town!" he announced at another point. Gathering Smith up in his arms, he headed for the door, but he stumbled from the drugs and the champagne and put her back down on the bed again, with a promise to return later.

The next person to arrive upstairs was Wagstaff, who had had his fill of the "smarty-pants set" and wanted to keep Smith company. She never tired of listening to Wagstaff talk, and while the party was still under way, he launched into a discussion of Brancusi, running his fingers across imaginary slabs of marble. "Do you know what Brancusi once said?" he asked Smith. " 'Don't look for mysteries—I give you pure joy!' Isn't that marvelous!" Eventually Wagstaff kissed her good night, and when he headed up to his penthouse Smith noticed him beaming like a proud parent. "Well," he said, in parting, "our boy is finally the belle of the ball."

Mapplethorpe achieved instant notoriety as the art world's enfant terrible. People were as fascinated with him as they were with his art. "Robert was the 1970s' leather-clad equivalent of the great dandies and decadents of the nineteenth century—Beardsley, Oscar Wilde, Huysmans," said Philippe Garner of Sotheby's. "What made his personality so intriguing were the same qualities found in his work—the chilling contrast between the viciousness of his sexuality, and the grace and finesse of his personal style." Arthur C. Danto, in his introduction to *Mapplethorpe,* wrote that Mapplethorpe embodied both Dionysian and Apollonian qualities—Dionysus being the "god of frenzy" and Apollo "the god of proportion and form."

Despite people's curiosity about Mapplethorpe, however, the two exhibits generated hardly any revenue for him. Holly Solomon was charging three hundred dollars for a unique framed piece, and one hundred fifty for the same photograph unframed, but some people complained that the framed pieces were too expensive while the photographs without the silk mats and exotic wood weren't compelling enough to buy. Mapplethorpe's framing costs were high, and he had been hoping to recoup some of his expenses; he was frustrated by his inability to make any money. Wagstaff served as a safety net, but Mapplethorpe wasn't sure how long he could depend on him, as he was still seeing the young architect.

Mapplethorpe knew the market for S&M pictures was a small one, and that people were reluctant to hang portraits of strangers, even rich and famous ones, on their walls. Hoping to broaden his commercial appeal, he made a concerted effort to take more flower pictures. A few days after the party at One Fifth, Paul Walter sent him a dozen tulips as a thank-you present, and with the new quartz lights Wagstaff had recently given him, Mapplethorpe began experimenting with photographing the flowers.

He needed to be in control, or at least maintain an illusion of control, at all times, and since he didn't know how to work the lights, he would never have exposed his technical inadequacies in front of a human subject. "I played around with the flowers and the lighting, so that was a good way to educate myself," he told *Print Letter.* "And what I came up with, I think, is as strong as any of the pictures I have done." In the case of Paul Walter's tulips, he transformed them into a dramatic diptych in which the viewer's eye is drawn to a solitary bud lunging from the bouquet.

For someone who was later acclaimed by art critic Peter Schjeldahl for creating "the most beautiful floral still-lifes ever taken,"

Mapplethorpe was curiously hostile toward flowers. Wagstaff wrote in a 1984 essay: "As an old-fashioned gesture, I once sent Mapplethorpe some flowers at Easter which, to my chagrin, were greeted with snarls. 'I hate flowers,' he said and pretended to spit on them. Now, if you will, he still spits on them but with his Hasselblad, or he does something perverse to them that nobody else seems to have thought of before." Many of Mapplethorpe's flowers appear to have lost their virginity, as though the photographer himself had defiled them in some exotic and unspeakable way. There was an air of the kidnaper about him as he rushed home from Gifts of Nature, a florist shop on Sixth Avenue, his arms laden with orchids, irises, and tuberoses. By the time he finished photographing his "gifts of nature" they had no connection to nature at all and had become, in Mapplethorpe's words, "New York flowers"—hard-edged and decadent. Like the hero of Joris-Karl Huysmans's novel *Against Nature,* Mapplethorpe despised "bourgeois blooms" and preferred orchids and lilies—the "princesses of the vegetable kingdom," or in his case, the "princes."

Flowers being the sex organs of plants, Mapplethorpe's view of botanical reproduction was colored by his own sexual interests; he transformed protruding pistils and stamens into male genitalia. "My approach to photographing a flower is not much different than photographing a cock," he told *The Print Collector's Newsletter.* "Basically, it's the same thing." Yet when Holly Solomon saw the flower pictures, she immediately agreed to exhibit them later in the year. "I hate flowers myself," she said, "but I hoped that by showing his pictures it would change people's perception of him. They saw Robert as a leather guy, and to have him do flowers, it was shocking—more shocking than the porno stuff. *That* was expected."

Mapplethorpe treated his flowers no differently than the men who modeled for him. He didn't know what to do with the flowers once he had taken their picture, and since he didn't want the responsibility of watering them, he tossed them in his garbage bin before they wilted and died. "I am obsessed with beauty," he explained to Anne Horton in a 1987 interview. "I want everything to be perfect and, of course, it isn't. And that's a tough place to be because you're never really satisfied."

. . .

A few weeks before her accident, Patti Smith had received a five-thousand-dollar advance from G. P. Putnam's Sons to write a book of poetry, and when William Targ, the editor on the project, learned she was confined to her apartment, he paid a visit to One Fifth Avenue. "You lucky bastard!" she snarled. "If I hadn't fallen off that stage, I wouldn't have had time to work on your book. But now I'm trapped." Targ recalled: "Patti was in this huge bed surrounded by floral arrangements, and the pages of the manuscript were all over the place. She was rather belligerent, and I couldn't understand why. I was there on a social visit. I didn't expect the completed book. But Patti had two sides to her. When I first took her to lunch at the Algonquin, she had been all shy and deferential, then I learned what a viper she could be."

Smith's ego was surprisingly resilient for someone who had taken such a battering with *Radio Ethiopia;* she truly believed in her own talent and surrounded herself with people who totally supported her artistic vision. Smith and manager Jane Friedman had a falling out, and she hired lawyer Ina Meibach to handle her career. The break was a painful one for Friedman, who had been with Smith since the beginning and who considered her a close friend. Smith was now spending all her time with a woman named Andi Ostrowe, whom she had met through a fan letter. Ostrowe had lived in Ethiopia as a Peace Corps volunteer, and both women were convinced that because of the Ethiopian connection their friendship was "destiny." Ostrowe, who was known as "Peace Corps Little Patti," worked as the band's roadie, moving and setting up their equipment; but after the accident she volunteered her services for free and sat by Smith's bed every day with a portable typewriter.

Smith's mind had become even more hallucinatory as a result of the Percodan tablets she was taking to control her pain; she composed the poems for the book she appropriately titled *Babel* by working herself into a trance while Ostrowe struggled to transcribe the rush of words:

> i haven't fucked w/the past but i've fucked plenty w/the future. over
> the silk of skin are scars from the splinters of stages and walls i've
> caressed. each bolt of wood, like the log of helen, was my pleasure. i

would measure the success of a night by the amount of piss and seed
i could exude over the columns that nestled the P/A . . . in heart i am
an american artist and i have no guilt.

In March Smith began a strenuous course of physical therapy that
combined exercise and weight machines. She was determined to re-
build her strength so she could earn money for the band by performing a "Resurrection" concert on Easter Sunday at CBGB. She
even had a new slogan: "Out of Traction, Back in Action." Mapplethorpe documented Smith's recovery by taking a picture of her sitting in bed, hair matted in pigtails, holding her neck brace in the air.

Mapplethorpe usually stopped by to visit her on his way to the
leather bars, and Andi Ostrowe remembered him sitting on Smith's
bed, his legs swaddled in leather chaps. He had impulsively called his
parents to invite them to come and see the Solomon show, and he
sorely regretted it. Wagstaff had left for Europe, and he was afraid of
facing his parents alone. "What am I going to say to them?" he
asked Smith, whose brother, Todd, was a roadie for the band and
whose mother was president of the Patti Smith Fan Club.

Mapplethorpe was so out of touch with his family that his mother
still thought he was married to Smith, and when the performer had
played a club in Long Island the previous year, Joan had taken her
friend Pat Farre to watch her "daughter-in-law." She had no idea
what Smith's music was like, and was horrified to see her stumbling
around the stage, spitting and scratching her crotch. Joan had
planned to go backstage afterward, but she and Pat Farre quickly
fled the club; Joan felt relieved she had not invited Harry to join
them.

The years had not been especially kind to Joan, and her once
vivacious personality had turned increasingly pessimistic and mo-
rose. Her routine hadn't varied much since the 1950s; she still went
to church, belonged to the bowling league, and had dinner on the
table at six for Harry, who was nearing forty years at Underwriters
Laboratories. She wasn't dissatisfied with any one aspect of her life;
it was just that she complained of feeling down all the time, and
eventually took the unprecedented step of consulting a psychiatrist,
who prescribed lithium for her manic-depression. Harry blamed
Robert for contributing to Joan's depression by never returning her

phone calls and ignoring the family on birthdays and Christmas. When Joan told him that Robert had telephoned to invite them to a show in the city, he had mixed feelings about seeing his son again, for it dredged up all the old grievances—the long hair, quitting ROTC, failing to graduate from Pratt. That Robert was having a show at a gallery only reminded Harry that his son had defied him by becoming an artist. Reluctantly, Harry agreed to drive Joan into the city on a Saturday before the exhibit closed, and while navigating the narrow streets searching for a parking spot, they both wondered why anyone would voluntarily live in such a dismal environment.

Robert, meanwhile, was pacing up and down West Broadway, smoking one cigarette after another and then grinding the butts into the sidewalk with the toe of his black Western boots. His chin was covered with a scruffy goatee that he knew his father would find objectionable, but to avoid a major confrontation he had left off the jewelry and attempted to hide his bloodshot eyes, the result of too many drugs and late nights, behind tinted aviator glasses.

Nevertheless, when Harry and Joan finally joined Robert at the gallery after parking the car, Harry still thought his son looked terrible, and there were several awkward moments when they stood around in silence; then Holly Solomon bustled into the room and introduced herself. Except for the art galleries in the mall stores that sold paintings of flowers, seascapes, and clowns, Harry and Joan had never been to a real gallery, and it was a little overwhelming to them. Robert led them from portrait to portrait, introducing them to Princess Margaret—"She's a friend from Mustique"—and John Paul Getty—"You know, *the* Gettys." Afterward he took his parents to lunch at a local restaurant, where Joan nervously chattered about her daughter Nancy, who had four children by then, and Susan, who had married her high school sweetheart and had a baby of her own, and Richard, whose marriage to his Korean war bride had ended in divorce, and who was now living in Los Angeles with his second wife, a Filipina named Jasmine. "You know," Robert interrupted, "*I'm* one of the best young photographers in New York." A skeptical Harry immediately began quizzing Robert about his technical expertise; he asked him if he knew the meaning of "depth of field." Harry was amazed by Robert's ignorance, and by the subsequent revelation that his son paid somebody else to do his printing for him. "How can you call yourself a photographer?" Harry demanded. "You don't even print your own pictures!"

Robert explained for the umpteenth time that he was an artist, not merely a photographer. "People don't have time to wait for somebody to paint their portraits anymore," he told Harry, "so the money is in photography. It's the perfect medium for our times, because it's of the instant." When Robert said good-bye to his parents after lunch, he realized it had been a mistake to invite them to the exhibit. His success hadn't altered their relationship at all, and if anything, it seemed to have made Harry even more contentious.

On the way back to Floral Park, Harry wondered how Robert managed to socialize with so many important people, as his son had never impressed him as being particularly charming or gracious. "What is it with him?" he asked Joan. "It's not like he's a conversationalist or anything of that sort." No matter what Harry's feelings were, Joan had been impressed by the exhibit, and while she had stared at the portraits on the wall she had come to the sad realization that perhaps they had no relationship with their son because they had nothing to offer him. "Maybe we're just not his type," she replied.

Harry may have begrudged Robert's success, but he later boasted about his son's exhibit to a fellow employee and camera buff, whose specialty was pictures of scantily clad women. The man was planning to visit Manhattan the following weekend and told Harry that he would see the show. When he arrived in the city, however, he found he had misplaced the name of the Holly Solomon Gallery. He picked up *The Village Voice* for the art gallery listings and, seeing Robert's name in connection with the Kitchen, went there instead. First thing Monday morning he confronted Harry with the news that while his son's portrait of Princess Margaret may have been hanging elsewhere, it was most definitely not on the walls of the Kitchen. Harry listened, repulsed, while the man described "Erotic Pictures" in detail—homosexual men, naked and in bondage. "Are you sure about that?" Harry kept repeating. He had always suspected that Robert was up to no good, but never in his wildest imagination did he think his own son would embrace the holy trinity of parental nightmares: he was an artist, a homosexual, *and* a pornographer. Harry would never be able to tell Joan, for she was depressed enough already, and this, surely, was enough to break any mother's heart.

CHAPTER FOURTEEN

"Do it for Satan."

—*Robert Mapplethorpe*

Mapplethorpe's "S&M period" reached its peak during the years 1977 and 1978, when he produced thirteen graphic images that were later packaged and sold as the "X Portfolio." The severity of the pictures, which included scenes of bodily mutilation, were shocking by nearly anyone's standards, but Mapplethorpe's explorations had taken him so far into the netherworld of sexual deviancy that almost nothing shocked him anymore. "All the great libertines who live only for pleasure are great only because they have destroyed in themselves all their capacity for pleasure," Georges Bataille wrote about the Marquis de Sade in *Eroticism: Death and Sensuality.* "That is why they go in for frightful anomalies for otherwise the mediocrity of ordinary sensuality would be enough for them." Mapplethorpe had grown bored with the "same old S&M schtick," so he needed to keep searching for newer and stranger aberrations.

"I had many affairs during that period," he explained in 1988, "but I was never into quickie sex. I've only slept with maybe a thousand men."

The end of the seventies coincided with the last gasp of the Sexual Revolution, and while most people did not push themselves to Mapplethorpe's extremes, both gays and straights alike were acting out their fantasies in ways that would have been inconceivable just a decade earlier. Heterosexuals had sex in the showers, steam room, and murky pool of a former gay bathhouse rechristened Plato's Retreat; watched sex shows like *Midnight Blue* on cable TV; placed ads in sex magazines for spouse swapping; rented pornographic tapes for the VCR; and consumed popular best-sellers with titles such as *The Joy of Sex* and *Everything You Always Wanted to Know About Sex*. The campy line "I have the feeling we're not in Kansas anymore" had been part of the gay vernacular for at least several decades, and Studio 54, which characterized the era's glorification of sex and cocaine, was dubbed the "Oz of discos" by *The New York Times*. Studio 54's glamorous image was cleverly crafted by owner Steve Rubell, who attempted to create an aura of chic bisexuality by denying entrance to straight-looking couples in favor of hot young men who energized the dance floor and fantastic creatures such as Rollerena, who was rumored to be a Wall Street broker by day but who regularly appeared at Studio 54 in a wedding gown and roller skates.

Mapplethorpe always made an appearance at whatever club was designated the current hot spot, and during this period he went to Studio 54 at least once or twice a week. But Studio 54 was more for socializing, not for serious sex, and he usually followed his visits to the disco with trips to the Mineshaft, a hardcore "leather environment" located in a slaughterhouse at the corner of Little West Twelfth and Washington Streets.

The irony of having so many gay bars in the heart of the meat-packing district was underscored by signs that read WELL-CUT BEEF and CHOPPED MEAT. Unlike the neighboring club, the Anvil, which had a stage show and dancing bar boys, the Mineshaft was considered the definitive S&M club; its theatrical lighting and minimalist music attracted everyone from art critics and movie directors to construction workers and short-order cooks. Yet ultimately it didn't matter what job someone held during the day, for the club was only about sex, and the desire to reach a state of mind-numbing ecstasy.

"The scene at the Mineshaft was not about conversation," recalled Peter Reed, a dancer Mapplethorpe photographed several times, who died of AIDS in 1994. "In fact, you'd be told to leave if you were standing around too long talking about the opera or something. It was a stalking animal thing. I think what happened was that in one concentrated period of our history a whole group of people became addicted to this concept of going out every night and getting laid. It wasn't even a question of getting laid, it was a question of having an orgasm. Some of the ways one would end up doing that might seem tragic if viewed from the outside, but it was just to experience that feeling—like the release one gets from exercise—then you could go home, go to sleep, and move on."

Mapplethorpe had a lifetime pass to the Mineshaft and was there so often he inspired the running joke "Who did you see out last night *besides* Robert Mapplethorpe?" Yet he rarely participated in any of the public orgies; he spent most of his time roaming the dimly lit passageways that led to rooms where men were being whipped and chained. There was a bathtub for "watersports" and a jail where "prisoners" were handcuffed or strapped to chairs, and leather slings to facilitate fisting. Mapplethorpe was constantly on the lookout for someone to take home, and the Mineshaft provided him with an opportunity to connect with other men who also venerated sexual excess. "If the average person had ever gone there," said an art critic and biographer, "they would have been horrified. You'd see these incredible models with these great bodies in a sling. They'd be completely drugged, their eyes rolled up in their heads . . . it would be two fists, three fists. In sexual terms, they saw themselves as Olympic athletes. The next day I'd see some of my female friends, and they'd tease me and say, 'I'm sure you were up to some terrible thing last night,' and I used to think, 'God, if they only knew, they would faint in horror at the extremities of it.' "

Among Mapplethorpe's first contacts at the club were two S&M specialists named Nick and Ray who conducted heavy-duty sex scenes in their apartment in between writing best-selling romance novels. Nick was the subject of several Mapplethorpe portraits; he had the menacing demeanor of a pit bull, and his swarthy face, with its dark brows and black eyes, was made even more ominous by the

flaming skull tattoo on his forehead. Once, when Nick and Mapplethorpe were at the Mineshaft, a mutual friend introduced them to
an enormously obese man who seemed pathetically eager for punishment. "I just planted a cigarette butt on top of his head," the
friend whispered to them. "Let's take him home."

First they stopped by Mapplethorpe's loft to pick up his camera
equipment, then they went to Nick's "dungeon," where, according
to Nick, a "nasty scene" developed. The corpulent man was forced
to sign a photo release, and he later threatened to sue Mapplethorpe. "The pictures were never released," Nick said. "God knows
what happened to them, but Robert got these calls from a lawyer the
next day, and he went into hiding and wouldn't answer his phone."
It was one of the few times Mapplethorpe ever photographed anyone against his will, although Nick believed the man, who later
complained of being tortured, had ultimately enjoyed the experience. "The little fatso had been to Robert's exhibitions," Nick said,
"and he was all goo-goo over him."

From Nick's hardened perspective, Mapplethorpe's approach to
S&M was more that of a sex-obsessed adolescent than of a serious
player. "He was always stoned on MDA or coke," he recalled, "and
he'd slither around the Mineshaft like a snake. I remember him
showing me a copy of this Satanic bible that was like something I'd
read in high school. Robert's pictures always struck me as an artsi-
fied version of S&M. They're not like photographs snapped during
an actual scene."

Mapplethorpe had never been interested in merely documenting
the S&M subculture, but in bringing his own aesthetic to bear on
scenes that many people would normally find sordid or repugnant.
A perfect example is *Jim and Tom, Sausalito,* one of the seven
photographs at the heart of the 1990 Mapplethorpe censorship trial
in Cincinnati; it shows one man urinating into the mouth of another
and was taken during a 1977 trip to San Francisco. Mapplethorpe
placed his two figures in an abandoned Marine bunker, where the
light from a nearby window floods the dingy space with a religious
glow. Instead of an angel appearing in the cell, however, there are
only Tom and the leather-hooded Jim transforming urine into
something like wine. "Can't you see the beauty in it?" Robert had
pleaded to his neighbors in Floral Park after showing them his Cu-

bist madonnas. Years later, he was still preoccupied with the same question, and in a 1988 interview with Janet Kardon he described another disconcerting image, of a man inserting a finger in his penis, as "a perfect picture, because the hand gestures are beautiful. I know most people couldn't see the hand gestures, but composition-ally I think it works. I think the hand gesture is beautiful. What it happens to be doing, it happens to be doing, but that's an aside." One suspects, however, that Mapplethorpe would have been slightly disappointed if anyone had looked at his photograph of fist-ing and had responded the way Janet Kardon had during the Cin-cinnati trial by discussing "the centrality of the forearm."

Mapplethorpe was fully aware that he was breaking taboos, and the act of transgression was central to his work. He pushed his sexual partners to transgress their own boundaries by repeating the phrase "Do it for Satan." He wanted to bring to light previously hidden sexual secrets, and often taunted the various men by telling them, "You know you're dirty." Once he had succeeded in breaking down their reserve, he often photographed the "secrets" and made them public. He was careful not to reveal anyone's identity, and while he never dreamed of blackmailing his subjects, the pictures gave him the sense of control he craved. "Robert was really interested in photographing people's private desires," explained Scott Facon, whose picture appears in the "X Portfolio." "He'd always tell you, 'Do it for Satan.' When he found out that I was into smells and odors, dirty jockstraps, and being submissive, he convinced me to wrap two jockstraps around my head for the picture. Actually my photograph should have been the piss one, but he'd already done that."

Mapplethorpe had recently seen a film that clarified his own hid-den desires. It was Pier Paolo Pasolini's *Salo,* which was loosely based on the Marquis de Sade's *120 Days of Sodom* and contained a scene in which four libertines torture eight innocent victims by forc-ing them to consume their own excrement. *Salo* initially ran afoul of Italian censors who found the movie "aberrant and repugnant," but not so Mapplethorpe, who proclaimed it a brilliant piece of film-making. He boldly advertised his own coprophiliac tendencies by wearing a belt that spelled the word "SHIT" in metal studs, yet he was evasive with people he thought might be repulsed by his activities, and coyly referred to his own fetish as "dirty." He hinted at the origin of his fixation, however, in a 1978 self-portrait that was taken at the prompting of a German art director named Helmut, who, after agreeing to reveal his "secret," pressed the photographer to divulge his own. Mapplethorpe inserted the handle of a bullwhip into his anus and glared defiantly at the camera.

He developed a worldwide network of coprophiliacs who visited Bond Street whenever they were in town, and who spoke of excrement as the "ultimate sacrament." He even gave a party at the loft of a New York pediatrician, sending out invitations with a photograph of Arnold Schwarzenegger on the cover that read "Hot Dirty Man, You are Invited to . . ." "It was great," Mapplethorpe said. "Whether it's an orgy or a cocktail party, I know how to do it." He often boasted about his sexual prowess and believed he had cultivated his senses to a far greater degree than anyone else he knew. Yet to reach a point where one can eroticize excrement involves a certain shutting down of the senses, and while Mapplethorpe proudly maintained he was not a voyeur, he derived his greatest pleasure from watching others consume his excrement—an act of perverse voyeurism. Perhaps his chilly detachment explains why many men found him to be utterly devoid of sensuality. John Richardson, for one, thought of him as a "cold-blooded angel figure, curiously unsexual for someone who was supposedly so sexual."

Mapplethorpe attempted to eroticize almost everything he photographed, turning the head and shoulders of a bald man into a penis and testicles, for example, or focusing on the sex organs of plants, but his photographs are rarely erotic. "The images don't register in the genitals," writer George Stambolian observed, "but go straight from the eyes to the brain. The gay sensibility of the 1970s was celebratory—men were dancing in the discos and going to the bars and sex became a kind of religious experience—but Robert didn't capture that ecstasy at all. Everything he did was cold, static, distanced." In a rare moment of self-reflection, Mapplethorpe confided that his goal in sex, and in art, was to stop himself from feeling: "When I have sex with someone I forget who I am. For a minute I even forget I'm human. It's the same thing when I'm behind a camera. I forget I exist."

. . .

Mapplethorpe had been with the Holly Solomon Gallery for less than a year, and although she lobbied successfully in the summer of 1977 to have his work included in Documenta 6, the prestigious international art show held in Kassel, Germany, he didn't think the dealer was adequately promoting him. Moreover, both he and Sam Wagstaff believed it would be more advantageous to have a gallery uptown so he could balance his raunchy image with a more conservative Fifty-seventh Street setting. Behind Solomon's back, they canvassed everyone they knew to determine which gallery best suited him and which dealers were sympathetic to his work. Klaus Kertess recalled: "Robert complained a lot about Holly, that she wasn't generating enough income for him, and that the portrait commissions she had promised hadn't come through, and that he wasn't crazy about her other artists. We'd go out to dinner and he'd complain that he wasn't making as much money as a painter would be in a comparable situation, and wasn't that awful? He didn't want to show with a photography gallery because he didn't want to be dealt with as a photographer. But he was a photographer, finally, and what he did well was photography. To put a triple frame around something isn't really what made it better art. I had a really soft spot for Robert, but at a certain point he began to wear me out."

Patti Smith, meanwhile, was "out of traction and back in action," and already planning her third album, *Easter*. During her recuperation she had completed most of the manuscript of *Babel* and had produced enough drawings for another show at the Gotham Book Mart. When Klaus Kertess learned that Robert Miller was planning to open a new gallery, he suggested that Miller look at Smith's new drawings. Miller, who was in his late thirties, had spent twelve years working for Andre Emmerich, but after a mysterious falling out with the dealer, in addition to a terrifying brush with death due to a brain hemorrhage, he decided to strike out on his own. With the financial support of his sister-in-law, who had married into the Johnson and Johnson family, he rented a space at 724 Fifth Avenue and immediately signed up Robert Zakanitch, who defected from Holly Solomon, and sculptor Robert Graham. Miller had liked Smith's *Horses* album, and at Kertess's suggestion he went to her show at the Gotham Book Mart. Impressed by the drawings and, no doubt, by the publicity value of her name, he offered to exhibit her work at his new gallery.

Smith knew how badly Mapplethorpe wanted to leave Solomon, so she accepted Miller's offer on the condition that he stage a joint exhibit of works by Smith and Mapplethorpe. Miller had met Mapplethorpe five years earlier through Wagstaff, but had thought little about him until he attended the twin openings at Holly Solomon and the Kitchen. "I found the work amazingly thrilling," Miller recalled. "I mean, where did this person come from? The portrait of Harry Lunn hanging in Holly's gallery was the most amazing presentation of the human head. Robert could make a picture of a person and do something incredible to it so it even had more of an edge than his sadomasochistic material. I knew nothing about photography then, but I was just knocked over by his photographs." Nevertheless, Miller was reluctant to take Mapplethorpe on; he had no experience selling photography, and he may have felt the S&M photographs would brand his fledgling operation a "gay gallery." Yet Smith, according to Mapplethorpe, pestered Miller until he finally agreed to include him in the show. It was not exactly the way Mapplethorpe had envisioned his triumphant move uptown, for he was still perceived as riding on Smith's coattails; but nevertheless, he had solved the "Holly problem" and had a gallery across the street from Tiffany's.

Solomon was already furious with Miller for taking Robert Zakanitch away from her, and during a heated phone call she had told him, "Hey, please don't come to my gallery anymore, because every time you walk in the door you steal an artist." She had no idea Mapplethorpe was planning to leave, too; he had kept his plans quiet so as not to jeopardize his flower show scheduled for November. A few days after the opening, however, he walked into the gallery and informed Solomon that he was going to Robert Miller.

Solomon was nearly beside herself. "My mother had recently died so it wasn't a very happy time for me," she explained, "then Robert told me he was leaving in the middle of the flower show, which wasn't exactly the nicest thing in the world. I said to him, 'Robert, this is dumb! I'll be happy to share you with Robert Miller. That way you can have galleries uptown and downtown.' But he left anyway.

Working with him had been a financial horror, but had he stayed at the gallery, I would have started to bring back some of the money that he drained. Did I feel used and abused? Yes! And it was rather nasty for him to leave when he did. It hurt my credibility as a dealer, which is very important to me. . . . But Robert was a very ungenerous man." He did give her a going-away present, although one with a decidedly mixed message. When the dealer unwrapped the photograph he had left at the gallery for her, she was confronted by Robert's rectum, with a whip snaking out of it. "I didn't know whether to be complimented," she said, "or insulted."

Sam Wagstaff turned fifty-six that November, and for his birthday Mapplethorpe gave him a card that featured a Mapplethorpe picture of a bust of Pan kissing a phallic flower pistil. Inside, he had written, "I love you as much as I can love anyone." It was a sad acknowledgment of his own limitations, and while their love might never have survived the daily strain of a live-in relationship, Mapplethorpe seemed almost wistful when he added, "I miss what we once had . . ." It was evident from Wagstaff's letters to Mapplethorpe that he still loved him very much; he reminded Mapplethorpe to take his vitamins, and to prepare the hot gruels he had taught him to make to ward off respiratory infections; he pleaded with him not to get depressed because he was "much too smart & sweet and getting so famous."

Wagstaff was becoming famous himself as one of the most knowledgeable and outspoken authorities in the photography field, and next to Chicago lawyer Arnold Crane, he owned the largest private collection of pictures in the United States—a total of five thousand images that dated back to photography's invention in the 1820s. Mapplethorpe frequently took Wagstaff to task for buying too many quirky pieces by unknown photographers, which, he felt, diluted the power of the collection. "Please stop this insane collecting," he pleaded in one letter. "It's really gotten out of hand. You are not discriminating enough. You're building a paper gravestone to yourself. . . . The photographs that are art have to be separated from the rest—then preserved—you have no right to treat art the way you do."

Wagstaff's pictures were piled haphazardly in his penthouse, and when friends came to visit he would throw hamburgers directly on the burner of his stove, open a tin of caviar, and pass around a bottle of Chateau d'Yquem before showing off his latest acquisitions. An art dealer recalled watching Wagstaff lay out several lines of cocaine on a nineteenth-century stereograph of the Crystal Palace, which then inspired him to give a lecture on the 1851 Crystal Palace Exhibition where stereographs were displayed for the first time. "Sam loved drugs," said Daniel Wolf, who sold and collected photographs himself. "Maybe he loved it for sexual reasons, I don't know, but he also loved the intellectual buzz it gave him, and the different angle at which to look at life. He used drugs to think, as well as to feel. Sam was a real pioneer. He was one of the first people to go to Paris and bring back pictures. Now everybody goes three times a year, but then it was a really different scene. There were just a handful of people in New York who really cared about photography, and we'd sit around and say, 'Isn't it amazing that nobody else appreciates it? What can we do to get it out there? What are the important ideas? Sam was the spiritual captain of the movement."

Wagstaff helped focus attention on vintage nineteenth-century prints and raised the profiles in the United States of such previously little-known photographers as Gustave Le Gray, a Frenchman noted for his haunting land-sea-sky compositions, and Nadar, whose pictures he lent to the Museum of Modern Art for inclusion in the photographer's first major show in the United States. By ignoring acknowledged masterpieces in favor of obscure images and pictures by anonymous photographers, Wagstaff celebrated the concept of the collector as artist; he presented his view of the world by carefully editing and selecting the views of others. He often described himself as a "collector of collectors," by which he meant that photographers themselves were involved in making similar aesthetic judgments every time they looked into the lens. He "collected" their collections and made them his own. "The common thread throughout is quality," he told *Art & Antiques*. "I don't collect by subject but by what interests me—a bare ass or a sunset, a waterfall or Lincoln, an American Indian or a dead soldier or Louise Brooks, who was one of the most beautiful women who ever lived. . . . You can't collect with someone else's eye. It's putting your own stake in the ground. . . . It's not about motherhood; it's not homogenized. It's about yourself, about ego."

Wagstaff's iconoclastic approach appealed to Jane Livingston, who was then curator of photography at the Corcoran Gallery of Art in Washington, D.C., where Mapplethorpe's "Perfect Moment" exhibit would later be canceled. Livingston had met Wagstaff at the Russian Tea Room in the early seventies, when she was having lunch with sculptor Tony Smith. "Here was this tall, slender, drop-dead beautiful man wearing a green velvet shirt and turquoise Indian jewelry," Livingston recalled. "At that time he had obsessively embraced Arica, and he was in a moment of sobriety and ecstatic straightness. I couldn't imagine Sam the crazed addict talking mostly about Arica, but I'd heard he was a little crazy. He was also wonderful and charming and opinionated and we all laughed and had a great time." In 1975 Livingston went to the Corcoran, but as her career up until then had been centered on contemporary art, she had no great interest in dealing with photography. "I'd been brainwashed into accepting the sixties feeling that photography wasn't high art," she explained. "People forget that the admission of photography as an art form into the hall of museums was a very recent development. It didn't really gain a full-fledged momentum until the early seventies, then it all happened very fast. In the course of getting into the photography world and having this very rapid and very passionate love affair with the medium, I crossed paths again with Sam." Livingston asked Wagstaff to organize a show based on his collection, and she and Wagstaff devoted a major part of 1977 to planning the exhibit. "We both agreed that we didn't want the exhibit to be a typical chronological, scholarly presentation," she said. "The whole point of Sam's collection—indeed, the whole point of Sam—was about appreciating individual objects for their own sake."

In conjunction with the show, Wagstaff was scheduled to publish a book of photographs from his collection, and he hired a young photographer named Gérald Incandela, whom he had met through the artist and filmmaker Derek Jarman, to help him select the pictures. As with all of Wagstaff's business dealings with young men, his motivations were mixed, and having lost interest in the architect, he was now taken with Incandela. He convinced him to move from London to New York and offered to help him in any way he could. "Sam needed a muse," said Norman Rosenthal, a curator at the Royal Academy of Art. "He needed someone young and beautiful to inspire him. He would have been lost without a Robert or a Gérald." Incandela was already involved in another relationship, and while he knew that being Wagstaff's "discovery" would benefit his career, he kept the friendship platonic. "I was a little nervous because I thought, I'm going to come out looking like a protégé of Sam Wagstaff, and I wanted to stand on my own two feet," Incandela explained. "I thought maybe Robert would feel threatened, and being a newcomer I didn't want to get into tricky water."

Mapplethorpe could handle the sexual jealousy, but the idea that Wagstaff was promoting the work of another young photographer sent him into an emotional tailspin. He was no longer the favorite child, and his position as Wagstaff's heir apparent was in jeopardy. "I once wrote a piece on Incandela for *Artforum*," Klaus Kertess recalled, "and Robert was furious about it. He never referred to him by name but only as 'that person.' "

The psychological war between the two photographers was staged, appropriately enough, on the battlefield of Wagstaff's photography book. He had arranged for each man to be represented by two pictures apiece, but had led Incandela to believe that one of his images would grace the cover in repayment for all the work he had done on the book. It would represent a triumph for the relatively unknown photographer, for it meant that among all the images in the book, Wagstaff, the ultimate arbiter of taste, would be telling the world, "Look at *this* one."

The exhibit of "Photographs from the Collection of Samuel J. Wagstaff," which opened at the Corcoran Gallery on February 3, 1978, was the high point of Wagstaff's life. Paul Richard, the art critic for *The Washington Post*, described the exhibition as "the finest show of photographs Washington has seen." Wagstaff's social credentials played an important part in helping to elevate the humble art form in the eyes of status-conscious Washingtonians. MAKING PHOTOGRAPHY SOCIALLY ACCEPTABLE was the headline of the *Washington Post* article, and Wagstaff was portrayed as "the collector the establish-

ment trusts . . . a Wagstaff of the New York Wagstaffs, Yale '44."
The bohemian Wagstaff had been temporarily replaced by a distinguished middle-aged man in a tuxedo, his long straggly hair
trimmed short for the occasion.

Prior to the opening, Wagstaff was honored at a candlelit dinner
at the Corcoran attended by 250 people, including politicians, dip-
lomats, and Robert Mapplethorpe and Gérald Incandela. Afterward,
Wagstaff gave Joan Mondale, wife of the current vice-president, a
personal tour of the exhibit. Contrary to his refined appearance and
social pedigree, the exhibit itself was an affront to establishment
taste. "Sam had an arrogant confidence in his own eye," Jane Livingston explained. "He trusted his own taste, his own judgment,
and didn't care what anybody else thought. He loved to find beauty
in the undervalued, the forgotten, the neglected, and the forbidden." Indeed, among the pictures in the Corcoran's majestic galleries was Mapplethorpe's photograph of the leather-hooded Jim in
Sausalito.

Wagstaff's intention was to "jolt" the audience by mixing glamorous portraits by Cecil Beaton and Baron de Meyer, for example,
with a grotesque medical study of a syphilitic man; a smiling hippo-
potamus; a cat named "Tweedle"; Baron Von Gloeden's Sicilian
boys; and a Larry Clark picture of a drug addict tapping a vein. He
contrasted the world's great wonders—such as Francis Frith's *Pyramids of Dahshoor*—with Roger Fenton's Crimean war photographs
and scenes from the Warsaw Ghetto.

Nowhere was Wagstaff's "compare and contrast" technique
more evident than in the work he exhibited in two separate rooms
adjacent to the main exhibit. In one space he presented Mapplethorpe's flower pictures, and in the other Incandela's conceptual
photographs—the old muse versus the new one. "Everyone was
speechless," said Anne Horton, who headed the photography department at Sotheby Parke-Bernet. "It meant that Gérald had really
come up quite fast in the world vis-à-vis Robert." Critic Ben Lifson
later wrote an article for *The Village Voice* in which he criticized
Wagstaff for using undue influence in promoting Mapplethorpe's
career. The next time Wagstaff saw Lifson, he shouted, "You naïve
bastard! How do you think anything gets done in the world if not by
power and influence?" It was a concept Mapplethorpe understood

only too well, and when Wagstaff's *Book of Photographs* was published, he had effectively bumped Incandela's work from its potential place of honor: the front and back covers of the book displayed two different tulip photographs by Mapplethorpe.

"This book is about pleasure," Wagstaff wrote in the preface, "the pleasure of looking and the pleasure of seeing, like watching people dancing through an open window. They seem a little mad at first, until you realize they hear the song that you are watching." Despite his whimsical introduction, a central theme of the book is the fragile nature of beauty, and in many cases it is male beauty that faces the most dire threat. Wagstaff opened the book with Thomas Eakins's photograph of male nudes at a swimming pool, which he placed next to Frederick Evans's *Tomb of Edward III*. The saddest and most prophetic pairing, though, is *Jim, Sausalito* with Nadar's harrowing picture of human skulls in the Paris catacombs. When Ben Lifson asked Wagstaff to discuss the two pictures, he replied, "Joy takes many aspects in photography—the joy of sadness, of forgetfulness, of outrageousness, the joy even of death."

Mapplethorpe's loft had become a port-of-call for men with every conceivable sexual perversion, and they arrived with suitcases, and sometimes doctor's bags, filled with catheters, scalpels, syringes, needles, laxatives, hot water bottles, rope, handcuffs, and pills. They dressed up as women, SS troopers, and pigs. One wore baby clothes and a bonnet, drank from a bottle, and defecated in his diapers. "Joe" appeared at the loft in a rubber body suit and Mapplethorpe took a picture of him kneeling on a bench; the tube inserted in his mouth was later connected to an enema bag.

Until now Mapplethorpe had attempted to steer clear of the "crazies"—men whose sexual proclivities included bodily mutilation—but he had already documented most forms of gay S&M, and since he didn't want to keep repeating himself, he was open to meeting people with extreme tastes. "Ken," for example, whose horrifying image is included in the "X Portfolio," enjoyed having people carve their initials into his skin. "I think he's probably dead now," Mapplethorpe told Joe Dolce, who interviewed the photographer for a master's thesis on S&M. "He was totally scarred, like a tree trunk, with initials. He'd just lay there like a piece of beef, and you could do anything you wanted to him. But there was no real energy there. He was a down trip."

At the time Mapplethorpe photographed "Ken," he received a call from an art critic who offered to introduce him to someone who derived sexual satisfaction by having someone slash his penis with a razor. Stoned on MDA, Mapplethorpe arrived at the appointed apartment with his camera and met "Richard"—a "mathematician and computer person"—whose penis was strapped into a stocklike device, with a hole in the center and bolts on the side. "Then the scalpel came out," Mapplethorpe told Dolce. "I was told I could be a participant or an observer. I managed to do both. It was hard to focus the camera, but I found I could really get off on this thing. Holding a scalpel in my hand and grazing a cock was a real turn-on. You could feel the energy in your fingers. Another guy went through his number. He came out of a bathroom with a wig, garish makeup, and leotards, but that wasn't my scene."

When he had finished taking pictures of Richard's "crucifixion," he waited for the other man to strap himself into the contraption so he, too, could submit to the ritual. "Then all of a sudden it was my turn," he told Dolce. "The other guys were older, and certainly as intelligent as I, and I had certainly been an active participant. But I thought, how am I going to deal with this?" He placed the device over his genitals and tried to divorce himself from the reality of the situation, which was that a man in a curly wig and tights, who was flying high on LSD, was holding a scalpel in his hands. "Okay," he said, panicking. "I'm not getting off on this. It's not my thing."

Mapplethorpe saw Richard several more times and later created a multipanel piece that detailed the progressive mangling of Richard's penis. But ultimately the mingling of blood and semen revolted him. "I had kind of exhausted the S&M thing," he concluded. "I had gone through it all both photographically and physically, and I was meeting too many guys like Richard. It was getting a little too crazy."

CHAPTER FIFTEEN

"Off we go to the land of love."

—*Patti Smith, "Frederick"*

"Love was impossible with him, because the only people he
wanted in his life were rich people, famous people,
and people he could have sex with."

—*Marcus Leatherdale, about Robert Mapplethorpe*

In mid-February 1979, Mapplethorpe took his new photographs of "Richard" to San Francisco, where he hoped to show them as part of his scheduled exhibit at the Simon Lowinsky Gallery. Lowinsky had first met Mapplethorpe through dealer Harry Lunn at the Basel Art Fair in 1976, and he offered to sponsor the photographer's debut exhibit in the Bay Area. "The pictures were remarkably strong and very mannered," Lowinsky recalled. "Of course they were also very decadent, but I thought it was important to show the tougher work as well as the flowers and portraits." Mapplethorpe's tougher work, however, had grown considerably more hardcore since then, and when Lowinsky saw the latest photographs, including "Richard," he told the photographer that he couldn't possibly hang them in his gallery.

What troubled Lowinsky even more than the graphic nature of the pictures was the Nazi symbolism appropriated by some of the leather men. As a heterosexual in a long-term relationship, he did not feign understanding of the gay S&M subculture, but as a Jew, he was offended by the swastika imagery, which, no matter what the sexual rationale, was abhorrent to him. Furthermore, while he liked both Wagstaff and Mapplethorpe, he had always been uncomfortable with what he described as their "neofascist politics." Numerous people characterized Wagstaff as anti-Semitic, although most were so enthralled by his "eye" they tended to forgive the uglier aspects of his personality. Mapplethorpe, who might otherwise have tempered his tongue, was encouraged by Wagstaff's example to voice his own prejudices, and he often referred to Jews as being money-hungry and vulgar. "I think Robert liked me," Lowinsky said, "but I knew he despised Jews, and I happened to be Jewish. We both felt uncomfortable with each other. I believed his pictures had to be shown—if we're dealing with artists, we have to be able to exhibit anything that anyone makes—but I just wasn't as committed to it as other dealers were."

Lowinsky rejected eighteen of Mapplethorpe's photographs before settling on a mixture of flower studies, portraits, and the relatively tamer sex pictures, including *Mr. 10½*. He planned to contrast them with the hardcore news photographs of Arthur Fellig, better known as Weegee, who, during the thirties and forties, documented the seamy underside of New York's nightlife. Mapplethorpe was furious with Lowinsky, for not only had the dealer spurned his sex pictures, but he now also expected him to share gallery space with a news photographer whose images bore such captions as "The Sixteen-Year-Old Boy Who Strangled a 4-Year-Old," and "Murder in Hell's Kitchen." He accused Lowinsky of censoring his work and complained to *The Advocate*, a national gay biweekly, of his difficulties in finding exhibition space for his S&M photographs. It was a clever strategy: he could not have realistically expected a straight photography dealer with an upscale gallery on Grant Avenue to jump at the opportunity to exhibit pictures of two-fisted anal intercourse. By giving Lowinsky the chance to reject his photographs, Mapplethorpe raised his public profile another notch and incited curiosity about the pictures that were "banned" in liberal San Francisco.

Mapplethorpe, meanwhile, sought the advice of Jim Elliott, Wagstaff's former colleague at the Wadsworth Athenaeum, who was now the director of the University Art Museum at Berkeley, where, not coincidentally, "Photographs from the Collection of Robert Mapplethorpe" was currently on view. Mapplethorpe's show of the vintage prints he had collected over the years was a junior version of Wagstaff's Corcoran exhibit, and in fact, many of the five hundred pictures had been gifts from Wagstaff. Worried that someone might steal the photographs, and unwilling to pay for insurance, Mapplethorpe prevailed upon Elliott to keep his collection on loan for several years. He now asked his help in finding an exhibition space for his own "censored" pictures.

Elliott put him in touch with Edward de Celle, who, with his partner Don Lawson, owned the Lawson de Celle Gallery on Kissling Street. "Jim brought Robert over to the gallery," de Celle recalled, "and I agreed to take him to lunch. I was curious to meet him, but he was not what I expected at all. I had imagined a much stronger physical presence. He was slight and shy and terribly polite and humble. We had a table where we could look at the photographs, and I remember opening this box. I had seen pornography before, but his pictures were really more graphic because they're better pictures and they draw you in more. The one that disturbed me the most was the man putting his finger into his urethra. I was revolted but I was also mesmerized. I kept staring at these things, and I purposely didn't react because I didn't want to seem, I suppose, unsophisticated. I kept thinking, There's something wrong with me if I can't just look at these pictures in an objective way. It's like the emperor's new clothes. You have to prove that you're unflappable. I was happy to put the lid back on the box, and I was kind of reeling. I thought, How can I show these pictures in my gallery? Because my immediate thought was not about the quality of the pictures, or whether or not they were art, but about the teacher from the local girl's school who always brought her class into the gallery. I kept seeing those little girls in their pleated skirts, and I thought, Oh my word!"

De Celle, nonetheless, was fascinated enough by the pictures that he told Mapplethorpe he would broach the subject of a potential show with Don Lawson. "No way!" Lawson said, after looking at the photographs. "Absolutely not! I couldn't live with myself if I did this." A disgruntled de Celle, then, took the portfolio to 80 Langton Street, a not-for-profit exhibition space funded by the National Endowment for the Arts, and after a spirited discussion with the board of directors, of which he was a member, he convinced them to stage the exhibit. Mapplethorpe insisted on calling the show "Censored" anyway, and on the cover of the invitation he placed his self-portrait with the whip.

Mapplethorpe's show of flowers, portraits, and milder sex pictures at the Lowinsky Gallery opened on February 21, followed by "Censored" on March 20; both exhibits attracted attention within the gay and art communities, but "Censored" drew the most colorful opening night crowd, with a cavalcade of leather men, in addition to the local chapter of the Hell's Angels, who roared up to the gallery on their motorcycles. "It was a wonderful mix of people," de Celle recalled. "I used my mailing list and included my card so that people would know I was personally involved. I have pictures of Robert with Anita Mardikian, who was a very popular San Francisco socialite, as well as with Chris Burden, the artist who crucified himself to the top of a Volkswagen. Everyone was just fascinated by the work, and I didn't have one negative remark. Now, maybe when they got home and told their best friend about it, they were revolted, but when you're in an art setting you want to appear sophisticated and broad-minded."

Thomas Albright, the critic for the *San Francisco Chronicle*, did not feel so constrained; he described the show at the Lowinsky Gallery "as pedestrianly conventional" and "somewhat melodramatically illuminated in the cliché style one might find in the commercial photography of the slick glamor magazines." *Artweek* dismissed it as the work of "a very young artist, seemingly propelled to exhibit publicly his sexual growing pains." Mapplethorpe's subsequent exhibit at 80 Langton Street was ignored by the press entirely except by a reviewer for *The Advocate* who compared the bloody "Richard" to a Willem de Kooning painting and, quoting the Roman playwright Terence—"I am a man; nothing human is alien to me"—praised the photographer for increasing "awareness of what it means to be a human being."

That sentiment was not universally shared by members of San Francisco's gay community, some of whom privately took Mapplethorpe aside and accused him of providing ammunition for orange juice pitchwoman Anita Bryant, who was then conducting a virulent antigay campaign. Mapplethorpe's "lecture" at a seminar sponsored by 80 Langton only enhanced his stature as a dangerous wild card, for he swallowed MDA beforehand and delivered a rambling talk about God, magic, and "getting off" on the energy of severe sex. "It was pretty much a disaster," de Celle said. "Robert wasn't what you might call a 'public speaker.' "

Sam Wagstaff had flown to San Francisco for Mapplethorpe's openings but returned to New York soon afterward. Gérald Incandela was still a touchy subject between them, and while Mapplethorpe had convinced Wagstaff to remove Incandela's photograph from the cover of Wagstaff's book, he had failed to oust Incandela from Wagstaff's life. One night at a Folsom Street leather bar, however, Mapplethorpe stumbled upon an ideal solution: a man to sexually distract Wagstaff from his infatuation with Incandela.

The man's name was Jim Nelson, and he was handsome in an effeminate way; no matter how much black leather he layered on his six-foot frame, he couldn't disguise his fragile personality. When he became overly excited, his pale hands fluttered and his Texas accent turned more pronounced. He was like a character out of a Tennessee Williams play, and more than one acquaintance offered the unflattering comparison to Blanche Du Bois. Like Blanche, Nelson was a dreamer without much to support his dreams other than a layer of pretension that made him appear childish and at times pathetic. He was completely starstruck and for years had such a crush on Loretta Young and Connie Stevens that he kept photo albums filled with their pictures and press clippings. He had a dog-eared map of the stars' homes tacked inside a closet and fantasized about living in a Hollywood mansion—his Belle Rêve.

Nelson's fantasies provided an antidote to the grim reality of his rural Texas childhood; he lost his mother at the age of two, and since his invalid father could not take care of him, he was exiled to foster homes. He later complained to his lawyer Leonard Bloom that he was taunted by the other boys there for being homosexual. At fourteen he moved to Los Angeles to live with his married brother, Art, a local deejay, who helped put him through cosmetology school; the two men eventually had a falling out over Jim's keeping late hours, and Art told him, "It's either my way, or the highway," so Jim left. He later worked at Elizabeth Arden in San Francisco, where he spent his days catering to the cosmetic fantasies of women and his nights submitting to the sexual fantasies of men. He was so desperately eager to please that he would have been willing to do anything Mapplethorpe requested of him. They spent several nights together before the photographer arranged for Nelson to rendezvous with Wagstaff in New York. "The persistent rumor was that Robert sent Jim to New York in an overnight express box," said Sam Green. "That's how Jim arrived at Sam's door—air freight."

When Robert Mapplethorpe and Patti Smith's joint exhibit, "Film and Stills," opened at the Robert Miller Gallery in June, it drew huge crowds and TV cameras. Smith had made a stunning comeback since her accident seventeen months before; *Easter,* her new album, had received the best reviews of her career, and she had a Top Ten single with "Because the Night," which she had cowritten with Bruce Springsteen. In addition, *The New York Times Book Review* had devoted two pages to the April publication of *Babel,* with reviewer Jonathan Cott describing it as an "alternately dazzling, uneven, arousing, annoying, imitative, original book." *Rolling Stone* featured Smith in a cover story entitled "Patti Smith Catches Fire" and illustrated the piece with a dramatic Annie Leibovitz photograph of the performer in front of several blazing barrels of kerosene.

Smith clearly was the star of the event, but the show itself celebrated her decade-long friendship with Mapplethorpe. The poster for the exhibit featured a photograph of Patti by Robert and a drawing of Robert by Patti, and the first image confronting viewers when they entered the gallery was a 1968 snapshot of the two artists taken in Coney Island. The couple arrived at the opening together, and they wore such radiant expressions that William Targ, who had edited *Babel,* compared them to a bride and groom on their wedding day. "It was everything we had ever hoped for," Smith later explained. "The two of us together in an art gallery."

Smith had the place of honor in the gallery's middle room, where her colored pencil sketches of Rimbaud, Pasolini, and Jane Bowles were hung salon-style in elegant gilt frames. Mapplethorpe's work was split between two smaller rooms, with his photographs in one and a sixteen-millimeter film, *Still Moving,* running on a continuous loop in the other. He had made the ten-minute movie with Smith the previous January, when he had given the performer MDA in order to capture her in "a state of total abandon," but she was already uninhibited enough without chemicals, and the drug reduced her to near-psychotic gibberish. Blindfolded, she stumbled around Mapplethorpe's studio offering stuttering pronouncements on God and the nature of evil. At times she could barely speak and kept touching her tongue as if she were trying to untwist it. Lisa Rinzler, a young camerawoman, actually shot the movie, while Mapplethorpe remained the cool, dispassionate photographer; he gave hand directions to Smith from behind his Hasselblad while she literally tried to climb the walls of his studio. *Still Moving* has a cruel and manipulative quality to it, but Mapplethorpe and Smith's relationship defied ordinary rules. They both accepted extreme behavior in the other, and among their half-dozen collaborations in the exhibit was his photograph *Richard, 1978,* which she had embellished by scribbling poetry around its edges.

"Their friendship is their masterpiece," René Ricard wrote in *Art in America.* "What's on show, the works, is documentation or artifact; its importance is that it was made by these people. This works doubly. Mapplethorpe photos are always beautiful, but a Mapplethorpe photo of Patti Smith is, well, history. By the same token even if Patti had no talent for drawing (it's only gravy that the drawings are fine) the lovely drawings of Rimbaud in the show would be something to have, the way a Verlaine or Rimbaud would be something to have. . . . Verlaine, Rimbaud, Smith, Mapplethorpe: we are dealing here with a network of homage and swapped destinies, like Piaf and Cocteau, people who would die within minutes of each other."

On June 15 Mapplethorpe went to Paris for the opening of a show of his work at the Galerie Remise du Parc. Sam Wagstaff had largely been responsible for the exhibit, as he had first shown Mapplethorpe's photographs to the gallery's co-owner, William Burke, whom he had met through a Detroit art collector. Burke thought the pictures were stylish and handsome and prevailed upon his part-

ner, Samia Saouma, to be the first European gallery to give Mapplethorpe a one-person show. The opening attracted the corps d'elite
of gay society, several of whom Mapplethorpe had corresponded
with regularly over the years so that he was current with the latest
gossip on which friend had suffered ruinous gambling debts at
Monte Carlo, which European ballet company had the sexiest dancers, and which royal was a closet gay. Galerie Remise du Parc sold
nearly all the photographs in the show, and among the buyers were
art collector Baron Leon Lambert, who added a Mapplethorpe to
his extensive holdings. "Robert's shows in Paris were always filled
with homosexual men," a prominent French photography dealer
recalled. "He was very connected to that whole leather world, and
these men always showed up at his openings. Personally, I always
thought he was an unsavory character, and I always wondered what
Sam was doing with him. I loved Sam. He was brilliant. But Robert
was simply dreadful, and I think that without the support of Sam,
and that whole homosexual sadomasochistic universe, no one
would ever have heard of him."

Before Mapplethorpe left for Paris he had given the keys to his
New York loft to a recent art school graduate whom he had met at
the Simon Lowinsky Gallery earlier that spring; the young man's
name, fittingly enough, was Marcus Leatherdale. When Mapplethorpe returned to New York at the end of the summer, he offered
Leatherdale a job as his office manager. The photographer had always been lax with his record keeping, and he often didn't know
how many numbered editions of each print he had sold. Moreover,
Wagstaff had given Mapplethorpe the money to build a darkroom,
and he now had two part-time printers in his employ and badly
needed someone to oversee his rapidly expanding business. Leatherdale seemed like the perfect choice; an aspiring photographer himself, he was totally in awe of Mapplethorpe, who, though only four
years older, was vastly more experienced in the ways of the art world,
and of the New York gay club scene.

To understand Mapplethorpe's attraction to the younger man,
one didn't have to look beyond the obvious: they could easily have
passed for brothers, and their physical similarity was stretched to the
point of foolishness when they began dressing in identical black
leather outfits. Leatherdale was Mapplethorpe's mirror image the

way Patti Smith had been, and when Mapplethorpe looked at him, he saw a younger, more innocent version of himself. He constantly teased Leatherdale about what he considered to be his puritanical sexual attitudes, and on their first evening together, he took him to dinner at One Fifth, then to the Mineshaft. "Whenever you make love with someone," Mapplethorpe advised him, "there should be three people involved—you, the other person, and the devil."

Sometimes Leatherdale slept with Mapplethorpe in his bedroom; other times, when one of Mapplethorpe's "tricks" stayed the night, he was relegated to the studio in the front room. Mapplethorpe's other sexual partners could not have been more physically dissimilar to Leatherdale—or to himself. His sex life had always been such a part of his work that since he had sworn off the "crazies," he needed something visually dramatic to replace their photogenic secrets. More and more, he began to search out models not for their sexual aberrations but for their physical appearance.

One night at a gay bar he noticed Robert Sherman, whose milky-white face and body were totally hairless. Mesmerized, Mapplethorpe trailed him from room to room, and eventually enticed him back to Bond Street. Sherman, who worked as a drag queen, suffered from a rare form of the disease alopecia, which had left him without any hair, including eyelashes and brows. Initially Sherman was intimidated by Mapplethorpe's hardcore reputation and by his sinister loft—"I had never seen a black leather bedspread before"—but the photographer was surprisingly sweet and gentle toward him. "Robert wanted to find out what it was like growing up without any hair," Sherman recalled. "He kept asking me, 'Did the kids make fun of you? Did they make you feel like a freak?' " But as tender as Mapplethorpe had been that night, he was all business the next morning, when he roused Sherman from bed at seven o'clock with a perfunctory "Get up." Naked and half-asleep, Sherman was then directed to crouch on the floor near a wall of vertical shadows that mimicked the bars of a cage, then Mapplethorpe photographed him. "Robert gave directions by just flicking his hands," Sherman recalled. "It was over very quickly. I knew he had wanted to take my picture, but I'd hoped he'd court me a bit."

Mapplethorpe didn't have time for courtship, however, for the elevator at 24 Bond Street was continually transporting men to his door. One, Larry DeSmedt, was a biker whose visual appeal to the photographer was enhanced by the Harley-Davidson tattoo on his bicep, the word "SEX" over his navel, and the missing finger on his left hand. "Robert was extremely promiscuous," Leatherdale recalled. "All through the night he'd come home with one person, then another. The next morning he'd wake up with somebody I hadn't even seen from the previous evening." Meanwhile, Mapplethorpe continued to go everywhere with Leatherdale, whom he was happy to help as long as the younger photographer kept his own ambitions in check. But the more serious Leatherdale became about his own work, and the more his pictures began to take on a distinct Mapplethorpe look, the more Robert reacted like a jealous older brother; he derided Marcus behind his back and called him "Marcus Leatherthorpe."

At first Leatherdale was baffled by Mapplethorpe's behavior, for he could not imagine how he could be a threat to him. He was just starting his career, while Mapplethorpe was already well established. But during the months he lived at Bond Street, Leatherdale noticed a side of the photographer few people were ever allowed to see. Mapplethorpe would emerge from his cagelike bedroom around noon, then walk into the living room, which was decorated with the Arts and Crafts pottery and austere Mission furniture he had been collecting over the past several years. His Morris chairs and Stickley settee had been upholstered in black leather, which, he believed, reflected an "amorous, masculine quality." He spent at least a half-hour rocking back and forth in one of the chairs, as if to make contact with that "masculine" power base. He then smoked several cigarettes, followed by half a joint, and snorted a line of cocaine while he distractedly picked at his face. "Robert was one of the most tortured, tormented individuals I've ever met," Leatherdale said. "He was a bundle of insecurities and always seemed ready to snap."

And snap he did, when Leatherdale accidently spilled coffee on the cover of one of his photography catalogues. An enraged Mapplethorpe slapped him hard across the face with the book. "He was in his dressing gown," Leatherdale recalled, "and he just whacked me like I was some kind of slave. I was ready to punch him in the face, but the guy who did his printing separated us." Leatherdale quit his job as Mapplethorpe's office manager and went to work for

Sam Wagstaff organizing his photography collection; after an initial cooling-off period, he and Mapplethorpe reconciled, and they continued to be friends for the next several years, but Leatherdale's feelings toward him remained ambivalent. "He was fun to be with, very gossipy," he said, "and when he focused on you, it was like you were the most important person in the world. But, unfortunately, that rarely happened because Robert wanted to be the most important person in the world. I was never in love with him, though maybe I thought I was in the beginning, but now that I know what love is—it wasn't what I felt for Robert. Love was impossible with him, because the only people he wanted in his life were rich people, famous people, and people he could have sex with."

During March 1979 Robert Mapplethorpe had three different photography shows in the city—uptown, downtown, and midtown. "Trade-Off" was the title of his exhibit at the International Center of Photography, at 1130 Fifth Avenue, where he collaborated with Lynn Davis in a "friendly" competition designed to compare and contrast each photographer's approach to the same sixteen subjects. Davis met Mapplethorpe in late 1976, when she was editing a small photography magazine; she had been fascinated by his work since first seeing the picture *Mr. 10½* in a European publication and had made an appointment to visit him at Bond Street. Davis, who was born in Minneapolis, had moved to New York in 1974 after living in San Francisco for nearly a decade. She considered herself a sophisticated woman, but nothing in her experience had prepared her for the raw power of the sex pictures. She was utterly enthralled by them—and by Mapplethorpe himself.

"I remember being at a cocktail party with her," photography critic Ben Lifson said, "and I heard one of the most worshipful accounts of Robert Mapplethorpe. It was like he had the same kind of awesome commanding presence as Timothy Leary did in the sixties. Robert was going to lead us into the great sexual beyond." Mapplethorpe was flattered by Davis's attention, and he began telephoning her to share news of his sexual experiences. "He'd call me up, and in this very cool tone, he'd tell me what he'd done the night before," Davis said. "I was frightened and excited by it. At the time it was as new to him as it was to me; he was taking pictures of things he'd never seen. Sometimes I'd get very physically uncomfortable looking at the sexual pictures. They brought out things in my own un-conscious that were terrifying."

Once a month Davis would stop by Bond Street to show Mapple-thorpe her latest pictures, then he would reciprocate. They took portraits of each other—Davis emphasizing Mapplethorpe's sensual beauty; Mapplethorpe highlighting Davis's handsome face and long, thick, dyed black hair. "I think our relationship worked be-cause it was centered on photography," she said. "I wasn't involved with him professionally or sexually. I didn't want anything from him." It was Davis, in fact, who had first been approached by Wil-liam Ewing, director of exhibitions at ICP, to do a one-person show, but she wanted Mapplethorpe and another friend, Peter Hujar, to join her. When Hujar declined—he didn't like the idea of a three-way competition—it came down to Davis and Mapple-thorpe.

The competition was conceived by Davis as a congenial one, but it soon became apparent that Mapplethorpe wanted to win at all costs. As part of the rules of the game, he and Davis both shot pic-tures of the same sixteen people, including Wagstaff, Leatherdale, Robert Sherman, dancer Peter Reed, gossip columnist Phyllis Tweel, and composer Philip Glass. "Robert got crazy over the ex-hibit," Marcus Leatherdale recalled. "Every time he'd take a pic-ture, he'd ask me, 'Is it better than Lynn's?' When it came time to hang the show, Mapplethorpe brought Wagstaff with him, and ig-noring Davis, they tried to claim the best spots in the gallery. "Right then I understood Robert's enormous competitiveness and his will to succeed," Davis said. "It taught me a valuable lesson about New York and the art world."

Ben Lifson in *The Village Voice* praised Mapplethorpe for his technical mastery of light and detail—"Mapplethorpe's skill over-whelms the show"—yet he took him to task for his slickness and inability to extract more than a narrow range of emotions from his sitters. Lifson thought Davis's pictures were rough and unschooled, although he commended her for touching "on emotions that elude Mapplethorpe, or which he avoids." Nevertheless, he was not overly impressed by either photographer and regarded the exhibition as a failure. "I was so devastated by the *Village Voice* article that I took to my bed for three days," Davis recalled, "but when I spoke to

Robert, he seemed totally unaffected by it. 'At least we got reviewed,' he said. That was pretty much his attitude about everything—he just wanted to keep moving ahead, and he moved like a speeding bullet train."

Carol Squiers had been commissioned to do an essay about the show for its catalogue, and she compared Mapplethorpe's pictures to the work of the gay artist Tom of Finland: "Mapplethorpe extends this tradition of forging and chronicling a public posture of gay men . . ." Mapplethorpe was furious with Squiers, and did not speak to her for weeks afterward. "Robert was working very hard to make it into the limelight, and already it was a problem because photography was not a first-tier art," Squiers recalled. "It didn't become anywhere close to that until the mid-eighties with Cindy Sherman and Barbara Kruger, so he had a lot of stuff going against him. On top of that, he didn't want to be ghettoized as a gay artist. Robert was adamant about not being identified with gays, or having gay subjects, but I didn't think you could leave that out. I mean, it would be like a truck driver who takes portraits of truck drivers. Would I have to pretend he wasn't a truck driver, and that all the guys in his pictures weren't truck drivers? No. So it was a dilemma."

Mapplethorpe was loath to be labeled a "gay artist," yet his rise to prominence paralleled the acceptance and assimilation of a gay aesthetic into the cultural mainstream. Frank Rich, in a 1987 essay for *Esquire* entitled "The Gay Decades," delineated nine episodes in "the homosexualization of America." These included Mart Crowley's *Boys in the Band;* the rise of Bette Midler and her campy bathhouse sensibility; rock music's "merchandizing of androgyny"; the American Psychiatric Association's 1973 resolution that homosexuality should no longer be classified as a psychiatric disorder; and Studio 54's institutionalization of gay chic. The gay rights and women's movements helped liberate the male nude; women could now look at photographs of naked men in magazines such as *Playgirl,* thereby blurring the lines between "the sex that looks," as art scholar Margaret Walters defined the traditional male voyeuristic pose, and "the sex that is looked at." George Stambolian, who taught a course in the male nude at Wellesley College, explained: "For years the male nude was repressed, and when one spoke about 'the nude,' one usually meant the *female* nude. But in the late seventies, all that began to change. The Marcuse Pfeiffer Gallery did a major survey on the male nude that included works by both male and female photographers, and that inspired a lot of debate about the sexist notions we held about male nudes versus female ones— men having to project a powerful image, women passive and power-*less.*''

During the forties and fifties, photographers such as Minor White and George Platt Lynes had purged traces of their homosexuality from public exhibits. Lynes is an interesting example in relation to Mapplethorpe, for both men were among the most successful New York photographers of their era; both chronicled the cultural scene through portraits of noted figures; and both had a passion for the male nude. But while Mapplethorpe's fame rested on his scandalous pictures, Lynes lived in fear of having his nude studies exposed to the public. The strain of living such a divided life, however, eventually wore him down, and growing disenchanted with his commercial fashion accounts, he moved to Los Angeles, and his once-successful career began to unravel. He declared bankruptcy, and in the remaining years of his life he took photographs for a Swiss homoerotic magazine under a pseudonym. Lynes often took great care to obscure the genitals of his models, but the subject itself was so incendiary that the only person who publicly collected his work was sex researcher Alfred Kinsey, who claimed a professional interest in documenting the homoerotic aesthetic. Lynes was diagnosed with cancer in 1955, and as if to make the point that his commercial career had been meaningless to him, he destroyed hundreds of negatives before he died at the age of forty-eight.

In contrast, Mapplethorpe was working at a time when many gay photographers were using their pictures to express both their public and private selves. Both Arthur Tress and Duane Michals analyzed their homosexuality through dreamlike images that borrowed from surrealism and Jungian psychology; Robert Giard took pictures of nude models in ordinary domestic settings, such as in the bathtub or reading the newspaper; Jimmy DeSana photographed S&M scenes in a crude, confrontational way that was the exact opposite of Robert's cool classicism; and Peter Hujar expressed his melancholy vision of the world through moody pictures of friends and lovers. "Male image art," as Samuel Hardison, a former interior designer, labeled it, had the potential to make money, so, in 1978, he opened the Robert Samuel Gallery. Its location at 795 Broadway made it an ideal meeting place for Greenwich Village gays who turned out in massive numbers for openings of work by such artists as Kas Sable, Rip Colt, Peter Hujar, Arthur Tress, and Paul Cadmus. "Everybody showed up, not so much to cruise, but to share in the common culture," George Stambolian explained. "You felt a sense of group pride in looking at pictures that helped define and telegraph a sense of the gay experience."

Despite his reluctance to be identified as a gay photographer, Mapplethorpe was not about to ignore such a potentially lucrative outlet for him, and he eagerly took part in a group show, "Seven Artists' View of the Male Image," which opened at the Robert Samuel Gallery on March 11. On the front of the invitation was a kitschy Mapplethorpe photograph of a phallic-looking banana encircled by a key ring. Robert Miller and his twenty-five-year-old gallery director, John Cheim, were extremely unhappy when they learned of Mapplethorpe's involvement in the downtown show, for hadn't he emphasized how much he wanted to be *uptown*? What they didn't realize then, but eventually understood, was that Mapplethorpe's intuitive sense of counterpoint was apparent in everything he did; he wanted to balance the Miller Gallery's aura of restrained elegance— what some dealers cattily described as designer-decorated art for high-class gays—with the more obvious and sexually graphic Robert Samuel Gallery. "A lot of gay artists at that time were shuttling between the classical traditions of Greek art and the pornographic," said George Stambolian. "Robert attempted to merge those two traditions in his art, and even in his choice of galleries." Whatever the creative rationale, John Cheim felt Mapplethorpe had nothing to gain by associating with a second-rate gallery. "Robert always walked the line between high and low taste," he said. "Hardison represented the appeal of low taste. It was a trashy gallery that specialized in homoerotic art, and Hardison showed too much of Robert's homosexual subject matter. I'd tell Robert, 'It's going to have a very bad effect and ruin your reputation.' But Robert liked torturing us. It's not that we weren't willing to show the explicit stuff, but Hardison was always willing to show more."

When Mapplethorpe's show "Contact" opened at the Miller Gallery on March 21, explicit images were hardly in short supply. On the advice of English photography dealer Robert Self, Mapplethorpe had created the "X Portfolio," a black-leather-bound album of thirteen pictures that included *Jim and Tom, Sausalito;* "Scott" bound by his jockstrap; the physically scarred "Ken"; a depiction of fist intercourse with "Helmut and Brooks"; "Richards' " slashed genitalia, and Mapplethorpe's self-portrait with the whip. In his introduction to the "X Portfolio," Paul Schmidt, a writer and Rimbaud translator, wrote, "In a secular age, these images are all we have left. Here are the images of our modern martyrdom: our Scourgings, our Crownings with Thorns, our Crucifixions." The "X Portfolio" was on view in a side gallery at Miller, but a selection of some of Mapplethorpe's other S&M pictures was hanging on the walls, the photographs resplendent in their ebony frames, silk mats, mirrors, and colored Plexiglas. These were interspersed with flower pictures and portraits, many of which were framed in the same decorative way.

Mapplethorpe was a savvy businessman who understood the importance of "propping up" his pictures. It was not enough to sell individual prints for five hundred dollars, then split the income with his gallery; he created diptychs and triptychs for which he could charge up to eighteen hundred dollars. Mapplethorpe's desire to create "unique objects" was not exclusively motivated by money; framing had always been an integral part of his art. But just as he never knew when to stop piling on junk with his assemblages, or layering too many fetish jewels around his neck, he may have erred on the side of excess with the "Contact" show.

Reviews ranged from mixed to downright hostile; Vicki Goldberg in *New York* thought his S&M pictures had the ability to "turn a brown paper wrapper blue," but complimented him for photographing such scenes "with a purity of technique and design that is positively elegant"—perhaps "too elegant for his own good," she concluded. What Goldberg found most interesting about Mapplethorpe's career was how it illustrated changing public attitudes: "Two years ago his portraits were shown in a respectable SoHo gallery, his black-leather men in the avant-garde Kitchen. Today both are on Fifth Avenue." Hilton Kramer in *The New York Times* concurred: "[The] very real interest of this show lies not so much in 'art' as in the way it somewhat redraws the boundaries of public taste. After Helmut Newton, perhaps Mr. Mapplethorpe's was the next logical step. But it gives one the creeps, all the same."

Ben Lifson, who only the week before had treated Mapplethorpe rather gently with his "Trade-Off" review, executed a dramatic about-face after he attended the "Contact" exhibit and met the photographer for the first time. "Robert walked in with Marcus Leatherdale, who was wearing leather chaps over his trousers," Lifson recalled, "and the chaps were held together on the inside seam by leather thongs. He had tied the thongs of the left leg to that of the right leg, so he could only walk a few inches. So there was Robert with this cross-gartered figure hopping around the room. The two of them were as dandified and foppish as anything I'd ever seen." Lifson hated the "Contact" show so much that he went home and wrote a scathing reassessment of Mapplethorpe in *The Village Voice* headlined "The Philistine Photographer": "Everything about this show is hostile. Mapplethorpe's subjects—fleshy, overblown, aestheticized flowers; fashionable people; gay men in the costumes and rites of sado-masochism—exist within a closed circle, are ringed about by Mapplethorpe's glamorous photographic style as surely as the images are framed by his expensive materials. His style equates these various subjects; they become a self-defined elite. Their haughty gazes, their overblown sensuality, their self-satisfied perversion warn us that we can't belong. Emotionally, we can't afford their sex any more than we can pay for their clothes or buy their fame—or Mapplethorpe's pictures. The exhibition condescends to our ordinary lives."

Mapplethorpe was shocked by the review, especially since Lifson had just declared him the "winner" of the "Trade-Off" competition. Yet he finally concluded that Lifson did not like his work because the critic was homophobic, although a reviewer for *Christopher Street,* a gay publication, had been equally appalled by the exhibit and had denounced Mapplethorpe as "a street kid who figures he can make a lot of money by packaging his slick portraits and S&M photographs as art." Lifson thought most of the S&M images weren't effective because they weren't "real" enough. "Actually, when I look back on that show, I think Robert's best picture was the one with the cock and balls and all the blood," he said. "It was a tough-minded observation of something that most people don't know anything about but something that obviously goes on. It was gritty and antiglamorous and it felt honest. The other pictures strike me as being made by somebody who fears what our imagination might make of the subject, and wants to foreclose the imagination's operation. It's like Robert didn't want to give us what he knew. In *Civilization and Its Discontents,* Freud talks about artists who descend into what he calls the maelstrom, meaning the unconscious, and they come back and tell us what was there. Robert went into the maelstrom, no question about it, but he came back with an elegant picture postcard—'Having a wonderful time, wish you were here. Love, Robert.' "

Four years earlier, Patti Smith had warned Clive Davis that she didn't have the strength to wait too long to become a star. Now that she had realized her dreams, she didn't have the stamina to sustain them. "To do this line of work is tough," she admitted in a radio interview for KSAN. "Look at Christ—he only lasted for thirty-three years." The popular success of "Because the Night" had placed enormous pressure on her, and while she publicly ridiculed the song as "commercial shit," the "field marshal of rock and roll" had celebrated her good fortune by purchasing a mink coat. Smith's contradictions had never been so blatantly obvious before. She insisted—some might say a little too stridently—on being viewed as an artist, yet she craved the kind of popular acceptance few artists ever achieve. Consequently, trashing Patti Smith became an increasingly popular sport in the press; critics who had admired her "rock-poetry" accused her of selling out, while those who thought *Easter* represented both an artistic and commercial breakthrough were baffled by her artsy meandering. Smith had ventured into rock and roll with the intention of "getting people to wake up"; it must have been a humbling experience then to realize that when she finally caught America's full attention, her message consisted of "because the night belongs to lovers, because the night belongs to love."

Smith had become increasingly frightened by what she considered the more psychotic strains of punk rock; what had started out as an exhilarating musical adventure had ended in punk's symbolic breakdown when Sid Vicious stabbed his girlfriend, Nancy Spungen, to death in the Chelsea Hotel. Two months later, free on bail, Vicious slashed Smith's brother, Todd, in the face with a broken beer bottle. Frightened and disillusioned, she expressed her feelings in her fourth album, *Wave*, when she recorded a version of the Byrds' "So You Want to Be a Rock 'n' Roll Star." ("But you pay for your riches and fame/Well, it's all a vicious game/It's a little insane.")

Still, she might not have removed herself so quickly from the "vicious game" had she not become involved with a man who roused her fantasies of unconditional love like no other boyfriend before him. Fred (Sonic) Smith had been the rhythm guitarist for the MC5, the Detroit-based group managed by White Panther leader John Sinclair. The "Five," as they were known, were expected to take his convoluted message of rock, dope, and armed self-defense to the airwaves. Sinclair had established a commune in Ann Arbor—"Trans-Love Energies"—where the band lived in an eighteen-room house with a group of women who, according to *Rolling Stone*, provided the "domestic energies" by cooking, cleaning, and sewing their clothing. "It was an astonishing thing," said Danny Fields, who had once promoted the MC5, "because here was this band preaching liberation of all aspects of humanity, of the races, of the sexes, of everything. Then the men would come back from a concert, and they'd sit at a table chomping on spareribs, and the women would be in the kitchen scurrying around. The women didn't eat with the men, except for John Sinclair's wife, who had gone to school and was tough. But the others were these little pansy types in flowered hippie dresses just cooking and serving their men. I don't know if Fred was married then, but they all had 'women.' You couldn't tell one from the other. They were like nonpeople."

The MC5's first and most successful album, *Kick Out the Jams*, was released in 1969, but when Sinclair was imprisoned for possession of marijuana—his conviction was later overturned—the band opted for a less radical direction. British rock critics Julie Burchill and Tony Parsons later vilified their second album, *Back in the USA*, as "pure pop pap sheep-dipped in transparent raiments of youth and rebellion." Their next album, *High Time*, didn't fare much better, and when the MC5 lost their recording contract, Fred Smith decided to strike out on his own. He formed the "Sonic Rendezvous

Band," but while Fred had a reputation as a first-rate guitar player, the group's performances were mostly limited to Detroit. Patti met him there in March 1976 at a record company party given in her honor, and even though she was clearly the Smith with the more promising future, she was immediately drawn to him. "The first night we met," Patti said, "he appeared onstage with us, and I could tell by the way he played what kind of a person he was—better than me, stronger than me."

Fred, who was in his late twenties, was a physical composite of all Patti's previous boyfriends: he had a lean build, sharp features, and center-parted hair that hung below his chin and gave him the appearance of an Amish farmer. There was something equally austere about his personality, as if he had lived too long in the insulated subculture of the MC5 and still longed for a protective cocoon. Fred was born in West Virginia but soon moved to Detroit, and having joined the MC5 when he was still a teenager, he had grown up listening to Sinclair's rhetoric about liberating culture through drugs and "high energy." Smith conducted a secret affair with him for two years, then, in the summer of 1978, she made the final break with Allen Lanier.

Mapplethorpe's friendship with Patti Smith had survived illness, suicide attempts, his revelations of homosexuality, and her reckless fame, but it reached a temporary impasse when Fred entered their lives. Mapplethorpe worried that Fred held too much influence over Patti, who seemingly needed to ask his permission for every move she made. Now that she was Fred's girlfriend, she declined to pose naked for Mapplethorpe and affected an air of modesty that some old friends found difficult to accept. Jim Carroll recalled that when he and Sam Shepard visited her backstage after a poetry reading she made a big issue of telling them to leave the room so she could slip off her jeans. "It wasn't like we hadn't seen her naked before," Carroll said, "and after some of the stuff she used to pull at the Chelsea, the whole virginal thing seemed pretty ridiculous to me."

When *Wave* was released in April 1979, it featured a Mapplethorpe portrait of the singer on the cover. The picture had been taken in Sam Wagstaff's apartment, against the same bare white wall that had served as the backdrop for *Horses*. Unlike the sexually aggressive pose of the first cover, however, Smith now wore a chaste white dress and balanced a pair of doves on her fingers. "I was deeply in love with Fred, and I was becoming more modest in my performing," Smith said. "I didn't have the desire to seduce an audience anymore. Those things were more personal." *Wave* made the Top Twenty after four weeks on the LP chart, and while some critics felt it was a lukewarm follow-up to *Easter*—*Rolling Stone* described it as a "transitional album in the most transient sense of the word"—Smith was satisfied that she had balanced the commercial, or "communicative," as she phrased it, with the artistic. *Wave* was her most personal album—a musical account of a gifted woman's struggle to reconcile her lofty ambitions with an even deeper need for an all-consuming love.

Smith no longer felt that she could give herself completely to the band, and she was so miserable during their five-month tour that she vented her unhappiness at close friends such as Andi Ostrowe. "Patti was absolutely brutal toward me," Ostrowe said. "We've since made up, but those last few months were among the worst of my life. She could rip you to shreds with a few words, and by the end of the tour, we weren't even speaking to each other." Smith was just as brutal toward the audience, and even though she claimed the local papers constantly misquoted her, the press accounts of the band's tour reflect her emotional turmoil. The *Minneapolis Tribune* reported that Smith seemed "dispirited" and quoted her as telling the audience at St. Paul's Civic Center, "I am extremely tired. If you don't like the tired aspect of it, go get your money back and leave me the f . . . alone." *The Boston Globe* complained of her "stream-of-conscious, oftentimes scatterbrained jabber" that produced a "flat, leaden spectacle." The *San Francisco Examiner* described her as looking "like a crazy woman," and reported that she threatened to slap a writer during a news conference. The *San Francisco Chronicle* described a poetry reading in which Smith failed to read a single poem, and instead "prattled on in a stoned manner before a standing-room-only crowd at the Boarding House." *Newsday* thought she seemed "closer to demagoguery than ever," and that "her ego seemed both monstrous and frayed." Several times she broke down in tears when reciting the opening lines of "Gloria"— "Jesus died for somebody's sins but not mine"—and eventually couldn't sing the song anymore. Curiously, she had recently added

Pope John Paul I to her pantheon of superheroes; he had died within a month of his election as pope, and Smith, who had watched him wave from a balcony in Rome the previous year, had been so taken by his simple piety that she wrote the song "Wave" for him. The album, which began with Smith's buoyant "Hi, hello" in the first cut, "Frederick," ended with the poignant words, "Bye papa."

At the end of the summer the band went to Europe, where she had been a bigger star than in the United States. Their final concert in Florence, Italy, attracted a massive crowd of eighty thousand—the largest Smith had ever played for—and she pulled herself together to give one of the most rousing performances of her career. She ended the set with Pete Townshend's "My Generation," and when the band unfurled an American flag, members of the audience began to rush the stage. At first the police pushed them back because they thought a riot had broken out, but it soon became apparent that Smith's fans loved her so much that they only wanted to be closer to her. Before the police cleared them away, they encircled the stage and sat, adoringly, at Smith's feet.

Later that evening, while members of the band were still riding high from the concert, Smith made a stunning announcement: she was abandoning the group. "We were sitting in the hotel watching TV," bass player and guitarist Ivan Kral recalled, "and she told us, 'Okay, boys, this is it.' I couldn't believe it. We had stood by Patti after she had broken her neck, and now that we were finally making some money after all these years, she was quitting on us. I was so frustrated I started to cry."

Smith's decision to abandon her career prompted speculation about her health, and it was widely assumed that she had a drug problem; but it was mainly her addiction to Fred Smith that resulted in her defection from the band. She had made the decision to leave even before she had recorded *Wave,* and while she kept her plans secret, she had scattered clues throughout the album. In addition to the record's title and the love song "Frederick," in which she bid farewell to her fans, she had included the following Rilke quote in the album's liner notes: "For one human being to love another, that is perhaps the most difficult of our tasks." She had always been susceptible to the notion that loving a man involved great self-sacrifice; now she had the opportunity to make the kind of grand gesture that would ensure her place alongside Modigliani's mistress, whose picture she had also featured in the liner notes. Many of her closest friends blamed Fred for the demise of her career; they believed he pressured her into quitting, and that their relationship was predicated on her acceptance of the traditional "little woman" role. Patti, however, was perfectly capable of romanticizing even the bleakest scenario. Two years earlier, in an interview with *Melody Maker,* she had talked of her fascination with Jeanne Moreau, and described a movie in which the actress played a chaste schoolteacher: "She zeroes in on this Italian lumberjack who's scorned by the town because he's coarse . . . but she really wants him. And by the end of the movie, she's so possessed that she'll do anything to get him. She, in the end, is going to be the victorious one because she came after him. And she's crawling because she *wants* to crawl."

So in the end Patti Smith traded her public life for a private one in Detroit, and in March 1980 she and Fred were married in a church ceremony with only their parents in attendance. For the first year she kept in touch with Mapplethorpe and other friends by telephone. During one conversation with Janet Hamill, she confided that she missed New York so much that she hadn't experienced such unhappiness since the revelation of Mapplethorpe's homosexuality years earlier. By the time she gave birth to her son Jackson in 1982, however, the phone calls had stopped; when friends tried to reach her, they discovered that she had changed her number to an unlisted one. Letters were returned "Addressee Unknown." Once, while in Detroit, Sandy Daley went looking for her, but Mrs. Fred Smith was nowhere to be found.

PART FOUR

Blacks and Whites

CHAPTER SIXTEEN

"He was looking for the Platonic ideal."

—*Kelly Edey, about Robert Mapplethorpe*

"Once you go black, you can never go back."

—*Robert Mapplethorpe*

The trajectory of Robert Mapplethorpe and Patti Smith's friendship had spanned nearly two decades, but as the eighties approached, their parallel lives diverged. She sought anonymity while he still coveted the limelight, and he was baffled by her calculated disappearing act. "Robert worried that Patti hadn't been strong enough to handle the fame," said writer Kathy Acker, who shared his fascination with the seamier side of downtown culture. "To me, she was the greatest, a really powerful woman, but Robert didn't see her that way. He told me, 'Maybe I shouldn't have pushed her to be a star.' I think he still really loved her, but he didn't understand the choices she had made."

Equally puzzling to Mapplethorpe was Sam Wagstaff's relationship with San Francisco hairdresser and makeup artist Jim Nelson, which, contrary to plan, had blossomed into something beyond a sexual dalliance. Mapplethorpe had succeeded in undermining

Wagstaff's friendship with Gérald Incandela, but now he had Nelson to contend with. Nelson had quit his job at Elizabeth Arden and was ensconced in Wagstaff's penthouse, cooking meals for the older man, taking care of his cats, and referring to him affectionately as "my Sammi." It was a plot worthy of a soap opera, and in fact, Nelson was doing hair and makeup for the TV soap opera *As the World Turns.* "Jim was a trick who ended up staying," Klaus Kertess explained. Indeed, Wagstaff was so embarrassed by him that many people didn't even know they were living together. Paul Walter recalled: "Sam once told me the only reason he was with Jim was that he didn't know how to get rid of him." But at fifty-five, Wagstaff may have wanted a marriage of sorts, and while Nelson could not hold forth on minimalism or quote Wallace Stevens, Wagstaff's favorite poet, he loved and adored his "Sammi."

Mapplethorpe had fashioned a life for himself that precluded love, yet he, too, sometimes worried that he would end up alone. "Just because I was out at the bars all the time didn't mean I wasn't looking for someone to love," he said. "I wanted that as much as anyone else . . . only it was hard for me." It was nearly impossible, in fact, for the same dramatic tension that pervades his work—the push-pull of black and white, good and evil, Catholicism and homosexuality—was emotionally tearing him apart. He was still the same fragmented man depicted in his 1971 self-portrait in which he had photographed three separate portions of his body, then enclosed them behind a paper bag "cage." Mapplethorpe wanted to escape, but to where, and to whom?

The answer was literally black and white, for he became infatuated with a Caucasian female bodybuilder at the same time he declared his passion for black men. In doing so, he had effectively solved two problems: he had found a new muse to replace Patti Smith, and a new area of sexual exploration to succeed the leather bars. Black, white, male, female—the possibilities were endless.

Mapplethorpe thought of himself as "mostly homosexual," but he enjoyed the company of women, and bodybuilder Lisa Lyon was the ultimate female consort. He met her in late 1979 at a SoHo party, where she caught his eye with a black rubber outfit that encased her powerful body like a second skin. In contrast to her strong physique,

Lyon had a surprisingly delicate face—reddish brown curls framed creamy-white skin, high cheekbones, and a chiseled jaw. Though she had recently won the "First World's Women's Bodybuilding Championship," she was hardly a stereotypical athlete, and regularly took the psychedelic drug PCP ("angel dust"); she quoted Carlos Castaneda, R. D. Laing, and William Blake; and she counted among her friends Henry Miller and former Black Panther leader Huey Newton.

Mapplethorpe invited her to Bond Street the following afternoon for a photo session, and she appeared at his door in a miniskirt, thigh-high leather boots, and a wide-brimmed hat decorated with feathers. He immediately responded to what was then an exotic notion—a muscular woman—by photographing her in the frilly hat, flexing her biceps. "I had never seen a woman like that before," he explained. "It was like looking at someone from another planet."

He had used the same words to describe Patti Smith, and while the two women were physical opposites, both had a proclivity for strange and unusual behavior. The daughter of an affluent Beverly Hills oral surgeon, Lyon had been an intellectually gifted child who, like Smith, had suffered from terrifying hallucinations. In attempting to gain control over her visions, Lyon developed compulsive rituals, such as running around the house counterclockwise, and tapping on furniture hundreds of times. Ultimately she would be diagnosed as having manic-depression, the disease Joan Mapplethorpe was thought to suffer from, but throughout high school and college she attempted to slow down her brain waves by taking large amounts of angel dust. She majored in anthropology at UCLA, where she joined the school's kendo team because the men reminded her of "ancient warriors in a Kurosawa movie." She was the only woman in the sport, and after collapsing in tears when a teammate repeatedly hit her with a bamboo sword, she vowed never to think of herself as a weak female again.

Lyon began working out at Gold's Gym in Santa Monica, which was owned by bodybuilder Ken Sprague, who was then attempting to transform the gym's gay beefcake image by attracting professional athletes such as Arnold Schwarzenegger and Lou Ferrigno. Gay or straight, however, Gold's was not receptive to the opposite sex, as women were thought to be hormonally incapable of building muscle mass, and Lyon, at five foot three, 102 pounds, was not a likely candidate to debunk that myth. Moreover, she didn't appear to be mentally tough enough. Her father was then dying of pancreatic cancer, and her brief marriage to a music-ethnology teacher had recently ended in divorce when her husband was jailed for selling heroin. Yet driven by her compulsive behavior, she began rigorously counting bicep curls and leg lifts, and when she was too wired to fall asleep at night, she exercised on the trapeze hanging from the ceiling of her apartment. Instead of steroids, she used LSD, which she claimed helped reprogram her cellular structure and made it possible for her to dead-lift 265 pounds and squat 285. "I was using LSD to resculpt myself," she said. "Not only was I leaping forward in my body, but I was having visionary experiences. I was going into zones you can't even talk about to people."

Lyon became an instant celebrity when she won the bodybuilding championship in 1979 and immediately signed up with the high-powered IMG sports-management group. Strong, yet feminine enough not to alienate the women who were beginning to incorporate weight training into their fitness routines, she was a potential marketing gold mine, and plans were quickly under way for an exercise book and even a new perfume. Lyon, however, was unwilling to play the game for even a short time, and convinced she would probably lose her title, she decided against defending it. Consequently she was a has-been even before her name received wide recognition, but she had never dreamed of being an athlete in the first place. She saw herself more as a sculptor who used her own body as raw material. Her meeting with Mapplethorpe, then, was serendipitous, for she was searching for a photographer to document her "work-in-progress."

Mapplethorpe, coincidentally, was searching for ways to change his gay S&M image, and as part of that effort, he had met several times with freelance editor Jim Clyne, who suggested he do a photography book on women. Mapplethorpe worried that he wouldn't be able to contribute anything original to the subject, and he confided to Clyne that the female pubic region was so unattractive to him that he couldn't imagine photographing full-frontal nudes. Eventually they arrived at an idea that appealed to Mapplethorpe's homoerotic aesthetic: a book entitled "Small-Breasted Women."

Subsequent brainstorming sessions were geared to defining "small-breasted." Mapplethorpe wondered if women who wore bras should be automatically disqualified, or if "small" meant totally flat. He even worked out on a piece of paper the exact nipple-to-breast ratio of the ideal candidate. Clyne sent numerous models to his studio, but after he had taken their pictures, he would reject their breasts for one reason or another. Luckily, during the interim, he met Lyon, and they began a photographic collaboration that would lead to the book *Lady*.

After their first photo session together, Lyon returned home to Los Angeles, but she spoke with Mapplethorpe regularly on the phone. His homosexuality was not regarded by either of them as a barrier to a potential romance. "I never thought of it as an issue," Lyon said. "It didn't matter. I was totally entranced by him. Everybody loved Robert in a weird way. When they got to know him better, they might hate him, but not in the beginning. He could be cruel and nasty, but you had to forgive him, because he was a genius, a visionary, a revolutionary; he did things other people would never dream of doing, violated every taboo. Wasn't it William Blake who said, 'The road of excess leads to the palace of wisdom?' "

During the past year Mapplethorpe's travels had taken him away from the predominantly Caucasian world of gay S&M to an even smaller subculture composed of gay white men attracted to black men. By 1980, in the throes of what he called "black fever," he claimed white men no longer interested him sexually. "Once you go black," he said, parroting the cliché, "you can never go back." He began frequenting Keller's, a former S&M bar on West Street that was now a social gathering place for men interested in biracial sex; whites were known as "dinge queens," blacks "dairy queens." Two thirds of the patrons were working-class blacks who were drawn to Keller's because it afforded one of the few opportunities to meet other gay men. John L. Peterson, in an essay, "Black Men and Their Same-Sex Desires and Behaviors," examines the difficulties faced by blacks in reconciling their sexual orientation with their racial identity. In addition to the antiblack bias of the gay community—Peterson described the process of "carding" nonwhites for admission to certain gay bars—blacks confront the antigay prejudice of the black community, which has been influenced by fundamentalist church teaching and by gender roles in black culture that stress the importance of marriage and procreation. This, combined with the high rate of unemployment among black men, which has stripped them of economic power, has further diminished their status.

Consequently, the scene at Keller's was complicated by certain realities prevalent in the culture at large; the white patrons had money; the blacks did not. What the blacks had, however—or so went the myth—was an exotic, "primitive" sexuality that lured the white men to Keller's the way affluent whites were once drawn to Harlem's Cotton Club. Mapplethorpe went to the bar at least four times a week, and was usually joined there by Winthrop "Kelly" Edey, an art historian and international authority on antique clocks, and John Abbott, who had recently left his job at the Sonnabend Gallery in Paris. Both men had impeccable social credentials and looked as if they would be more comfortable at the Union Club than at a seedy bar on West Street, but they, too, had been infected by "black fever" and spent hours with Mapplethorpe discussing their favorite subject: the physical superiority of the black male.

Once Mapplethorpe began photographing blacks, he found to his delight that he could extract a greater richness from the color of their skin. Kelly Edey shared Mapplethorpe's feelings: "For one thing, the texture of a black man's skin is different. The most beautiful black bodies have a thin layer of fat all over them which gives an amazing consistency to the musculature and to the surface of the body. Another thing about black bodies at their best is the broadness of shoulders in proportion to the narrowness of the hips. Then, of course, there's the size of the cock. The average black cock *is* bigger. I don't think people realize how hard Robert worked to find the perfect one. He examined thousands and thousands of them."

George Stambolian once heard Mapplethorpe describe the perfect black phallus in such detail that he had even worked out the ideal measurement of the tiny opening at the tip of the glans through which the urethra carries urine and semen. "Robert had drawn a picture of a penis on a chart," Stambolian recalled, "and he was like a surgeon, using medical terms like 'corpus spongiosum.' I was impressed by his dedication." But in those rare instances when Mapplethorpe found the ideal phallus, he was usually dissatisfied with another part of the man's anatomy. Perhaps he had too much of a "prison build"—the upper body too large for the hips—or perhaps his skin color was too muddy, or his legs too short. "When the ancients did a painting or a sculpture of a god," Edey explained, "they often took parts from different models—a hand, or a leg, or a face. Robert couldn't do that as a photographer, so he needed to find everything in one person. He was searching for the Platonic ideal."

Mapplethorpe's method of seduction varied little from night to night; since black leather was not standard attire among black gays, he dressed in jeans and a simple shirt, then, arriving at Keller's after midnight, he would order a beer and stake out a position in front of the bar so he could watch the men walk in the door. He had nicknames for all the regulars—"Pail and Shovel," "Mutton Chops," "Pigeon." After twenty minutes of gossiping with Kelly Edey and John Abbott, he would saunter to the far end of the bar, light a cigarette, and fix his eyes on the most desirable person in the room, staring so intently the chosen man was compelled to approach him. "Robert's eyes just blazed whenever he saw a person whom he thought was spectacularly beautiful," Edey said. "I was trying to find a word for that intense look on Robert's face, and I finally realized it was the same word they used to describe Michelangelo's eyes—*terribilità*."

Mapplethorpe's charisma was enhanced considerably by the vial of cocaine he kept in his back pocket and waved at the appropriate moment. Some of the men at Keller's were there for the sole purpose of procuring drugs, and even if they weren't homosexual, they were amenable to trading sex for coke. Others went home with Mapplethorpe because they knew he was a photographer and they hoped they might be able to make some money modeling for him. Curiously, while Edey maintained that both he and Mapplethorpe longed to be "swept away by a black superstud," the men Mapplethorpe wound up with were often small and slightly built.

One of his first black lovers was Phillip Prioleau, who had a slender, nicely proportioned body and a sweet, melancholy face. Prioleau needed money, so Mapplethorpe hired him to spot his prints, which involves correcting the tiny white marks that result from specks of dust on the negative. He occasionally modeled for him, too, and in one picture he climbed atop an oak plant stand and posed as a bronze on a pedestal. This, and other photographs, gave rise to the criticism that Mapplethorpe exploited and objectified his black models. Recognizing the possibility of a racist interpretation of his work, he discussed the situation with David Hershkovits in *Soho Weekly News:* "It has to be racist. I'm white and they are black. There is a difference somehow, but it doesn't have to be negative. Is there any difference in approaching a black man who doesn't have clothes on and a white man who doesn't have clothes on? Not really, it's form and what you see into that and do with it. I do the same thing. I'm not trying to do it a different way."

What happened when black men ceased to be "form" was a different matter entirely. Mapplethorpe referred to his Platonic ideal as "Super Nigger," and told John Abbott he longed to find a black man who was "free enough" to allow him to repeat the pejorative word in bed. "I've always liked to talk dirty," he explained. "It's like magic words, forbidden words. The idea that someone white would call them 'nigger' worked consistently with blacks. It made their cocks jump." When he discussed his work with art critics and journalists, he addressed the aesthetics of dark skin, but with friends at Keller's he talked about the way blacks smelled different from whites; the size of their lips and genitals; how he could always "catch a nigger with coke"; and which blacks were "gorillas." He and his friends weren't interested in middle-class blacks, because then, according to Abbott, "they weren't black anymore." Consequently it was nearly impossible for Mapplethorpe to find someone who could fit comfortably into his social world. "Robert's leitmotif was how unbelievably and impossibly stupid they all were," said Edey. "We called it 'the curse of beauty.' There was an inverse proportion between mental development and cock size. The most beautiful ones didn't seem to develop their brains much. Robert came to just accept it as a fact of life that the ones he was attracted to sexually and as a photographer weren't going to have much upstairs. So we did a lot of sitting around wringing our hands. And then somebody would walk through the door, and we'd say, 'My God, did you see that?' There was a sense of obligation. If somebody is that beautiful you have to capture them on film, like catching a total solar eclipse."

. . .

From the time Mapplethorpe entered his "black period," he made a concerted effort to study the work of other photographers who had taken pictures of black male nudes. He didn't regard this as "stealing" other photographers' ideas or techniques, but rather as creating a library of images in his subconscious from which he could occasionally borrow. "I like to look at pictures, all kinds," he said in *Portrait: Theory.* "And all those things you absorb come out subconsciously one way or another. You'll be taking photographs and suddenly know that you have resources from having looked at a lot of them before. There is no way you can avoid this. But this kind of subconscious influence is good, and it certainly can work for one. In fact, the more pictures you see, the better you are as a photographer." Photographic images of the black male nude, however, were relatively rare. Of the 134 images in Constance Sullivan's *Nude: Photographs 1850–1980,* the black male is not represented at all. Given the taboo against male nudity in general, white heterosexuals were not inclined to celebrate the erotic properties of the black male body. And since blacks rarely had the financial resources to become art photographers, it was left to gay white men to present their vision of the black male nude.

F. Holland Day, who had shocked nineteenth-century Boston with his staged crucifixion scenes, was one of the first Americans to photograph the black male nude. Day's fascination with male beauty was evident in the highly stylized portraits of black models that comprised the "Nubian series." His photograph of a black man dressed as an Ethiopian chief in a striped African robe and feathered headdress was featured by Alfred Stieglitz in the October 1897 issue of *Camera Notes;* Day's biographer, Estelle Jussim, cited the picture as "one of the first photographic embodiments of the idea that 'Black is beautiful.' " In his photograph *Ebony and Ivory,* Day further explored the erotic properties of the black body by contrasting the model's dark skin with the white figurine he holds in his hand. Allen Ellenzweig, in *The Homoerotic Photograph,* emphasizes Mapplethorpe's debt to Day: "Certainly Day proffered the black male as a desirable sexual object, aesthetic in himself, worthy of admiration, and, to those open to the possibility, likely to spur sexual longing. What we have here is a forerunner of Robert Mapplethorpe."

In the years between Day and Mapplethorpe, the black male nude was largely invisible, and the pictures that existed were usually done in secret. George Platt Lynes took photographs of black nudes in the early 1950s, but these didn't surface until several decades later. With so few historical antecedents, Mapplethorpe turned to the work of such contemporary photographers as Craig Anderson, who produced pictures of black men for several pornographic magazines. Anderson lived in San Francisco but regularly visited Keller's to search for models. He and Mapplethorpe were planning to produce a pornographic magazine themselves, but after the two men had a falling out, the project was discontinued. "The magazine wasn't going to be an art piece to be exhibited at the Whitney," said Kelly Edey, "but real porn to be sold on Forty-second Street."

Through Edey, Mapplethorpe made contact with Miles Everett, a seventy-year-old retired electrical engineer from Los Angeles who was considered "the grand old man of the black male nude." Everett was a member of a club called Black and White Men Together (BWMT) and had been photographing black men since the early thirties, when he was employed by the Defense Department. He kept his photographs private for fear of losing his job, but among gay white Americans attracted to blacks, he was an underground celebrity. Mapplethorpe flew to Los Angeles to meet Everett and purchased twenty of his prints. At Everett's suggestion, he eventually began to photograph his black models against black backdrop paper instead of gray, to enhance the skin's highlights.

George Dureau was another photographer whose work attracted Mapplethorpe's attention; Dureau, a resident of New Orleans, had a curious relationship to his models, many of whom were dwarves and amputees. "I ran a little kingdom where I was an esteemed patriarch," he said, "and the blacks were like natives of my village." Dureau often met his models by driving through the city in his pickup truck and offering to give them a ride; his photographs were strategically placed in the backseat. "They'd look at them and say, 'What a coincidence! I have a missing leg, too,' " Dureau explained. "Then I'd offer to photograph them. Almost everyone on earth wants to be remembered." When Mapplethorpe saw a picture of Dureau's longtime lover, Wilbert Hines, nicknamed "Wing Ding," whose left arm had been amputated at the elbow, he wrote to the photographer and asked if he could buy the photograph. He then invited Dureau to New York, where the two men discussed their approach to the subject of black men. Dureau explained that he viewed his models' handicaps as visual metaphors, and that despite their disabilities, he saw them as vibrant, sexual creatures. Dureau spent only a short time taking pictures; most of his efforts, he said, were directed at understanding the model as a human being. "Okay," Mapplethorpe interrupted, "but what's your feeling about their armpits?" Dureau was appalled by his single-minded focus on sex. "I was searching for the greatest universal truths," he said, "and Robert was searching for pungent armpits."

Mapplethorpe's decision to photograph black men made him even more particular about the quality of his prints, and while he had worked with various printers over the years, he had finally settled on one—Tom Baril, a recent graduate of the School of Visual Arts, who had turned to printing to support his own fledgling photography career. Mapplethorpe had hired Baril in June 1979, based on a ten-minute interview during which he had set forth the ground rules: "My lifestyle is bizarre, but the only thing you need to know is where the darkroom is. You come in, you print, you go home."

Thus began a strange ten-year relationship between two people who could not have been more opposite. Baril was a hard-drinking, good-old-boy type who referred to gays as "fags" and who thought Mapplethorpe's lifestyle disgusting. "All Robert wanted to do was to fuck his models, then photograph them," Baril said. "He was documenting his life and sticking it in front of everybody's faces, daring them to say something about it." Perhaps sensing Baril's hostility, Mapplethorpe confined him to the darkroom, but Baril, knowing his employer was too intimidated to confront him directly, delighted in disobeying him. Mapplethorpe, then, would send a message through a third party directing Baril to "stay in the darkroom." From Mapplethorpe's perspective, it was the ultimate put-down, as he derived great pleasure from having made a name for himself as a photographer without ever making a print.

Mapplethorpe avoided the darkroom, but he had definite ideas about printing. "He wanted everything to look beautiful," Baril said. "Flowers . . . faces . . . blacks—it all had to look beautiful." Taking a cue from classical sculpture, he expected white skin to approximate marble, and black skin the color of bronze. Baril was directed to "dodge" (selectively lighten) the white faces to obscure any imperfections, and to "burn in" (selectively darken) the blacks; he then printed portraits of whites on Ilfobrom, a "cold" paper, and blacks on Portriga-Rapid, which Mapplethorpe preferred for its warm tones. Eventually the two men worked out a system that allowed them to keep contact to a minimum, and days would go by without Mapplethorpe having to say anything more to Baril than "dodge" or "burn." Baril attributed the success of their long collaboration to his own detachment from Mapplethorpe's photographs. "It might have been more difficult working with stuff I cared about," he said. "This way I only had to worry about making technical judgments. Is it a good print, or not?"

Mapplethorpe's show "Blacks and Whites" opened at the Lawson de Celle Gallery in San Francisco on March 25, exactly two years after Don Lawson had rejected the "Censored" exhibit. Lawson was not much happier with the new pictures and, according to Edward de Celle, strenuously objected to three images—*Bobby and Larry Kissing,* a photograph of Mapplethorpe's friends Bobby Miller and Larry DeSmedt kissing each other on the lips, and two pictures of erect penises. "During the reception, Don was made so uncomfortable by the pictures that he wouldn't go into the room where they were hanging," de Celle recalled. "I remember someone shouting, 'Ann Getty is coming up the stairs!' Well, Don was horrified. He said, 'Ann Getty can't come in here and see this, it's horrible.' Well, the next thing I know Don and several other gay men who knew Mrs. Getty socially were running down the fire escape."

De Celle understood the importance Mapplethorpe placed on being surrounded by the "right people," so he arranged for him to stay in a small cottage on Nob Hill that was owned by Anita Mardikian, and he gave the photographer a dinner party to which he had invited Lita Veitor and Katharine Cebrian, two of the city's grande dames. De Celle also set up a portrait shoot with Cebrian, although afterward he had second thoughts about it. "Katharine was San Francisco royalty," de Celle explained. "Everybody always wanted to do her portrait, and she usually turned them down. She abhorred bad manners and anything she considered 'inappropriate.' " De Celle trusted that Mapplethorpe would have the good sense to forgo his black leather jacket in favor of the green velvet he sometimes wore for social occasions—"the Bill Blass," as Mapplethorpe called it. De Celle was horrified when the photographer arrived at Cebrian's door in black leather and studded "SHIT" belt. "I held my breath," he said, but then Mapplethorpe worked his quiet charms on the elderly woman. He toured her house, admired the Renoir and Titian, and continued talking softly to her while he set up his tripod in the sitting room. Cebrian was attending a black-tie benefit at the Convent of the Sacred Heart later that evening, so she was dressed in a long, flowing black caftan accessorized with an ornate gold-and-coral necklace. Mapplethorpe placed her in a window seat, with her face in profile. He liked to begin with a profile shot because he thought it was the most natural, and from there he could rotate the head to locate the most becoming pose. He usually found the three-quarter angle flattering to most people, but in Cebrian's case he remained with the profile, as it emphasized her distinctive nose, with its suggestion of nobility and power.

Cebrian enjoyed the photo session so much that afterward she asked Mapplethorpe to escort her to the Convent of the Sacred Heart benefit. "I do wonder if he has something else to wear?" she whispered to de Celle, but Mapplethorpe went to the benefit dressed exactly as he was, and although one society figure turned her back on him, Cebrian introduced him to all her friends. "You wouldn't think Robert would go to a benefit at a Catholic girls school," de Celle said, "but he never turned down an opportunity to see different worlds. He was such an excellent observer, and he showed more interest in other people than anyone I've ever met. That's what made his pictures so good, and why so many different people responded to him."

Lisa Lyon had attended the "Blacks and Whites" opening, and afterward she and Mapplethorpe drove to the Joshua Tree National Monument near Palm Springs, where they had hoped to do a photo session in the desert. Mapplethorpe had never learned how to drive, so he sat in the passenger seat as Lyon navigated the car directly into a sandstorm; by the time they finally arrived at Joshua Tree, it was nearing sunset, and Mapplethorpe had to move quickly to take advantage of the remaining light. The desert was studded with huge geometric boulders shaped like pyramids, ovals, and cylinders, and even though Mapplethorpe had never been to Joshua Tree before, he had obviously seen similar landscapes in Edward Weston's photographs. He began climbing the rocks with his camera and tripod while Lyon undressed in the car, and having no time to put on cosmetics, she attempted to make her body gleam by pouring a bottle of baby oil over it. Naked and shivering in the forty-degree weather, she scrambled atop the rocks, and with the wind blowing sand in her face she struck a series of bodybuilding poses. Mapplethorpe then directed her to lie down on a boulder, and, as with a Weston nude, he drew an analogy between the curve of her body and the sculptural form of the landscape.

Afterward, covered in scrub brush, sand, and black leather, they checked into a Palm Springs hotel, where the management at first was reluctant to give them a room. "I looked in the mirror, and I was completely covered in oil," Lyon recalled, "and my black leather pants were sticking to my skin. Everybody was giving us the strangest looks, so we took acid to make it okay." That night they celebrated their creative union by making love, and even though Lyon was worried that Mapplethorpe might react by emotionally withdrawing from her, she found him to be "gracious and respectful the whole way." They fantasized about getting married and moving to a big house where they could live in separate wings. "He was really sweet," she said. "He'd do things like hold my hand, and I think we truly loved each other. But it was hard, because he never really expressed his emotions in words, and you were left deciphering his silences."

When Mapplethorpe returned to New York after several weeks in California, he fell back into the routine of going to Keller's every night. He was becoming so obsessed in his pursuit of black men that if he saw an attractive candidate in a club or a restaurant he would abandon his companions in midsentence and take off like a hunting dog. Tom Baril witnessed a steady parade of black men entering and leaving the loft. "If Robert spent the night with someone," Baril said, "he'd totally ignore them the next morning. He was just using these guys." Mapplethorpe told his friend Bobby Miller that he sometimes became so desperate for sexual contact that he prowled the Bowery picking up homeless black men. "Don't you care about getting diseases?" Miller asked him, but Mapplethorpe dismissed the notion. "They're okay if you give them a bath," he said, "and besides, they're the least likely people to have diseases because nobody else wants them."

By the end of the summer he had grown more despairing about his inability to find his Platonic ideal. "I was having a conversation with Robert and Craig Anderson about how difficult it was to find the perfect body," Kelly Edey recalled. "We spoke of this as a manifestation of the divine. If you're of a religious temperament, then insofar as you live your life through your eyes, you will believe that these glimpses of beauty are manifestations of God. Craig then went to Boston for a week and discovered a beautiful model named Carlos. 'I've found God in Boston,' he told us. Robert and I cried endlessly on each other's shoulders about the impossibility of that happening to us, because we, too, wanted to worship the body of a god."

CHAPTER SEVENTEEN

"He had the face of a beautiful animal."

—*Robert Mapplethorpe, about Milton Moore*

Robert Mapplethorpe found "god" in a gay bar called Sneakers one drizzly September evening in 1980 after leaving Keller's. He looked in the window of the bar and saw a young black man staring forlornly at the legion of gay men walking up and down West Street. Overcome by a sudden urge to take the stranger home, Mapplethorpe slipped into the bar, and leaning against a wall, he fixed his "Michelangelo" gaze in the man's direction.

Milton Moore had just finished playing pinball, and he was resting a few minutes before taking the subway to a friend's apartment on the Upper West Side. Turning around to pick up his jacket, he noticed a scrawny white man smoking a cigarette, his eyes ablaze. The intensity of Mapplethorpe's stare frightened him, so he quickly left the bar and began running up Christopher Street toward the Sheridan Square subway station. Mapplethorpe chased after him, dodging the other men sauntering up and down the sidewalk. Mapplethorpe was panicked that he would lose sight of the man, that he would disappear into the subway and be gone forever. Catching up with Moore before he crossed the street, Mapplethorpe fumbled for his business card. "I'm Robert Mapplethorpe," he said. The name meant nothing to Moore, who instinctively backed away from him. "Please," he implored. "I don't want no trouble."

Mapplethorpe offered a few soothing words and invited him to dinner at a coffee shop near the subway station. It was three A.M., and when Moore told him, "I've already had dinner," Mapplethorpe quickly adjusted the plan to include a "late-night breakfast." Over French toast and coffee, he learned the basic facts of Moore's life: he was twenty-five years old, a native of Jackson, Tennessee, and one of thirteen children. He had recently left the navy and needed to find a job, as he was quickly running through his small savings. "Have you ever thought of modeling?" Mapplethorpe casually asked. Moore admitted that even though his specialty was radio tele-type he had indeed taken a few modeling courses at the Barbizon School in San Diego. That was all Mapplethorpe needed, and he immediately offered to help Moore put together a portfolio. "When do you want to do that?" Moore asked, to which Mapplethorpe replied, "Well, we could do it now."

Bond Street's eerie atmosphere made Moore uncomfortable, and he wondered if he had misjudged his new friend. His head buzzed from the cocaine Mapplethorpe kept offering him, and he sat in a chair in the living room, gripping the armrests with his fingers. Moore later claimed that he had never had a homosexual relation-ship before, and while his presence in a gay bar might indicate other-wise, he seemed genuinely confused by Mapplethorpe's advances. His naïveté deeply touched Mapplethorpe, who was even more con-vinced that he had discovered the "primitive" of his dreams. "When I looked into his eyes," he gushed, "I saw a pure soul."

What he experienced when he finally coaxed Moore into disrob-ing was an even greater revelation: he possessed the only phallus that had ever approximated the photographer's ideal. But, embarrassed by his generous proportions and afraid of disgracing his family, Moore wouldn't allow Mapplethorpe to take pictures of him until the photographer agreed that he would never show his face and genitals together in the same photograph. Disappearing into the bedroom, Mapplethorpe returned with a pillowcase, which he then placed over Moore's head before proceeding to shoot several rolls of film. Afterward he had Moore sign a release form in which he granted "Robert Mapplethorpe, a photographer, the right to take photographs of me."

When Mapplethorpe returned to Keller's, he told Kelly Edey and John Abbott that he had found the "great love of my life." In addition to Moore's physical attributes, including legs that Mapplethorpe likened to those of a horse, and "the face of a beautiful animal," he had a sweet, innocent personality that fed into the stereotype of the noble savage. Mapplethorpe wanted to protect him from the world, and he was given an opportunity to do that when Moore reluctantly admitted that he was AWOL from the navy. Having already served one term of duty, Moore had reenlisted so he could visit the Far East again, but when the navy stationed him in Virginia he felt betrayed and ran away to New York. "Had I known about it when I first met him," Mapplethorpe said, "I probably would have stayed away. I'm not attracted to disasters." But his emotional entanglements had always been marked by high drama, and in choosing Moore he had set himself up for the biggest calamity yet. The idea of Moore behind bars struck at the heart of Mapplethorpe's noble-savage fixation; he could hardly sleep at night worrying that naval authorities would swoop down on Bond Street and whisk the "pure soul" off to jail.

Mapplethorpe had become friendly with Cuban-born artist Agustin Fernandez and his wife, Lia, and often turned to the middle-aged couple for advice. Lia put him in touch with a lawyer in Alexandria, Virginia, who was willing to handle Moore's case, and then arranged for Moore to stay with Ramon Osuna, a Washington art dealer and Agustin's cousin.

Since Mapplethorpe had a show at the Galerie Jurka in Amsterdam on November 2, he couldn't accompany Moore to Washington. "Please, don't let me go alone," Moore begged him. But Mapplethorpe couldn't disappoint Rob Jurka, who had been one of his earliest supporters in Europe, having exhibited his work the previous year and published a catalogue of it. So Moore went off alone to face his court martial, and Mapplethorpe went off to Amsterdam with Sam Wagstaff for the opening of "Black Males." No sooner had they arrived in Amsterdam than Mapplethorpe received a telephone call from a frantic Lia Fernandez telling him that Moore refused to meet with naval authorities and was threatening to return to New York. "Ask him what it will take for him to stay in Washington," Mapplethorpe said. "I'll do anything." A few days later Lia called back with Moore's request: he wanted a brand new military uniform for the hearing. Mapplethorpe sent him the money, then nervously awaited the results of the navy's investigation. Moore spent a week at Bethesda Naval Hospital under psychiatric observation, then two months in a detention center, after which he was awarded a medical discharge. "Milton was very pleased he didn't have to go to jail," said his lawyer, Michael Leiberman. "He left the navy feeling he hadn't been disgraced."

Moore returned to New York at the beginning of 1981, but his erratic behavior did not bode well for the New Year. He would lapse into a trancelike state for hours at a time, then suddenly become so agitated he would rip the clothing off his back. Mapplethorpe rationalized the dramatic change by chalking it up to Moore's inability to adjust to his new environment. "He had come from a straitjacketed military life into my world," he said. "And mind you, I was also feeding him drugs." Mapplethorpe's sexual activities, no doubt, added another layer of stress, for not only was Moore subjected to the word "nigger," but he also had to cope with his lover's coprophiliac tendencies. Furthermore, he was trapped in a bizarre comedy of manners inspired by the photographer's relationship with Wagstaff. "It was the first time in my life I could have helped somebody," Mapplethorpe explained.

So just as the patrician collector had once helped the aspiring artist from Floral Park, the artist attempted to educate the sailor from Tennessee. Mapplethorpe hired an English tutor for him and, acting upon Wagstaff's ludicrous advice bought him Charles Dickens to read, and John Milton's *Paradise Lost*. The relationship had a doomed quality to it, and Wagstaff cautioned Mapplethorpe about expecting too much from a simple country boy from the South. Perhaps sensing Wagstaff's disapproval, Moore, who carried a paperback dictionary with him everywhere, began referring to him as "Samuel Viperous Wagstaff III." Mapplethorpe was quick to remind Wagstaff that he, too, was involved in a socially inappropriate affair with "Dumb Dora," as he called Jim Nelson, who would soon reach the pinnacle of his career when he was hired to do hair and makeup for *Cats*. At least Moore, Mapplethorpe insisted, was not a screaming queen but a man of rare physical beauty and grace. He encouraged Moore to take advantage of his "natural rhythm" by presenting him with a pair of tap shoes and setting up appointments with several choreographers. When it came time for Moore to audition for them, however, he refused to leave the bedroom despite Mapplethorpe's increasingly emotional entreaties to "dance, Milton, dance."

Mapplethorpe's love/obsession for Moore reached its fullest expression in the photograph some consider his masterpiece—*Man in Polyester Suit*. The picture came about when Moore proudly showed him the three-piece suit he had bought several years before in Korea. It was the most expensive piece of clothing he owned, and he was saving it for a special occasion. Mapplethorpe immediately spotted the flaws in the tailoring, and after persuading Moore to model the suit, he purposely emphasized the shoddy workmanship by lining up Moore's thumb so that it pointed to the spot where the seam ended abruptly on the jacket. "Wouldn't a nigger wear a suit like that?" he commented to John Abbott, when he first showed him the picture. In the photograph, Moore's semierect penis is seen rising from the suit, as if escaping its humble origins. The phallus is the centerpiece of the picture, and Mapplethorpe obviously took great care to arrange the trousers and jacket to highlight what he believed to be Moore's best feature.

He cropped the photograph at Moore's neck according to their agreement, but by isolating the genitals he seemed to be pandering to the notion that blacks existed only as sexual objects. The black gay writer and activist Essex Hemphill delivered the following comments at the OUT WRITE '90 conference: "Mapplethorpe's eye pays special attention to the penis—at the expense of showing us the subject's face, and thus, a whole person. The penis becomes *the* identity of the black male, which is the classic stereotype re-created and presented as *art* in the context of a *gay* vision. . . . What is insulting and endangering to black men on one level is Mapplethorpe's conscious determination that the faces, the heads, and by extension, the minds and experiences of some of his black subjects were not as important as close-up shots of their penises. It is virtually impossible to view Mapplethorpe's photos of black males and avoid confronting issues of exploitation and objectification."

Edmund White, in the introduction to the "Black Males" catalogue published by Galerie Jurka, expressed the opposite view:

When Robert Mapplethorpe looks at black men, he sees them in two of the too few modes of regard available to a white American today: he sees them either esthetically or erotically. . . . There are those liberationists, of course, who would say that whenever a white desires a black some sort of "racism" is occurring, just as supposedly whenever someone older longs for someone younger he must be guilty of "ageism." But such assertions, fine and ringing as they may sound as parade-ground rhetoric, never stand up to the individual case. Because sexual desire, finally, is a form of love. . . . Not love in the sense of sustained social responsibility but love as passion, as appetite, as irrepressible yearning.

White visited Mapplethorpe not long after he had taken *Man in Polyester Suit,* and he was surprised by the depths of the photographer's emotion. Mapplethorpe was telling him about his relationship with Moore when he decided to illustrate the story with the portrait of his lover's genitals. "Now you know why I love him so," he said, his eyes brimming with tears.

The affair with Moore had altered the dynamics of Mapplethorpe's personal relationship with Lisa Lyon, and while he was still fascinated by her body, he was no longer inclined to daydream about marrying her. Their romance had culminated in the desert at Joshua Tree; yet Lyon was a formidable ally, and in the fall of 1980 she had arranged with Ingrid Sischy, who had recently been appointed editor of *Artforum,* to publish a portfolio of Mapplethorpe's pictures of her. Lyon then used the photographs to persuade Viking Press to give them a contract to do *Lady.* She and Mapplethorpe would spend two years working on the book, which Sam Wagstaff later described in the foreword as a "whirlwind tour of one lady's anatomy, and other eccentricities." She posed for Mapplethorpe as a bride, a boxer, a biker, a moll, a fortune-teller, an archer, a scuba diver, and a choir girl; he covered her body with graphite, green clay, leather, and silk, and, in one memorable shot, draped an eighty-five-pound python around her neck. By the end of their "whirlwind tour," however, he had exhausted all the possibilities of Lyon's body, and the highs and lows of her personality were grating on his nerves; he thought she did too many drugs, and at times he could barely follow her manic chatter. During a photo session at the Terry Hill Zoo in New Jersey, he placed her next to an epileptic tiger who had a seizure in the middle of the shoot. "Wouldn't it be great if the tiger ate Lisa," he whispered to Bobby Miller, who was serving as the hair and makeup artist. "That would be the perfect ending for *Lady*."

The book was only one of Mapplethorpe's projects, and his fame was growing both in the United States and Europe. Unlike a painter or a sculptor, he could produce enough work for multiple shows each year, which, in turn, generated reviews and more publicity. His press books were bulging with articles about him. During 1981 he had ten one-person exhibits in five different countries; between February and April alone, his work was shown at the Nagel Gallery in Berlin; the Contretemps Gallery in Brussels; and the Kunstverein in Frankfurt. The Kunstverein published an important catalogue of his work, with an essay by Sam Wagstaff, and organized a traveling show that went to Hamburg and Munich; Graz and Vienna, Austria; and Basel and Zurich, Switzerland.

By art photography standards, Mapplethorpe's career was an enviable one, but he had developed an expensive cocaine habit and constantly complained that he didn't have enough money; he often couldn't pay Tom Baril on time. What made his financial situation even more depressing to him was the hype surrounding the neo-expressionists, whose bold, emotive paintings appealed to art collectors who had grown bored with the spartan style of minimalism. Julian Schnabel, whose career was a paradigm of the 1980s, was commanding fifteen thousand dollars for a painting, while Mapplethorpe could charge only two thousand dollars for a photograph.

In March he agreed to show portraits of such punk celebrities as Patti Smith and Debbie Harry in a group exhibit, "New York/New Wave," at P.S. 1, along with Jean-Michel Basquiat, whose graffiti-inspired paintings were being seen for the first time. At thirty-four,

Mapplethorpe was a decade older than Basquiat, and clearly the most established artist in the show. "Robert didn't have to be there," said Diego Cortez, who curated the exhibit. "All the right people already knew his name, but he never missed an opportunity to promote himself."

Mapplethorpe felt he had no other choice, because otherwise he wouldn't make a living at all. "I had to sell a lot of photographs to make the kind of money a painter made from selling just one painting," he explained. "I just couldn't sit back and hope for the best." He repeatedly expressed his dissatisfaction with the Miller Gallery, and it was Wagstaff's job as Mapplethorpe's "handler" to deliver periodic lectures to gallery director John Cheim for not devoting enough time to the photographer. Yet the Robert Miller Gallery and Robert Mapplethorpe constituted an ideal 1980s marriage, for the gallery's emphasis on expensive framing and glossy catalogues mirrored the photographer's own obsession with style. Moreover, despite Mapplethorpe's complaints of being ignored, the gallery had demonstrated a strong commitment to photography by setting up a separate department headed by twenty-six-year-old Howard Read, a close friend of John Cheim's from their student days at the Rhode Island School of Design. Read was the consummate yuppie salesman, and he hustled photographs the way a commodities dealer might hawk pork bellies. With his hair slicked with gel and his custom-tailored suits, he didn't subtly woo his clients but verbally assaulted them, his blue eyes throbbing to the beat of his rapid-fire delivery. He was a living, breathing, selling machine, and people often made jokes about his crassness and manic personality. Mapplethorpe detested him, in fact, and behind his back called him "the used-car salesman." Yet the photographer himself was equally motivated by money, and whether or not he realized it, the two men were soul brothers of a sort.

Read had his work cut out for him in merchandising Robert Mapplethorpe, for the photographer's sales figures had never been as high as his public profile. In fact, his initial value to the Miller Gallery was not his ability to make money for them, but his ability to bring "traffic" to the gallery. People came to see Mapplethorpe, and even if they didn't buy one of his pictures, Read would then steer them to something by Diane Arbus, Man Ray, or one of the other photographers whose work the gallery represented. "Robert was a fluke in a sense," Read explained. "People were totally fascinated by him as a person. You'd show them a picture and they'd want to know everything about him. They'd want to swallow him up and eat him. But ask them to pull out their checkbooks and forget it."

"Black Males," which opened at the Miller Gallery in May, was Mapplethorpe's most successful show to date. Although it consisted of pictures of young black men, many of them nude and endowed with muscular bodies and generously proportioned sexual organs, the exhibit hit a nerve with Read's predominantly white buyers. The dealer eventually sold all twenty images at two thousand dollars apiece. Unlike the previous exhibit, "Contact," in which Mapplethorpe's inherent classicism was nearly overwhelmed by his garish frames, he focused his energy on the photographs themselves. They were larger than usual—some measured thirty by forty inches—and by placing them in simple black frames he didn't detract from the raw visual power of such images as *Man in Polyester Suit*. The most striking series of photographs was four views of the model "Ajitto" hunched on a pedestal, which simultaneously evoked Hippolyte-Jean Flandrin's *Naked Boy Sitting on the Seashore*, Baron Von Gloeden's *Male Nude Seated on the Rock*, and Edward Weston's peppers.

People who walked through the Miller Gallery to see such beautiful black bodies as "Ajitto" had no idea the man who took the pictures referred to his subjects as "niggers," or that he subscribed to racist ideas. "Robert's obsession with blacks was a little scary, a little on the edge," said Diego Cortez, "but basically the work reads pure. Sometimes art goes beyond the artist's own narrow-mindedness." Most viewers focused on the gleam of black skin and the sculptural form of the muscles underneath. *New York*'s Kay Larson complimented Mapplethorpe on his technical control: "The grain of each photograph looks burnished, as if it were possible to polish silver oxide with a hand tool." Allen Ellenzweig, in *Art in America*, wrote: "Mapplethorpe signals unambiguously that we are here to inspect: the body is its own unapologetic event. Accordingly, we have no sense of an attempted mediation between Sex and Art—the esthetic object *is* the sexual object, and vice versa. Without any pretense of a sociological pose, this exhibition accurately taps into prevailing cultural values: sex is beautifully packaged and objectified; you can even take it home and put it on your walls." However, Fred McDarrah of *The Village Voice* used blunter language: "Main picture here is a big black dude seen in an expensive vested gabardine suit with his fly open and his elephant cock sticking out. The picture is ugly, degrading, obscene—typical of the artist's work, which appeals largely to drooling, lascivious collectors who buy them, and return to their furnished rooms to jerk off."

Mapplethorpe took Moore to see "Black Males," and true to his word, he never showed his lover's head and genitals in the same photograph. Moore was either the nameless "man" in *Man in Polyester Suit,* or else a sweet-faced sailor saluting for the camera. Mapplethorpe had literally split him in two: a head or a body. In real life, Moore's divided self was not so easily dealt with, and while Mapplethorpe proclaimed him a great "sexual receptor," he didn't know what to do with him during the daylight hours.

He suggested Moore apply for unemployment insurance, but Moore never seemed to be able to find the appropriate office. Week after week he would return to Bond Street empty-handed, thereby precipitating a huge fight with Mapplethorpe, which frequently ended with Moore losing control of himself, then lapsing into a kind of catatonic trance. Nevertheless, Mapplethorpe persisted in placing Moore in stressful social situations by taking him to dinner parties with art critics and collectors. Studying his dictionary beforehand, Moore would become so nervous that he would sometimes write down words or phrases on the palm of his hand. "He would get along really well with someone," Mapplethorpe explained, "if they talked to him and allowed themselves to be fascinated by this primitive. But other times it was a little iffy."

In July Lia and Agustin Fernandez invited Mapplethorpe to stay at their house in San Juan, but when he arrived with Moore, Lia was relieved when they checked into the Hilton Hotel instead. She considered Moore "dangerous and totally paranoid"; he told her how much he hated Sam Wagstaff and Lisa Lyon, and even though he had never met Patti Smith, he was convinced her spirit was haunting Bond Street. His harshest words, though, were directed at his lover. "Milton didn't like to be photographed," Fernandez recalled, "and he'd say things like, 'Robert is using me. I'm smarter than he is. Why is *he* the photographer and not me?' He'd get so worked up that I worried for Robert's safety."

Mapplethorpe had given Moore a skull necklace and photographed him on the beach at San Juan, the death's-head dangling from a silver chain around his neck. Right after the picture was taken, Moore disappeared and Mapplethorpe spent the entire day searching for him. He found him later that night, but the vacation was ruined, and the tension between the two men was so palpable that Lia Fernandez vowed never to invite them anywhere together again. "Robert kept complaining that Milton would only eat 'nigger food,' and that he couldn't stand it anymore," she said. "Robert's relationships with blacks were all terribly sexual, but he didn't actually *like* them. He constantly called them 'niggers,' and said they were stupid. He may have been in love with Milton, but it was very different from the love other people feel."

The word "love" didn't even begin to describe Mapplethorpe's complicated passion for Moore, which fluctuated between despair and rapture. Not long after their disastrous trip to Puerto Rico, they were invited to spend a weekend in the Hamptons with *Artforum* editor Ingrid Sischy, who, with Klaus Kertess, picked them up at the train station. Emerging from a sea of Ralph Lauren polo shirts and Topsiders, Mapplethorpe and Moore stepped off the train into eighty-degree weather in matching black leather outfits. "We drove directly to the beach," Kertess recalled, "and everybody was in bathing suits except for Robert and Milton, who were still dressed in black leather. This was not exactly a normal sight for the Hamptons, but then Robert took Milton's hand and they began to skip along the shoreline. I'll never forget the image: Robert and Milton on the beach, skipping and holding hands like they were the two happiest people in the world."

Such rare moments of joy were outweighed by days and weeks of anguish, as Moore's emotional health deteriorated and Mapplethorpe refused to recognize the severity of the problem. In mid-September Mapplethorpe nearly suffered a catastrophic fire at Bond Street when Moore threw a lit cigarette into a wastebasket. The fire department arrived early enough to save most of his negatives, although some were destroyed by water damage. "What happened?"

Tom Baril asked when he arrived at Bond Street to find Mapple-thorpe picking through the debris. "Oh," he sighed. "Milton."

The fire showed Mapplethorpe that his life was truly out of con-trol, and attempting to impose some order on Bond Street, he im-mediately hired a studio manager named Betsy Evans, who had once worked for Simon Lowinsky in San Francisco. By her own definition she was "Little Miss Prep," and life at the Mapplethorpe studio was a revelation to her. Mapplethorpe delighted in teasing her by drop-ping contact sheets of penises on her desk and asking her to pick out her favorites. Eventually she grew accustomed to his perverse sense of humor, and responded to his adolescent behavior by "playing Mama" for him. Mapplethorpe seemed incapable of handling even the most basic tasks: he couldn't compose business letters, so she wrote them for him; he couldn't be bothered to eat lunch, so she went to the corner deli to bring him a bologna sandwich on a bulky roll. His photographs were in such disarray that she spent the first three months sorting through the stacks of prints on the floor. "Robert kept very bad records," she explained, "and he didn't know which gallery or museum had what print. I had to do a lot of research trying to figure out where they went."

At the end of October Mapplethorpe flew to Paris for an opening of his work at the Galerie Texbraun, which was owned by Hugues Autexier and François Braunschweig, whose early beginnings selling vintage photographs at the flea market at Porte de Clignancourt had inspired Mapplethorpe and Wagstaff to call them "the fleas." Autexier and Braunschweig were a gay couple who frequented the Mineshaft and other international leather bars; Braunschweig would die of AIDS in 1986, and Autexier, HIV positive himself, would commit suicide a few weeks later. For Mapplethorpe's exhibit in 1981 they dressed, as they often did, in black leather and welcomed a crowd that included others in similar garb. Photography dealer Monah Gettner recalled bumping into Harry Lunn, who offered the cynical assessment: "Gay is in, didn't you know?"

The following month Lunn had a show of Mapplethorpe's work at his gallery in Washington, D.C., where he hung the photogra-pher's "X" and "Y" portfolios on the walls, in addition to the re-cently completed "Z Portfolio," which comprised pictures of black men. When asked by *The Washington Post* why he felt the need "to include the banal sadomasochism" in the exhibit, Lunn was bluntly honest: "I think the work is interesting and I can make money on it."

Mapplethorpe's frequent trips away from New York increased the strain on his relationship with Moore, and every time he left him alone, he worried that he might destroy the loft. But even when Mapplethorpe was home to supervise, it was becoming clearer that Moore couldn't cope in his current environment. From the time he woke up in the morning he was plunged into the frantic world of the Mapplethorpe studio, with its jangling telephones and obtrusive employees. Sometimes he was so unnerved by the fast pace of Mapplethorpe's life that he stayed in bed and watched the activity from behind the chicken-wire cage.

In November Mapplethorpe rented a studio apartment at 88 Bleecker Street so he and Moore could live together without the distractions of the business. He transformed the small space into a showcase for his Mission furniture, American earthenware pottery, and his newest collection of Scandinavian glass and ceramics. He had purchased most of his pieces at Fifty 50 in Greenwich Village, where he spent at least an hour every Saturday afternoon sizing up the new merchandise. "He'd come in around five P.M., light up a joint, and start looking," said owner Mark Isaacson, who died of AIDS in 1993. "Nothing escaped him. He'd put a vase under a spotlight in the shop to see how the light fell across the surface. He was constantly visualizing the pieces in terms of his photography, and sure enough, they began appearing in his pictures. Since the vases were stark and symmetrical, his floral arrangements became increasingly austere—a single orchid, for example, versus a bunch of tulips. It was interesting to me to see how that happened, because I felt a little bit part of the creative process myself." The shelves in the new apartment were soon weighed down with bulbous vases in shades of brown, mustard, sea green, and periwinkle blue, and Moore was instructed to keep his hands off them.

During the early months of 1982 Moore tried as hard as he could to play by the rules, and at Mapplethorpe's suggestion he even enrolled in a photography course at Parsons School of Design. But ultimately he couldn't tolerate the pressure of attending class, and he simply stopped going. Mapplethorpe had paid $3,600 for

Moore's legal bills, and now that he was renting an apartment for a thousand dollars a month, he expected Moore to bring in some money, even if it was only an unemployment check. When Moore failed once again to make an appearance at the unemployment office, Mapplethorpe became so frustrated he began to cry. "I'm doing everything for you," he lamented. "When you wanted to sing, I got you Barbra Streisand's coach. When you wanted to dance, I got you the best choreographers in the city. What do you want from me?" Moore grabbed a kitchen knife from the dishwasher and began randomly stabbing the air until Mapplethorpe wrestled it away from him. He then attempted to quiet Moore, who had collapsed on the floor, sobbing and talking gibberish.

Mapplethorpe was so afraid Moore might hurt himself that even though he had once saved him from jail, he now kept him locked in the apartment. "Robert had this poor black kid from the South cooped up in what looked like a showroom for a glass company," said Bruce Mailman, who owned the Saint, a gay dance hall, and the New St. Mark's Baths, and who died of AIDS in 1994. "It was like keeping a tiger on a leash in your apartment."

Mapplethorpe was scheduled to be in Atlanta on April 2 for the opening of his work at the Fay Gold Gallery, so he asked Edmund White to baby-sit Moore while he was away. "I thought he was very sweet and kind," White recalled, "more like a difficult child than anything else." A few weeks later Mapplethorpe returned to Bleecker Street one evening to find the window of the apartment wide open and Moore gone. Mapplethorpe ran to the local police precinct, but he couldn't summon the nerve to give them Moore's name. "I knew they were going to tell me he was dead," he said, "and I just couldn't bear it." So he returned to the loft, crying to friends on the telephone that Moore was dead. He waited for him throughout the night and the next morning, and just as he was about to go to the police precinct again, Moore sauntered into the apartment; his pants were a mass of wrinkles, and he wasn't wearing a shirt. "My God, where have you been?" Mapplethorpe shouted. Moore calmly explained that he had always wanted to see New Jersey, but since he didn't have the money for transportation, he had decided to swim there. "You *swam* to New Jersey?" Mapplethorpe wailed. "Why would you do such a crazy thing?" Milton shrugged his shoulders. "Well," he said, "it was warm in the apartment, so I opened the window, then jumped out."

Mapplethorpe immediately telephoned Ingrid Sischy and asked if she could recommend a psychiatrist for Moore. "I was stunned that Robert was willing to go that far," Sischy said. "Robert was a real meat and mashed potatoes guy—Mr. Nonanalytical—and that he would do this for Milton revealed his determination to make the relationship work." Mapplethorpe and Moore attended several sessions together, but Moore was reluctant to continue, and perhaps sensing that the dynamics of their relationship might require hundreds of hours to sort out, Mapplethorpe soon gave up the idea.

Moore, meanwhile, began to vent his anger at Mapplethorpe, whom he targeted as the source of all his problems. His comments were perceptive and, at times, hysterically funny for a "primitive." He taunted Mapplethorpe with threats of inviting his own parents to New York so they could see for themselves the kind of debauched life their son was forced to lead. "You can call them 'Mother and Father Moore,'" he instructed. "We can take them to a few Broadway shows, then to the Mineshaft. Won't that be *marvy?*" Other times, however, he lashed out at Mapplethorpe for referring to him as "nigger," and made threatening phone calls to Sam Wagstaff in the middle of the night. Jim Nelson was furious at Mapplethorpe for destroying their domestic tranquility. "Thanks to you," he complained, "we're all going to be murdered in our beds."

Mapplethorpe was so consumed by Moore that he solicited advice from friends and strangers alike. Lawyer Michael Ward Stout remembered listening to Mapplethorpe pour his heart out at the TriBeCa restaurant the Odeon. The dinner had been arranged by Bruce Mailman, for whom Stout had acted as legal advisor when Mailman opened the Saint and the New St. Mark's Baths. Stout would later become executor of the Mapplethorpe estate and president of the Mapplethorpe Foundation, but at the time he barely knew the photographer, and the two men looked as if they'd have little to say to one another. At thirty-nine Stout was only three years older than Mapplethorpe, but his imperious manner and imposing girth gave him the appearance of a Roman emperor. He usually dressed in conservative three-piece suits and relaxed by playing Beethoven and Scriabin on the Steinway piano in his Upper West Side apartment, which was decorated to simulate the refined atmosphere of a European hotel suite. Yet both men, according to Stout, shared a "lust for excess and exotica."

Stout was born in Lake Mills, Wisconsin, and moved to Manhattan soon after his graduation from the University of Wisconsin Law School. He befriended Micky Ruskin and became a regular at Max's Kansas City, where he first noticed Mapplethorpe. It is doubtful, though, that Mapplethorpe paid much attention to him, for the lawyer's evening attire was the same as his conventional daywear. "I didn't have time for two wardrobes," he said. Nevertheless, he persisted in working for a discreet Park Avenue law firm by day and socializing with his friends in the art world by night. In 1975 he was introduced to Salvador Dalí, who was struck by the lawyer's resemblance to his own father—Dalí's wife, Gala, thought that Stout, then thirty-one, was in his sixties—and immediately offered him a job. He began spending months in Europe with the Dalís and their entourage. "Once I became involved with Dalí," he said, "I lost some of my friendships and business relationships in the art world. They thought Dalí was pretentious, commercial, money-hungry—just the worst! But I thought he was really fascinating, a genius." Because the artist was too free with his signature—for a time he was signing blank pieces of paper—the market in forged Dalí lithographs boomed. Stout played a critical role in distinguishing the authentic Dalís from the fakes, and earned a reputation as an expert in art fraud.

Mapplethorpe was toying with ways to commercialize his career and was interested in hearing about Dalí's lucrative licensing deals. But when he arrived at the Odeon, he was so obsessed by Moore that he immediately launched into a history of their relationship. Stout, who had been prepared for a business dinner, was immediately drawn into the vortex of their troubled affair. "I'm having a lot of problems," Mapplethorpe said, by way of introduction, and for the next several hours he barely touched his food. Stout watched, fascinated, as cigarette ashes formed little pillars on Mapplethorpe's dinner plate. "Milton was jumping out the window," Stout said, "or had just jumped out of the window, or maybe someone had thrown him out the window. I don't remember the exact details, but something very dramatic was going on."

"So what should I do?" Mapplethorpe asked him. "Throw him out or keep him?" Stout, whose traditional appearance belied a wicked sense of humor and a love of gossip, found Mapplethorpe's plight intriguing. He did not, however, have an easy answer. "When you love someone it's torture," he counseled. "You just have to wait until it wears off."

Mapplethorpe made one last effort to save the relationship by traveling to Tennessee with Moore in an ill-conceived effort to understand his roots. Nothing in Mapplethorpe's experience had prepared him for this voyage home. The Moore family lived in a squalid housing project where dozens of people were crammed inside rooms the size of the Bleecker Street studio. "It was a tenement!" Mapplethorpe explained. "Poverty row!" Immediately regretting his decision to stay the night, he temporarily escaped the apartment by offering to take photographs of Moore's young nephews and nieces who were playing on a rusty chair outside. The trip was difficult for Moore, too, and unnerved by Mapplethorpe's sudden intrusion into his old life, he lapsed into gibberish, an angry scowl spreading across his face. His family ignored him and spent the evening watching a small black-and-white TV set as cockroaches scurried across the screen.

Later that night Moore's mother showed Mapplethorpe to his bed, a small cot with a mattress so thin the springs of the frame poked through the fabric. He knew he would never fall asleep—a fact reinforced by the sudden appearance of Moore, who stood in the doorway of the bedroom with a loaded rifle in his hand. "Nigger, nigger, nigger," he said, his voice growing louder with each repetition. "Nigger, nigger, nigger . . ." Mapplethorpe attempted to calm him down but Moore was beyond soothing. "I'm going to tell my mother I'm a homosexual, and that you're my lover," he said. "Then I'm going to tell her what we do in bed, and that you call me 'nigger.' " Mapplethorpe didn't know if he was more afraid of the gun or of Moore's threat to expose his unorthodox sex life. "Please," he begged, "quiet down." But Moore kept repeating the word "nigger" and calling for his mother. "My God! They're going to lynch me!" Mapplethorpe thought. The next morning, he practically ran out of the apartment and fled back to New York.

Several weeks later Moore appeared at Bond Street to claim his property—two television antennas and the soundtrack of the movie *Fame*. He told Mapplethorpe to keep the Capezio tap shoes. "We never really had what you might call a real relationship," Moore later explained. "I think he saw me like a monkey in a zoo."

CHAPTER EIGHTEEN

"You know, faggots are dying."

—*Robert Mapplethorpe*

Mapplethorpe was devastated over losing Milton Moore and mourned the end of their relationship like a bereaved spouse. "Robert was absolutely grief-stricken," John Abbott recalled, "and I empathized with his sadness because he had found his sexual deity. Milton was Super-Nigger, so Robert overlooked the fact that he was also, perhaps, schizophrenic." The experience had taught him the drawbacks of living with a "primitive" and he vowed that his next black lover would be someone who felt more comfortable in polite society.

He was heading to a black-tie party when he saw Jack Walls on the street; unlike his experience with Moore at Sneakers, it was not an epiphany, but rather a routine pickup, in which Mapplethorpe hastily slipped Walls his business card and directed him to "call me." Several days later they met for coffee at the Pink Teacup, where Mapplethorpe was forthright about his newest requirements for a lover. "I'm not interested in being with a nobody," he warned Walls, who confidently replied, "That's okay, because I'm not going to be a nobody. I'm going to be a star—and a star of some magnitude."

Walls was then a clerk-typist, but, at twenty-three, he imagined himself capable of almost anything: he wanted to write, paint, dance, sing, and act in the movies. Mapplethorpe liked his bravado, if not his physical appearance, for Walls, unfortunately, was not a deity. At five feet nine inches tall, he had a scrawny frame and skinny bowed legs, and while his face was cute and expressive, it lacked Moore's haunting poignancy. But Walls was smart, funny, and had a streetwise hipness that had been honed to perfection through his years with a Chicago street gang. He had eight sisters and brothers, one of whom had been shot and killed in a gang fight, and although his mother cautioned him about getting into trouble himself, he was caught with a .32 automatic while still a sophomore in high school. He spent three months in a juvenile detention center, and upon his release he quit school and began teaching the Hustle at a local Fred Astaire Dance Studio. "I also dealt drugs—heroin, mescaline, coke," he said. "I had guns put to my head. People shot at me. It was a really crazy life. I'd go from beating up someone to teaching the Hustle. I also taught Spanish salsa, too."

Walls might have become a career criminal, except for a chance encounter with a group of gay men who opened up a whole new world of books and old movies. He soon realized he was gay himself and didn't feel compelled to hide the information from the members of his gang. "I said, 'Yo! I'm gay,' " he explained, "and they said, 'Hey, that's cool.' I wasn't swishy and didn't go flaming down the street, so I had total respect within the gang system of Chicago." At eighteen he enlisted in the navy, and after three years in the Far East, he lived in San Diego until he heard singer Grace Jones on the radio one day. "I said to myself, 'I'm leaving,' " he recalled, "because she was *so* New York."

Within several months of his arrival Walls met Mapplethorpe, and he was suddenly thrust into a world of A-list parties, gallery openings, and weekends in East Hampton. That he could handle himself without recourse to dictionaries and crib notes heartened Mapplethorpe, who felt comfortable taking him almost anywhere. Still, the relationship was not without its problems. "Robert not only chose to be with men," said his lawyer Michael Stout, "but he picked *black* men. It's a real specialized neurosis. Having a Jack or a Milton on your arm isn't exactly a ticket to society." Amy Sullivan, whom Mapplethorpe had known since Max's in the early seventies, once invited them to her house in East Hampton, where they spent the evening with photography collector Paul Walter. "Jack suddenly disappeared," Sullivan recalled, "and Robert found him pacing up and down the driveway. Jack simply couldn't sustain those kinds of events. If he could find a common ground with someone, he was okay, but what could he say to the Paul Walters of the world? Maybe Robert thought being with blacks enabled him to keep a certain power structure intact. These men weren't doctors or newscasters, but poor, lost-in-the-city kids, and Robert could control them."

When Walls expressed an interest in fashion design, Mapplethorpe convinced Sullivan, who was director of the Agnes B. clothing boutiques in the United States, to hire him as a sales clerk at the SoHo shop. Walls was often late for work and blamed his delinquent behavior on Mapplethorpe. "We had to have sex every night," he explained. "Sometimes I'd have to say things like, 'Please, I have a headache,' but then he would whine like a baby if you refused him." Mapplethorpe also expected Walls to pay his dues as a model, but their collaboration was not as inspired as the photographer's pictures of Milton Moore. "In the body department," Mapplethorpe complained, "Jack just didn't have it." Consequently Mapplethorpe was not motivated to place him on a pedestal or idolize him in any way. The photographs he took of Walls on Fire Island that summer only served to emphasize his model's physical limitations.

One picture of Walls in Bermuda shorts focuses attention on his bowed legs, which are made to look even more crooked by the straight lines of the plywood decking and white railing. By contrast, a similar photograph of Moore shot from the waist down reveals each sculpted curve in his flexed quadriceps. Mapplethorpe's conclusion that "Jack wasn't Milton" was obvious from the pictures, yet he tried to convince himself that he was infatuated with him. "I think I'm in love," he would periodically announce to Walls in a tone that indicated lukewarm feelings at best. "You *think?*" Walls replied, after one such temperature reading. "Let me know when you're head over heels."

The photographer was still going to Keller's and taking men to Bond Street for late-night photo sessions. Because his pictures required a certain intimacy, he had never worked with an assistant before, but in April he suddenly introduced Betsy Evans and Tom Baril to his newest employee, a young man named Ed who had dark brown hair, intense blue eyes, and seemingly no last name. "It's just Ed," Mapplethorpe told them. *"Ed."* It did not take long for Betsy and Tom to discover that Ed was Mapplethorpe's twenty-one-year-old brother, who had been born when Robert was already fourteen years old and a high school student. Ed had just graduated from the State University of New York at Stony Brook, Long Island, where he had majored in photography and wrote his thesis on Robert Mapplethorpe. "I don't particularly care to have my brother working for me," Robert told Ed upfront. "But I barely know you, so maybe it will be okay."

Studying Robert's photographs for his school paper was about as close as Ed had ever been to his brother; Robert had moved to Manhattan when Ed was in first grade. His most vivid recollection of Robert was the time he appeared at Ed's Catholic grammar school graduation looking like Marlon Brando in *The Wild One*. Ed later sneaked off to Manhattan to see Robert's exhibits at the Solomon Gallery and the Kitchen, but waited another year before summoning up the nerve to visit him at Bond Street. By then Robert had assumed larger-than-life proportions in Ed's mind, so when he walked toward Bond Street on that cold, rainy day and saw a sinister figure in black standing on the fire escape, he had an urge to run in the opposite direction. But Ed took the creaky elevator upstairs, where Robert, refusing to compensate for the gloomy weather by turning on a light, sat in the semidarkness and smoked a joint. "Robert didn't say a word," Ed recalled, "so I had to do all the talking, and I worried the whole time that I wouldn't have anything interesting to offer him. I didn't want him to think I was like the rest of the family. I wanted to impress him." At the conclusion of Ed's rambling monologue, Robert handed him a portfolio of S&M pictures and watched, silently, as Ed looked at each one. "That was something to do to your kid brother," Ed said. "I was really disturbed when I left the loft. I told my friends that I went to see Robert, but I kept the other stuff to myself."

Ed, who was then sixteen, didn't grasp Robert's complicated sexuality, but he did somehow accept the darker side of his brother's nature and admired him for escaping the stultifying environment of Floral Park. He hoped to be a more gentle version of Robert, and he took the first step toward realizing his goal by majoring in photography. Such hero worship did not sit well with their father, who worried that he would lose another son to art, and perhaps to homosexuality as well. When Ed graduated from college in the winter of 1982, Harry urged him to forget about a photography career and focus his efforts on finding a "real job." Ed knew that Robert had endured the same lecture, so he called him for some advice, and to his amazement, his brother offered him a job. "I later found out my mother had pressured him into it," Ed said. "I wish she hadn't done that, because it would have been nicer if I'd known it was Robert's own idea." Since Ed was still living at home, Robert warned him that he didn't want his business discussed at the dinner table. "The last thing I need," he said, "is to have a link to Floral Park."

During the first few months of his employment, Ed mounted his brother's prints and helped organize his files; careful to observe Robert's privacy, he crept around the loft as if he were walking on glass. Robert's postcoital photo sessions were sacred to him, and while they usually took place at night, Ed never knew for sure what he might stumble upon the next morning. Even when Robert shot portraits of people he wasn't sexually involved with, he liked to have at least forty-five minutes alone with his sitters. It was then that he attempted to establish a connection with the other person through some common experience—perhaps a mutual friend, or a shared interest in collecting pottery. Robert was shy, but he had a talent for putting others at ease because he conveyed the impression he would never betray anybody with an unflattering image. He was only interested, he often said, in capturing the "best" of someone.

Cocaine was an integral part of Robert Mapplethorpe's creative process, and friends and colleagues described his drug habit as "highly controlled." Betsy Evans explained: "He used it like a cup of coffee. Just a little bit, then a little bit more. It was amazing." But one of his coke dealers maintained that Mapplethorpe was seriously addicted to it. "He worked so hard at being aloof that he was able to disguise it," the dealer said. "But the reason I know he was addicted was that I helped procure it for him many, many times. He always came alone when he bought it from me, so it's not something anybody else would know about." He almost always used coke during a shooting and frequently offered it to his sitters. Perceptively, *ARTnews*, in 1977, had complimented the photographer for his ability to create "light effects that are the visual equivalents of certain psychological states induced by cocaine." Indeed, the wide-eyed stare that became a distinguishing characteristic of his portraits was often the result of cocaine, and when it wasn't, the photographer seemed to be aiming for a sharp "coke look." His portrait sitters were never caught in a wistful reverie, but rather, they often seemed poised on the edge of an invisible line from which they were about to spring. Mapplethorpe's portrait of Iggy Pop, mouth agape in a mute howl, is terrifying in its desperate, live-for-the-moment immediacy. His portrait of Alice Neel is terrifying in a different way, for he photographed the elderly painter right before she died, and her face wears the exhausted, open-mouthed expression of a woman about to evaporate into another state of being.

Mapplethorpe was not an intrusive photographer; he barely raised his voice above a whisper and gave directions by just flicking his hands. He didn't ask his portrait sitters to jump in the air or wear funny clothes. If they were photographed with props in their hands, it was usually because they devised the idea themselves. Sculptor Louise Bourgeois arrived at the loft with one of her own phallic pieces under her arm. "I thought it was going to be a catastrophe," she said about the portrait sitting in a BBC interview, "and I prepared for it." But people usually went to Bond Street equipped with only their psychological armor—the shield of beauty, talent, or wealth that made even private faces seem like public ones. Even though Mapplethorpe rarely exposed his sitters' vulnerabilities, he was, at times, capable of piercing to the heart of things. Right-wing lawyer Roy Cohn, who vigorously denied his own homosexuality, posed for him in 1981, and few pictures of Cohn better summarized his snarling, hypocritical personality than Mapplethorpe's portrait of his disembodied head floating in a black Hell, his eyes spitting venom at the viewer. "I don't know why my pictures come out looking so good," Robert once confided to Ed. "I just don't get it."

Ed didn't understand it, either, for his brother's working methods were haphazard at best. He didn't bother with light readings, nor did he test the setup beforehand by taking Polaroid pictures of his models. He simply turned his monolight on at full power and kept the aperture of his camera at f16. Eventually, as Robert became more comfortable with Ed, he allowed him into the studio to help set up the equipment, but expected him to leave immediately afterward because he was afraid he would destroy the magic. So Ed waited outside the door until Robert called for him again, but he was running back and forth so often that his brother finally agreed to let him stay in the studio and assist full-time. With Ed's encouragement, Robert began doing light readings and taking Polaroids and even bought a secondhand strobe light, which was more complicated to use than the monolight, as it involved an electronic flash unit. "Robert was really afraid of anything too technical," said photographer Gilles Larrain, whom Mapplethorpe had met when he needed someone to take over a commercial job he couldn't do himself. "I always felt his reluctance to get involved with printing, for example, stemmed from his intuition that his career might be very short. It was like he couldn't be bothered, because he just didn't have the time. Once I went out to dinner with Robert, and a friend of mine suddenly asked him if he was happy. He looked at her as if she had suddenly started speaking Chinese. 'Happiness?' he said. 'No . . . it's not there for me.' "

At the beginning of the eighties AIDS was a distant drumbeat—a few rumbling noises about a new illness among gay men that was then known as GRID (Gay-Related Immune Deficiency). By the spring of 1982, though, the rumbling had grown louder and more ominous: the Centers for Disease Control had reported 285 cases of GRID in seventeen states, with half diagnosed in New York City. Mapplethorpe had been hearing stories of people he knew from the Mineshaft and the San Francisco leather bars suddenly developing swollen lymph nodes, severe hepatitis, pneumonia, a rare skin cancer called Kaposi's sarcoma, and a battery of other opportunistic infections rarely seen in the United States. Betsy Evans, whose brother actor Peter Evans was ill himself, always knew when Mapplethorpe received news that someone had been hospitalized, because the color would drain from his face, and his hands would tremble. In May, Mapplethorpe auctioned off his photography collection at Sotheby's to help pay the rent on his Bleecker Street apartment. GRID was obviously on his mind, for he described collecting pictures as if it were a horrible illness. "I get sick to my stomach when I buy," he told *Maine Antique Digest*. Amy Schiffman of *American Photography* elaborated on Mapplethorpe's statement that collecting was a "disease" with an even more dramatic and morbid comparison of her own: "With the money he made selling off his first bout with the virus, he should be able to supply himself with plenty of antibiotics in the future."

Mapplethorpe, in fact, was then taking the antibacterial drug Flagyl for treatment of amebiasis, a gastrointestinal disease that had plagued him for several years now. Randy Shilts, in *And the Band Played On*, related the frequency of such enteric disorders among the gay population to the increase in anal intercourse and more exotic sexual practices. Dr. Larry Downs, who was then Mapplethorpe's physician, repeatedly advised him to stop his obsession with feces, but since he failed to follow the doctor's advice, he was continually battling parasites and spreading them to his sexual partners. Worn down by stomach cramps and diarrhea, he nevertheless kept up a grueling exhibition schedule, with shows opening nearly every other month—at Larry Gagosian in Los Angeles in June; Tokyo's Galerie Watari in September; Amsterdam's Galerie Jurka in October.

By November, when a show of his work opened at the Contemporary Arts Center in New Orleans, Mapplethorpe was clearly exhausted, but he and Jack Walls flew down to attend the exhibit. They stayed with Mike Myers and Russ Albright, an interior decorator and radiologist, who lived in a three-story Empire-style house that was reputedly haunted by black slaves tortured to death by the original owner. It was known to the public as the "Haunted House"; Mapplethorpe had been a guest earlier in the year when he celebrated Mardi Gras by picking up a succession of black men and taking them back to the house. This time, however, he was un-characteristically lethargic; he didn't have the energy to stay out at night, and he complained of flulike symptoms. Albright made an appointment for him to see a colleague, Dr. Brobson Lutz, who took a medical history from him and inquired about his drug use. "I don't use recreational drugs," Mapplethorpe replied, "except for cocaine, hallucinogens, and nitrites."

Dr. Lutz admitted him to Southern Baptist Hospital, where he was diagnosed with a bacterial ear infection and swollen lymph nodes. By then the acronym GRID had been changed to the more neutral Acquired Immune Deficiency Syndrome, or AIDS, but the HIV virus had yet to be isolated, and accurate antibody tests wouldn't be available until 1984, two years away. "Robert was in a panic about having AIDS," Lutz recalled, "but he had a normal chest X-ray and showed no signs of pneumonia, so we reassured him based on what we knew at the time. In retrospect, the kind of ear infection he had was rare for a thirty-six-year-old adult. I'm sure if they'd had a blood test for HIV back then, Robert would have been positive."

When Mapplethorpe returned from New Orleans he immediately arranged for a health insurance policy for himself, but he didn't want to talk about AIDS or his recent hospitalization to anyone. However, during a breakfast meeting with Jim Clyne to discuss his participation in the book *Exquisite Creatures,* Mapplethorpe sud-denly blurted out the sad truth. "You know," he said, "faggots are dying."

Mapplethorpe liked having multiple shows in the springtime, and in March 1983 he had three exhibits at three separate galleries in New York. "You could not ride the subway without hearing his name," said Howard Read. On March 1 an exhibit of Mapplethorpe pic-tures of black men, dye-transfer prints of flowers, and sex pictures opened at the Robert Samuel Gallery, recently renamed Hardison Fine Arts. The sex pictures were the most curious of all, for Mapple-thorpe, having turned his attention away from gay S&M scenes, had recently taken up heterosexual pornography, as if that might offer him some safety from AIDS. The pictures featured Marty Gibson, a young black Coast Guard from Virginia, who had sent Mapplethorpe nude photos of himself and had promptly received an invitation to New York. Mapplethorpe had spent a weekend with him at Bruce Mailman's house in Fire Island, then asked if he would pose for some experimental photographs with a self-proclaimed "sexual revolutionary" named Veronica Vera, who prided herself on having "the best vulva" in the porn business. She arrived at Bond Street with a trunk filled with lacy lingerie, and after selecting a red velvet corset, black stockings, and high heels, she performed sex acts for Mapplethorpe's camera. "The shoot was a little uncomfortable," Gibson explained, "because she was coming on to me, but I tried to be professional about it."

Before Gibson left New York, Mapplethorpe promised to send him copies of the photographs. "What should I do with them?" Mapplethorpe called out as Gibson climbed into a cab. "Put them in a museum," Gibson joked. Six years later *Marty and Veronica* was part of the Mapplethorpe retrospective at the Whitney Museum. "Marty had stuck his head between my legs," Vera recalled, "and that was the picture that got in the Whitney."

Andy Grundberg of *The New York Times* struggled valiantly to come to terms with the Hardison show in a review headlined "Is Mapplethorpe Only Out to Shock?" He wondered if Mapplethorpe's "continued fascination with pornography could be seen as part of a pioneering bid to 'decode' pornographic imagery by mimicking its 'look'—just as Cindy Sherman, for example, has mimicked the look of 50's film stills." Yet he quickly dismissed that notion, "because any evidence of a critical distance from his material is lacking. . . . Rather than educate, these pictures titillate; rather than addressing the conventions of pornography, they *are* pornography." Even *Screw* magazine sent a reviewer to cover the exhibit: "Maplethorpe's [*sic*] strategy is, in a sense, cynical. The denizens of the upper class wouldn't be caught dead sloshing around in the anonymous spurt of peep shows and smut shops, yet they are in need of images to fuel their sexual shadow lives, same as the rest of us. If they won't go to the porn, Maplethorpe [*sic*] will bring the porn to them."

This time Mapplethorpe didn't bring the porn to the Miller Gallery; he showed his sculptural wall pieces instead. Viewers who attended the March 1 opening saw only four Mapplethorpe photo-

graphs but over a dozen "frames" shaped like crosses and penta-
grams. "Basically, it had to do with Robert's whole thing about not
just being a photographer," Howard Read explained. "It was like
he was saying, 'I can prove it. Go see my show. There aren't any
photographs in those pieces.' " Grundberg wrote that it was "difficult to fathom from these works alone what Mapplethorpe has in
mind," though he wondered if the cross-and-star motif suggested
"a perverse Oscar Wilde–meets-Duchamp reworking of the highly
charged imagery of church and state."

The third and most interesting show was at the Leo Castelli Gallery, where the photographs from *Lady* were exhibited to coincide
with the book's release. Lisa Lyon flew from Los Angeles to accompany Robert to the opening, but she was hardly a walking advertisement for the new, self-made woman featured on the gallery walls.
She had married a French rock singer, Bertrand Lavilliers, from
whom she was now divorced, and their breakup had precipitated a
nervous collapse. Lyon was now living with her mother in Los Angeles, and she weighed a skeletal eighty-six pounds. Critics were
hostile, and seemingly threatened by the whole notion of Lyon as a
"new woman." Grundberg focused attention on her "hermaphro-
ditic build," "bulging biceps," and "protruding forearm veins and
unshaven underarms." *People* wondered if *Lady* represented some
"kind of sick joke about the blurring of sex roles?" Mapplethorpe's
concept may well have been ahead of its time, for ten years later
Madonna and photographer Steven Meisel would essentially create
a pornographic version of *Lady* when they collaborated on *Sex*, the
rock star's pictorial fantasies of bondage, bisexuality, and biracial
sex. That book became a publishing event, and Madonna's muscular
body was viewed as a triumph of discipline, whereas Lyon was castigated as a freak.

Some critics, though, were not so threatened by Mapplethorpe's
depiction of a powerful woman as they were turned off by his sexist
ideas. "How new is it for a woman to crouch, bare-assed, on her
hands and knees in a lacy corset?" asked Carol Squiers in *The Village
Voice*. "To expose her breasts, wear dark glasses, or stare coldly at
us, dressed in gorgeous clothing? Despite all the accepted cant
about newness, Lisa Lyon's supposed multifaceted portrait collapses
into one long, stereotyped vision of women."

ROBERT MAPPLETHORPE

Holly Solomon Gallery	The Kitchen

Saturday, February 5, 1977

Through Feb. 26	Through Feb. 19

| 392 West Broadway
Phone: 925-1900
Tues.-Sat. 10:30-6:00
Wed. 10:30-9:00 | 484 Broome Street
Phone: 925-3615
Tues.-Sat. 1:00-6:00 |

Mapplethorpe's invitations to his dual openings at the
Holly Solomon Gallery and the Kitchen revealed an uncanny awareness
of how he planned to market his work and his
"uptown" and "downtown" lifestyles.

Mapplethorpe's dark sexual urges led him to explore the subterranean
world of sadomasochism. "Other people might have been overwhelmed
by such a powerful sexual drive," said writer George Stambolian,
"but Robert found a way to make art from it."

Holly Solomon, Mapplethorpe's first art dealer, "auditioned"
the photographer by asking him to do her portrait.

A BOOK OF PHOTOGRAPHS

When Mapplethorpe learned that Wagstaff was thinking of using
another photographer's picture for the cover of his book, he made sure
that one of his own flower photographs received the honor instead.
Then he conspired to replace the photographer in Wagstaff's affections
with San Francisco hairdresser Jim Nelson (*below*).

Mapplethorpe believed he had found "God" when he met
Milton Moore, the only model whose physical attributes approximated
the photographer's ideal.

Body builder Lisa Lyon was Mapplethorpe's ultimate female consort.

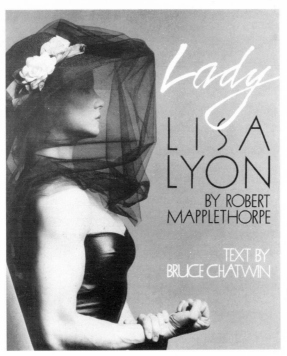

Mapplethorpe hoped to alter his gay S&M image by collaborating with Lisa Lyon on *Lady*.

The staff of the Mapplethorpe studio in a spoof of Mapplethorpe's picture with Lisa Lyon. *From left:* Mapplethorpe's brother Edward Maxey, studio manager Betsy Evans, and printer Tom Baril.

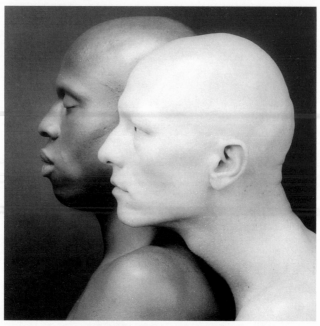

Models Ken Moody and Robert Sherman both suffered from alopecia, a disease that left them without any hair. Mapplethorpe likened their skin to bronze and marble.

Thomas Williams, an exotic dancer and porn star, was Mapplethorpe's last muse. Williams's "perfect" body inspired Mapplethorpe to create a series of geometric studies that underscored his obsession with the classical form.

"I'm not interested in being with a nobody," Mapplethorpe told Jack Walls, to which Walls replied, "I'm going to be a star." But Walls soon realized that the photographer didn't want an equal relationship.

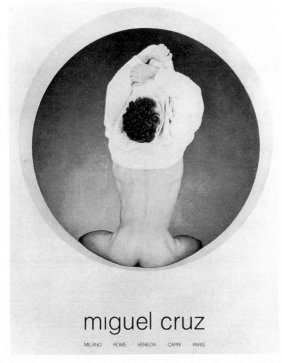

miguel cruz

MILANO   ROME   VENEZIA   CAPRI   PARIS

Mapplethorpe was drawn to advertising work because of its lucrative fees, but the ad he created for Miguel Cruz illustrates why he would never be a successful fashion photographer.

Though Mapplethorpe and Wagstaff were involved with other people,
Wagstaff still doted on his protégé and gave him $500,000
to buy a new loft on West 23rd Street (*below*).
House & Garden linked Mapplethorpe's "aesthetic genealogy"
to Oscar Wilde, Aubrey Beardsley, and Jean Cocteau.

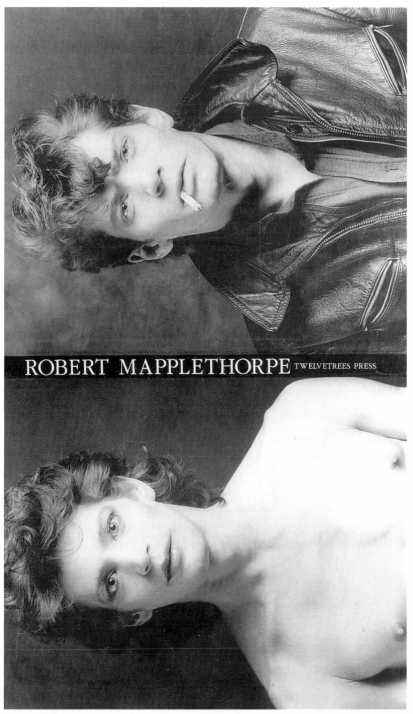

ROBERT MAPPLETHORPE TWELVETREES PRESS

Mapplethorpe assumed both masculine and feminine identities for the front and back covers of *Certain People,* his first book of portraits.

Mapplethorpe took this picture for the cover of Patti Smith's comeback album, *Dream of Life*. He didn't like the photograph because it wasn't "perfect" enough.

Mapplethorpe's portrait of Philip Prioleau appeared in his *Black Book*. "I can't even look at the pictures in the book anymore," he lamented. "It seems like most of the men in it are dead."

Contrary to Mapplethorpe's fears that rumors of AIDS would ruin his career, the disease only served to increase his sales potential. "AIDS," said his dealer Howard Read, "had a terrific influence."

SAMUEL J. WAGSTAFF, JR.

1921 – 1987

Mapplethorpe's 1978 portrait of Sam Wagstaff graced the cover of Wagstaff's memorial card.

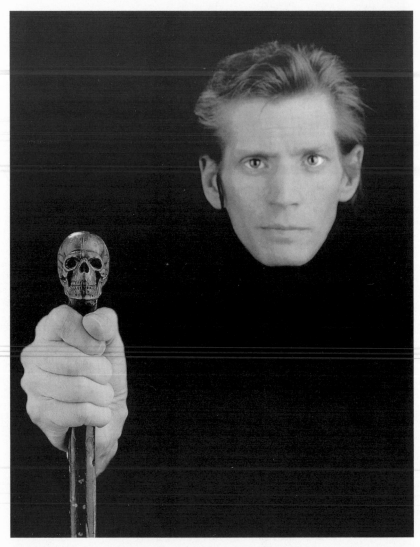

"I just hope I can live long enough to see the fame," Mapplethorpe said.

The Mapplethorpe retrospective at the Whitney Museum was the
highlight of the photographer's life. In this photograph, by Jonathan
Becker, he is pictured with his friends and admirers, including stylist
Dimitri Levas (*center*). When the photo later appeared in *Vanity Fair*,
Mapplethorpe was devastated by the harsh reality of the image.

Mapplethorpe took this picture of his brother Ed Maxey and his girlfriend Melody Danielson, who was one of the photographer's
favorite models. "If I hadn't been gay," Mapplethorpe said,
"I would have picked a woman like Melody."

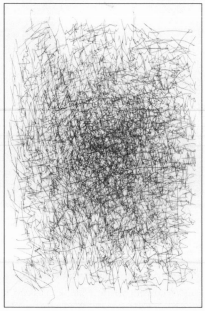

The photographer's final days were spent at Deaconness Hospital in
Boston. Unable to take photographs, he whiled away the time by
drawing in a sketchbook. Among the last entries were these two pages
covered with his signature. In the one shown at right, the name
Mapplethorpe has been reduced to a blur.

Mapplethorpe and his mother were buried together in her parents'
plot in Queens. The photographer's name has never been
inscribed on the tombstone.

Slides of Mapplethorpe's photographs were projected onto the facade of
the Corcoran Gallery of Art in Washington, D.C., as part of a
staged protest against the museum's cancellation of the
"Perfect Moment" exhibit. Mapplethorpe's self-portrait is seen
floating above the demonstrators.

Mapplethorpe had still not entirely forgiven Squiers for making an issue of his homosexuality in the piece she wrote about the "Trade-Off" exhibit in 1978, and he felt doubly betrayed by the *Village Voice* review. He refused to speak to her for years afterward, which, considering they often showed up at the same openings, was extremely awkward for Squiers. "It was like I'd humiliated him in front of the entire art world," she said. "He'd already gotten two bad reviews from Ben Lifson in *The Village Voice*, and it was like the newspaper had waged a concerted attack on Robert Mapplethorpe. He was really upset, and it had a terrible effect on me. Finally, I ran into him at a club a couple of years later, and I walked up to him and said, 'I'm so sorry I wrote what I wrote,' and we embraced and he said, 'Oh, it's okay.' Robert had the capacity for genuine affection, only it couldn't last too long, because obviously his primal scene was loving someone and being betrayed—and he just kept replaying that over and over again."

Mapplethorpe spent several weeks in Europe that spring with Lyon on a promotional tour for *Lady,* and while they played up their symbiotic relationship by dressing alike in black leather and flirting for reporters, he planned to break off their strained relationship once the tour was over. He complained that Lyon hadn't capitalized on her bodybuilding career, and he couldn't understand why she persisted in labeling herself a "performance artist" when she could have been a female Conan the Barbarian. But it was more than Lyon's faltering career that bothered him; having built her up to near perfection, he hated that his picture-book Amazon had a drug problem and emotional difficulties. It was the "curse of beauty" all over again, the toppling of the gods from his self-created Mount Olympus. "I know I disappointed Robert," Lyon said, "because I didn't live up to his ideal. But what person on this planet could have?"

Certainly not his dealer Howard Read, who no matter how hard he tried couldn't extract a word of praise from the photographer. "He tortured and tormented me," Read said. "I'd tell him, 'I've just gotten you this great museum show,' and he'd go, 'Yeah? . . . Anything else?'" Mapplethorpe met with other dealers behind Read's back, and before leaving for Venice in August, where an exhibit of his work was scheduled to open at the Centro di Documentazione di Palazzo Fortuny, he asked Peter MacGill to represent him. MacGill had recently opened Pace MacGill on East Fifty-seventh Street with his partner, Arnold Glimscher, but he didn't feel strongly enough about Mapplethorpe's photographs to risk alienating Read. "Except for *Man in Polyester Suit*," MacGill said, "there's not a lot of genius pulsating from the pictures." So Mapplethorpe stayed at the Miller Gallery, but not a day went by when he wasn't tearing Read to pieces. "Robert would hang up the phone and scream, 'I'm so mad at Howard,' " Betsy Evans recalled. "He just hated him."

Mapplethorpe's relationship with Jack Walls was yet another source of frustration. The two men had been living together on Bleecker Street for nearly a year now, but Mapplethorpe was still not in love with Jack. "I thought Jack was the perfect boyfriend for Robert," Lisa Lyon said, "but he was never able to love him, because it was a rebound situation. He was still in love with Milton, which, in my opinion, was like a DNA thing—you can never explain why. So it was really hard for Jack. He was trying a lot of different things, but instead of Robert encouraging him and believing in him, he kind of *defied* him to be successful, and that didn't work." Walls had to listen to Mapplethorpe lecture him about his worthless life, and how, with the right discipline, he, too, could become successful. But Walls could hardly muster the discipline to hold down a job—he was fired from Agnes B.—and his worsening drug problems made it unlikely his situation would improve. "Robert said he wanted me to be successful," Walls explained, "but he really didn't. If I'd done anything to outshine him, anything at all, it would have been the end of us."

While Mapplethorpe may have been unrealistic about Walls's career potential, the latter was equally foolish in expecting Mapplethorpe to remain monogamous. "You don't want someone you love to have sex with someone else," Walls said. "I had opportunities to go to bed with other people, but I didn't because Robert was not an anonymous person, and I didn't want people to say, 'Yeah, I slept with Jack Walls, and you know he goes out with Robert Mapplethorpe.' To this day, hardly a person in the city of New York, or the state of New York, or even the whole country, could admit to sleeping with Jack Walls. I didn't want a reputation as a slut, and I didn't want Robert to be known as a slut, either."

Mapplethorpe, nevertheless, carried on affairs with dozens of his models, including a young man named Dennis Speight, who appeared in a series of pictures he contributed to the Terrae Motus Collection in Naples, Italy. Terrae Motus had been conceived by Neapolitan art dealer Lucio Amelio, who persuaded numerous artists to create works based on their reaction to the 1980 earthquake that had devastated parts of southern Italy. Mapplethorpe had visited Naples in August, and when he returned to New York he constructed a panel of five pictures that centered on an image of a stone death's-head. Photographs of Dennis Speight, in which he held a spray of thorns and Easter lilies, anchored each end of the panel.

Walls was extremely jealous of Speight, and learning that Mapplethorpe was photographing him one afternoon, he called the studio. "How could you do this to me?" Walls shouted into the telephone. "I'm so upset I'm going to kill myself." When Mapplethorpe failed to respond, Walls grabbed one of Mapplethorpe's precious glass vases from the shelf and dangled it out the window. "I've got your glass," he threatened, "and unless you come home right now, it's going to be shattered into a million pieces." Mapplethorpe immediately dropped the phone and sprinted down Bond Street toward the apartment, where he found Walls perched on the window ledge. "Don't do it," Mapplethorpe begged him. *"Don't drop that vase!"*

Mapplethorpe was in London for his thirty-seventh birthday on November 4, 1983, and he celebrated the event with his biggest career triumph to date—the opening of a thirteen-year retrospective of his work at the Institute of Contemporary Art. British newspapers had aroused the public's curiosity with articles that described him as New York's "bad boy" and a "one-man cult." Lines formed outside the ICA to gain entrance to the show, which critic C. S. Manegold attributed "to a silly but perverse fascination with New York City's wild side, with . . . Homo New Yorkus."

Sandy Nairne, the ICA's exhibitions director, had purposely included the S&M pictures in the hopes of sparking a debate on the 1970s, and the decade's impact on sexual stereotyping. "I was a great fan of Robert's work," said Nairne. "Of course I didn't like all of it. I found the flowers to be dull, and his pictures of children too cutesy-pie. And I thought his attempts at straight-sex pictures were ludicrous. But the S&M pictures were important for the issues they raised about the seventies." Nairne realized that some of the photographs would be controversial, and because the ICA occupied a prominent position on The Mall, leading to Buckingham Palace, he took care to post a sign at the entrance to the exhibit prohibiting minors. Nevertheless, even before the show opened Heathrow Airport customs officials seized six Mapplethorpe photographs, among them *Man in Polyester Suit* and the portrait of Louise Bourgeois with her phallic sculpture. "The selection didn't reflect any national policy on obscenity," Nairne explained, "but merely what an individual customs agent deemed 'obscene.'" Nairne had three choices: he could send the photographs back to New York; watch the customs agent set them afire; or contest the obscenity charge at a hearing in a magistrate's court near the airport. Advised by his lawyers that he would lose if he contested the case, Nairne exercised the first option, then asked a friend at the New York bureau of the London *Sunday Times* to send the pictures back to him in the newspaper's overnight pouch. The expurgated Mapplethorpe photographs arrived at *The Times* the following day and went directly to the ICA. "I was later talking to the crime writer for the *Daily Mirror,* who told me the Criminal Investigations Department had purposely checked out the exhibit," Nairne said, "but wisely decided not to make an issue out of anything."

Mapplethorpe appeared at an ICA symposium with photographer David Bailey, but unfortunately Nairne's anticipated "stimulating debate" fell short of its purpose. C. S. Manegold recorded the following exchange:

Questioner: "When Marlon Brando's film *The Wild Bunch* [*sic*] came out, I think the projectionist in England was jailed for having shown it. Now in this exhibition you've got that fist-fucking picture. Now how much further do you think we can actually go?"

Mapplethorpe: "Actually, I have one with two [fists] . . ."

Questioner: "Seriously, how much further? It's amazing to me that the ICA is showing that picture, and I think that's great in one respect. But how much further do you think we can go just in terms of shocking people?"

Mapplethorpe: "I don't know . . . I mean, that's not my kind of . . . issue. . . . I mean, I'm not trying to . . . I recorded that because it happened to me. . . . In fact . . . the *fist* in that picture belongs to an art director for one of the better art fashion magazines . . . they were friends of mine. I mean, I wasn't making a point of how far . . . I also have a photograph with a lot of blood in it. I don't know what the point is that you are making."

Later that evening Mapplethorpe, who arrived at the opening with Jack Walls in tow, was so stoned that Sandy Nairne could barely carry on a conversation with him. He then left the ICA to attend a dinner party given for him by one of his newer English acquaintances, Francesca Thyssen (the daughter of the German industrialist and art collector Hans Heinrich Thyssen), who had hosted Mapplethorpe and Lisa Lyon at her home in Jamaica the previous year. "I was struck by how important it was to Robert to maintain those social ties," observed Nairne. "He deliberately selected pictures of his London friends for the portrait section of the show, because, after having spent so much time playing with that set, I think he wanted a way to bring them back into his life. When I spoke to Robert about any of his pictures, he could never seem to disentangle his personal relationships from the images. When we were first planning the show in 1982, he had wanted a big section on Lisa Lyon, then the next time I met with him, he said, 'Well, let's save some space.' By the time the show was going up he only wanted a few pictures of her, and the reason was not that he didn't like the photographs, but that he was 'fed up' with her. That was the only way he seemed to be able to discuss and evaluate his work; it was whether or not he liked the people, not the pictures."

Nairne was miffed that after he spent so much time planning the exhibit and producing a sixty-four-page catalogue Mapplethorpe never bothered to thank him, or to send a follow-up note. Nine months later, during a chance encounter with Mapplethorpe in New

York, the photographer asked, "Where have you been? I told your secretary I wanted to take your photograph." Nairne had never received the message but understood that Mapplethorpe's offer to do his portrait was meant as a thank-you. He agreed to be photographed but made a silent vow that he would not allow himself to be transformed into a stark and formal Mapplethorpe creation. He purposely wore a loose-fitting Katharine Hamnett jacket to the photo session, and while Mapplethorpe smoked a joint, the curator projected a mental image of himself as someone relaxed and friendly. When they moved from the sitting room into the studio area, however, Nairne noticed that Mapplethorpe no longer seemed stoned, and that his blurry eyes had assumed an expression of steely intensity. He began firing instructions at Nairne in a soft but commanding voice: "Move your hands before your lapel . . . turn your head to the left . . . shift your eyes to the right." Before Nairne had time to think about what was happening to him, he had abdicated control of his own body. "I was suddenly part of the process," he explained, "and I felt myself becoming stiff and formalized. Robert was sculpting me into a Mapplethorpe photograph as surely as if I'd been a piece of stone."

The spring of 1984 marked Edward Mapplethorpe's two-year anniversary as his brother's assistant, but the adulation he had once felt toward his older brother had turned to profound disappointment. He had been careful to play by Robert's rules; he respected his privacy and never asked for help with his own career. There were times when he even thought Robert liked having him around, especially at the end of a day when they would share a joint and laugh together. It came as a shock, therefore, when Robert invited him to breakfast one morning and calmly ordered scrambled eggs and coffee before delivering a vitriolic lecture. It seemed that Robert had learned that dealer Sam Hardison had invited Ed to exhibit one of his pictures in a group show at his gallery. Robert's pictures were featured in the same exhibit, so the invitation listed two Mapplethorpes. "I'm not going to have my kid brother come along and ride off my energy," he scolded Ed. "I want you to change your name." Ed was totally unprepared for Robert's edict and told him that he wouldn't even know what name to substitute. But Robert had thought of everything. "Mom's maiden name is Maxey," he suggested. "Why don't you use that?"

Thus Edward Mapplethorpe became Edward Maxey, but the transition was not a smooth one, and Ed was puzzled and angered by his brother's reaction. "How could I be a threat to him?" he wondered. "Robert was having museum shows, and I was just starting my career." At the end of March, Ed took a trip to Los Angeles to visit friends and to see if he liked the city well enough to move there. Though he hadn't told Robert yet, he wanted to quit his job and start his new life as Edward Maxey somewhere else. First, however, he had agreed to rendezvous with his brother in L.A. to assist him in taking pictures for *A Day in the Life of Los Angeles,* a book project that involved sending a hundred photographers to cover the city between the hours of 12:00 A.M. and 11:59 P.M. on March 30. Robert was staying at the Hyatt Hotel on Sunset Boulevard with the other photographers, and when Ed met him in the lobby, he was already complaining that he shouldn't have accepted the assignment. "What am I doing here?" Robert grumbled. "I'm not a photojournalist." Later that evening the brothers attended a reception at the G. Ray Hawkins Gallery, where Robert picked up his identification badge, then directed Ed to drop him off at a gay bar. When Robert woke up the next afternoon at one o'clock, he was the only photographer involved in the project to have spent twelve of his twenty-four hours in L.A. having sex and sleeping.

He had arranged to take portraits later that night of artists David Hockney, Ellsworth Kelly, and Ed Ruscha at a dinner party given in his honor at the home of art collector Dagny Corcoran. But when the living room proved too congested, the photographer placed his tripod on the lawn, where he kept getting electrical shocks every time he pressed the button controlling the strobe unit. "Robert was terrified he was going to get electrocuted," Ed Maxey said, "and by the time we finished the portraits we didn't even make the official deadline. Robert didn't care. He just wanted the whole thing to be over."

So did Ed; during an emotional confrontation at the Hyatt Hotel the following day, he told Robert that he was moving to Los Angeles. Robert exploded, and in an angry voice that reminded Ed of their father's, he attacked him for being selfish and inconsiderate.

"How dare you!" Robert yelled. "I've put energy into training you, and now you're repaying me by quitting your job. You're never going to get anywhere in life if you don't live up to your obligations. Remember, you're *my* employee." Ed was so shaken by his brother's assault that he burst into tears. "I've been good to you these last few years," Ed cried. "But I want my own life. I want to establish myself as a person. You're just thinking of yourself and the problems it's going to cause for you."

Indeed, Robert's technical setup had become more complicated since Ed had joined him, and he was now using several strobes, a hair light, and diffusion filters to soften the faces of his portrait sitters. He could not take pictures without an assistant anymore, and realizing it would be difficult to find a replacement for Ed, he persuaded his brother to continue working at the studio until the right person came along. "I can't just have anybody assisting me," Robert informed him. "I need somebody who I can really communicate with."

Ed remained in L.A. several days longer than Robert, and when he returned to Bond Street he was amazed to find that his brother had already replaced him. "I'd like you to meet Javier Gonzalez," Robert said, introducing Ed to his new assistant. "He's just a Spanish street kid but he's very ambitious." Robert had met Javier in February when he traveled to Madrid for an opening of his photographs at the Fernando Vijande Gallery, and attracted by the young man's classical profile and punk haircut, he had offered to give him a job one day. "He doesn't speak English," Robert informed a disbelieving Ed, "but I don't think it should take longer than a week for you to train him. He's got a dictionary." And so Ed's final assignment was to teach someone who didn't speak English how to assist his finicky brother. "Javier was a smart kid," Ed said, "but a lot of the terms weren't even in the dictionary. Everybody in the studio thought it was just another example of Robert's craziness."

For Jack Walls it was the final straw, and even though Mapplethorpe explained that it was primarily a business arrangement, Walls observed him dipping into his bank account to pay for his new assistant's English lessons and dental bills. Walls responded by sinking deeper into drugs and, finally, by stealing money from the photographer's apartment. Mapplethorpe retaliated by evicting him from Bleecker Street and telling everyone he knew that Walls was a thief and a liar. "I was happy to get away from him," Walls said, "because, frankly, his lifestyle was gross, and I had my own reputation to think of."

CHAPTER NINETEEN

"Ultimately he treated people the way he treated a statue or
his collection of pottery. People were either subjects for his
photographs, or they were in his life the way his
collections were in his life."

—*Paul Schmidt, about Robert Mapplethorpe*

I n June 1984, two months after his brother left for Los Angeles,
Robert Mapplethorpe faced another defection: Sam Wagstaff suddenly sold his photography collection to the J. Paul Getty Museum
in Malibu.

The sale had been part of a secret package deal brokered by Daniel
Wolf, who brought together nine collections, including those owned
by Arnold Crane and André Jammes, to provide the Getty with a
total of eighteen thousand photographs. What made the $20 million
package deal so unusual was that none of the sellers knew the identity
of the buyer until after the transaction had been completed. Consequently, while Wagstaff received $4.5 million for his photographs,
he suffered a temporary blow to his ego when he realized that his
pictures would be merged with thousands of others. "Sam told me
he had wanted the Wagstaff collection to remain a separate entity,"

George Rinhart recalled. "He was very upset when he learned what happened."

Wagstaff's collection had become a burden to him, however, and he was relieved that someone else would now bear the responsibility for it. "Sam had a lifelong pattern of developing huge obsessions, then walking away from his commitments," said curator Jane Livingston. "He did it with his contemporary art collection, and now photography. Sam told me, 'I'm getting pissed off having to take care of it.' He had to rent another apartment to house the photographs, and he was always worried about someone breaking in. He didn't want the hassle. Sam may have been a voracious collector, but he never wanted to be tied down by his possessions. In some ways, Sam was just one massively spoiled brat."

Among the photographs that remained with Wagstaff in New York were his collection of Mapplethorpes, which, according to Daniel Wolf, he had refused to part with, even though the dealer had badly wanted them for the Getty. Wagstaff's relationship with Mapplethorpe, though, had been rooted in photography, and while he had divested himself of most of his pictures, perhaps the sentimentalist in him could not let go completely. But just as Wagstaff didn't need to give outraged speeches on photography's behalf anymore—the public had grown considerably more enlightened about photography as art—he no longer needed to promote Mapplethorpe's career; it, too, was doing fine without him. "I used to think of Sam and Robert as being like Brian Epstein and the Beatles," Howard Read said. "But after a while it became sad, because Sam would come into the gallery, and Robert would tell him, 'Shut up! You don't know what you're talking about.' Robert thought Sam's advice was getting old and tired, and he didn't need to consult a broken record anymore." Yet for all Mapplethorpe's complaining, he was so emotionally tied to Wagstaff that he experienced a twinge of regret when he first learned of the Getty sale; it signaled a bittersweet ending to that part of their lives together. Then, when Wagstaff declared his newest passion—American silver from the nineteenth and early twentieth centuries—Mapplethorpe responded like a jealous lover and proclaimed it "hideous."

Wagstaff had long been fascinated with silver, and when dining with friends he occasionally rummaged through their cupboards searching for heirlooms. From time to time he had purchased a few silver pieces at auction, such as a Tiffany water pitcher encrusted with spider chrysanthemums, but such an ornate and dowdy object seemed an unlikely prize for an ex-curator of contemporary art. Wagstaff delighted in confounding people's expectations, however, and American Victorian silver was regarded as so vulgar in its design and in the way it paired silver with copper, or even silver plate, that he decided to adopt it. The silver was something he could promote the way he had photography, or the career of Robert Mapplethorpe. It was yet another manifestation of his Pygmalion fantasy; finding neglected pieces in junk shops and flea markets, he could take them home, polish them up, and show the world how brightly they shined.

His penthouse was soon transformed into a sparkling silver vault, and dozens of eccentric objects piled up on the floor: cheese scoops decorated with cats and mice; condiment services embellished with crabs and fish; an 1870 Gorham yacht trophy with a mermaid perched as a handle; a silver bowl with icicles and polar bears inspired by the 1867 U.S. purchase of Alaska; countless cake baskets, compotes, fruit bowls, butter dishes, and napkin rings. Ingrid Sischy described her experience of Wagstaff's whimsical lair for *HG:* "Despite the chicness, some problems with air trapping had developed between the floor boards and the white linoleum. Walking around was like treading on Bubble Wrap, and the sound of popping would punctuate conversation. So at his place even the acoustics contributed to the Wagstaff electricity, the expectation that he would unwrap and reveal something amazing. I was never disappointed. In a way, it was permanent Christmas up there."

Mapplethorpe, whose own spartan aesthetic did not encompass silver-plated inkwells shaped like cats and dogs, thought Wagstaff was wasting his money. Meanwhile, he had turned to collecting modernist glass by Venini and Murano, and his cramped Bleecker Street apartment was now overflowing with turquoise decanters; garnet handkerchief glass vases; leaf-shaped dishes; paperweights; and dozens of vases in red, amber, brown, and blue. "The Venini glass really caught Robert's attention," recalled Mark Isaacson, who sold him many of the pieces. "He bought at least a hundred of these really elegant bottles and vases because there was something about the hardness and the softness of them—the combination of opaque and translucent—that really captivated him. I think it was the whole experience of collecting that cemented his relationship with Sam, although they pursued it in different ways. Robert didn't care to know the history of the pieces—the dates and the names of the manufacturers. It was purely a visual thing with him. Those times I didn't have anything specific to show him he'd go crazy and pace up and down the shop. 'Don't you have *anything*?' he'd snap at me. Robert was like a drug addict who needed his fix. Whenever I'd get a new shipment of glass, I'd call him up, and he'd be down at the store in less than an hour. He'd try to be casual about it, but I'd see the excitement in his eyes, like he was already anticipating the incredible rush he'd get from buying something."

The image of Mapplethorpe and Wagstaff nearly buried in their pharaoh's tomb of treasures was symbolic of a decade in which more people had more money to buy things than at any other time in the country's history. Nowhere was this phenomenon more evident than in the art world, which, in a Faustian bargain with Wall Street, had begun catering to the newly rich arbitrageurs, corporate raiders, and mergers-and-acquisitions specialists who needed material objects—paintings, sculptures, photographs—to fill their newly renovated Park Avenue co-ops. SoHo, in the words of Maureen Dowd in *The New York Times Magazine,* had become a "blue-chip bohemia where artists talk tax shelters more than politics, and where American Express gold cards are more emblematic than garrets." It was a dramatic reversal from the days of Max's Kansas City, where famous artists had traded their work for a bar tab. But Max's had been replaced as an artists' hangout by the elegant Mr. Chow's on the Upper East Side, and the art stars of the eighties were not reclusive intellectuals, but people such as Keith Haring, who would later open a shop that sold T-shirts, shoelaces, and wallpaper that featured his trademark doodle designs.

Throughout 1984 Mapplethorpe was determined to reap the financial rewards of the booming art market; he created a limited edition, phallic-shaped coffee table that was distributed by ARC International, and arranged to have his flower lithographs decorate the walls of Morgans, the new minimalist hotel owned by Studio 54's Steve Rubell and Ian Schrager. "My theory about creativity," he told *Photo/Design,* "is that the more money one has, the more creative one can be." He watched other photographers, such as Bruce Weber, win highly lucrative fashion accounts, and he wondered why he wasn't able to do the same, especially since Weber's work often glorified the male body in a distinctly homoerotic way. Yet Weber managed to obfuscate the issue by choosing models that were paragons of all-American heterosexuality—Olympic athletes, surfers, and U.S. Marines—who, as Allen Ellenzweig has pointed out, were likely to be homophobes in real life. "I find the work intellectually dishonest and cynical," Ellenzweig said, "because Weber is clearly appealing to a homoerotic sensibility. But who does he use as his models? In many cases, it's straight men who live in a segregated male universe, and who probably think of gays as 'faggots.' In any minority community, there's a lot of self-hate, a lot of unresolved psychological issues about power, for however much we admire powerful men, they are often the ones who treat us badly, deny us our rights, and beat us up. For that reason, I think Robert's work is so much more honest than Weber's."

For the past year Mapplethorpe had been working with Art & Commerce, an agency that specializes in the editorial and advertising side of a photographer's career. But unlike other clients, such as Steven Meisel and Annie Leibovitz, Mapplethorpe was not an easy sell, and Anne Kennedy, who owned the agency with her partner Jimmy Moffat, had problems convincing American clients to hire him. "In the beginning we would send out these huge portfolios filled with his pictures," she said, "but people just didn't get it. Robert was perceived as being a photographer out on the edge. We did more work with the European magazines, which, generally, are a little more creative and daring than the American ones. But Robert really wanted to work for the American magazines, and America mostly means Condé Nast. Robert's pictures, though, were too hard and specific for them. I thought Robert was the great portraitist of our time, but that doesn't necessarily mean his pictures had any place in those magazines. They wanted things that were funnier and lighter, more amusing, and Robert was not really about that."

No matter whose portraits he took, or whose products he pro-

moted, his pictures always seemed to be more about Robert Mapplethorpe than anything else. Asked to photograph a pair of high
heels for the German magazine *Stern,* for example, he balanced a
shoe on the buttocks of a naked black man; for *Vogue Italia,* he
accessorized a black model's body with diamond jewelry; later, for a
Japanese department store, he photographed the same black model
bound by leather belts. The real message of the pictures wasn't
about fashion, but power and submission, especially as it related to
black men, whom Mapplethorpe regarded as the ultimate acces-
sory—a fetish equal to a high-heel shoe, or a diamond elephant pin.

Mapplethorpe's detractors frequently characterized his work as
being too cold and unemotional—all surface and no heart; yet one
sensed a combustible blend of emotions just beneath the exterior
that threatened to blow the glassy perfection to smithereens. There
was something disquieting about his pictures, even the commercial
ones, and that element did not lend itself well to American consumer
culture. "Robert was very Catholic in his way," said Paul Schmidt,
who had written the introductory essay to the "X Portfolio." "We
had several talks about it, because I'd grown up Catholic, too, and I
often wondered if Robert's pictures were his mechanism for dealing
with his sexual guilt. When a kid exposes himself in the third grade,
it's an act of aggression, and within that context, it's also a desire for
retribution and punishment. It's 'Fuck you,' then it's 'Punish me,
I'm a bad boy.' Because the iconography of sex had never been dealt
with in such a way in our society, he became famous for opening up
a whole theoretical field of speculation. But I think Robert, at first,
was dealing with the sexual imagery in a very subconscious way,
then, once he realized he could get away with it, he was like a kid in
a candy store. Ultimately I think he was miserable though, and without sounding condescending, somewhere in Robert is a shriveled
soul crying out for affection."

Perhaps that's why Mapplethorpe decided to forgive Jack Walls,
who after stealing money from him had managed to insinuate himself back into the photographer's life. This time Mapplethorpe was
convinced that Walls had the potential to be the "new Ben Vereen,"
and arranged to launch Walls's career in tandem with the December
10 premiere of his own eight-minute film, *Lady,* which featured Lisa

Lyon. He had rented the club Private Eyes for the movie screening, and when the film was over, Walls was scheduled to sing—except that he was ninety minutes late for his own debut, and Mapplethorpe was seething. For its patience the audience was rewarded with Walls's nearly tone-deaf interpretation of "Chicago," after which he left the stage to a modest smattering of applause.

"It was a nightmare," recalled Mark Isaacson, "and everybody was sitting around, whispering, 'Oh my God!' and wondering why Robert would embarrass himself like that. I mean, we're talking about the art snob community of New York—a bunch of piranhas—and I'm sure people looked at Jack, as they did Milton, and thought, Why doesn't he just drop his pants, because that's obviously the only thing he has to offer."

Not long after the debacle with Walls, Mapplethorpe encountered Fern (Urquhart) Logan, his friend from Pratt, and complained of his inability to find a suitable partner. He now wanted someone rich, he said, and professionally accomplished. Fern, who was a photographer herself, had divorced Tom Logan, Mapplethorpe's nemesis from the Pershing Rifles, and she was searching for a boyfriend, too. She invited him to attend a yacht party that had been advertised as a social evening for women looking for black millionaires. "I wanted one," Logan said, "and he wanted one." But when they arrived in black-tie at New York harbor, there wasn't a millionaire in sight. "It's a disaster," Mapplethorpe complained. "They're all in *sales.*"

At one point during the evening he advised Logan to carve out a professional niche for herself as a female photographer specializing in black male nudes. "They're black, and you're black," he said, "so you'll probably have an easier time convincing them to take off their clothes." He then asked if she knew how stimulating the word "nigger" was during sexual foreplay. "Let me get this straight," she said, dumbfounded. "You're looking for an intelligent, successful black millionaire who wants you—a white man—to call him 'nigger'?" Mapplethorpe patiently explained that she hadn't grasped the whole concept. "I wouldn't call him 'nigger' all the time," he said, offended. "Only during sex."

. . .

Mapplethorpe's personal life was a paradigm of chaos, yet somehow he managed to keep his studio running fairly smoothly. Tina Summerlin, who had previously worked for Annie Leibovitz, had replaced Betsy Evans as his studio manager; she, too, was blond and well educated, and in her role as Mapplethorpe's front woman, she helped offset his sinister image with a veneer of normalcy. Javier Gonzalez had learned English, and although no one fully understood the dynamics of his relationship with Mapplethorpe, he proved himself an able assistant. As for Tom Baril, he still detested his employer, yet he continued to produce such magnificent work for him that the photographer was universally lauded for the quality of his prints. "Robert was very good at knowing how to use people," said Howard Read, "and that takes a certain talent, too."

Mapplethorpe's gift was much in evidence with Dimitri Levas, a prop stylist whom he had first met at the 80 Langton Street exhibit in 1978, then again in 1983, when they struck up a conversation in SoHo about their mutual interest in 1950s glass. Levas was an inveterate flea-market shopper, and he began selling Mapplethorpe pieces he had discovered on his rummaging trips. Impressed by his eye and foraging ability, Mapplethorpe encouraged him to buy flowers so he could photograph them, and before long Levas was arriving at Bond Street with bouquets of tiger lilies and tulips. There was something of a courtship ritual in his efforts, and he confessed to being completely starstruck by the photographer, whose work he greatly admired and whose glamorous life served in sharp contrast to his own. Levas had worked for the Charles Cowles Gallery, then assisted John Loring, design director of Tiffany's, but the jobs were low-paying ones and he was often strapped for money. He lived in a small apartment bordering SoHo, where Mapplethorpe's photograph *Jim, Sausalito* was among his prized possessions. He was of average height, with a stocky build; he had dark brown hair, dark eyes, and a pleasant face. Both physically and temperamentally he was ideally suited to play the secondary role of Mapplethorpe's faithful sidekick. After he left his job at Tiffany's he began receiving styling assignments from magazines, but what he loved best was working for Mapplethorpe, even though the photographer rarely paid him and frequently denied him styling credit. "I was really intent on making his photographs better," Levas explained. "I saw the pictures that I thought were really good, and I tried to push him to maintain those standards. I'd get possessed about bringing him the right flowers and the right vase."

Contrary to Mapplethorpe's reputation for being totally career-driven and a perfectionist, he was often lazy about coming up with ideas, and would photograph almost anything Levas brought him—fruits, flowers, vegetables. His social life was more interesting to him than taking pictures, and to that end he maintained a frenzied schedule. He was out every night at parties and openings, then off to Keller's. "I used to say to him, 'Take some nudes of white men for a change,' " Levas recalled, "but he was attracted to black men, and he wasn't the kind of person who'd go after models for pictures; for years, he had gone after them for sex, and then had taken their pictures."

AIDS, however, had impacted the way Mapplethorpe approached his photography, and while he would not sacrifice Keller's, he more willingly photographed models whose bodies appealed to him aesthetically, rather than sexually. It was Levas, in fact, who discovered the bodybuilders Ken Moody and Lydia Cheng, who became two of the most visible Mapplethorpe icons of the mid-eighties.

Moody was a black physical trainer whose extraordinary body was rendered even more photogenic by the disease alopecia; without hair, his skin gleamed like bronze, and Mapplethorpe photographed him regularly between 1983 and 1985. While Moody admired the book *Lady,* he was generally offended by the photographer's depiction of blacks, particularly *Man in Polyester Suit,* and he made it clear that frontal nudity was off-limits. Mapplethorpe instead focused on what Stephen Koch in *Art in America* described as "the black body graphic" as distinct from the "black body erotic." Moody existed as a way to demonstrate color and form; for one photograph, Mapplethorpe covered his head and shoulders with white talcum powder; for another, he paired him with Robert Sherman, the white model with alopecia, to heighten the dialectic between the tonal properties of black and white.

Unlike Lisa Lyon, whose *Lady* photographs revealed a woman steeped in the seventies sex-and-drug culture, Lydia Cheng lived with her husband, who owned a bookstore near Columbia University, and was scrupulously health-conscious. Robert thought she was too much of a yuppie for his taste, and made no effort to get to know her at all. She was merely a body to him, and a headless one at that, for he thought her Asian facial features limited the universality of her beauty, and usually photographed her from the neck down. He wanted Cheng to represent a timeless, racially neutered feminine ideal—one he would not have been capable of creating earlier in his career, when his ideas of beauty were inextricably bound to his homosexual obsessions.

Mapplethorpe attempted to heighten the visual properties of his photographs by experimenting with platinum printing, which, unlike the photo norm of silver, produces a more expansive range of tones between black and white. Instead of using commercial paper, the images are printed on watercolor paper that has been coated with a platinum emulsion, which attaches itself to the fiber as if becoming part of the material itself. The end result is a softer, more velvety finish capable of seducing the eye more effectively than ordinary silver prints. The process is complicated, however, and since Tom Baril wasn't equipped to do it in the darkroom at Bond Street, Mapplethorpe collaborated with Martin Axon, a master printer from England who was now living in New York. In preparation for a show at the Miller Gallery in May 1985, Mapplethorpe went over his photographs with Axon to see which ones would work best in platinum, and among the images they selected were those of Lydia Cheng, and Ken Moody and Robert Sherman. In September, encouraged by his successful foray into platinum, Mapplethorpe presented fifty photographs using fourteen different printing processes, including silkscreen, lithography, and rotogravure, at the Barbara Gladstone Gallery. "Considering the technical challenges involved in these exotic printing processes," John Tavenner wrote in the *New York Native,* "Mapplethorpe's role was probably one of selecting and approving, rather than getting his hands dirty. One is left with the impression that Mapplethorpe has stepped back, turned inward, and feels less. . . . The detached air that hangs over these photographs implies a retreat into safety after years of dangerous acts."

The specter of death was everywhere that year. In May, Joan Mapplethorpe collapsed and was taken to the hospital, where she was diagnosed with emphysema. Joan's mother had died of lung cancer, and now Joan herself was in danger of dying from a respiratory disease worsened by her lifelong addiction to nicotine. Robert sent flowers to the hospital, but did not visit his mother until July, when she had already been in the intensive care unit for several months. He rented a limousine and drove to Winthrop Hospital in Mineola, Long Island, with Anne Kennedy, who waited in the car while Robert went inside to find his brother Richard weeping at his mother's bedside. Richard lived in Los Angeles, and since he came home only once a year, he was afraid he would never see her alive again. Robert lingered outside the door until Richard was finished, then, taking his brother's place beside Joan, he was stalwart and unemotional. His sisters were struck by the contrast between the two men, and how, when they brushed past each other in the doorway, it was like two strangers passing on the street. The rest of the family hoped Robert might return with them to Floral Park, but unnerved by the grim image of his mother hooked up to a respirator, he immediately headed back to Manhattan.

He did not find much solace there, however, for Jim Nelson, Sam Wagstaff's lover, had recently been diagnosed with AIDS, and while neither Mapplethorpe nor Wagstaff cared to discuss it, the reality of the disease was now hitting precipitously close to home. Wagstaff and Nelson spent most of the summer in Oakleyville, where Wagstaff had recently paid $300,000 for a dilapidated, hundred-year-old house whose previous owner had died of AIDS. "The place was more like a beach shack," recalled neighbor Sam Green. "It was damp and smelly and the roof leaked—not a place anyone would want to live." Yet Nelson tried as best he could to transform the house into a comfortable home; he hung curtains, dressed the table with elegant linens, and hired a gardener to plant a rose garden. But deer persisted in chewing up the bushes, and no matter how many times he replaced the plants, each new day brought a diminished supply of flowers. The sad tale of the roses was a metaphor for Nelson's failing immune system, and perhaps without realizing what he was doing, he battled the deer as if his life depended on it. Periodically throughout the summer, Sam Green heard the wailing sound of "My roses, my roses" coming from Nelson's garden.

Wagstaff spent his days combing the beach for pottery shards that had filtered down from the local dump. He later commissioned an artist, Carol Steen, to make the pieces into jewelry, which he gave to friends for Christmas and birthdays. He called his designs *"bijoux des plages."* More perplexing was his passion for collecting the tiny scraps of metal believed to be nail remnants of ancient ships. He and Nelson would wait for the tide to come in, then sift through the sand for hours searching for the microscopic specks of gray metal. A French art dealer who knew Wagstaff well was horrified when he first saw his collection of metal scraps, which he displayed in tea cups scattered around the house. "Sam had an absolutely brilliant eye," he said, "and I almost wanted to cry when he showed me these pebbles and things. I couldn't understand it at all." But Pierre Apraxine, curator of the Gilman Paper Company and also a long-time friend, joined Wagstaff on one of his scavenger hunts that summer, and he marveled at Wagstaff's conviction that it was possible to achieve a heightened state of consciousness merely by looking at things.

Mapplethorpe blocked his anxiety in the usual method—by going to Keller's—but the bar's convivial atmosphere had grown more sober. One summer evening, when he greeted Kelly Edey, whom he had not seen since the erudite antique clock collector had settled down with a fragrance factory worker several years before, he casually inquired, "How's your lover?" "He's dying of AIDS," came the anguished reply. Edey immediately apologized to Mapplethorpe for injecting a note of tragedy into their usual conversation about black sexuality. "I shouldn't have subjected you to that," Edey said, "because I heard you were going through a period of terrible suffering, too." He was referring to Milton Moore, whose ill-fated romance with Mapplethorpe had become part of Keller's lore. "I still am suffering," Mapplethorpe replied. Edey thought he looked older and more haggard than he remembered, but attributed Mapplethorpe's careworn appearance to cocaine. "Keller's is still the best place to go for black men," Mapplethorpe told Edey, though both men were puzzled by the dwindling number of them at the bar.

Several of Mapplethorpe's friends warned him that his sexual behavior was tantamount to suicide. Confronting him at a party one night, Fran Lebowitz told him, "You're like a kamikaze. Why don't you just jump off a building instead?" Art dealer Barbara Gladstone refused to leave a taxi one evening when Mapplethorpe stopped it to drop her off at her apartment, then directed the driver to go to West Street. "I know where you're going," she said. "Don't you think it's really stupid?" He stared coldly into her eyes. "I think you should mind your own business," he replied. Gladstone stepped out of the cab, and he continued on his way.

Mapplethorpe had always maintained that sex was more important to him than anything in his life, and even if the consequences of his actions now carried a greater risk, he refused to alter his behavior. Perhaps because he rarely engaged in anal intercourse, the method of transmission of AIDS most frequently cited by health professionals, he believed he wasn't in danger. Or perhaps he was in such a state of denial he believed himself invincible. Writer and editor Steven Aronson, who had known Mapplethorpe since 1970, recalled a conversation he had with him at a lunch party given by jewelry designer Kenneth J. Lane: "We were leaving the party together, and Robert told me, 'Gee, this AIDS stuff is pretty scary. I hope I don't get it.' And I thought, 'Oh my God, if there are three people in this city who are going to get it, one of them is going to be him.' In my mind's eye, I saw the geese walk over the grave."

CHAPTER TWENTY

"I'm not in a high-risk group."

—*Robert Mapplethorpe*

The Robert Mapplethorpe who turned thirty-nine in November 1985 was a considerably more respectable figure than the one who had first terrorized the art world with pictures of gay S&M sex. His birthday coincided with the publication of *Certain People: A Book of Portraits,* which earned high marks from no less an establishment newspaper than *The New York Times.* Five years earlier the paper had denounced him for "redrawing the boundaries of public taste"; now *Certain People* was mentioned in its *Book Review* as a possible gift idea for Christmas, and the photographer was heralded by critic Andy Grundberg as "the best portrait photographer to emerge in the last 10 years."

Jack Woody, who published *Certain People* under his own Twelvetrees Press imprint, had conspired with Mapplethorpe to keep the overtly sexual material out of the book. They wanted to draw in a wider audience to his work, then, according to Woody, "blow everyone's minds away" by publishing a second volume of X-rated photographs. Consequently, of the ninety-five pictures in *Certain People*, the only direct allusion to gay S&M is the portrait of a leather-clad couple staring at the camera with an American Gothic solemnity that is almost farcical, given the bizarre drawing room setting and the Houdini-like shackles worn by one of the men. Woody never published a second Mapplethorpe book, however, for by the time he had finished working on the first volume, the two men despised each other. Woody had played a large role in helping to validate homoerotic photography with his 1981 book on George Platt Lynes, and he believed Mapplethorpe had been strongly influenced by Lynes's work, as well as by other photographers he had been exposed to through Wagstaff's collecting. "I wanted to include some of the earlier, rougher portraits to show the changes he'd gone through as a photographer," Woody explained. "But Robert would have none of that. The earliest portrait he agreed to include was one taken in 1976. Robert was very afraid of people saying that Sam had created him, and he was very calculating in the way he attempted to distance himself from Sam. He wanted to make people think he had come down from the sky on angels' wings, or, rather, more accurately, up from the ground. Image was everything to him."

The title *Certain People* implied an exclusivity that reflected Mapplethorpe's lifelong desire to be regarded as a "special person" himself, and he celebrated his initiation into that fraternity by placing self-portraits on the back and front covers of the book. These photographs from 1980 showed Mapplethorpe's awareness that his own uniqueness derived in part from his willingness to cross the boundaries of sexuality, class, and gender. For the book's cover he had selected a photograph that revealed him to be the epitome of 1950s masculine cool, in a black leather jacket and a greased pompadour, a cigarette hanging from his mouth. The picture on the back cover exposed another side; bare-chested and heavily made-up, his lips pliant and quivering, he is, like Marcel Duchamp's feminine alter ego, "Rrose Selavy," a man's version of a woman. "The message that Mapplethorpe delivers," David Joselit wrote in the "Perfect Moment" exhibition catalogue, "is that the experience of any masculine or feminine identity is the sensation of an unstable, constantly

readjusted succession of poses." As Mapplethorpe oscillated between male and female postures, he wavered between two ends of
the social spectrum—"New York squalor," as Stephen Koch defined it, and "New York glamour." The two universes collided in
Certain People to produce a democratic mix of rich faces (Francesca
Thyssen, Doris Saatchi, the Lambton sisters); famous faces (Richard
Gere, Kathleen Turner, Donald Sutherland); and obscure but unforgettable faces (Nick with a skull tattooed on his forehead; a regal-
looking porn dealer; a stripper in a gargantuan headdress).

From the time Mapplethorpe had taken many of the portraits,
however, the balance had tilted in favor of "glamour," and at the
publication party for his book, he unveiled his new $500,000 loft,
which had been purchased for him by Wagstaff with proceeds from
the Getty sale. The loft was located at 35 West Twenty-third Street,
two blocks away from where Mapplethorpe had once lived with
Patti Smith above the Oasis bar. Unlike its squalid predecessor, the
new loft merited a layout in *House & Garden,* which traced his "aesthetic genealogy" from Oscar Wilde and Aubrey Beardsley through
Christian Bérard and Jean Cocteau. The photographer's creation of
"little altars," which merged religious and occult items, had been
part of his decorating scheme since Pratt, but now that he had more
money to invest in his props, glowing Jesus statues and plastic devils
had been replaced by ivory crucifixes, marble satyrs, a bust of Mus-
solini, and an Ed Ruscha screenprint consisting of the word "EVIL"
in black and red. His black-leather-upholstered chairs had been
dressed up with pillows in strié silk taffeta from Scalamandre, and his
taste in furniture had evolved from the simplicity of the Mission style
to Biedermeier and Regency. Looming over the sitting room adjacent to his bedroom was the ultimate symbol of his success—a Warhol silkscreen portrait of Mapplethorpe himself.

The objects in the loft were so carefully composed that it was not
surprising Mapplethorpe did not want to shatter their perfection by
inviting Jack Walls to move in with him. "Don't get any big ideas
that it's your place, too," Mapplethorpe warned him after Walls had
spent the day helping him pack up his belongings to move. Increasingly, Walls resented the way Mapplethorpe accepted handouts
from Sam Wagstaff while lecturing him on the virtues of self-reli-
ance. Clearly, it was a no-win situation, and tired of Mapplethorpe's

promiscuity and needling accusations, he broke off their relationship and flew home to Chicago on Thanksgiving Day. "It wasn't like I had anything to be grateful for," Walls said. "Robert was having a feast, and I was getting thrown the scraps."

One reason Mapplethorpe had maintained his relationship with Walls was that he hated attending social functions by himself, and Walls was a convenient if not always reliable date. But in the true spirit of the decade, Mapplethorpe had formed a bond with his interior designer, a fifty-year-old, flame-haired divorcee named Suzie Frankfurt, whose reputation as a contemporary Auntie Mame rested on her close friendship with Andy Warhol and several decades of party-going that had left her addicted to alcohol. By the 1980s Frankfurt had reformed her destructive ways, but still relished her position as one of the city's preeminent social animals. She threw lavishly catered black-tie dinners at her East Side townhouse, which had been decorated, she told *W,* to evoke the resplendent ballroom scenes in Tolstoy and Pushkin. Mapplethorpe was enthralled by her ostentatious display of wealth. "He really enjoyed coming to my house," Frankfurt said. "It was like a palace . . . all very grand and formal, and I'd always be wearing big gowns. Everything was very well organized because I had a lot of staff, and Robert liked the idea of having servants. The way he treated all his black friends, it was sort of servantlike, so if he'd had the money, he surely would have had a butler and footman and everything else."

That Mapplethorpe was now being squired around town by Suzie Frankfurt struck many of his friends as odd if not two-faced, for the photographer had always been highly critical of "fag hags," women whose lives revolved around homosexuals, and Frankfurt had a history of falling in love with gay men. "I'd broken up with Andy," she explained, "and Robert took his place. I thought he was beautiful, and that he had a real rock-star charisma. Our relationship was very romantic, although I don't think I even kissed him on the cheek." Frankfurt took Mapplethorpe to the opera and ballet; to lunch at Mortimer's, the clubby restaurant on the Upper East Side; and to the furniture auctions at Sotheby's. She wrote him romantic little notes and gave him intimate presents, such as a silk paisley bathrobe designed by Gianni Versace. Having become a Catholic convert, she urged him, unsuccessfully, to return to the Church, and to face up to the health hazards of his sexual behavior. He told her not to worry. "I'm not in a high-risk group," he explained. Mapplethorpe's logic was preposterous, and while Frankfurt knew he was in deep denial, she was infatuated with him nonetheless. "Suzie was passionately, desperately in love with Robert," said Michael Stout. "She did a lot for him, commissioning him to do portraits, and getting her fancy friends to do the same."

On New Year's Day, 1986, Frankfurt telephoned to tell Mapplethorpe she had met Cuban financier Roberto Polo the night before at his annual party at Le Cirque and learned he was looking for someone to shoot fashion advertisements for Cuban designer Miguel Cruz. "I told him, 'You've got to hire Robert Mapplethorpe,' " Frankfurt recalled.

Even for the 1980s, Polo's Cinderella story raised eyebrows among members of Nouvelle Society who themselves had made quantum leaps from rags to riches. No one, though, had vaulted higher and faster than Polo; he had been living in a modest Upper East Side one-bedroom apartment when he suddenly purchased a Gothic-style townhouse, which he decorated with priceless art and antiques in only six weeks. He then purchased an antiques shop on Madison Avenue, as well as an obscure fashion house headed by Miguel Cruz. Polo would later be arrested for misappropriating $110 million of his investors' money and end up in an Italian jail, but when Mapplethorpe first met him at his opulent townhouse, the photographer was suitably awestruck. Polo explained that he wanted to transform Miguel Cruz into an international design star, and Mapplethorpe's assignment was to pique the public's imagination with a slightly scandalous ad campaign in the spirit of Bruce Weber's pictures for Calvin Klein. The work Mapplethorpe did for Miguel Cruz illustrated why he would never be a successful fashion photographer, for he paid no attention to the clothing whatsoever. His most famous picture for the Cruz campaign consists of a naked male model pulling a sweater over his head; the focus is not on the sweater, however, but on the way the model is sitting so that his back, buttocks, and legs form a gigantic phallus.

Mapplethorpe shot the Miguel Cruz ads for three seasons, but eventually quit after a dispute with Polo, whom he suspected, correctly as it turned out, of being a fraud. "The whole thing was just hideous," said agent Anne Kennedy. "The ads looked for the most part embarrassingly awful. The clothing was awful, and the people were awful. But it made Robert an enormous amount of money." And money, according to Kennedy, was his sole criterion in accepting commercial jobs, even if they were detrimental to his reputation. The more Kennedy worked with Mapplethorpe, the more ambivalent she felt toward him. She loved the Mapplethorpe with whom she could reminisce about her Catholic upbringing and laugh uproariously at shared stories of punitive nuns and priests. But there was another side to his personality she didn't like at all. He wasn't the only artist who yearned to make a lot of money, but his greed was coupled with social pretension and a hunger for publicity that increasingly made him a figure of ridicule in the art world. "I'd hear people talking about him and snickering at his pretense," Kennedy said. "The way he sometimes carried on was sort of pathetic and undignified for an artist."

Yet while making money was foremost in Mapplethorpe's mind, he was one of the few photographers accepted by the art world, and in recognition of this, Whitney curator Richard Marshall asked him to shoot portraits for the book *50 New York Artists*. Consequently, in addition to meeting with Roberto Polo, he spent three weeks in January taking pictures of Willem de Kooning, Mark di Suvero, Elizabeth Murray, Eric Fischl, Malcolm Morley, Richard Serra, Louise Nevelson, Red Grooms, and Sandro Chia. His own place among the artists he photographed was solidified by a self-portrait that ran alongside this personal statement: "I see things like they've never been seen before. Art is an accurate statement of the time in which it is made."

It was also an accurate statement of his obsessions at any given time, for while Mapplethorpe was creating a series of embarrassing ads for Miguel Cruz he took the same circle prop he used in the fashion photographs to produce the visually striking *Thomas in Circle*. The difference was that Thomas Williams was black, and Mapplethorpe was in love with his lean and sinewy body. Williams, a physical trainer, exotic dancer, and porn star, was Mapplethorpe's frequent companion throughout the spring and summer, and while no one realized it at the time, he would also be the photographer's last muse. Mapplethorpe never cared for him the way he had for

Milton Moore, or even Jack Walls, but he admired Williams's classical form and the glossy perfection of his skin. He was not so enchanted by the size of his head, which he deemed too small for the rest of him. Mapplethorpe dealt with the problem the way he had always dealt with nature's disappointments: he simply removed the flaws. Williams is often represented in photographs by only his torso, or with his head obscured. Mapplethorpe then complained that Williams was too small-minded for him, but since he couldn't fix that as easily, he did not foresee them having a long future together.

Nevertheless, he invited Williams to be his date at a black-tie dinner given in his honor at Suzie Frankfurt's house on May 10 to celebrate an opening of his work at the Palladium. The former concert hall had recently been transformed into a state-of-the-art club by Steve Rubell and Ian Schrager, and "art" was indeed the operative word there. Rubell had designed his club to appeal to artists—"the rock stars of the eighties"—and, more important, to the Wall Street types who bought the art. "God forbid a banker doesn't get in," Schrager told *New York,* explaining the Palladium's door policy. It was precisely this glitzy marriage of art and commerce that made Mapplethorpe think nothing of attending a black-tie dinner at Suzie Frankfurt's townhouse, then taking a limousine to the Palladium, where Patti Smith had once belted out the lyrics to "My Generation," the Who's famous anthem to youth rebellion. Times had changed, and Mapplethorpe had adapted himself to the zeitgeist, though he was still enough of a rebel to enjoy the shocked looks on people's faces when he showed up at social functions with a black man on his arm.

He captured that visual jolt in the photograph *Thomas and Dovanna,* in which a naked Williams dances with a beautiful white woman dressed in cotillion attire. What worked in a photograph did not work in his relationship with Suzie Frankfurt, however, and the decorator was appalled when she learned that Mapplethorpe had invited Williams to the dinner. "There were the names of all these couples on the guest list," Michael Stout recalled. "Lia and Agustin Fernandez . . . Robert and Thomas. When I met Suzie for lunch, she kept repeating, 'Robert and Thomas? . . . Robert and Thomas? Robert is *my* date.' She asked me to explain it to her a hundred times, and I told her it was basically bad manners. Robert should have had enough insight into the very society he was trying to break into to know how to behave at a dinner party. Suzie was so destroyed. She realized how silly she was giving this big party for Robert Mapplethorpe, and he was bringing a date."

Frankfurt remained friendly with Mapplethorpe, but after the Williams incident their "romance" was never the same. "Robert was like a drug," she said. "After you were with him for three hours, you just couldn't wait to get away, then you went through withdrawal, and wanted to see him again. But there was no give in that relationship, it was all sort of take."

Paul Schmidt pointed to Mapplethorpe's self-portraits as a key to his egocentricity. "They are really what it's all about," he explained. "The camera looks at me, I look at the camera, and everybody else is peripheral." Certainly the self-portraits served to dramatize each distinct phase of his life: the sexual confusion of the early Polaroids; the giddy happiness of his life with Sam Wagstaff as seen in the 1975 photograph Roland Barthes praised for its "blissful eroticism"; the S&M implications of the self-portrait with the whip; his obsession with blacks in a picture of the photographer performing oral sex on a man, probably Milton Moore; and most recently, a photograph of himself as social dandy, in a satin dinner jacket and bow tie. Tom Baril recalled that after he had developed that last self-portrait Mapplethorpe was more sensitive than usual about the lines on his face, and told Baril to erase as many as possible. "Well, you know, as you get older, all of a sudden you're doing bleaching and more diffusion," he told Anne Horton in a 1987 interview, in which he complained about the extra flesh under his chin that marred the self-portrait. "But it's not bad. I am sure the time will come when I say . . .'I like the way I used to look better.' But until then I'm okay."

Mapplethorpe was not okay, and no amount of diffusion and bleaching could help him. He was waking up in the middle of the night drenched in sweat; his lymph glands were swollen, and he had stomach pains and diarrhea. Sam Wagstaff had spent the past decade looking after Mapplethorpe's interests, but since the two men had built up a protective wall around the subject of AIDS, he did not insist that the younger man get tested for it. Wagstaff himself was suffering from chest pain and shortness of breath, and Jim Nelson had developed Kaposi's sarcoma, the purplish cancer lesions that are among the most frightening manifestations of the disease.

That Mapplethorpe managed to go about his business as though no one was suffering from anything more serious than a common cold was a testament to his denial and determination. He even agreed to be interviewed by TV España for a documentary on his life, and when asked if his portraits served as a chronicle of the era, he responded, "I just try to live my life and do my thing." He had always relied on Wagstaff to provide the subtext for his work, and that June he arranged for the Spanish reporter to visit Wagstaff at his penthouse, where he described the photographer as someone who "plays with danger a great deal." He used the analogy of the "bad boy" who skates where the ice is thin, unlike the "clunks . . . the ordinary people" who skate only on the thick part. Wagstaff, too, had made a career of skating on thin ice, and despite his sixty-four years, he had the look of a seditious prep school boy, a cherry bomb hidden in his navy blazer. He was still remarkably good-looking, as evidenced in the documentary, and gave the appearance of a man in robust health. His friends, therefore, were shocked when he was suddenly taken to St. Vincent's Hospital at the end of the month and diagnosed with tuberculosis. For someone with Wagstaff's refined aesthetic, the disease was suitably romantic-sounding and genteel, and he was not ashamed to tell people that he was "suffering from a touch of TB." What he did not mention was that tuberculosis, once viewed in the nineteenth century as the ailment of writers and poets, had now become an opportunistic infection associated with AIDS.

Mapplethorpe spent the Fourth of July weekend with Ingrid Sischy and Amy Sullivan in East Hampton, but he was so exhausted he fell asleep for several hours on the beach one afternoon. Sullivan tried to shield his fair skin from the sun by covering him with a towel, but his feet poked through and he received a bad burn on them. Mysteriously, his skin was even redder the next day. "I remember being so frightened because I'd never seen a sunburn get worse," said Sullivan. "I guess his immune system was failing him, and he couldn't fight the burn." Two days later, Sullivan and Sischy accompanied him to a party for the French fashion industry at Lincoln Center, where the paparazzi scanned the stylish crowd for any famous faces. Normally Mapplethorpe enjoyed the attention, but the scene turned nightmarish when they surrounded him with their cameras, and the lights burned his skin. "I have to get out of here," he whispered to Sullivan. "The flash hurts me."

The nightmare continued when he learned that his brother Richard had been diagnosed with lung and brain cancer. His last encounter with Richard had taken place exactly a year ago at Joan's hospital bedside, when Richard had feared he would never see his mother again. Ironically, Joan had recovered, and it was Richard who was now dying in the hospital. The illness had descended so quickly that the Mapplethorpes could barely digest the information provided by Ed, who served as the family's link to Richard in Los Angeles. Ed's news bulletins were devastating: "Richard has lung cancer . . . it's metastasized to the brain . . . he's losing his memory . . ." No one knew exactly what had happened to Richard; he, too, was a heavy smoker and perhaps he had inherited his mother's and grandmother's respiratory weakness. In late July, when doctors gave Richard only a few weeks to live, Ed summoned the family to Los Angeles. Since Joan could not breathe without an oxygen tank, she remained behind with Harry, but Susan, Nancy, and James met Ed at the hospital. "When we all walked into the room," Nancy said, "Richard just started crying and kept moving his hands. I don't know if he knew us or not. I don't even know if he realized he had cancer. The nurses would try to help him walk, but he could hardly move. Then he'd say strange things. I knew after the five days I spent with him that I'd never see my brother alive again."

Robert had begged off the tragic family reunion, blaming too many commitments in New York. Yet on August 8 he flew to L.A. to shoot architect Frank Gehry for *House & Garden,* and asked Ed to assist him. Ed waited until the end of the photo session to broach the delicate subject of whether Robert intended to visit Richard in the hospital. He was flabbergasted by his brother's response. "I'm not going," Robert declared. "If I were dying, I wouldn't want him to see me like that. Besides, we're not close." Robert made a minor concession to Ed by sending his dying brother a copy of *Certain People,* which he coldly inscribed, "For Richard, Robert." Richard had the book with him in his hospital room when he died on August 24. "My sister saw Richard in the casket," Nancy said, "and she told me he didn't have any hair and that he looked like an old man. He was only forty-one."

The Mapplethorpe family had a funeral Mass for Richard at Our Lady of the Snows, and while Joan left a message at Robert's studio with the details, she never heard back from him. He was not at the church when the family filed down the center aisle, nor was he evident among the other mourners. Ten minutes into the Mass, however, Nancy heard someone coughing so loudly the sound threatened to drown out the priest. She turned around in the pew to see a frail figure in black, doubled over in a spasm of coughing, a tissue covering his mouth. When the man lifted his head, she saw that it was Robert, and her heart sank. "Instead of thinking of the brother I had just lost," Nancy said, "I kept thinking of Robert, and it was like, 'Oh God, not him, too.' "

In late September Mapplethorpe, who was so weak he could barely leave his bed, conceded to Dimitri Levas that he might have pneumonia—"but not the AIDS kind." If he needed a reminder that his pneumonia very likely was the "AIDS kind," he had only to flip through the pages of the *Black Book*, which was about to be published by St. Martin's Press. The photographer had been sexually involved with at least 75 percent of the men in the book, and many of them, according to Mapplethorpe, were rumored to have AIDS. A handful of models, including Phillip Prioleau, whom he had photographed on the pedestal, were already dead.

Levas considered Mapplethorpe his best friend and felt stymied in his efforts to help him. "Robert was just getting sicker and sicker," Levas said, "and he wasn't getting the right care." One night, when Mapplethorpe was in especially bad shape, Levas ran into Mark Isaacson, whose twenty-year-old lover had AIDS and was then in the care of Dr. William Siroty at Beth Israel Hospital. "Mark, you've got to help me," Levas implored. "Robert is really sick, but he's denying it. Can your doctor get him into the hospital and check him out?" Isaacson called Siroty and made arrangements for Mapplethorpe to be admitted to Beth Israel that evening, then he and Levas went to pick him up. "I'm not going, I'm not going," Mapplethorpe shouted when they told him of their plans. Levas and Isaacson were utterly disbelieving. "You heard me," he yelled again. *"I'm not going!"* Levas was so upset his heart pounded and his skin turned cold and clammy. "You're crazy!" he shouted back. "We've made all the arrangements. You're going to go." Mapplethorpe, however, refused to budge from the bedroom, and finally Levas and Isaacson, realizing they couldn't force him into the waiting car, left him alone.

The next morning Levas checked to see how Mapplethorpe was feeling. "Not great," he said, a little sheepish. "I'll go now." Immediately upon Mapplethorpe's arrival at Beth Israel, Dr. Siroty ordered a bronchoscopy to biopsy the lung tissue to see if he had AIDS-related Pneumocystis carinii pneumonia (PCP). Levas and Amy Sullivan were with Mapplethorpe when Dr. Siroty returned with the results. "Well," Mapplethorpe said. "I've got it."

PART FIVE

The Perfect Moment

CHAPTER TWENTY-ONE

"Everybody's got it."

—Sam Wagstaff

Patti Smith was in the kitchen of her home in St. Clair Shores, Michigan, when she received a call from her lawyer, Ina Meibach, informing her that Robert Mapplethorpe was in the hospital with AIDS-related pneumonia. He had passed the word through his lawyer Michael Stout, who then called Meibach on his behalf.

That Mapplethorpe and Smith were now communicating through their lawyers showed how estranged they had become over the years. In fact, Smith's life was so isolated that the only way she kept up with old friends was through the obituary page of the newspaper. Drugs had claimed an alarming number of lives in the seventies; now, in the eighties, it was AIDS, but the epidemic had little to do with Smith's experience as a suburban wife and mother, and she hardly ever thought about it. In June 1986, however, one obituary caught her eye: Mario Amaya, who had given Mapplethorpe a show at the Chrysler Museum, had died of AIDS, and from then on she began to worry about Mapplethorpe's health.

Ironically, when Smith heard the bad news she was in the process of planning a trip to New York to record her comeback album, *Dream of Life*. Fred Smith had granted his permission for Mapplethorpe to shoot the album cover, and she was just about to call him to arrange their reunion, and to share a secret: at forty, she was happily pregnant again. Now she was afraid to make the phone call for fear Mapplethorpe was dying in the hospital. Instead, she telephoned Sam Wagstaff to learn more details of Mapplethorpe's condition, but since she hadn't spoken to either man since 1982, their conversation left her feeling like Rip Van Winkle. "How's Robert doing?" she asked Wagstaff, who would soon be hospitalized himself for the second time. "He's doing better than I am," he replied. "I've got it, Jim's got it, everybody's got it."

When Smith finally spoke to Mapplethorpe she was surprised by how little he seemed to have changed. He was cranky and depressed but certainly not defeated, and they scheduled a visit for the first week of December. Surprisingly, he never asked her to justify her disappearance back in 1979, and she never offered a reason. It was enough for him that she was back.

No sooner had Mapplethorpe received his AIDS diagnosis than he immediately rallied his friends to the hospital. Though he didn't realize it at the time, his world was slowly contracting, and his relationships with people such as Michael Stout, Dimitri Levas, and photographer Lynn Davis would become more important to him with each mounting crisis. Mapplethorpe had kept his life so compartmentalized that it was the first time many of his friends had met one another, and over the next few days he was deluged with art books, joints, jelly beans, cigarettes, pizzas, and floral arrangements by the dozen.

Lisa Lyon had recently been released from a psychiatric hospital in Pasadena and was now involved with septuagenarian scientist and drug pioneer Dr. John Lilly. When she heard about Mapplethorpe she jumped on the next plane to New York, but soon after takeoff she lapsed into a Carlos Castaneda–style trance, in which voices instructed her to disfigure her face with lipstick and eye pencil. She

entered Mapplethorpe's hospital room looking like one of the Cubist madonnas he had drawn in his childhood and, holding out her
arms like a character in a Greek tragedy, began crying, "Robert
. . . Robert." She then disappeared into the bathroom to smoke
angel dust, and the following day collapsed in the hospital waiting
room, where she slept for six hours. It was all too much for Mapplethorpe, who had been watching Lyon self-destruct for years and
now considered her beyond redemption. With as much authority as
he could muster given that he was eating pizza at the time, he cast
her out of his life. "I never want to see you again," he said. "I've
had it."

He was hardly at a loss for female admirers, however, and among
the most persistent was twenty-eight-year-old Alexandra Knaust,
whom he had met in the early eighties when she worked for photographer Gilles Larrain. That relationship had ended in a lawsuit, and
Knaust then became fixated on Mapplethorpe, her affection for him
bordering on the obsessional.* "I was in love with him," she said.
"Robert was the most appealing man I'd ever come across. One
time I told him how I felt, and he said, 'Oh, Alex, if you were only a
black man.' My relationship with Robert was very complex." Mapplethorpe complained about her incessantly and often refused to
take her phone calls, yet he had always been drawn to complicated
personalities, and Knaust, for all her determination and bravado,
was as fragile as Milton Moore. Pretty, with honey-blond hair and
high cheekbones, she looked up to Mapplethorpe as an all-knowing
mentor figure, and in 1984 he responded to that devotion by offering to let her be his agent in London. Knaust combined almost
superhuman tenacity with a high-strung intensity that often frightened people. Anne Kennedy, for one, was disturbed by her professional attachment to Mapplethorpe and couldn't understand the
purpose she served.

*In 1990 Knaust became involved in a four-year legal battle with Michael Stout
and the Mapplethorpe Foundation over Mapplethorpe photographs that Stout
claimed were still in her possession. Knaust then sued the Foundation for over
$2 million worth of fees that she felt were owed to her for services as Mapple-
thorpe's agent in the United Kingdom. The jury voted in favor of the Foundation,
and Knaust was ordered to return the photographs.

Knaust, nevertheless, worked tirelessly on Mapplethorpe's behalf in London, and after he was diagnosed with AIDS she further insinuated herself into his life by learning everything she could about the disease. She then volunteered to manage his health care for him, and amazingly, she made contact with all the top AIDS officials in the United States, including Dr. Sam Broder, the clinical director of the National Cancer Institute. Broder arranged for Mapplethorpe to meet Dr. Michael Lange, who was then conducting experimental trials of AZT at Roosevelt–St. Luke's Hospital in Manhattan. Though AZT had not yet been approved by the Food and Drug Administration and was only available in clinical trials, Mapplethorpe had a childish belief in the restorative power of science. "I'm so lucky they've found a cure," he told Lia Fernandez, who didn't know anything about the drug herself, but assured him, "Yes, you are very, very lucky."

On December 11 Mapplethorpe took a cab to the Mayflower Coffee Shop on Central Park West for his reunion with Patti Smith. Of all the pictures he had ever taken of her, the image that remained in his mind was the *Horses* cover from a decade ago. It must have been a shock, then, when he saw the middle-aged woman seated at the corner table. Smith's waist-length hair was now streaked with gray, and her eyes were hidden behind glasses. She was flanked by her husband, Fred, and son, Jackson, who kept pulling at the sleeves of her black turtleneck, crying "Mommy." She was relieved to see Mapplethorpe looking surprisingly fit, and he explained that with AZT and his weekly vitamin B_{12} shots, he felt better than he had in years.

His relationship with Smith had always been a private, one-to-one affair, so it was difficult for him to talk freely with Fred next to her. He was struck by how she still deferred to Fred about every detail of their lives, and how, when it came time to discuss shooting the new album cover, she kept looking to her husband as if seeking his approval. Yet Mapplethorpe hoped he'd be able to rekindle their special magic when he took her picture. Smith looked forward to the photo session as well, for she suspected it would be the last time a Mapplethorpe portrait graced one of her album covers, and she wanted to remember it as their best collaboration ever.

Mapplethorpe had become considerably more professional since the days he chased Smith around the loft with Sandy Daley's Polaroid, and the minute she entered his pristine new space she realized that intimacy and spontaneity were things of the past. Mapplethorpe had replaced Javier Gonzalez with a handsome young assistant named Brian English, whom he had hired without realizing that he had only been shooting photographs for several months. "We didn't talk about photography at all during my interview," English recalled. "He was impressed with me because I knew about computers. So in a matter of a day I went from doing nothing to working for him. I had to wing it." English turned out to be even more of a perfectionist than the photographer, and during the shoot with Smith, he fussed endlessly with the lights while a hair stylist and makeup artist stood ready with crimping irons, lipsticks, and powder brushes. Smith hated makeup, but endured the transformation for Mapplethorpe's sake, and after an hour of preparation she finally stepped in front of his camera.

Mapplethorpe's eye immediately noticed a tiny brown spot on her right hand; he was convinced he'd never seen it before, and when he asked her about it, she told him the mark had mysteriously surfaced right after her son was born. The brown spot bothered him, not only because he hated imperfections of any kind, but also, no doubt, because it reminded him of Patti's life with Fred. He had always admired her graceful hands for their resemblance to those of Georgia O'Keeffe, and he was probably thinking of Stieglitz's famous model when he directed his own muse to spread her unblemished hand across her chest in a gesture that evokes countless Stieglitz-O'Keeffe photographs. Smith noticed that Mapplethorpe was unusually quiet during the shoot, and she wondered if he was thinking the same thing, that one day the only evidence of their relationship would be the photographs they had created together. "Oh, Robert," she sighed, and he looked up briefly at her face. "I know," he said. "I know."

When Smith saw the picture a few days later, she was disappointed by it. Mapplethorpe had made her look beautiful—far more beautiful than she looked in real life. He had banished the wrinkles and hollows under the eyes and had transformed her into a vision of the perfect madonna, crimped hair cascading down her chest. But the woman in the picture didn't reflect the philosophy of *Dream of Life,* and its emphasis on the power of motherhood and the collective strength of the people to affect social change. She could not bear to hurt his feelings, however, so she agreed to use it, but she left New York feeling depressed for reasons even she did not completely understand.

Sam Wagstaff had been hospitalized for pneumonia in late November, and upon his release he spent his days planning a silver show at the New-York Historical Society that was scheduled to open in March 1987. Perhaps because he knew it would be his last exhibit, he was totally obsessed by it, and telephoned the society's director, James Bell, at all hours of the night and day to discuss his latest ideas. He wanted Mapplethorpe to take pictures for an exhibition catalogue, but the silver had always been a sore subject between them, and the photographer did not want to waste his time on it. Under the provisions of Wagstaff's will, Mapplethorpe stood to inherit the bulk of the Wagstaff estate, and he worried that unless Wagstaff stopped buying pieces for the show he'd be left with nothing but a clattering heap of nut bowls and soup tureens. Yet the silver was the only thing in Wagstaff's life that gave him any pleasure; he had a yeast infection that blanketed the inside of his mouth so that he could not eat solid foods, and he was so weak he needed crutches to walk from the bedroom to the living room. The disease had also ravaged his good looks, and Samuel J. Wagstaff, the handsomest man in New York, was no longer evident in the mirror. The silver could be invigorated with a touch of a polishing cloth, however, and propped up in bed, he shined the butter knives and Stilton scoops until they gleamed.

Wagstaff had everything he needed for the exhibit but still felt something was missing—the pièce de résistance. For years he had been hearing stories of an extraordinary 1881 Gorham centerpiece, a show-stopping Flo Ziegfeld concoction that was supported by four costumed elephants and draped with a Persian blanket. When an enterprising young dealer named Ron Hoffman managed to locate it for him, Wagstaff was ecstatic. He insisted on getting out of bed to greet Hoffman in the living room, and balancing himself on his crutches, he asked the dealer to rotate the object in the sunlight so he could admire it from every angle. "How wonderful!" he enthused. "I'll float gardenias in it for the show. Can't you just see it?" That night Wagstaff took his silver talisman to bed, where it rested on the pillow next to him.

Yet the magic object could not impede the relentless progression of his disease, and on December 12 he was back at St. Vincent's Hospital. It was there Patti Smith saw him for the first time since 1979, but lacking the energy for one of his diverting monologues, he spoke as if he had pared down his thoughts to the bare essentials. "I had three great loves in life," he confided. "My mother, art, and Robert." Smith was still in the room when Mapplethorpe dropped by. Incensed by the eighty-thousand-dollar price tag attached to the elephant centerpiece, he had envisioned a line of silver dealers stretched out into the corridor, but he immediately softened when he saw how poorly Wagstaff was doing. He reached out to take his hand, but Wagstaff was embarrassed by an ugly rash on his skin and pulled his hand away. Smith heard Mapplethorpe whisper "Don't be silly" before he grabbed Wagstaff's hand firmly in his own. Later, when Mapplethorpe and Smith left St. Vincent's, they couldn't stop thinking about John McKendry and another hospital visit years ago. "It's all so stupid," Mapplethorpe had said at the time, only now he used the same words to describe Wagstaff's predicament, and his own. As they stood on the sidewalk outside the hospital he told Smith, "This is going to happen to me, too."

Wagstaff was at home for the holidays, but the penthouse, which had once evoked images of a year-round Christmas, had the desolate air of Good Friday about it. His death was inevitable; it was only a matter of waiting. The vigil was hardest on Jim Nelson, who watched the unfolding drama from a mattress on the living room floor, where he slept amid the silver, which was strewn everywhere in the apartment. Nelson's Kaposi's sarcoma lesions were spreading on his foot, but he was not yet as sick as Wagstaff, and he had to endure the invasion of visitors and private nurses into his home. "Doesn't anyone care about me?" he would sometimes scream in frustration, but the truth was that Nelson had always been perceived as a bit player in Mapplethorpe and Wagstaff's life, and AIDS had done nothing to change that. Anne Ehrenkranz, Wagstaff's doting research assistant, was the frequent recipient of Nelson's anger, and one afternoon he became so hysterical he threatened her with a kitchen knife.

Mapplethorpe and Ehrenkranz were uneasy allies during Wagstaff's ordeal, and the photographer worried that since she was on the board of the New-York Historical Society she might be encouraging Wagstaff to acquire more silver for the show. Mapplethorpe believed that Wagstaff was suffering from AIDS dementia, for he seemed to make little sense at times and would suddenly burst into screaming rages. Wagstaff, however, was not being defrauded by a horde of greedy silver dealers. In fact, Ron Hoffman was the only dealer invited to the penthouse. As late as the second week of January 1987 Wagstaff was still so preoccupied by the exhibit he asked Hoffman to bring several pieces to the apartment for his consideration. This time Wagstaff did not have the strength to leave his bed, so Hoffman carried the objects into his room on a breakfast tray. "He was too weak to even lift the pieces up," Hoffman recalled, "but he was still able to discriminate between what he liked and what he didn't like. It was so sad to see him struggling that I broke down and had to leave the room."

Several days later Wagstaff lapsed into a coma, and Ehrenkranz, who had taken care of him for months, gathered together the diverse group that constituted his family. The very proper Mrs. Judith Jefferson found herself jockeying for space at her brother's deathbed with a photographer known for his pornographic pictures; a hairstylist and makeup artist for *Cats;* and a Manhattan lawyer's wealthy wife, who was seemingly infatuated with the dying man. "I think," Wagstaff's sister remarked at one point, "that we'll probably have a small family service." Mapplethorpe whispered to Ehrenkranz, "I'm sure they'll really appreciate having a Jew and two faggots show up."

At eleven P.M. Mapplethorpe left the apartment with Ehrenkranz and Jefferson, and Nelson and the night nurse maintained the vigil. For the last eleven years Wagstaff had been Nelson's family, and while the relationship had been far from ideal, it had provided Nelson with an illusion of happiness. He lived in a Manhattan penthouse with a wealthy lover who resembled a movie star. It was everything the orphan from Texas could have hoped for, and now it was all coming to an end. Nelson did not want to let go, so he held the dying man in his arms for the next hour. When Wagstaff died a little after midnight on January 14, Nelson was still holding on for dear life.

"Sam's dead," Mapplethorpe told Patti Smith in a mournful voice, yet two days later, on January 16, he attended a dinner for the artist David Salle at Mr. Chow's and acted as if nothing had happened. Andy Warhol refused to sit next to him because, as he later recorded in his diary, "he's sick." Indeed, rumors about Mapplethorpe's health began to circulate in the art world from the moment Wagstaff's obituary appeared in *The New York Times*. The cause of death was given as pneumonia, but everyone suspected he had AIDS, which ultimately led to gossip about Mapplethorpe's HIV status.

While the photographer had been candid with his friends, he naïvely hoped he could keep the information a secret from the public. He feared jeopardizing his commercial work and didn't even tell his studio employees. Suzanne Donaldson, who had recently been hired as Tina Summerlin's replacement as studio manager, unwittingly confirmed a newspaper report of Mapplethorpe's hospitalization, and he reduced her to tears by screaming, "How could you do such a thing?" Donaldson suspected that he had AIDS and was terrified by his outburst. "I thought, 'Who needs this?' she explained. "Why should I walk into somebody's life who's very sick and who hasn't bothered to tell me a thing about it?"

Eager to escape the rumors and prying phone calls, Mapplethorpe left for New Orleans on January 19 to shoot pictures of the Louisiana bayou for *Condé Nast Traveler*. Mapplethorpe disliked shooting on location, so in addition to Brian English, Lynn Davis joined him on the expedition. "We stayed at this funky little motel on the bayou," Davis recalled, "and this redneck guide who owned several pit bulls, one of which chased Robert, took us out on a boat." Even in the middle of a swamp, Mapplethorpe's aesthetic superseded nature's, and among the lush color photographs that appeared in the April issue was an alligator's head that resembled one of the black vases in the photographer's collection.

Mapplethorpe then stayed in New Orleans for a week with Mike Myers and Russ Albright at the "Haunted House." The couple had recently opened the Julia Gallery, where, as a favor to them, Mapplethorpe had agreed to show his work. Myers was struck by the dramatic change in Mapplethorpe's personality, for instead of being cold and emotionally withdrawn, he was seething with rage. He hated the phoniness of the art world, he said, and cursed out his dealers. He wanted to move from New York, and even contacted several real estate agents in New Orleans about buying a loft there. "Robert was really running away," Myers explained. "He was so angry I kept waiting for him to explode."

And explode he did, by rampaging through the gay bars to pick up black men. Mapplethorpe had confided to several friends that he blamed a black man for infecting him with the AIDS virus, but given his boast of having had sex with an estimated thousand men, he couldn't possibly know for sure. Still, he approached his task like an avenging angel, picking up one black man after another with offers of cocaine, then baiting them with the word "nigger." One man screamed at him to stop, but when Mapplethorpe still kept repeating the word, the man grabbed his clothes and ran out the door. "You're evil," the man shouted, in parting. *"Evil!"*

Artist George Dureau was appalled by Mapplethorpe's behavior, and on several occasions tried to divert his attention from sex by keeping him out as late as possible. No matter what the hour, though, Mapplethorpe would always make a detour to the black bars. It's impossible to know whether he practiced safe sex, but to observers such as Dureau there was something terrifying about his aggression. "I asked myself several times," Dureau said, " 'Does the man have any morals at all?' "

Mapplethorpe returned to New York for the reading of Wagstaff's will and learned that he had inherited three quarters of the Wagstaff estate, ultimately worth upward of $7 million, while Jim Nelson received the remaining 25 percent. Judith Jefferson, Wagstaff's sister, was left a relatively paltry ten thousand dollars, and she immediately contested the will; both Wagstaff's heirs had terminal illnesses and her brother's money would ultimately fall into the hands of lawyers. Even Michael Stout was sympathetic: "You had a hairdresser with Kaposi's sarcoma all over the place, and an S&M photographer who was always in the gossip sheets—who could blame her?" But since the will would now be tied up in probate court, neither Mapplethorpe nor Nelson had access to the money, although Wagstaff, anticipating his sister's reaction, had left instructions for them to receive a monthly stipend of several thousand dollars apiece. Nevertheless, Mapplethorpe, as executor of the Wagstaff estate, decided to raise more money by selling the penthouse, which meant Nelson would now lose his home. Understandably distraught, Nelson turned to lawyer and gay activist Leonard Bloom to negotiate a settlement with the Wagstaff estate.

Bloom found the situation a fascinating study in human psychology—a love triangle with Wagstaff at the apex and Mapplethorpe and Nelson at opposite ends of the base. Consciously or not, Wagstaff had picked two men who were both emotionally crippled, and who relied on him for financial and parental support. "Some of what Sam saw in Robert," Bloom explained, "he saw in Jim. They both suffered from a lack of self-worth. Look at Robert—he took a picture of himself with a whip up his ass. Sam enjoyed being dominant; he liked controlling Jim, and to a lesser extent Robert. And the way he did that was through his money." Mapplethorpe attempted to carry on the tradition by painting Nelson as a hopeless spendthrift bent on frittering away his inheritance. "If you give him too much," he lectured Bloom, "he'll only squander it." Yet Mapplethorpe had to make some provision for Nelson, and ultimately he agreed to a cash settlement of $500,000 and ownership of the beach house in Oakleyville. Mapplethorpe hated the house anyway, but it held great sentimental value to Nelson, who was determined to make one last attempt at planting a rose garden the next summer. He hoped his ashes and those of Wagstaff would be intermingled there one day.

Wagstaff was destined for a grander resting place than Oakleyville, however, and his remains were deposited in the Wagstaff crypt at the Church of Heavenly Rest, on Fifth Avenue and Ninetieth Street in New York. On March 2 Mapplethorpe led a memorial service at the Metropolitan Museum of Art, where several hundred people gathered to remember Wagstaff and to praise his unique vision. The photographer read a poem that Patti Smith had written in which she compared the collector to a "tulip in the black wind." Afterward, Mapplethorpe and Nelson hosted a small memorial dinner at Il Cantinori, one of Wagstaff's favorite Village restaurants, and the guests toasted his memory with several bottles of his beloved Chateau d'Yquem. The situation impressed Mapplethorpe as macabre, and turning to Sotheby's Anne Horton, he whispered, "How can you give a dinner for someone who isn't here?"

At the end of March Mapplethorpe and his assistant Brian English flew to Palm Springs to shoot desert blooms for *Condé Nast Traveler*. They were joined by Ed Maxey, who had driven from Los Angeles. The three men trudged through the desert for several hours, Mapplethorpe in black leather and high-heeled Western boots, until they found an elderly park ranger who told them the bad news: the spring weather had been so dry that all the flowers were dead. They retreated to Los Angeles, where Patti and Fred Smith were renting an apartment while finishing *Dream of Life* at the Record Plant. Mapplethorpe knew Patti was unhappy with the first picture, and although he liked it himself, he arranged to do a second shoot to please her. She was only a few months away from giving birth, and her stomach bulged under a loose crewneck sweater. Inspired by the painter Frida Kahlo, she had woven her hair into a series of skinny braids, and, sitting under a palm tree in the backyard, the sun highlighted the lines in her face and her dry, chapped lips. While Brian English set up the equipment, Mapplethorpe rested beside her. He had lost the false bloom of health that had followed his AIDS diagnosis, and when he stood up to take her picture, his hands suddenly began to tremble, and he dropped the light meter on the ground and broke it. Up until now the disease hadn't affected his picture-taking abilities, and he was subdued for the rest of the shoot. Without the light meter he couldn't accurately calculate the exposure, and he knew the pictures wouldn't turn out well. When he returned to New York several days later he wasn't surprised when Tom Baril advised him of the poor quality of the negatives. "It's not what I wanted it to be," a disappointed Mapplethorpe told Smith over the telephone. "They're not good enough."

The record company needed the cover art by the end of the week, so Smith reluctantly prepared to mail them the first portrait, but before she went to the post office, Mapplethorpe telephoned her again. "Hold off for one more day," he said, mysteriously. The next morning she received a Federal Express package from him, and when she saw the picture inside she immediately began to cry. Technically, the portrait wasn't up to Mapplethorpe's high standards; her face was washed out and the background was blurry, yet she loved it all the more because it wasn't perfect. Mapplethorpe had even refrained from airbrushing out the brown spot on her left hand. "Certainly it's not a glamorous picture," Smith said, "or the most flattering. But Robert knew it was the image I wanted. It was his gift to me."

CHAPTER TWENTY-TWO

"I just hope I can live long enough to see the fame."

—*Robert Mapplethorpe*

Mapplethorpe had once told his Pratt roommate Harry McCue that he was willing to sell his soul for fame, so the irony of his current predicament was not lost on him. Contrary to his fears that rumors of AIDS would ruin his career, the disease only served to increase his sales potential. He was already one of the most visible photographers in the world, and during the past decade his work had been the subject of sixty-nine one-person shows, five books, and fifteen catalogues. But AIDS would soon catapult him into another realm of celebrityhood; unfortunately, nothing enhanced his life more than the prospect of his leaving it. "I don't think it's impossible to sell a million dollars' worth of Robert's pictures," Howard Read boasted to dealer Peter MacGill. "He's ill."

Prices often escalate after an artist's death—"the deader, the better" goes the art world saying—so Mapplethorpe's terminal illness had, according to Read, created a "built-in market condition," whereby people purchased Mapplethorpe photographs in anticipation of his demise. "AIDS," Read said, "had a *terrific* influence."

Lisa Lyon recalled a photography dealer calling her up to see if she'd sell some of her Mapplethorpe photographs from *Lady*. "The dealer said, 'You know, Robert's dead,'" she explained, "so I immediately got crazy and said, 'What do you mean he's dead?' Then the dealer told me, 'Well, he's dead . . . in terms of the market.'"

Janet Kardon, who was then director of the Institute of Contemporary Art in Philadelphia, had admired Mapplethorpe's work, but it wasn't until he had been hospitalized for pneumonia that she began seriously thinking about a retrospective. She approached him in the early spring about doing a show that would originate in Philadelphia, then travel to six cities throughout the United States. Meanwhile, the Stedelijk Museum in Amsterdam had announced a planned Mapplethorpe retrospective for early the next year, and Alex Knaust had arranged with Robin Gibson, the director of London's National Portrait Gallery, to do a show there. "The weird part about it was when I first started working for Robert," Suzanne Donaldson said, "there was nothing really going on. And then within six months everybody wanted to buy his pictures; galleries and museums were having shows, and everything really started to happen.".

In April Mapplethorpe had a show of platinum-on-canvas prints at the Robert Miller Gallery, which had moved to a second-floor space at 41 East Fifty-seventh Street. It had just been vacated by art dealer Andrew Crispo, who had been linked to the brutal sadomasochistic slaying of a young Norwegian model. Although never indicted, Crispo had been accused of playing S&M games in the gallery, where Mapplethorpe was now exhibiting his lush photographs of flowers, a bust of Mercury, and *Thomas in Circle*. Andy Grundberg wrote in *The New York Times*, "Mr. Mapplethorpe's longterm devotion to the classical ideal emerges with a new and surprisingly Platonic clarity. Classicizing style and Minimalist presentation mate perfectly." The show was so successful that by the end of the exhibit Read increased prices for the unique pieces from $10,000 to $15,000. "By this point you could presell everything right away," Read explained. "In fact, the show was oversubscribed. It really hit a high note."

The genesis of the platinum-on-canvas concept went back to 1985, when Mapplethorpe and the printer Martin Axon began discussing ways to further heighten the physical appearance of his photographs. Though Mapplethorpe's platinum prints were normally 22½ by 25 inches, he toyed with the idea of making them as large as 4 by 6 feet. When he realized that wasn't economically feasible—Axon would have needed to build a gigantic darkroom—he settled on the idea of making his pictures look more like paintings by printing the images on canvas. No other printer, to Axon's knowledge, had ever used this technique, and he spent most of 1986 researching and refining the process. Mapplethorpe then collaborated with framers David Cochrane and Ken Perkins to render the pieces even more graphic by surrounding the images with silk and velvet fabric. It was all part of Mapplethorpe's preoccupation with blurring the distinction between painting and photography. "Some people say to me, 'Oh! I love your painting,' " he told Martin Axon, "and they are talking about a photograph. I am still a snob a little bit about painting versus photography, and I would say that it is a compliment when they call it a painting and I know it is in fact a photograph. To make pictures big is to make them more powerful." In this regard Mapplethorpe was in sync with a new generation of photographers, such as Cindy Sherman and Doug and Mike Starn, who created unique, large-scale works that could hold the wall with equally large contemporary paintings and who commanded prices that had once been unthinkable in photography.

In May Mapplethorpe had a relapse of pneumonia, and while it wasn't serious enough for him to be hospitalized, he then developed neuropathy, an inflammation of the nerves that caused terrible burning in his feet. Alex Knaust, who was commuting back and forth from London, was still overseeing Mapplethorpe's health care; she switched him to a doctor at Memorial Sloan-Kettering Hospital, and suggested numerous antiviral remedies, including AL-721, an egg lipid concoction manufactured in Japan, and thiocitic acid, which supposedly protected AIDS patients from the toxic effects of medication. Mapplethorpe was an extremely passive patient; he took whatever pills anyone recommended to him, and even though several doctors warned him that using cocaine would further damage his immune system, he still snorted coke and smoked nearly two packs of cigarettes a day.

He had stopped seeing Thomas Williams immediately after learning he had AIDS, but he never bothered to tell him that he had been hospitalized with PCP. It was a cruel oversight, for Williams wondered why the photographer was suddenly ignoring him, and worried that he had done something wrong. He was later diagnosed with AIDS himself, and in 1993 he complained to *New York* that even though he was one of the photographer's most visible models, the Mapplethorpe Foundation, which awards grants to AIDS-related causes, refused to help him.

Mapplethorpe's racism intensified with the progression of his disease, and Kelly Edey, who had presumably heard everything, was so startled by Mapplethorpe's venomous comments that he noted one incident in his diary. Mapplethorpe was standing outside Keller's on the evening of August 2 when he suddenly began to shout, "This is the sleaziest corner in New York. How can it be that I'm standing here in the midst of all this human garbage? They're so stupid, every last one of them is so unbelievably stupid." And yet he kept returning to Keller's, hoping his demigod might rise from the debris. "A lot of people yelled at him for continuing to go to the bars," Mark Isaacson explained. "But he looked at it, like, well, that's their problem—if they're not protecting themselves, why should I worry about it? When Robert first got sick, I said to him, 'You've got to stop your old lifestyle,' and he said to me, 'If I have to change my lifestyle, I don't want to live.' "

Mapplethorpe derived a morbid pleasure from hearing stories of other people with AIDS, and he always inquired about the health of certain friends whose medical history paralleled his own. He took an especially keen interest in fifty-year-old photographer Peter Hujar, whose career was a shadow version of Mapplethorpe's. The relationship between the two men might be compared to that of Mozart and Salieri; both photographed the male nude in a bare studio setting, but while Hujar's prickly personality antagonized dealers and gallery owners, Mapplethorpe played the game brilliantly. Hujar grew to despise his younger rival, whom he regarded as a hustler and plagiarist, while Mapplethorpe viewed the older man as a textbook case of how *not* to become famous; he could think of nothing worse than to fall victim to what Stephen Koch characterized as Hujar's "secret fame."

The two photographers were diagnosed with PCP within two months of each other, but while Mapplethorpe still aggressively pursued his career, Hujar never picked up his camera again. Neither would he take AZT, and in his typically idiosyncratic way, he explored such remedies as crystal cures before converting to Catholicism. Lynn Davis was also a friend of his, and she tended to him until he died, on Thanksgiving Day. Mapplethorpe was among the 150 mourners who attended the Catholic funeral at St. Joseph's Church in Greenwich Village. Writer Vince Aletti and artist David Wojnarowicz, who had been Hujar's lover, carried the photographer's remains in a simple pine coffin, which they placed in the center aisle of the church. After the funeral Mapplethorpe saw Pratt alumnus Kenny Tisa on the church steps, and in response to Tisa's question about his health, replied, "I just hope I can live long enough to see the fame."

The fame, however, did not come without a price, and when Mapplethorpe saw the cover story about himself in the January 1988 issue of *American Photography,* he picked up the telephone and lambasted senior editor Carol Squiers. "I can't believe you've done this to me," he shouted. "I know everyone in the business, and I'm going to make sure nobody ever hires you again." This was the third time Squiers had been subjected to Mapplethorpe's ill temper, but she had never heard him sound so vindictive before. "It was just this barrage of sheer venom coming through the receiver," she said. "Being threatened by a dying man wasn't anything I had bargained for. I was so upset I was beside myself."

The object of Mapplethorpe's ire was an article entitled "Mapplethorpe: The Art of My Wicked, Wicked Ways," written by Australian art critic Paul Taylor, who had been assigned the piece by Squiers. Though Taylor admired the photographer's work, he had managed to alienate Mapplethorpe within the first few minutes of the interview by demanding, "I want to know about the AIDS thing." He then asked about Sam Wagstaff's role in his career, and the disposition of the Wagstaff estate. In a bit of revisionist history, Mapplethorpe had recently begun to deny Wagstaff's influence on his career, and he angrily told Taylor he would have Michael Stout kill the piece unless he dropped the objectionable questions. "I just want to be written about as a normal artist," he pleaded.

Mapplethorpe cooperated with Taylor, but he was concerned the piece would be a hatchet job and he steeled himself for the attack. Ultimately, Taylor's article was rejected by *American Photography* for being too reverential, and his material was then combined with previous interviews by Squiers and Stephen Koch, whose 1986 Mapplethorpe profile had already been killed by the magazine. Considering the number of writers involved, the cut-and-paste article was surprisingly fair and well balanced, and Squiers couldn't imagine what had triggered Mapplethorpe's hysteria. She later discovered he hadn't even bothered to read the article prior to their phone conversation. He was upset by a caption—the caption next to Wagstaff's portrait that described him as the photographer's "lover." Even after all this time Mapplethorpe was afraid his parents might learn of his homosexuality, and while they didn't read art magazines or *The New York Times,* they might spot *American Photography* in the local drugstore and wonder who Sam Wagstaff was.

Ed was the only family member who knew Robert had AIDS, and he had recently returned to New York to help his brother. But Robert was so afraid his parents might suspect something was wrong if they learned Ed had moved from Los Angeles that he convinced Ed to take part in an elaborate charade that involved keeping an answering machine hooked up to his old phone number. Ed regularly called into the machine to get his messages, and whenever he received one from his mother, he had to pretend he was still in L.A. That Ed was willing to play along with the ridiculous game showed how much he still longed for his brother's approval, but he was drawing from the same empty well.

Robert allowed Ed to live rent-free at Bond Street, where he still kept his darkroom and staff, and he paid him a modest salary to assist in the studio, but Robert seemed no more grateful to Ed than he did to his other employees. "Ed really adored Robert and, in a sense, wanted to be Robert," said Brian English. "I don't think it was healthy. He was working for him and living in his loft with all the old S&M stuff under the bed, and all these Mapplethorpe photographs staring down at him. Ever see one of those pictures where no matter where you are in the room, the eyes are looking at you? That's what it was like for Eddie."

Complicating matters even more, Ed was sharing the loft with a Mapplethorpe model named Melody Danielson, whose serendipitous arrival in his life had been carefully choreographed by the photographer himself. "If I hadn't been gay," Robert said, "I would have picked a woman like Melody." Certainly, she possessed all the right qualities; Truman Capote may have gathered his "swans" from the ranks of the stylish rich, but Robert Mapplethorpe's were drawn from punk rock, Gold's Gym, or, in Danielson's case, the world of professional sex.

Danielson had worked as a dominatrix, servicing a clientele of high-profile New York businessmen who paid her five hundred dollars an hour to incite their submissive and often bizarre fantasies. She had been asked to pretend that she was a cheerleader, a little boy, or, in one instance, a chirping cricket. Danielson had recently renounced the business to start a line of couture country-and-western clothes under the label of "Hillbilly Heaven," but Mapplethorpe loved hearing stories about her dominatrix experiences, and how, when she was a teenager, she and her con artist father engaged in numerous get-rich schemes in South America. More important, he was fascinated by her androgynous beauty; thin to the point of appearing emaciated, she had close-cropped hair that changed color on a moment's whim, and amazingly white skin so perfect it already seemed airbrushed. In full makeup, her heavily lined eyes and mouth in sharp contrast to her pale face, she looked like a young boy pretending to be a woman, and in fact, numerous people remarked on her resemblance to Mapplethorpe's own self-portrait in drag.

Robert had invited Melody to his forty-first birthday party on November 4, 1987, hoping Ed would be attracted to her; given that she bore Robert's imprimatur, as well as a strong resemblance to him, it was not surprising that Ed fell in love. Consequently, Melody, who had quit her job as a dominatrix because she longed for a more stable life, became caught up in the crazy turmoil of Robert's. "Ed was really dedicated to his brother," said Danielson, who died of cancer in 1993, "so I knew if I got involved with him, I'd be getting involved with Robert, too. But Robert's life was so complicated and, at times, so screwed-up I'd say to myself, 'Well, you might as well be tying up guys with Mickey Mouse shoestrings again.' "

A few weeks after Ed moved from Los Angeles, Jack Walls, who had been halfheartedly pursuing a movie career there, returned to New York as well. Perhaps because Robert realized the odds of finding another lover were growing slimmer every day, he invited Walls to share the Twenty-third Street loft and paid him three hundred dollars a week to supervise the household. In a reprise of their old relationship, the two men immediately began squabbling, with Mapplethorpe accusing Walls of buying drugs instead of laundry detergent, and Walls denouncing Mapplethorpe for throwing away his money on more Venini glass. They smuggled their respective purchases into the loft, stashing them in secret hiding places, until one or the other discovered proof of wrongdoing, and then pandemonium would break loose. Inevitably, the arguments ended with Walls storming out the door, only to reassume his salaried position as Mapplethorpe's domestic and bedmate hours later.

Mapplethorpe had always relished the freedom to come and go as he pleased, but his illness made him accountable to Walls, who lectured him on spending money; to various doctors, who frowned on cigarettes and cocaine; to well-meaning friends, who suggested he try yoga, meditation, and vitamin therapy; and to Michael Stout, who suggested he write a will. After a year of legal wrangling over the Wagstaff estate, Sam's sister, Judith Jefferson, had decided to drop her lawsuit, and Mapplethorpe was a wealthy man. No sooner had he received the money, however, than he had to think about giving it away, and he hoped he'd live long enough to spend at least some of it on himself.

Yet his neuropathy was worsening, and fevers and diarrhea prevented him from sleeping at night. Alex Knaust had arranged for him to meet with doctors at the National Cancer Institute in Bethesda, Maryland, and had even flown to Paris to consult with researchers at the Pasteur Institute, but no one had anything more promising to offer than AZT. Mapplethorpe hated going to Sloan-Kettering for his checkups because he was used to being treated as a celebrity and didn't like having to wait to see the doctor, who never offered him any encouraging news. In mid-February, when he went to the hospital with Lia Fernandez, he vowed never to go back. "So what did he say?" Fernandez asked Mapplethorpe as he emerged from the doctor's office. "It's got me," he said, reaching out to hold her hand. "I'm just sort of disappearing."

Mapplethorpe had never been more visible to the art world, however, and in addition to Janet Kardon's ICA retrospective, which she had titled "The Perfect Moment," he was to be honored by one at the Whitney Museum. It was highly irregular for two major museums to be holding retrospectives, especially since Kardon had already approached the Whitney about taking "The Perfect Moment" as part of the ICA's traveling exhibit. But Whitney curator Richard Marshall had collaborated with Mapplethorpe on *50 New York Artists* and had close ties to the Robert Miller Gallery through his friendship with its director, John Cheim; he felt he could do a better job himself, and went about planning an independent Mapplethorpe retrospective. Worse for Kardon, Marshall scheduled his show for July—seven months before "The Perfect Moment" was to be unveiled in Philadelphia; in effect, she had been scooped by another museum curator, and her retrospective was in danger of being old news.

Ironically, "The Perfect Moment" would ultimately receive more attention than Kardon would have dreamed possible when, in the summer of 1989, the Corcoran Gallery of Art in Washington, D.C., canceled the exhibit and provoked a furious censorship battle that was front-page news for the next year.

At the time, however, Kardon faced the possibility of having no show at all when Mapplethorpe threatened to cancel "The Perfect Moment" himself because he worried that he didn't have the energy for both retrospectives. Though he had long considered the Whitney a second-rate institution, he badly wanted his retrospective to be shown in New York and was crushed when the Metropolitan Museum's photography curator, Maria Morris Hambourg, decided against taking "The Perfect Moment" as part of the ICA's traveling exhibit. But Hambourg had never been a fan of Mapplethorpe's work and certainly wasn't about to put herself on the line for it. "I couldn't take a bloody penis to my director and say, 'I want to show this,'" she explained. "The time is not here for that; if it ever will be, it's not going to be in the next ten or fifteen years. I made that very clear to Robert, and I don't think he ever got over it."

Eventually Kardon persuaded Mapplethorpe that he couldn't abandon the project, and he agreed, in part because it gave him an added incentive to keep fighting his disease. He now treated each retrospective as a goal he needed to reach in order to stay ahead of his illness. Since "The Perfect Moment" wasn't scheduled to open until December, he felt confident he wouldn't die until he had witnessed the last vestige of fame.

Meanwhile, he had more immediate goals, such as attending the opening of his show at the Stedelijk Museum on February 27. Even though no one expected him to feel well enough to travel to Amsterdam, he took Lynn Davis and Jack Walls with him and went anyway. "Robert had always loved Amsterdam," Davis said, "and at the opening he was surrounded by all his old friends, like Rob Jurka, who had been one of his earliest champions. He was really weak, but we spent one afternoon looking at the van Goghs, and that seemed to cheer him up." When Mapplethorpe returned, he switched to a new doctor, Barbara Starrett, who had been recommended to him by actress Susan Sarandon, whom he had occasionally escorted to black-tie fund-raisers over the years. Dr. Starrett, whose practice consisted mainly of AIDS patients, was willing to make house calls and to work with Alex Knaust in finding experimental drugs for Mapplethorpe. After examining him, she wrote down in her chart that he appeared to be suffering from "wasting syndrome"—an insidious condition marked by weight loss and chronic diarrhea that resulted in patients literally wasting away. Meanwhile, she kept him on AZT, in addition to pentamidine, an antiprotozoal medication; Zovirax for herpes; and Elavil for his neuropathy.

On March 14 he complained to Starrett of terrible abdominal pains and nausea, yet on the twenty-second of the month he managed to board a plane to London for a week of Mapplethorpe-related events staged by the indomitable Knaust. "I wasn't really thinking along the lines of Mapplethorpe at all," admitted Robin Gibson, director of the National Portrait Gallery, "because we're a very British institution, and it's not the type of thing we normally do. But then Alex turned up at the doorstep one day and asked if we wanted a Mapplethorpe show. It was a little nerve-racking, because we really didn't know what position Alex held within the Mapplethorpe organization, and Robert would never say anything about her. She convinced us that we needed to drape lots of gray silk moiré fabric on the walls because it was his favorite color, so we had all this expensive fabric, and then, a month before the show, she disappeared on us. We then learned she had been detained at Heathrow Airport as she was carrying Mapplethorpe's photographs into the country, and customs officials thought some of the pictures might possibly be obscene. We really weren't sure there would be a show until the pictures were actually hanging on the walls. It was really rather extraordinary."

Mapplethorpe arrived at the National Portrait Gallery show with a phalanx of supporters, including Michael Stout, Jack Walls, Dimitri Levas, Alex Knaust, and Howard Read. There was a huge banner outside the gallery that read MAPPLETHORPE, and plastered to the entrance gate were rows of posters bearing a 1987 self-portrait of him. Inside, Mapplethorpe's own portrait hung alongside pictures of such notables as Lord Snowdon, Norman Mailer, Truman Capote, William Burroughs, Francesco Clemente, Peter Gabriel, Richard Gere, Glenn Close, Iggy Pop, and David Byrne. It was as if Mapplethorpe was celebrating his parity with them, and Sandy Nairne, who had curated his 1983 show at the Institute of Contemporary Art, was amazed by how differently people were now treating him. "He was like a rock star," he said. "Young kids were clamoring to meet him and asking him to autograph their catalogues. But there was something rather spooky about it, because they knew he was dying."

John Russell Taylor, in a review of the show for *The Times,* attributed the sudden surge of interest in Mapplethorpe not to his talent, which he found to be on the level "of the average photographic graduate from art school," but to the elaborate myths surrounding his career: "Certainly no photographer of recent times—perhaps no photographer ever—has been so ruthlessly hyped, so skillfully merchandised." The issue of Mapplethorpe's impending death from AIDS only served to enhance the myth.

When Mapplethorpe appeared at the Hamiltons Gallery in Mayfair for yet another show arranged by Knaust, Tim Jefferies, the gallery's co-owner, was stunned by the huge crowd at the opening. "I suppose a certain percentage of them came out of morbid curiosity," said Jefferies, who had been unfamiliar with Mapplethorpe's work. "But it was like 'Robert Mapplethorpe Week' in London and he was a lot more celebrated than any of us expected."

That was due, in part, to a documentary on Mapplethorpe's life that was shown on BBC television the same week, which had also been initiated by Knaust. According to producer Nigel Finch, he found the experience a nightmare. Knaust accused him of trying to create an "AIDS exposé," and received a court order preventing the BBC from airing the documentary unless they expurgated any references to the disease. Hours before the show was scheduled to air, she sat in the editing room with him and demanded appropriate cuts. "Alex destroyed the film," Finch said. "I was interested in placing Mapplethorpe within a larger social context of which AIDS was a crucial part. I wanted it to be a chronicle of a decade. I understood that Robert didn't want to be known as an 'AIDS artist,' and during my interviews with him, he didn't once mention the word 'AIDS.' But because of Alex, we even lost a bit of Robert's interview in which he talked about mortality."

On March 27, two days after Mapplethorpe returned from London, he was at the Miller Gallery for the opening of "New Color Work," which comprised twenty dye-transfer prints of flowers. He had made sporadic attempts at color throughout his career, but the results had never totally satisfied him. Color had never been his strong suit, and he didn't respond to color photography in general. Yet, through his advertising work, he had been doing more of it, and now that he had the money to invest in the costly dye-transfer process, he began photographing calla lilies, tulips, roses, and orchids against backgrounds of deep purple, magenta, and black. Howard Read quickly sold out the show, with one client from Japan purchasing all twenty photographs. "We did them in editions of seven," Read explained, "and they went so fast it was unbelievable."

Art collector Marieluise Black, who owned a large collection of Mapplethorpes, discussed the color work with Robert during an interview in June. Black thought Mapplethorpe's photographs lost their impact in color, but he insisted, "I really think they do work. Because I'm not somebody that would ever be attracted to color photography, I've always stayed away from it in terms of other people's photographs as well. Maybe because it's my own, I really appreciate my color pictures. I haven't done much of it. It's just starting."

Mapplethorpe's ability to discuss his work in terms of "just starting" was an example of how he truly believed in the magic power of his own creativity, and how, despite his deteriorating body, he was still capable of expanding the boundaries of his vision. Physically, however, he was like the photograph of Thomas Williams trapped in the circle. The neuropathy was spreading from his feet to his legs, and from his fingers to his hands. Since Mapplethorpe had long defined his identity in terms of sex, it must have terrified him to imagine a nerve disorder traveling to his genitals, and he obsessed on the idea that when it struck the center of his body, it meant he would no longer exist.

Yet AIDS had already diminished his sexual desire, and in response, he wasn't focusing on black nudes anymore. "I'm over that phase," he told Janet Kardon. "I'm not photographing anything naked these days. That isn't to say I won't again, but I haven't been concentrating on bodies recently." Instead, he turned his attention to marble statues—"chilly white icons of desire," as art critic Kay Larson described them.

In doing so, Mapplethorpe had come full circle, for having once excelled at transforming his models into pieces of sculpture, he was now attempting to breathe life into stone. Most of the statues he photographed were nineteenth- and twentieth-century reproductions of classical gods, which Dimitri Levas bought for him at Malmaison and Niall Smith. Mapplethorpe purposely sought the reproductions because the ancient classical figures were rarely in perfect condition, and he did not want to own them if they were missing "noses and things." Yet even his reproduction gods failed to measure up to his exacting standards, and discovering a slight mark on the bridge of Apollo's nose, he sent the statue out to be professionally cleaned. He then began sending all his statues out for cleaning until Levas finally put a stop to it. "This is ridiculous," he said. "You're ruining the beautiful patina and making them look like brand-new statues. It doesn't make any sense."

While it might seem that Mapplethorpe's inability to accept the ravaging effects of age indicated an unwillingness to confront his own mortality, that was not the case at all. He didn't like talking about death, yet his photographs could be seen to symbolize a progressive move from the world of the flesh to that of the spirit. His portraits of women began to look more and more like angels, and even Princess Gloria von Thurn und Taxis, who, as "Princess TNT," was renowned in the 1980s as a royal party girl, was transformed into a celestial being as luminous as the string of pearls at her neck. Kay Larson noted the "new morbidity" in Mapplethorpe's work, and certainly one of the most macabre images was the photograph he took of a human skull. It was, for him, the purest sculptural image of all; neither hair nor flesh spoiled its clean lines, and everything, literally, was stripped to the bone.

He had been drawn to skull imagery from the time he first turned his pet monkey, Scratch, into a musical instrument, but never before had he used the death's-head symbol to make such a powerful statement about the terrifying process of bodily decay. He returned to the same theme in a more personal way with *Self Portrait, 1988*, one of his finest photographs, and certainly the most intimate. At first he had only intended to take a picture of one of his walking canes, which had a carved skull at the top, but while Ed Maxey and Brian English were busy setting up the shot, he suddenly disappeared into the bedroom and emerged, five minutes later, in a black turtleneck. He knew that by dressing in black the body could be made to appear almost invisible—he had used the same technique to great effect in his portraits of Doris Saatchi and Roy Cohn. Intuitively, Ed understood what Robert was trying to do, and as he photographed his brother, he focused the camera on the hand holding the skull cane, leaving Robert's blurred face to drift into the darkness.

The portrait reflected the way Mapplethorpe was currently approaching his work, for while each photograph bore his signature, as the months wore on he was slowly receding from the creative process. The portraits were the exception because then he was obliged to interact with the person on the other side of the camera, but many of the still lifes were now being photographed by Maxey or English. For years Dimitri Levas had been responsible for selecting the vases and flowers, then styling the pictures himself. The Mapplethorpe style had become so formulaic that Mapplethorpe needed only to approve a Polaroid of the setup before delegating the actual picture-taking responsibilities to someone else. "After a while it got to be so standardized that it was almost like a factory," Levas explained. "And you would think, oh well, it really doesn't have that much to do with Robert. But from the beginning, he had set up a certain process with Tom and me and his assistants, so that no matter what, it was really about his statement."

In fact, even when Mapplethorpe wasn't involved in the pictures, his vision was so controlled and precise that both Maxey and English felt as if they were forced to see the world through his eyes. "It was really kind of neurotic," English said, "because whenever I took a picture it was like being inside his head. That was part of Robert's whole thing—people would spend time thinking about who he was, then project their image of him onto the pictures. It didn't matter who did what, because it was all about Robert Mapplethorpe . . . all our names were Mapplethorpe."

May and June were roller-coaster months, as excitement over the forthcoming Whitney retrospective was offset by Mapplethorpe's failing health. He couldn't maintain his weight, and from a high of 120 pounds in March he had dipped to a skeletal 113 pounds. Dr. Starrett urged him to hire a private-duty nurse, but refusing to surrender the little freedom he had left, he continued to rely on the unreliable Jack Walls, who regularly deserted him in the middle of the night to buy drugs. Walls blamed his drug problem on having to sleep in the same bed with an ailing man. "Who wouldn't need a little something to sedate themselves?" he said. "He was sweaty and sick to his stomach all the time, and it was awful." Worse for Mapplethorpe than Walls's drug habit was the unsettling idea that he was losing his iron grip on him. "Robert would never have put up with the relationship if he'd been well," Lynn Davis observed. "Jack continually stole money from him. He forged Robert's name on things, but he also provided Robert with the illusion that he was still a sexual being."

Actually, if Mapplethorpe had not been diagnosed with AIDS, he probably wouldn't have spent so much time with most of the people who now comprised his inner circle, but each served a specific purpose. Michael Stout handled his legal matters; Dimitri Levas supervised his work; Alex Knaust was in charge of his medical treatment; his brother Ed helped shoot his pictures and provided a semblance of family life; and Lynn Davis served as a nurturing mother figure. Since the 1970s Davis's long hair had turned totally white, and it draped down her shoulders like a veil. Mapplethorpe called her "my Jewish saint," for she was untiringly devoted to him, and she radiated a sense of spirituality. Mapplethorpe felt better just being around her, and sometimes the two friends would just sit together holding hands. "I thought Robert handled his illness with such dignity," Davis said. "My friendship developed into a real respect for him. I never once saw him throw a fit; he never raged or screamed. He remembered what Sam had been like toward the end, and I think he made a private vow to restrain himself."

Mapplethorpe showed different sides of himself to different people, however, and just as Davis and Patti Smith brought out his sweetness, others drew his wrath. Many times he pushed his friends and employees to the limit. He rarely expressed his gratitude, and the highest compliment he offered anyone was volunteering to do his or her portrait. He was so reluctant to work gratis, though, that he made Stout pay for his picture and, after offering Levas a portrait in lieu of payment for designing his stationery, he procrastinated for five years before reluctantly fulfilling his obligation. He showed no interest in photographing his brother and seemed to derive a perverse pleasure from knowing how much Ed wanted a picture. "Robert knew he had the power to crush Eddie with a glance," Melody Danielson explained, "and it was sad because Eddie was so completely dedicated to him."

Both Ed and Melody always made sure Robert had company at night and often stayed with him until he fell asleep. Invariably, he would ignore Ed and spend most of the time talking to Melody—a situation that left Ed feeling even more depressed and inadequate. Finally, he and Melody decided to take a break from Robert and they left for Los Angeles at the end of May.

A few weeks later, Jack Walls declared that he, too, had had enough of Mapplethorpe. He persuaded studio manager Suzanne Donaldson to write him a check from the photographer's business account, and he went to L.A. as well.

Walls's departure left Mapplethorpe without anyone to care for him, but he still wouldn't hire a nurse, and he expected Suzanne Donaldson and Brian English to assume the responsibilities of a home-care attendant. They cleaned his house, washed the dishes and laundry, placed cold compresses on his head when he was feverish, and escorted him to the bathroom when he was too weak to walk there himself. "It was one of the worst times of my life," English said. "Every day instead of shooting pictures I'd be scrubbing his toilets and taking care of him. I just couldn't believe I was working for a dying man. What was I supposed to do if he suddenly keeled over on the floor?"

The question weighed heavily on Michael Stout, who realized he had to put Mapplethorpe's affairs in order. For the past several months he had been talking to Mapplethorpe about ways to preserve his archive of photographs, as well as to lessen his taxes. On May 27 Mapplethorpe signed documents creating the Robert Mapplethorpe Foundation and set up the guidelines for administering the organization's funds. At the time Mapplethorpe wasn't interested in using the foundation's money for AIDS research and wanted it to go exclusively toward photography-related projects. His first gift went to Philadelphia's Institute of Contemporary Art to assist them in producing the catalogue for his forthcoming show. In addition to Stout, Mapplethorpe asked Lynn Davis and Dimitri Levas to serve on the board. "Robert set up the foundation thinking that it was never going to be in action, because he wasn't going to die," Davis said.

Mapplethorpe was so determined to live that even though he was vomiting nearly everything he ate, he still insisted on going to restaurants with Davis. "We'd have Italian food at Il Cantinori and Da Silvano," she said. "He ate until he couldn't eat anymore." On June 22, Dr. Starrett admitted him to St. Vincent's Hospital, where a Hickman catheter was implanted in his chest. A flexible white tube was then inserted in the catheter, through which an intravenous protein drink could be regularly administered. When he returned home the next day he was severely depressed by having tubes jutting out of his chest, and he had no choice but to hire a private duty nurse to supervise his complicated feeding system. Kitchen utensils had now been replaced by hypodermic needles, and a nurse had to clean his catheter with alcohol and Betadine before mealtimes. "I'm like a space creature with all these tubes coming out of me," he lamented. "It's hideous."

Despite the Hickman catheter and the loss of his independence, Mapplethorpe was still remarkably feisty for someone in such poor health, and he was now battling the New-York Historical Society for the return of Wagstaff's silver collection. The silver had been on loan to the institution since the opening of the Wagstaff show in March 1987, but when Michael Stout asked for it back, James Bell, the society's director, produced a letter from Wagstaff extending the loan from eight months to five years. Mapplethorpe sued the society, claiming Wagstaff had not been capable of making rational judgments when he signed the letter from his hospital bed on December 15, 1986. When Mapplethorpe gave a deposition to the society's lawyers on July 1, however, his answers were extremely vague. In fact, though he claimed Wagstaff was not capable of making rational judgments, he never questioned his judgment concerning issues beneficial to himself, such as the trust agreement of January 1987 that provided him with six thousand dollars a month until the Wagstaff will was admitted to probate. In truth, Mapplethorpe didn't know what future plans Wagstaff had had for the silver, but according to James Bell, who labeled the photographer a "pathological liar," Wagstaff had wanted it to remain at the Historical Society, where it would be regularly displayed in the "Samuel Wagstaff Gallery."

Luckily for Mapplethorpe, the lawsuit coincided with a number of highly embarrassing disclosures in the press about the Historical Society's financial mismanagement and curatorial blunders. James Bell subsequently resigned, and the interim director had enough publicity problems without being involved in a lawsuit with someone battling AIDS. The Historical Society returned the silver to Mapplethorpe, who then promptly arranged with Christie's for the sale of the "Samuel J. Wagstaff Collection of American Silver," which would bring Mapplethorpe nearly a million dollars.

During the heat of the silver controversy, Mapplethorpe had discussed the lawsuit with a reporter writing a piece for *New York*, but as the July 11 publication date approached, he worried that someone might make a reference to Wagstaff's death from AIDS—or worse, his own infection with the HIV virus. He did not want to be a spokesman for the disease any more than he had wanted to be labeled a "gay photographer." Yet he couldn't keep refusing to discuss his illness, especially with all the upcoming publicity generated by the Whitney retrospective, and he felt he had no choice but to let the word out.

First, however, he telephoned Ed in Los Angeles and tentatively announced, "Well, I guess Mom and Dad have to know." It didn't take Ed long to realize that even though he was three thousand miles away he was the one Robert expected to break the news. Since he couldn't imagine telling them over the telephone, Ed first called his sister Nancy, who, after listening to his quivering voice and remembering Robert's feeble appearance at Richard's funeral, interrupted him. "It's AIDS, isn't it?" she said.

Before Nancy told her parents, she drove into the city to see Robert over the Fourth of July holiday. Mentally prepared for the worst, she still stifled a gasp when her brother shuffled down the hallway into the living room. Nancy had always felt close to Robert and had named him the godfather of one of her sons. She realized he probably thought her current life was boring, so hoping to spark some shared memories, she surprised him with one of their old family albums. They looked at the pictures together, and noticing tears welling up in his eyes, she longed to put her arms around him but was afraid of being rebuffed. She stayed for less than an hour, and as she was saying good-bye, she realized she hadn't asked the question everybody in the family had always been afraid to ask. "Robert," she said, "are you a homosexual?" He slowly exhaled the smoke from his cigarette before murmuring a barely audible "Yes."

Two days later Nancy picked up Susan and James, and together the three siblings drove to Floral Park to tell their parents about Robert. They didn't call ahead because Joan was still dependent on her oxygen tank and rarely left the house. When they arrived Joan was drinking coffee in the kitchen and Harry was smoking a cigarette in the backyard. Joan immediately knew something was wrong and instinctively sought sanctuary in the cheery living room. She offered a silent prayer—"Please God, no more bad news"—then confronted her three children, lined up on the bright sunflower couch. "Okay," she said, "who's got the problem now?" Nancy, the oldest, answered first. "Mom, we all do," she replied. "Robert's really sick . . . he's got AIDS."

Joan didn't respond at first, then suddenly she let out an anguished sob. "Oh God, no!" she wailed. "Not my favorite one!"

When details of the family meeting filtered back to Mapplethorpe, he could only express amazement that he was his mother's favorite. "How come I didn't know that before?" he asked. Still, he was a nervous wreck when he learned his parents were planning to visit him, and Ed and Melody returned to New York to help him through the ordeal. He had once boasted to his father that one day he would own the most beautiful loft in New York, and he arranged his photographs on the display ledge near the kitchen according to the ones he thought his parents would like best. How could they not be impressed by the Warhol portrait of him in the "Suzie Frankfurt Room"? Or the James Ensor, the Edouard Vuillard, and the Tony Smith—paintings and a sculpture he had inherited from Wagstaff? Nevertheless, he worried that his success would mean nothing to them, because "the cat was finally out of the bag . . . at best, I was a bisexual."

The day Mapplethorpe had been dreading for years came and went without a dramatic confrontation. No one brought up AIDS or Robert's homosexuality. Melody served tea while Ed engaged in idle banter with his parents, and occasionally Robert said a few words about his Whitney show. Afterward, he described his parents' visit as "nothing"—the exact same word Harry used to describe his experience of seeing Robert again.

Later that afternoon, when Joan returned home, she telephoned Nancy and expressed her regret that she had not asked Robert point-blank if he was gay. "Listen, Ma," Nancy said, exasperated. "I already told you . . . *Robert is gay!*" But Joan still had her doubts. "No," she replied. "I don't think so."

Even with the Hickman catheter, Mapplethorpe continued to lose weight, and he still had high fevers and recurrent vomiting. A few days after his parents' visit, on July 11, he was admitted to St. Vincent's Hospital, where he was diagnosed with mycobacterium avium-intracellulare (MAI), a bacterial infection Dr. Starrett considered an "end-stage disease," as it frequently appears in AIDS patients whose immune systems are severely compromised. Mapplethorpe was terrified of being in St. Vincent's and kept flashing back to Wagstaff's stay there. It just so happened Patti Smith was in New York doing publicity for *Dream of Life*—the album was about to be released by Arista—and now she was sitting at the edge of Mapplethorpe's bed, as she had sat at Wagstaff's. Visitors to Mapplethorpe's room were touched to see her vigorously massaging his legs and feet one afternoon, perhaps hoping to spark some life into his nerve-deadened limbs.

Mapplethorpe had angrily denounced Jack Walls for skipping out on him, but Walls was optimistic that the photographer would forgive him for going to Los Angeles. He appeared at the hospital one afternoon, expecting Mapplethorpe to give him the keys to the loft. "Are you crazy?" Mapplethorpe shouted from his hospital bed, and he threatened to call the police if Walls ever entered the building. With his talent for the dramatic gesture, Walls then moved into an abandoned tenement, where he lived with a group of vagrants. "I went from being with Robert, and doing what I could for him, to *poof!*—walking down the street with my clothes in a bag," Walls said. "I hadn't saved any money. I hadn't thought about my future. I was, like, flipping out."

When Walls complained to Lynn Davis that he was having a nervous breakdown, she took him to Beth Israel Hospital, where he checked himself into the psychiatric ward. "It was nut city," Walls said. "I realized I wasn't crazy—I just needed a place to live." He left after five days and moved into Michael Stout's apartment until Davis appealed to Mapplethorpe to provide Walls with rent money. "For better or worse, Robert had taken me to be, like, his fucking spouse," Walls explained, "so the least he could do was support me."

Writer Steven Aronson stumbled upon a bizarrely intimate scene when he visited Mapplethorpe one afternoon at the hospital and Walls was there rubbing his feet. "I was never so uncomfortable in my life," Aronson said. "Robert was moaning and making the kinds of sounds you make when you're having sex. I finally asked him, 'Well, is that painful or pleasurable?' and Robert said, 'It's in between.' And I realized that's what he liked, something between pain and pleasure."

When word spread through the floor that Robert Mapplethorpe was occupying a bed, he received visits from other AIDS patients who felt a special kinship with him. One developed a crush on the photographer and kept dropping by the room. "He won't leave me alone," Mapplethorpe complained to Steven Aronson. "And he has terrible taste . . . just look at his slippers!" But Aronson suspected Mapplethorpe was secretly flattered by the attention and by his status as the celebrity on the ward. A visit with another AIDS patient, though, left him badly shaken. The man's name was Howard Brookner, and he had just finished directing *Bloodhounds of Broadway*, starring Matt Dillon and Madonna, before going blind from complications of the disease. To be a blind film director was just as frightening as being a sightless photographer, and after Brookner was released from the hospital, Mapplethorpe was upset when nurses moved him into the room Brookner had vacated.

The Whitney opening was only two weeks away, and Mapplethorpe constantly inquired of his visitors, "You think I'll make it, don't you?" He was referring to the show, but some friends wondered if he was going to make it out of the hospital. "All through Robert's illness," Dimitri Levas explained, "there were moments when he would become very sick, and you'd wring your hands and say, 'This is it,' then he would bounce back again. Each time he was a little bit weaker, but he still had that amazing comeback ability. But at the hospital, he was in the worst physical shape he'd ever been in. . . . It didn't look good."

Rumors began spreading that Mapplethorpe wasn't expected to leave the hospital alive, and while he defied the skeptics by returning home on July 18, it seemed unlikely that he would have the strength for the Whitney show on the twenty-seventh. When Dr. Starrett paid a house call on the night before the opening, Mapplethorpe was still vomiting and so weak he couldn't leave his bed. Yet he had already planned what he was going to wear—a purple satin dinner jacket, white tuxedo shirt, and velvet shoes with his initials monogrammed in gold.

CHAPTER TWENTY-THREE

"Mapplethorpe captures the peak of bloom, the apogee of
power, the most seductive instant, the ultimate present that
stops time and delivers the perfect moment into history."

—*Janet Kardon*

"You know what they say about Robert Mapplethorpe. . . .
Here today, here tomorrow."

—*Sam Green*

The Mapplethorpe opening at the Whitney was one of the
most eagerly anticipated events of the summer of 1988—the last big
party before the galleries closed for August and the art world moved
to Bellport and the Hamptons. It was an opening Mapplethorpe
wouldn't have missed even if he hadn't been the star attraction, and
nothing short of his death would have kept him away. He arrived early
by limousine so the other guests wouldn't notice the accessories of his
illness—the wheelchair and oxygen tank that were now as integral to
his life as the jaunty brass-tipped cane he carried. Accompanied by
Lynn Davis, her white hair streaming down her shoulders, and a
beautiful black female nurse, whose head was swathed in a turban, he
stepped gingerly out of the car and steadied his body against the two
women. He shunned the wheelchair, and taking a deep breath, he
tottered toward the Whitney, and his moment of fame.

A couch had been set up for him in the center of the exhibit—

ninety-seven pictures that provided a visual diary of his life, from the collages and Polaroids of the early seventies to his most recent photograph of a bust of Apollo. Interspersed among the S&M pictures, flowers, and black nudes were fifteen years of self-portraits. The real-life Mapplethorpe provided the conclusive image in the series; gaunt and cadaverous, he was barely recognizable as the Mapplethorpe on the walls. Yet, in his withering away, he had achieved a kind of perfection. Whitney director Tom Armstrong hadn't been sure whether or not Mapplethorpe would be well enough to attend, and when he saw him gallantly perched on the couch, he blinked back tears. "I want to thank you for all this," Mapplethorpe said, straining to lift himself up to shake the director's hand. "I just lost it right there," Armstrong recalled. "His courage was extraordinary."

People poured into the exhibit by the dozens, until Mapplethorpe was nearly engulfed by a crowd that numbered sixteen hundred. The museum's air-conditioning was malfunctioning, so the rooms were sweltering, and the fashionably attired guests were soon complaining that the museum felt like a sauna. Meanwhile, paparazzi encircled the couch hoping to capture what was fast becoming a new genre of celebrity portraiture—the AIDS shot. Printer Martin Axon heard one attempting to persuade Mapplethorpe to move in front of his 1987 self-portrait for a glaring before-and-after comparison. "I found the whole experience really nerve-racking," recalled Dimitri Levas, who spent the evening at Mapplethorpe's side. "He was like a frail little bird being surrounded by a herd of buffalo."

It was Mapplethorpe's night, however, and he was determined to enjoy it. His fingers burned from the neuropathy, yet he shook hands with every important person who was whisked to his side, and throughout the evening he could be seen chatting with artists Francesco Clemente, Ed Ruscha, Robert Rauschenberg, Brice Marden, Barbara Kruger, and Louise Bourgeois, and dealers Leo Castelli, Tony Shafrazi, and Holly Solomon. Some were placed in the humbling position of having to lean down so far in front of him they appeared to be kneeling at his feet. "Robert lived for the adoration," Levas observed. "He loved that—all those people loving him." Sadly, the ones who mattered most weren't in attendance. Sam Wagstaff had been dead for over a year now, and Patti Smith didn't feel she could leave her family again since she had just returned to Detroit two weeks earlier. Jack Walls was boycotting the show for personal reasons—"I didn't want to see all those ultraboring people pretending to be ga-ga over Robert."

Mapplethorpe had sent an invitation to his parents, but Joan didn't feel strong enough to put up with the crowds, especially since she, too, was dependent on a wheelchair and oxygen tank. But Nancy, Susan, and James had driven into the city, and standing on the sidelines, they witnessed the full measure of their brother's celebrity. Nancy had already been forewarned by Ed that Robert wouldn't have much time to talk to her, and later, she was pleasantly surprised to see that she had been caught by one of the paparazzi's cameras. The picture says it all: Nancy is trying to get her brother's attention, but he is locked in a double handshake with Robert Rauschenberg and doesn't notice her.

Midway through the event Mapplethorpe felt lightheaded and feverish, and he moved to a back room to escape the crowd. He instructed Levas to guard the entrance and to keep everybody out except the chosen few. It was typical of Mapplethorpe that no matter how sick he was he still had to create the ultimate VIP room, and he periodically called out to Levas, "Get Brice," or "Where's Francesco?" He was having such a good time that he didn't want to leave, and it was only after the museum guards began clearing people out that he reluctantly said good night. Someone from the Whitney suggested he use his wheelchair, but Mapplethorpe replied, "I can walk," and he left the museum as if buoyed by a pair of wings—or so it seemed to Levas, who described him as floating on air.

"Mapplethorpe mania has arrived in New York," Andy Grundberg wrote in his review of the show for *The New York Times,* and indeed the Whitney retrospective cast such a bright spotlight on Mapplethorpe that hardly a day went by without his name appearing in the papers. He was the subject of a *Newsweek* article headlined "Walk on the Wild Side," which described him as a "lightning rod for an urbane cultural attitude—a mirror of contemporary narcissism." *Time*'s Richard Lacayo suggested that "with the era of sexual extremity now closed, some of Mapplethorpe's pictures look even more loaded and unnerving than they once did." *The Nation*'s Arthur C. Danto maintained that "a show of Mapplethorpe is always timely because of his rare gifts as an artist . . . but circumstances have made such a show timely in another dimension of moral reality." Kay Larson in *New York* noted that Mapplethorpe had "ridden a cultural curve that began in the seventies and eighties with the various movements toward sexual liberation and now seems on the downward swing toward fear and death."

Clearly, AIDS had made Mapplethorpe's work more relevant, and perhaps because he was known to be seriously ill with the virus, he was treated more gingerly by critics than he had been in the past. But the question of whether he was an important artist or a medio-cre one had long been clouded by larger issues—the relationship between photography and art, for example, or between art and por-nography. Moreover, Mapplethorpe's work had become so identi-fied with the gay S&M subculture that reactions to it often depended upon whether the viewer was conservative or liberal, gay or straight. In addition, since he straddled the territory between photography and other art forms, he was never accepted by the straight photography world of Garry Winogrand, Lee Freidlander, or William Eggleston, nor was he fully at home in the world of con-temporary painting and sculpture. "It doesn't take a genius to figure out that Robert wasn't a genius," said Jane Livingston, who none-theless agreed to show Janet Kardon's "Perfect Moment" exhibit at the Corcoran Gallery. "But there are a lot of artists who are better liked and have bigger reputations who are not as good as Robert Mapplethorpe. It's all about marketing and building up a myth."

"Ultimately one doesn't know how Robert Mapplethorpe will be perceived by future generations," said Philippe Garner of Sotheby's. "I think many people purchased his flower pictures for the frisson of owning a Mapplethorpe—the tip of the sinister iceberg, as it were. Many of them would never have hung his sexual pictures on their walls, but with Robert's flowers, they could flirt a bit with that world. The whole subject of exploring sexuality is a very important one in photography, and Robert will certainly be regarded as a piv-otal figure."*

*In the five years since his death the Mapplethorpe myth has continued to flour-ish, with exhibits of his photographs in France, Spain, Switzerland, Germany, Den-mark, Mexico, Japan, Belgium, Sweden, Israel, and Australia.

• • •

"Did you see any more stories about me?" Mapplethorpe would ask Jack Walls, whose frequent assignment was to scour the newsstands. Mapplethorpe skimmed many of the articles, as he had done with the essays in the Whitney catalogue. Though Ingrid Sischy was a friend of his, he pronounced her piece "A Society Artist" unreadable and complained that she got too bogged down in words; he couldn't make any sense of Richard Howard's essay either, and wondered if the critic himself understood it. But ultimately the only words that were important to him were "Robert Mapplethorpe," and each time his name appeared in the paper he reacted as if he'd just received a shot of vitamin B_{12}. "Can you imagine all the money I'd be making if I was doing commercial work right now?" he boasted to Anne Kennedy, who suddenly found her client more popular than ever. The Gap, the clothing chain, wanted him for a lucrative still-life campaign. "Everybody," Kennedy noted, "was just dying to work with him."

Mapplethorpe wasn't well enough to take advantage of the offers, however, and he spent August and September imprisoned inside his loft. He had always hated sunlight, and having lived most of his life in the photography studio or in dark bars, he had grown oblivious to seasonal variations. But now he suddenly became nostalgic for the fresh air and sunshine and longed to plunge into New York's street life again. Before his illness, he had walked so rapidly that friends could barely keep up with him; he would race from store to store, club to club, in pursuit of his momentary obsessions—a ceramic vessel, a Venini vase, a black man with lustrous skin. Trapped indoors, he amused himself by watching situation comedies on the new TV set Lynn Davis had bought him. His favorite show was *The Golden Girls*. Other times he played music on the stereo, and one afternoon he became teary-eyed listening to Al Green's rendition of "Tired of Being Alone." He confided to Davis that his biggest regret in life was that he hadn't managed to have a successful relationship with anyone. He contemplated buying a puppy because he wanted something to cuddle at night, but friends convinced him to choose a pet that required lower maintenance, so he settled on a snake. But he didn't want an ordinary snake, he wanted a special one, so he asked Steven Aronson to do the research for him, and

Aronson presented him with the most regal specimen he could find—a Sonoran Mountain king snake for six hundred dollars. The snake, however, began developing physical problems of its own; though it eagerly devoured the squirming mice it fed upon, it was shedding its skin too rapidly and losing its luster. Mapplethorpe asked Aronson if he could perhaps trade it in for another pet.

Steven Aronson kept him company nearly every weekend throughout the summer and early fall. He was in the city caring for his American water spaniel, Rory, which was now seriously ill, and which Mapplethorpe had once memorably photographed. Aronson's quick wit, sharp tongue, and wicked talent for mimicry made him the ideal court jester for Mapplethorpe, and before long the writer was swept up in the intrigue of the photographer's court.

"Robert was lyrically selfish—that's when you're selfish to the point where it becomes a kind of poetry," Aronson said. "But he did face the humiliations and ignominies of his disease with great courage. If someone came to see him, he went right into his host mode. He made an heroic effort, he put on his silk robe and combed his hair. He would stumble into the living room smoking his cigarette. It was quite a performance. In some ways, he was an old-fashioned gallant. In others, he was the savviest reptile of the modern age. He'd greedily swallow every press clipping, annoyed there wasn't more that day. He'd already engorged acres of articles, and still it was never enough. All his primordial defects and attributes were magnified and exaggerated by the illness—maybe because when you're dying you want to cram *all* the things you are into what little time you have left."

Mapplethorpe kept mental tabs on who had given him what gifts, and how much they cost. When Robert Rauschenberg sent him one of his photographs, he was outraged. "Yuch!" Mapplethorpe said, unwrapping the picture. "He should have given me a painting, or at least a drawing." Each time Aronson visited, Mapplethorpe inquired about his dog's health, and when the animal rallied, he'd lash out in frustration, "*He's* getting well, and I'm not. Why aren't the pills working for me?"

Mapplethorpe was equally curious about the health of ex-rival Jim Nelson, who had used a portion of Wagstaff's estate settlement to fulfill a lifelong dream of traveling first-class to London on the QE2 and booking a suite at the Ritz. By the time he was ready to go, however, Nelson could barely walk, so his lawyer Leonard Bloom had to wheel him up to the gate in a wheelchair, then watch his client practically drag himself on board. "I don't care if I die on this ship," Nelson declared. "I'm getting on it." Nelson was sick throughout most of the trip, and when he returned to New York that June, the Kaposi's sarcoma lesions had invaded his internal organs, and he was given only a short time to live. In early October he was taken by ambulance to New York Hospital for a blood transfusion, but since there weren't enough available beds, he was placed in a corridor next to a patient dying of stab wounds. Finally, Leonard Bloom took Nelson home and asked if he wanted him to notify Jim's brother Art in California. But Jim had spent a lifetime denying his homosexuality to his family; he wrote them letters about his girlfriends, and even moved out of Wagstaff's penthouse into another apartment when a nephew visited him in New York. "I can't face them now," he told Bloom, who eventually convinced Nelson that his brother should be summoned to New York. By then, Nelson lay dying in a small studio apartment several floors below the one he had once shared with Wagstaff; he had painted the walls maroon to match a pottery shard from Pompeii that Wagstaff had given him, and two Mapplethorpe portraits, including one of Nelson in better days, were hanging near his bed. When Art Nelson and his family arrived, Jim could hardly speak, yet he was so deeply ashamed of his predicament that when his niece bent over to kiss him, he managed to gasp, "Didn't you hear?—You're not supposed to touch people like me." Those were among the last words Jim Nelson ever said. He died the next day, October 8, and following his instructions, Leonard Bloom carried his ashes to Oakleyville, where he scattered them in the barren rose garden.

Mapplethorpe's reaction to Nelson's death was characteristically blasé; he had never professed to like him, so he wasn't about to become overly emotional now that he was gone. Furthermore, he had recently learned that Harry and Joan were going to see the Whitney retrospective, and he agonized over the suitability of some of the S&M pictures. "Do you think it would be all right if I called the Whitney and asked them to take some of the pictures down?" he asked Steven Aronson, who told him, "Well, there *are* some pictures not even a mother could love." Nevertheless, Aronson advised him to leave them on the wall. "Although Robert was by now sophisticated to a certain extent and also had achieved a certain stature in the world," he observed, "his parents were still the punishing priests of his childhood, and he was still the guilt-ridden little kid."

Yet if Mapplethorpe was expecting to be castigated by his parents, he didn't receive even that satisfaction, for neither Harry nor Joan professed to find much that was offensive in the show. In fact, Joan sent him a lovely note afterward in which she praised him as "the best photographer in New York." Perhaps the same blocking mechanism that prevented her from admitting his homosexuality blinded her to such photographs as *Richard, 1978* and *Jim and Tom, Sausalito*. Or perhaps, in her own way, she had always loved and accepted him. Harry's low opinion of his son was such that he expected the photographs to be even more sensational and wondered if the museum had purposely removed "the really offensive ones" for their visit. It is difficult to know how much more offensive he thought they were going to be, but his torpid reaction pointed to the reason Robert may have taken the pictures in the first place. "No big deal," Harry said, explaining his reaction to the show.

Mapplethorpe equated publicity with life itself, so when his name receded from the newspapers he glumly told Jack Walls, "Well, I guess that's it." To make sure he wouldn't be forgotten entirely, however, he had agreed to be interviewed by Dominick Dunne for *Vanity Fair*. Numerous friends had advised him not to cooperate with the magazine, because Dunne couldn't be expected to treat him reverentially. But Mapplethorpe needed something to look forward to, and since the magazine had agreed to publish a portfolio of seven portraits to accompany the piece, he scheduled shootings with Jack Walls; Ed Maxey and Melody Danielson; Susan Sarandon's daughter, Eva Amurri; Carolina Herrera; actor John Shea; and author Dunne.

Mapplethorpe had once prided himself on approaching his work with a minimum of fuss, but the disease created so many complications that he was exhausted even before he shot the first roll of film. First, he had to arrange his appointments so they wouldn't interfere with his intravenous schedule or coincide with the times he vomited most frequently. Since he didn't want anyone to see him hobbling from the bedroom to the living room, he usually made sure his nurse helped him into his Mission oak chair so he'd already be seated when visitors arrived. Conversation mostly consisted of him struggling to control his coughing—a brutal congestive rattle that sounded as if his body was being split in half. He didn't have the strength to take pictures standing up anymore, so he sat in an adjustable chair with wheels and depended on Brian English or Ed Maxey to move him around. "It was like the human spirit adapting to the decaying of the physical body," observed John Shea. "As I looked into the camera, I saw this frail little spirit being wheeled backwards and forwards, and I found myself filling up with tears because this guy was dying before my eyes. Just then I looked at Robert, and he took the picture. He saw exactly what was happening to me, and I think he knew why, because he immediately pushed the chair backwards. It was just too powerful a moment for him."

Mapplethorpe decided to include a self-portrait among his pictures for the magazine, and Maxey and English photographed him in the uniform of his illness—a fifteen-hundred-dollar silk paisley robe from Sulka given to him by Michael Stout, and a pair of velvet slippers with gold crowns. His image of himself as a dandified aristocrat is touching in its pretension; it calls to mind Dirk Bogarde as the dying Gustave Aschenbach in *Death in Venice,* in which he is sitting on the Lido, perfumed and pomaded, watching the beautiful young Tadzio wrestle on the sand.

Coincidentally, a week after Mapplethorpe had his portrait taken, he, too, made a haunting appearance on the beach. Art dealer Barbara Gladstone had rented a limousine for the day, and offering to take him anywhere he wanted, she found herself going to Coney Island with Mapplethorpe, Walls, and a nurse. Dressed in a black cashmere overcoat and bright red muffler, a polished mahogany cane in his hand, Mapplethorpe shuffled up and down the sidewalk, stopping every few minutes to catch his breath and look around him. Off-season, Coney Island was a ghost town, and the garish rides, such as the Wonder Wheel and the Hell Hole, were gruesome in their stillness. Yet his eyes immediately lit up when he saw the sign

NATHAN'S FAMOUS. He had not eaten solid food for months, but he asked Walls to order him a hot dog and french fries, while he waited outside inhaling the pungent aroma of salt air and sizzling meat. "I don't think this is a good idea," Walls warned him, returning with a hot dog heaped with mustard and relish, and a plate of ketchup-soaked fries. Mapplethorpe devoured the food in a matter of minutes and was about to order another round when Nathan's suddenly began to swim in front of him and, clutching his stomach, he vomited everything on the sidewalk. He was mortified and quickly returned to the car, where he hardly said a word on the way home.

All signs indicated that Mapplethorpe was a dying man, yet no matter how many times he doubled over in spasms of vomiting, he believed, in the end, that he would be saved. His bathroom, with its mounted shark over the tub, was filled with his newest collection of objects—plastic pill bottles that were lined up in rows according to shape and size. None of the medicines seemed to be doing him any good, but he was convinced that a cure for AIDS existed, if only he could wait it out.

On November 2 he started a course of hyperimmunotherapy, by which HIV antibodies taken from healthy HIV-infected individuals are recirculated into patients with more progressive symptoms. He was one of the first people in the United States to receive the treatment, which was administered to him by a doctor from London. Immediately afterward he reported to Dr. Barbara Starrett that he was feeling better; he had color in his cheeks and appeared more animated and energetic than he had in months.

Two days later Mapplethorpe celebrated his forty-second birthday by inviting 250 people to his loft. In a scene worthy of a Fellini movie, guests milled from room to room dipping into huge tins of buluga caviar, sipping Dom Perignon, and spotting the celebrities Mapplethorpe had once photographed, including Sigourney Weaver, Susan Sarandon, and Gregory Hines—one of the few black men at the party. People showered Mapplethorpe with gifts and flowers; they complimented him on his appearance; they sang "Happy Birthday" and presented him with a cake. He gamely blew out the candles and made a silent wish while everyone applauded.

He was made happy by all the attention he received, and by the fact that he could still throw a stylish party. "Look at all the people," he said, beaming at a guest. "I still have the magic."

Later, when all the guests were gone, Mapplethorpe opened his presents, and surrounded by a heap of wrapping paper and ribbon, he expressed his dissatisfaction with his birthday offerings by groaning, "Ick!" Nothing in the pile appealed to him. What did he want with more ivory crucifixes, devil figurines, and cashmere mufflers? Over the next several days he received more flowers from people thanking him for the party, and he hated those, too. Lying in bed, breathing from an oxygen tank, he motioned to Dimitri Levas to remove a bouquet of red roses that his nurse had placed on the bureau directly opposite him. "The container," he gasped. "It's *plastic*!"

Mapplethorpe's eyes were one of the few parts of his body relatively unaffected by the disease, and his compulsion to weed the ugly from the beautiful was the only way he could still exert control over his life. Fittingly, his last self-portrait was a picture of his eyes only—an eerie close-up that was taken by Ed, whose shadowy reflection is imprinted on Robert's iris. Ed watched his brother die the way he had watched Richard, and from his intimate vantage point he was expected to provide his family with news of Robert's condition. Robert avoided his mother's phone calls, so she relied on her youngest son for comfort. "Do you think Robert still goes to church on Sunday?" she asked him. "Do you think he prays?" On Robert's behalf, she had offered a novena to St. Jude—patron saint of impossible causes—but she couldn't bear the thought of him dying without last rites, so she telephoned Father George Stack, the priest from Robert's childhood, and asked if he would visit her son.

A few days after Thanksgiving, Father Stack rode the elevator up to Mapplethorpe's loft and entered the "Suzie Frankfurt Room." The afternoon light filtered through the silver blinds and illuminated the bronze Mephistopheles in the corner; the ivory crucifixes and African masks; Tom of Finland's pornographic drawings; Baron Von Gloeden's Sicilian boys; and several skulls, with empty eye sockets and grimacing mouths. Seated in front of Ed Ruscha's *EVIL* silkscreen, Mapplethorpe, in his silk finery, was smoking a cigarette and coughing mucus into a plastic container.

The priest was mesmerized by the objects in the room, for, outside of religious art, he had never seen the battle of good versus evil depicted in such a decorative way. He couldn't imagine the life the photographer had led, and while he had come with the idea of offering to hear his confession, he decided to wait for a subsequent visit. Instead they spent ninety minutes reminiscing about Floral Park and their mutual friends from the Columbian Squires—boys named Tommy, Terry, and Philly, who were grown men now, and whose exploits interested Mapplethorpe only so far as he could measure his greater success against theirs. Before Father Stack left, he asked Mapplethorpe if he believed in any concept of a God at all. "I don't know," he answered. "I don't believe in dogmas and theologies. I just believe in being a good person. I've always been honest with people. I've never lied. I think I've lived a moral life." The priest hoped he would be invited back so they could talk further, and he was pleased when Mapplethorpe asked, "Can I see you again?"

Yet the photographer derived his true solace from the knowledge that sales of his prints had reached a record high. The escalating numbers had become a kind of religion to him, and whenever he spoke to Howard Read on the telephone, he would interrupt the conversation to announce to anyone who happened to be in the room, "Another twenty-five thousand . . . another fifteen thousand. . . . That's forty thousand dollars in two hours alone!" Ever since the Whitney show, and the subsequent articles about Mapplethorpe's illness, Read had sold several million dollars' worth of Mapplethorpe prints, and the market was still going strong. "We had a huge run-up in sales," Read said. "It was like Wall Street, except in this case people were buying against death, and they were really buying and buying."

Given the demand for Mapplethorpe photographs, Read hounded the studio to ship prints to the gallery as fast as possible. "It had become an assembly-line process," said Tom Baril, "and some prints that weren't perfect got pushed through." Suzanne Donaldson was so disturbed by Read's orchestration of the Mapplethorpe feeding frenzy that she complained to Mapplethorpe that he was turning the studio into a poster factory. "You are a fine-art photographer," she told him, "and the love and appreciation of your work seems completely at odds with Howard's need to entertain his clients." Mapplethorpe attempted to soothe her, but he didn't seem to mind Read's hard-sell tactics at all. "In two years we did three exhibitions, which is unbelievable," Read boasted. "If Robert had lived another six months, and from his bed, he'd have said, 'I've just taken pictures of my pillow and I want to do another show,' we probably would have done another show."

Read made hasty arrangements for an exhibit of Mapplethorpe's pictures of busts and religious icons that opened at the Robert Miller Gallery on November 29. Gallery-goers meditated on Mapplethorpe's photograph of a crucified Christ figure as if they were studying the Pietà. One man swore he could see a real tear in the eye of an African bronze. "The pictures were really just a production thing," Brian English explained. "Howard said, 'We're going to have a show of sculptural objects, so shoot them.' I shot them under Robert's direction. We printed up ten of each, and Robert sold them . . . *boom!* I don't think he got a thrill out of that one, though. It was kind of hollow." Dimitri Levas agreed: "It was not a good show, and it made me very sad, because it was all about confinement—the objects selected to be photographed were all within his narrow reach. Maybe it had to be that way because of his illness, but if Robert had been on his toes, he would not have done it."

"The Perfect Moment" was scheduled to open at the Institute of Contemporary Art in Philadelphia on December 9; it was Mapplethorpe's final goal for 1988, and he did not want to miss it. But this time there was no remarkable comeback; the hyperimmunotherapy had not proved to be an AIDS miracle after all, and he was vomiting so badly he couldn't even hold down his AZT tablets. While his friends took the Metroliner to Philadelphia, he remained in New York, the phantom of "The Perfect Moment." Afterward he watched a videotape of the event, in which guests were asked to look at the camera and speak directly to him. "It was like being at my own funeral and listening to people talk about me," he said. "It made me so sad, I cried."

Mapplethorpe's inability to attend the "Perfect Moment" exhibit sent him into the worst depression of his illness. He developed a fear of the darkness and would often lie awake at night and ruminate about his life while his nurse Tom Peterman tried to comfort him.

Though Peterman was Mapplethorpe's age, they could not have been more opposite; physically, the nurse was average-looking, yet he had devoted his life to the extraordinary task of taking care of terminally ill patients. Peterman wasn't sure whether or not he even liked Mapplethorpe, but nevertheless he sat by his bedside and listened to his fears. "I'm going to die," Mapplethorpe anguished one night. "I know it's going to happen, and I don't want to die." Peterman assured him that "nobody wants to die, and besides, you're not dead yet."

Still, Mapplethorpe knew it wouldn't be long and voiced regrets about his inability to connect with the right partner. He had recently received a disturbing letter from Milton Moore, who had been convicted of murdering a man with a lead pipe and was serving time in an Alabama prison. He asked Mapplethorpe if he could lend him three thousand dollars because he was in an "awkward situation." Jack Walls had recently borrowed three hundred dollars and used the excuse that he needed to visit his ailing mother in Chicago to help her move "from one tenement to another." Levas had suspected that Walls wasn't going to Chicago at all and needed the money for drugs, but he couldn't persuade Mapplethorpe that he was being taken advantage of. "That's the one thing that really bothered me about Robert and the disease," Levas said. "He started to believe only what he wanted to believe instead of seeing the whole picture. But I couldn't keep pointing to Jack all the time and saying, 'Look, he's stoned, he's stealing your money, he's lying to you.' So I let it go."

On Christmas Eve, Levas prepared an elaborate goose dinner, but the strong odor made Mapplethorpe so queasy he remained in bed. Levas shared his feast with Walls, Knaust, and Maxey and Danielson, and they dined in front of an evergreen tree decorated with Polaroid pictures of Mapplethorpe photographs. New Year's Eve was even bleaker. Lia Fernandez spent an hour with Mapplethorpe at the loft, where he and Levas were sitting in the living room. "It was terrible," she said, "because you couldn't very well wish him 'Happy New Year.'"

The month of January passed in the same dreary fashion, and nothing could cheer Mapplethorpe up. Read had sold a staggering $500,000 worth of photographs in December alone, but what did money mean to Mapplethorpe now? There was no pleasure to be found anywhere; he couldn't enjoy sex, drugs, or food. Cigarettes were the only relic of his hedonistic lifestyle, and he adamantly refused to give them up. "I need *something,*" he told Tom Peterman.

Mapplethorpe had naïvely thought the *Vanity Fair* article might make him feel better, but it only confirmed his worst fears. The cover line read "Robert Mapplethorpe's Long Good-Bye," which made him feel like an inconsiderate dinner guest. "The *long* good-bye?" he kept repeating. "Would *Vanity Fair* like me to speed things up? Am I dying too slowly for them?" He was even more upset when he turned to the article and read the breathless caption: "Here, as he courageously orchestrates his own exit from the world stage, he talks to DOMINICK DUNNE." Even worse was Jonathan Becker's photograph taken at the Whitney opening, which ruthlessly detailed every flaw and disfigurement on Mapplethorpe's skin. The magazine also published his own dandified self-portrait in the silk dressing gown, but it was the photojournalist's picture of him that captured the harsh reality of his condition—the image people would remember as they mentally scrolled through the "after" pictures of famous AIDS casualties. It didn't matter that Dunne's piece painted a fairly sympathetic portrait of him, for he couldn't see beyond the photograph. He once described the paparazzi's job as "stealing secrets," and he believed he had been robbed of his last vestige of dignity. "It's freakish," he lamented, "like Diane Arbus."

Not long after the *Vanity Fair* piece came out, Mapplethorpe recounted the following dream: "I was surrounded by dozens of frightening people . . . Mongoloids . . . women with bad teeth and skin . . . people who had escaped from insane asylums. They were screaming and grabbing me around the legs, and they wanted to pull me down, and I didn't want to go with them into that kind of Hell."

The *Vanity Fair* piece produced an extremely hostile reaction among readers; Mathilde Krim, director of the American Foundation for AIDS Research, wrote a letter to the editor in which she castigated Dunne for implying a causal link between Mapplethorpe's private life and AIDS. "To allude to such a link even as a possibility," she wrote, "amounts to sanctioning some of the most ignorant and harmful beliefs regarding the cause of AIDS." Others were appalled by Dunne's account of Mapplethorpe's sex life, and criticized the magazine as sick and depraved for devoting space "to a man who worshipped the anus." But ultimately what seemed to unnerve readers the most was that Mapplethorpe, unlike Rock Hudson or Ryan White, wasn't a sympathetic AIDS victim.

Many of Mapplethorpe's friends hoped that the Mapplethorpe Foundation would support AIDS research in addition to photography, but he was primarily interested in using his money to perpetuate his name. He thought of creating the equivalent of the Academy Awards for photography, and instead of an Oscar, winners would receive a Mapplethorpe—a trophy of his own design. But in January he suddenly decided to allocate a portion of the funds to AIDS, and a year after his death, the foundation would give Beth Israel Hospital $1 million to establish an AIDS health care facility; today it is known to its staff and residents as "Mapplethorpe."

"Now there's nothing to look forward to," Mapplethorpe had said after the *Vanity Fair* article came out, but on February 1 he surprised everybody by announcing that he would attend the opening of the Andy Warhol retrospective at the Museum of Modern Art. Warhol had died in 1987, and Paul Morrissey, the director of Warhol's films, had described the event to *The New York Times* as a "gathering of the clan." Though Mapplethorpe had not been a member of Warhol's inner circle, he was part of the extended tribe. He had originally come to New York to find Warhol, and while he had never penetrated the artist's glacial exterior, he had located the Warhol in himself. Mapplethorpe, too, had a gift for self-promotion, and his art was marked by a similar detachment. Warhol longed to be a machine; Mapplethorpe found comfort behind one.

He dressed for the occasion in the same purple dinner jacket he had worn to his own Whitney opening, but unlike at that event, he was not the star attraction and the reception he received from the other guests was polite but not effusive. Some pretended not to notice the wizened figure in the wheelchair, while others dashed off a breezy, "How are you doing?" Mapplethorpe's truthful response of "Not great" usually evoked silence, or in one case, "Let's have lunch." Nevertheless, he stayed for two hours while Tom Peterman wheeled him past Warhol's celebrity icons—the Ten Lizes, the Gold

Marilyn, the Silver Marlon, the Red Elvis, the Sixteen Jackies. Peterman found the whole event distasteful, for clearly Mapplethorpe was yesterday's story, and by fame's mercurial standards he had outlived his moment. But to Peterman's surprise, Mapplethorpe didn't seem to notice.

The strain of his "long good-bye," however, was taking its toll on his employees. No one wanted to desert him, but Suzanne Donaldson and Brian English didn't know how much longer they could continue working at the studio. "You'd go from rooting him on to live," English explained, "to wishing he was dead already. Then you'd feel guilty about feeling that way, but you'd realize you were only trying to protect yourself. I wish he hadn't been sick, but he was, and it was miserable." Jack Walls had also grown weary of the prolonged deathwatch and looked forward to the day when he could finally announce, "It's over." Alex Knaust was the only one who refused to accept Mapplethorpe's imminent death, and her all-consuming need to keep him alive had reached a fever pitch. Donaldson refused to take Knaust's phone calls, and even Mapplethorpe whose life she was trying to save, had instructed her to "see a psychiatrist or don't come back." Yet Knaust was so unbelievably persistent that she hacked her way through a jungle of red tape to get him the most advanced AIDS treatment available.

Since Mapplethorpe couldn't hold down his AZT tablets, she received special permission from Burroughs-Welcome for him to receive the drug intravenously, and then arranged for him to photograph Surgeon-General C. Everett Koop for *Time*. She knew Mapplethorpe would be too intimidated to discuss his condition with Koop, so she planned to attend the photo session and talk to the surgeon-general herself. But perhaps fearing she might make a scene, no one at the studio bothered to alert her of Koop's arrival on February 3, and as she predicted, Mapplethorpe didn't address his illness at all. Instead he focused his camera on the robust man who had surprised conservatives by advocating condoms in AIDS prevention, and fulfilled his last portrait assignment.

Furious with the studio for failing to tell her of Koop's visit, Knaust immediately accelerated her efforts to have Mapplethorpe included in the human trials of a new drug, CD-4, which were already in progress at Boston's New England Deaconess Hospital.

The drug was a copy of the CD-4 receptor found on the surface of many cells of the human immune system and the brain, and it was thought to act as a decoy, latching on to the AIDS virus and providing the cells with complete protection. Dr. Jerome Groopman of Harvard Medical School was supervising the trials, and after eight months of Knaust's badgering, he was finally persuaded to provide Mapplethorpe with the drug. Knaust was convinced it was the miracle they had been waiting for, and even though Mapplethorpe didn't want to leave his home for a hospital in Boston, he believed that he had been granted a last-minute reprieve. On February 14, a week before he was scheduled to leave for Boston, however, he began coughing up thick green sputum. Dr. Starrett placed him on antibiotics, and by February 20 he had improved, but the doctor thought he might have bacterial pneumonia.

Patti Smith hadn't seen Mapplethorpe since June, but she spoke to him several times a week on the telephone, and their conversations invariably cheered him up. Smith had a warm, mellowing voice, and knowing how much he was suffering, she carefully avoided discussing her own problems. Restrained by her responsibilities to Fred and their children, she had foolishly opted against touring to promote *Dream of Life*, and the album was a commercial failure. She had been gone from the music scene for nearly a decade, and even though she was idolized by many younger bands, she couldn't generate record sales on her cult reputation alone. When Smith heard that Mapplethorpe would soon be leaving for Boston, she asked Fred to drive her to New York so she could personally wish him good luck. She arrived several days before he was scheduled to go and found him arguing with his brother Ed over his shoulder-length hair. "It looks awful that way," Mapplethorpe scolded him. "You look like a girl." A few seconds later Mapplethorpe shook his head and smiled. "I sound just like my father, don't I?" he said.

Eventually Ed left them alone, and Mapplethorpe and Smith spent the rest of the afternoon together. Michael Stout had given him a copy of an old *Life* magazine that bore the date of his birthday and featured a desert scene on its cover. "We stared at the picture for a long time," Smith recalled. "It was like the photograph had opened up and we had entered the scene." In the middle of their reverie Mapplethorpe was seized with gastric pains, and a nurse led him to the bathroom. When he emerged a few minutes later, his eyes were glassy and feverish, and he could barely maintain his balance. "Patti," he said, "I'm dying."

Smith looked down at his hands, which had once been so beautiful, and saw that his arthritic-looking fingers had retracted into something resembling baby's fists. Tears stung her eyes, and although she tried to fight them back, she began sobbing and couldn't stop until Mapplethorpe suggested they go into the living room. He took a seat in his favorite chair while she sat opposite him on the couch. The Christie's catalogue of Sam Wagstaff's silver was on the coffee table in front of them. Mapplethorpe felt bad that he hadn't complied with Wagstaff's wishes and taken the pictures for the catalogue. "It should have been better," he said. Smith tried to convince him that he had done the best he could, then they both lapsed into silence. "There's nothing more to say, is there?" Mapplethorpe said. Smith began crying again, and Mapplethorpe got up from his chair to sit next to her on the couch. Resting his head on her shoulder, he tried to comfort her, but a few minutes later, Smith realized that he had fallen asleep. For the next two hours she sat very still so as not to awaken him and listened to his labored breathing and the faint beat of his heart. She retraced their lives together, flashing back to their first opening at the Miller Gallery, to Max's Kansas City and the Chelsea Hotel, and finally to Brooklyn, when she first saw him sleeping in his bed. They had come full circle. "I'd never felt so young," she said, "and so old."

On February 21 Mapplethorpe traveled to Boston in a Trailways touring bus that Knaust had rented for him in Woodstock, New York. The bus had once belonged to the band Jethro Tull, and it came equipped with a TV and VCR, on which Mapplethorpe watched *The Prophesies of Nostradamus*. In addition to Knaust, joining him on the four-hour trip were Lynn Davis and Tom Peterman, who had agreed to remain as his private-duty nurse. Mapplethorpe had asked Jack Walls to come to Boston with him, but Walls declined, offering countless feeble reasons why he needed to remain behind. Their relationship had always been a contest of wills, and in a last display of one-upmanship, Walls had spurned him.

Mapplethorpe had barely settled into his large private room on the eleventh floor of Deaconess Hospital when he received the first piece of bad news. Dr. Groopman hadn't been aware that Mapplethorpe had bacterial pneumonia and told him that he couldn't possibly administer the CD-4 until he first controlled the lung infection. For the next five days Mapplethorpe received intravenous antibiotics and waited for the CD-4. He had left strict orders with Suzanne Donaldson that he didn't want visitors, so he spent his days with Knaust and Peterman. Lynn Davis had returned to New York, but kept in close touch with Knaust by phone. Walls called to ask him for ten thousand dollars and Peterman overheard Mapplethorpe telling him, "You're nothing but a hustler." But he agreed to give him the money, admonishing him to do something with his life because, he said, "I'm not going to be around forever." Mapplethorpe's parents didn't visit him because Joan had just been released from the hospital and was recuperating at home. One afternoon a nurse presented him with a modest floral arrangement that he might otherwise have thrown in the trash, except for the inscription on the card that read "Love, Mom and Dad." He knew his mother was ill so it meant Harry had sent the flowers himself, and moved by the gesture of reconciliation, he turned to Knaust and said, "Do you believe my father took care of this?" A few minutes later, the nurse reappeared and apologized for the mix-up. "The flowers," she explained, "were meant for the patient across the hall."

On March 5, the day Mapplethorpe was scheduled for the CD-4, he suddenly began bleeding from his gastrointestinal tract and doctors forced tubes down his throat to drain his stomach. His throat was raw from a yeast infection, and he screamed in pain. "Please," he begged Knaust afterward, "don't let them hurt me anymore." Further tests showed that his immune system was so badly weakened that no amount of drugs could save him. "His body was being attacked from every side," Knaust said. "It was like watching a friend being machine-gunned." She didn't have the heart to tell him that Groopman wouldn't be administering the CD-4 after all, and explained that he had developed some complications that would delay the treatment a few more days. Meanwhile, she placed urgent calls to his friends in New York, and on March 7 a group that included his brother Ed, Dimitri Levas, Amy Sullivan, Ingrid Sischy, Lynn Davis, and Michael Stout rallied to his side. Even Jack Walls made the effort; sauntering into the room in a gray sharkskin suit, he saluted the photographer with a jaunty, "Hey, Big Daddy!"

Mapplethorpe didn't want any more members of his family at the hospital, and he was annoyed when he learned that Ed had alerted their sister Nancy to his condition. She had risen at five A.M. to drive to Boston with her son, but when she arrived at the hospital, she felt out of place. Mapplethorpe was surrounded by his surrogate family, and they encircled the bed, massaging his legs and hands. The previous Christmas he had sent her a thousand dollars, and after paying the bills, she had a little left over to buy herself a marcasite ring as a memento of him. She made a point of showing it to him at the hospital, for the ring seemed to be the only concrete evidence of their relationship. She stayed for several hours, and when she finally said good-bye, she knew she would never see him again. "He had the same look that Richard had," she said. "I can't explain it, but it was like a veil had come over his eyes." Before she left, she whispered in his ear, "Is there anything you want me to tell Mom and Dad?" He replied, "No, nothing."

Patti Smith knew Mapplethorpe hadn't been able to receive the drug treatment, but she wasn't emotionally prepared for his sudden decline. Amy Sullivan answered the phone when Smith called on March 7, and all Sullivan heard were wrenching sobs until Smith finally composed herself: She and Mapplethorpe had referred to their art as their "children," and in their last conversation together, he made her promise that she would write the introduction to his forthcoming flower book. And then he said good-bye.

Throughout the week Mapplethorpe had whiled away the time by drawing pictures in a sketch pad, and among the last images was a faint self-portrait, followed by his signature—"Robert Mapplethorpe . . . Robert Mapplethorpe . . . Robert Mapplethorpe"—until his name was reduced to a blur. There was nothing more for him to do.

On March 8 paralysis set in on the left side of his face. One eye closed shut. He couldn't speak anymore and the only sounds he made were low-pitched groans. Doctors increased the dosage of morphine, but he still fought to remain awake. "He was not ready to die," said Alex Knaust, who had moved a bed into his room to be with him. "He was putting up one hell of a fight."

Several times during Mapplethorpe's hospital stay, Tom Peterman had tried to broach the subject of death by telling him of his experiences with other patients who often dreamed of walking down a long tunnel and seeing a light at the end of the darkness. "That was usually a way for me to get a person to talk about death," Peterman explained, "but Robert wasn't interested." By the evening Mapplethorpe was fading so quickly that Ed fulfilled a promise he had made to his mother by notifying the hospital chaplain, who administered the last rites. Knaust stayed with Mapplethorpe until four the next morning, but finally left when Peterman advised her to get some rest. The nurse knew she was exhausted and didn't think she could handle Mapplethorpe's death. "If Robert wakes up," she pleaded, "tell him that God is with him. I don't want him to think he's alone."

Mapplethorpe didn't wake up, and at 5:30 A.M. on March 9, he suffered a violent seizure that racked his body with convulsions. Peterman had witnessed similar episodes before and understood that the body's frantic thrashing movements were a symptom of brain dysfunction. But in his heart he believed Mapplethorpe had been fighting his own private battle, struggling, in those final moments, toward the light.

EPILOGUE

May 22, 1989

Robert Mapplethorpe's memorial service at the Whitney Museum was a "guests only" affair, and several of the photographer's friends who wanted to pay their respects had to sneak past the Mapplethorpe sentinels at the door. Music executive Danny Fields, who had been the first person to befriend Mapplethorpe and Patti Smith at Max's Kansas City, was confronted by a woman demanding "Where's your ticket?" When he confessed he didn't have one— "It's a memorial service," he said, "not a rock concert"—he was informed that without a ticket he couldn't have a seat, although standing room was still available in the back. "One of the ushers was a friend of mine," Fields recalled, "so I told him, 'This is embarrassing . . . get me a seat.' Then I looked around me, and I couldn't figure out what any of the people had to do with Robert's life. There were no black men, and I didn't see any of the gay crowd from the Eagle's Nest or the Mineshaft. It was mostly art dealers in suits and leaders of fashion society, and you could almost see prices climbing in everybody's heads. It was like an auction at Christie's."

Mapplethorpe's flower photographs were hanging on the walls, and two enormous glass vases filled with lilacs flanked a podium in the center of the room. Michael Stout, Dimitri Levas, and Lynn Davis, of the Robert Mapplethorpe Foundation, had organized the memorial—a suitably dispassionate event that included remarks by Whitney director Tom Armstrong; AIDS researcher Dr. Mathilde Krim; dealer Harry Lunn; former Sotheby's employee Anne Horton; and writer Fran Lebowitz. Apart from Ingrid Sischy, who spoke movingly of Mapplethorpe's inherent elegance and grace, Patti Smith was the only speaker to evoke any real emotion from the crowd. She had arrived at the Whitney with Fred, and overwhelmed at seeing so many friends from the past, she couldn't stop crying. When she finally stepped up to the podium, she looked as if she might collapse, and for a few awkward moments, her mouth quivered, and she stuttered. Yet she pulled herself together as she usually did and performed a song she had written for Mapplethorpe, her "green-eyed bird."*

Afterward, waiters served champagne to the guests, many of whom then rushed off to fulfill other commitments. Photographer Sheila Metzner was overheard saying, "I feel bad that Robert's dead, but I'm just glad to be alive." A photographer from British *Vogue* wept into her champagne glass; it was unclear whether she had even known Mapplethorpe, but she was trying to get pictures of the memorial for the magazine, and the celebrity count was on the low side. The photographer glanced at Mapplethorpe's mother, then looked away.

Joan was in a wheelchair, hooked up to an oxygen tank, and her face looked pallid against the vibrant teal of her dress. Robert had not left his parents anything in the will, but if Joan was hurt by the multimillion-dollar slight, she didn't make an issue out of it. All she wanted from his estate was a pair of rosary beads she had given him, a coffee table he had designed, and his ashes. Harry worried that she

---

*Fred Smith died of heart failure on November 4, 1994—Mapplethorpe's birthday. Exactly a month later, Patti's brother, Todd, died of a heart attack. Both men were in their mid-forties.

had been too weak to travel into the city and had advised her to stay home, but Joan had been praying that God would let her live long enough to attend her son's memorial service.

Joan died three days later, and Harry prepared for another funeral at Our Lady of the Snows. Ed asked Michael Stout if the Mapplethorpe Foundation would finally return Robert's ashes, which, for lack of a more suitable place, were being kept in a box on Lynn Davis's mantel. No one had claimed Mapplethorpe's remains, so Davis had flown to Boston to pick them up from the crematorium. "Robert was in this little bag," she said, "and when I looked inside, there was nothing but bone chips." Davis had been searching for a beautiful object to hold Mapplethorpe's ashes and had finally located an exquisite silver box. She wanted to place the box in a crypt so that Mapplethorpe would have his own shrine. "Lynn didn't want to give the ashes to me," Ed recalled, "because she didn't think Robert would have wanted it that way. When I picked up the box at her house, she couldn't stop crying." Ed took the ashes home to Floral Park, and his brother's remains were placed in the coffin next to Joan's body. They were buried together in St. John's Cemetery in Queens, where Harry, "for private reasons," declined to put his son's name on the tombstone.

A month later, on June 22, slides of Mapplethorpe's photographs were projected onto the facade of the Corcoran Gallery of Art as part of a staged protest against the museum's cancellation of the "Perfect Moment" exhibit. Mapplethorpe's self-portrait in the leather jacket, cigarette dangling from his mouth, was seen floating above the demonstrators, as if the photographer himself had risen from the dead to skywrite the name Mapplethorpe over Washington, D.C. Finally, the ghostly image flickered away, and Mapplethorpe's picture of a tattered American flag, all bright stars and ragged stripes, took its place.

Chronology of the "Perfect Moment" Controversy

December 9, 1988: "The Perfect Moment" opened at the Institute of Contemporary Art in Philadelphia. Among the 150 photographs and objects in the show was the "X Portfolio"—thirteen images of men engaged in sadomasochistic activities. The pictures were smaller in scale than the other photographs in the exhibit, and were displayed alongside the "Y" and "Z" portfolios on a separate viewing table. The show closed in Philadelphia without incident on January 29, 1989; it then was scheduled to travel to five other cities in the United States.

April 1989: The American Family Association, a conservative watchdog group headed by the Reverend Donald Wildmon, of Tupelo, Mississippi, initiated a campaign to censor "blasphemous" art. The AFA targeted a New York artist named Andres Serrano, whose *Piss Christ*, an image of a crucifix submerged in a yellow liquid, had been exhibited several months earlier at the Southeastern Center for Contemporary Art in Winston-Salem. (Serrano described *Piss Christ* as a protest against the commercialization of sacred imagery.) The SCCA show, like "The Perfect Moment," had been partially funded by a grant from the National Endowment for the Arts. Wildmon, who had led boycotts against Martin Scorsese's *Last Temptation of Christ,* sent a letter and reproduction of *Piss Christ* to every member of Congress.

May 18, 1989: Thirty-six senators signed a letter indicating the need for changes in the NEA's grant-making procedures so "that shocking, abhorrent and completely undeserving art would not get money."

June 12, 1989: Christina Orr-Cahall, the director of the Corcoran Gallery of Art, stunned the art community when she canceled "The Perfect Moment," which was scheduled to open on June 30. The exhibit had already traveled to the Museum of Contemporary Art in Chicago, where it had attracted record crowds and no protests. But Orr-Cahall decided to cancel the Corcoran show because, she said, she didn't want "The Perfect Moment" to endanger NEA appropriations in Congress.

June 30, 1989: Slides of Mapplethorpe's photographs were projected onto the facade of the Corcoran Gallery as part of a protest against the gallery's cancellation of the exhibit. A crowd of seven hundred people waved placards and shouted "Shame, shame, shame" at the Corcoran.

July 22, 1989: "The Perfect Moment" opened at the Washington Project for the Arts, an artist-run organization, which had stepped in after the Corcoran's cancellation.

July 26, 1989: The Senate approved restrictions proposed by Senator Jesse Helms, Republican of North Carolina, that would bar the NEA from supporting "obscene" or "indecent" work—"including but not limited to depictions of sadomasochism, homoeroticism, the exploitation of children, or individuals engaged in sex acts; or material which denigrates the objects or beliefs of the adherents of a particular religion or nonreligion." The Senate also voted to limit funds to the Institute of Contemporary Art and SCCA for exhibiting the Mapplethorpe and Serrano shows. Helms had engineered a voice vote on the amendment by showing Senator Robert Byrd, the powerful Democrat of West Virginia, a selection of Mapplethorpe pictures, including *Mr. 10½*. Byrd replied, "Whoa! We funded that? I'll accept your amendment."

September 7, 1989: The Whitney Museum of American Art placed an ad in *The New York Times* that featured a Mapplethorpe photograph of a wilted parrot tulip. The ad was headlined "Are You Going to Let Politics Kill Art?"

September 19, 1989: Christina Orr-Cahall, of the Corcoran Gallery, expressed regret at offending members of the arts community with her cancellation of "The Perfect Moment." "Our course in the future," she said, in a written statement, "will be to support art, artists and freedom of artistic expression."

September 29, 1989: The Senate voted down Jesse Helms's amendment to restrict federal grants for "obscene or indecent" art. Once again, the senator had come to the debate equipped with Mapplethorpe photographs and had called upon "all the ladies" to leave the chamber while he passed the pictures around. Nevertheless, senators rejected the amendment, sixty-two to thirty-five, and eventually agreed on milder restrictions that would prevent the NEA from supporting "obscene" art for one year, based on the standards set by the Supreme Court's 1973 decision *Miller* v. *California*.

December 18, 1989: Christina Orr-Cahall resigned from the Corcoran Gallery of Art.

March 1990: Cincinnati's law enforcement officials, antipornography groups, and business leaders began an active campaign to pressure the Contemporary Arts Center into canceling the upcoming Mapplethorpe show. "The Perfect Moment" had recently been shown in Hartford and Berkeley, where it caused few problems, but conservative Cincinnati, with its stringent pornography laws, had been preparing an attack for months. The city's police chief, Lawrence Whalen, vowed to examine the exhibition and seize any photographs considered obscene. "The people of this community," he said, "do not cater to what others depict as art."

April 6, 1990: A municipal judge rejected a petition by the Contemporary Arts Center for a jury trial to determine the issue of obscenity. The CAC had taken the measure in fear of police action.

April 7, 1990: "The Perfect Moment" opened at the Contemporary Arts Center; police and sheriff's officers ordered four hundred visitors to leave while they videotaped Mapplethorpe's pictures as evidence to support obscenity charges. An angry crowd outside shouted, "Gestapo, go home!" and *"Sieg heil!"* Dennis Barrie, the director of the CAC, was charged with obscenity and misuse of a minor in pornography. Seven works were deemed offensive, among them portraits of "Rosie" and Jesse McBride, and five pictures from the "X Portfolio." Barrie faced a maximum penalty of six months in prison.

May 29, 1990: "The Perfect Moment" ended its run in Cincinnati; it drew bigger crowds than any exhibition in the city's history.

June 19, 1990: Judge David J. Albanese ordered Dennis Barrie and the CAC to stand trial on obscenity charges; the CAC was the first gallery in the United States to face prosecution for the art it displayed.

September 28, 1990: The Mapplethorpe obscenity trial opened in Cincinnati; the jury was composed of four men and four women from working-class backgrounds with little knowledge of art. In effect, Mapplethorpe's work was being judged by the same type of people he had grown up with in Floral Park. It was the jury's task to determine whether the average person, applying community standards, would find that Mapplethorpe's pictures appealed to prurient interests, depicted sexual practices in a patently offensive way, and lacked serious artistic value.

October 5, 1990: Dennis Barrie and the CAC were acquitted in the obscenity case. The prosecution had failed to come up with any credible witnesses to convince the jury that Mapplethorpe's photographs lacked artistic merit. In fact, the prosecution called only four witnesses to the stand: three police officers and Judith Reisman, of the American Family Association, who had once worked as a song-writer for the *Captain Kangaroo* TV show. The defense, mean-while, presented a battery of art world experts who testified that Mapplethorpe was a brilliant artist, and that his pictures of sexual acts were "figure studies" and "classical compositions." Robert Sobieszek, senior curator of the International Museum of Photogra-phy at the George Eastman House in Rochester, New York, com-pared the tormented aspect of Mapplethorpe's work to "a search for understanding, not unlike Vincent van Gogh painting himself with his ear torn off." The jury was unanimous in deciding that Mapple-thorpe's pictures appealed to a prurient interest in sex, and that they were patently offensive, but they couldn't agree that they lacked artistic merit. "I'm not an expert," said juror James Jones, a ware-house manager. "I don't understand Picasso's art, but I assume the people who call it art know what they're talking about."

Notes

Most of this book is based on interviews with Robert Mapplethorpe (RM) and with several hundred others who provided information on his life. Unless otherwise noted, the reader should assume that all quotations from Mapplethorpe come from my interviews with him during the period from September 1988 through February 1989. The same holds true with Patti Smith (PS), whose quotations are drawn from the numerous interviews I did with her over the past four years. Because of the frequency of those conversations, I have not attempted to date Smith's quotations. Except in a few cases, all other interviews are dated.

PROLOGUE

page 4 "*New York Times* obituary portrayed him as an aesthete . . .": *The New York Times*, March 10, 1989.

page 4 " 'work that is ultimately about no coverup, no censorship, no shameful secrets.' ": Ingrid Sischy, "A Society Artist," in the catalogue for the 1988 Mapplethorpe retrospective at the Whitney Museum of American Art.

page 4 ". . . calling for Salman Rushdie's death.": See "Cat Stevens Gives Support to Call for Death of Rushdie," *The New York Times*, May 23, 1989.

PART ONE: DARK SECRETS

Chapter One

page 11 " 'I got that feeling in my stomach . . .' ": See Ingrid Sischy, "A Society Artist."

page 11 " 'Nothing much happened.' ": Harry Mapplethorpe to PM, November 19, 1988.

page 13 "Joan understood that mothers weren't supposed to prefer one child over the others . . .": Joan Mapplethorpe to PM, November 19, 1988.

page 13 "The neighborhood was so saturated in 1950s conformity . . .": Jim Cassidy to PM, November 12, 1988.

page 14 "Residents nicknamed Floral Park the 'Lost Community'. . .": See "The Lost Community Finds Its Way Back into City," (New York) *Herald Tribune,* March 19, 1964; "Stepchild of Queens Fights City's Neglect," *Newsday,* February 13, 1978.

page 14 ". . . the area had to endure the humiliation of being constantly compared to its more affluent next-door neighbor . . .": See "A Very Fine Line Divides Floral Park From Floral Park," *The New York Times,* November 2, 1977.

page 15 " 'The first time I went over to Joan's house . . .' ": Pat Farre to PM, October 18, 1989.

page 15 " 'It was like someone had pressed a panic button.' ": Joan Mapplethorpe to PM, November 19, 1988.

page 15 "Several decades later, Joan would seek psychiatric help . . .": Pat Farre to PM, October 18, 1989.

page 16 "Both she and Harry were heavy smokers . . .": Harry Mapplethorpe to PM, October 20, 1989.

page 16 " 'I think she was an addictive personality.' ": Pat Farre to PM, October 18, 1989.

page 16 " 'A couple of times her father went into shock . . .' ": *Ibid.*

page 17 "She called him her 'skinny willy'. . .": Joan Mapplethorpe to PM, November 19, 1988.

page 17 "Both father and son had extremely poor appetites . . .": Harry Mapplethorpe to PM, October 20, 1989.

page 17 ". . . he kicked the bedroom door with the heels of his shoes . . .": Joan Mapplethorpe to PM, November 19, 1988.

page 17 ". . . his father once forced him to eat burned eggs . . .": Dimitri Levas to PM, January 24, 1989.

page 17 " 'A church has a certain magic and mystery . . .' ": RM to Ingrid Sischy, "A Society Artist."

page 18 " 'Robert didn't take his religion lightly.' ": Bill Cassidy to PM, January 13, 1989.

page 19 " 'Robert wasn't handsome like his brother . . .' ": Linda Bahr to PM, January 24, 1991.

page 20 " 'Whenever I think about Robert . . .' ": Tom Farre to PM, September 28, 1989.

page 20 Gays and athletics: See Brian Pronger, *The Arena of Masculinity.*

page 20 "He positioned himself in full view of the living room . . .": RM to PM.

page 21 "Robert had an excellent reproductive style.": Jim Cassidy to PM, November 12, 1988.

page 22 " 'My mother's just a baby producer.' ": *Ibid.*

page 22 " 'With all that equipment in the house . . .' ": Harry Mapplethorpe to PM, November 19, 1988.

page 22 " 'Almost all the fraternities were closed . . .' ": Jim Cassidy to PM, November 12, 1988.

page 23 " 'Here was this gentle, creative person . . .' ": Father George Stack to PM, December 8, 1988.

page 23 " 'I'll never do that again!' ": Terry Gray to PM, January 31, 1989.

page 25 " 'It was like a fairy-tale romance.' ": Jim Cassidy to PM, November 12, 1988.

page 25 " 'It was clear Harry favored Richard.' ": Marylynn Celano to PM, January 17, 1991.

page 25 "Robert and Terry Gray had attended a neighborhood party . . .": Terry Gray to PM, January 31, 1989.

page 25 ". . . the alcohol had unleashed a swarm of furies . . .": Nancy Rooney to PM, December 10, 1988.

page 26 "[The magazines] were all sealed . . .": RM to Ingrid Sischy, "A Society Artist."

Chapter Two

page 28 " 'Robert was a little too intense . . .' ": Nancy Nemeth to PM, July 26, 1990.

page 29 " 'We were the tough guys . . .' ": Tom Logan to PM, January 4, 1989.

page 30 "From the moment he arrived . . .": Peter Hetzel to PM, July 20, 1989.

page 31 " 'I can't go through with it.' ": Victor Pope to PM, January 20, 1989.

page 31 ". . . they bound the pledges' penises with rope . . .": Tom Logan to PM, January 4, 1989.

page 31 ". . . they were told to eat excrement . . .": Fern Logan to PM, November 23, 1988.

page 32 "Pop art was labeled 'cool art'. . .": See Irving Sandler, "The New Cool-Art," *Art in America* 1 (1965).

page 32 " 'And if I do that . . .' ": Marylynn Celano to PM, January 17, 1991.

page 33 " 'We all envied Tom.' ": Stan Mitchell to PM, July 20, 1989.

page 33 " 'Poor Bob wanted to fit in so badly . . .' ": Bonnie Lester to PM, January 12, 1989.

page 33 " 'There was a group of these women . . .' ": Tom Logan to PM, January 4, 1989.

page 34 " 'Bob told me his parents rejected him . . .' ": Rosita Cruz to PM, April 22, 1989.

page 34 " 'Bob threw a temper tantrum . . .' ": *Ibid.*

page 34 "Mapplethorpe similarly embarrassed himself . . .": Fern Logan to PM, November 23, 1988.

page 35 " 'Bob was one of the nicest people . . .' ": Linda Lee to PM, November 13, 1991.

page 35 " 'He simply wasn't as good . . .' ": Bob Jacob to PM, December 15, 1988.

page 36 "One evening, at the Cruz sisters' apartment . . .": Rosita Cruz to PM, April 22, 1989.

page 36 "Returning home drunk one night . . .": Tom Logan to PM, January 4, 1989.

page 37 " 'Nothing about him really stands out . . .' ": Nancy Nemeth to PM, July 26, 1990.

page 37 " 'She was one good-looking woman.' ": Bob Jacob to PM, December 15, 1988.

Chapter Three

page 38 " 'Robert's transformation was remarkable.' ": Kenny Tisa to PM, March 30, 1989.

page 38 " 'Eve of Destruction' ": See Todd Gitlin, *The Sixties: Years of Hope, Days of Rage*.

page 39 " 'We were the hip ones . . .' ": Kenny Tisa to PM, March 30, 1989.

page 39 " 'You did this without telling me?' ": Harry Mapplethorpe to PM, October 20, 1989.

page 40 "One teacher sarcastically labeled them . . .": Harry McCue to PM, January 12, 1989.

page 40 " 'You don't think I'm any good . . .' ": *Ibid.*

page 41 "The studio was soon covered in urine and feces . . .": Stan Mitchell to PM, July 20, 1989.

page 41 " 'Whenever I'd see him, my heart would sink.' ": *Ibid.*

page 41 " 'Scratch is dead!' ": Harry McCue to PM, January 12, 1989.

page 41 "Mapplethorpe had beheaded Scratch with a kitchen knife . . .": RM to PM.

page 42 "Mapplethorpe took his first LSD trip . . .": RM to PM.

page 43 " 'Everybody was doing so many drugs . . .' ": Claude Alverson to PM, July 26, 1989.

page 43 "Acid-inspired art was becoming so common . . .": Sam Alexander to PM, April 18, 1989.

page 44 "He vowed that when he moved to Manhattan . . .": Rosita Cruz to PM, April 22, 1989.

page 44 " 'We wanted the power of Satan . . .' ": Harry McCue to PM, January 12, 1989.

page 45 ". . . Mapplethorpe eventually opted to swallow a tab of acid . . .": RM to PM.

page 45 " 'You look like a girl.' ": RM to PM.

page 45 ". . . Harry was infuriated by Robert's latest revelation . . .": Harry Mapplethorpe to PM, October 20, 1989.

page 45 " 'He wasn't even enrolled in the class . . .' ": Sam Alexander to PM, April 18, 1989.

page 46 " 'Bob was a caring, sensitive guy . . .' ": Harry McCue to PM, January 12, 1989.

page 46 " 'Harry completely freaked out.' ": Pat Kennedy to PM, October 11, 1989.

page 46 " 'He was totally dismissive of me.' ": Harry McCue to PM, January 12, 1989.

Chapter Four

page 48 "Eager to be rid of her date . . .": PS to PM.

pages 49–50 "Female": See Patti Smith, *Seventh Heaven*.

page 50 ". . . she became pregnant . . .": Janet Hamill to PM, March 24, 1989.

page 51 " 'It was a long railroad apartment . . .' ": Pat Kennedy to PM, October 11, 1989.

page 52 " 'It was difficult to tell where Robert began . . .' ": Judy Linn to PM, November 21, 1988.

page 52 " 'Patti really hated women . . .' ": Margaret Kennedy to PM, October 10, 1989.

page 53 " 'When I work, and in my art . . .' ": PS to PM.

page 53 " 'I always thought he had an incredibly refined aesthetic . . .' ": Kenny Tisa to PM, March 30, 1989.

page 53 ". . . she supplemented her income by failing to ring up purchases . . .": RM to PM.

page 54 " 'They were both totally enraptured by the idea . . .' ": Janet Hamill to PM, March 24, 1989.

page 54 " 'I was with another kid from the neighborhood . . .' ": James Mapplethorpe to PM, November 4, 1990.

page 54 " 'She was a mess, a slob.' ": Harry Mapplethorpe to PM, October 20, 1989.

page 55 ". . . she had once worked as a prostitute.": RM to PM.

Chapter Five

page 56 " 'Nineteen sixty-eight had the vibrations . . .' ": See "1968—The Year That Shaped a Generation," *Time,* spring 1989 (special collectors edition).

pages 56–57 " 'For Patti, having a boyfriend . . .' ": Janet Hamill to PM, March 24, 1989.

page 57 " 'Howie was sweet . . .' ": *Ibid.*

page 57 ". . . he found Smith to be more 'far out . . .' ": Howie Michels to PM, August 29, 1989.

page 57 " 'Please don't go.' ": RM to PM.

page 57 " 'I was crazed . . .' ": Carol Squiers to PM, February 13, 1990.

page 57 " 'I'll never forget it.' ": Bob Barrett to PM, January 25, 1989.

page 58 " 'I have to find out if I'm gay . . .' ": Judy Linn to PM, November 21, 1988.

page 58 San Francisco gay scene: See Randy Shilts, *The Mayor of Castro Street.*

page 58 " 'I flew out to San Francisco . . .' ": See Victor Bockris, "Robert Mapplethorpe."

page 59 " 'Even by the standards of the sixties . . .' ": Tony Jannetti to PM, August 9, 1989.

page 59 " 'He disappeared the minute he got there . . .' ": Judy Linn to PM, November 21, 1988.

page 60 ". . . he immediately went home to make a collage . . .": PS to PM.

pages 60–61 ". . . 'untalented artist with an edge of darkness . . .' ": Howie Michels to PM, August 29, 1989.

page 60 " 'Patti was suicidal.' ": Janet Hamill to PM, March 24, 1989.

page 62 " 'I was crawling in the grass. . . .' ": See Dave Marsh, "Her Horses Got Wings, They Can Fly," *Rolling Stone,* January 1976.

page 62 "A neighbor was murdered across the hallway . . .": PS to PM.

page 62 See Patti Smith, *Babel,* "Sister Morphine."

page 63 "Then she marched into the office of the hotel manager . . .": PS to PM.

page 63 ". . . they made a solemn pact . . .": *Ibid.*

PART TWO: PATRON SAINTS
Chapter Six

page 68 " 'Both Robert and Patti came across as stylish . . .' ": Stanley Amos to PM, March 8, 1989.

page 68 " 'I knew Robert and Patti were brilliant . . .' ": Sandy Daley to PM, December 29, 1988.

page 69 " 'We talked about every aspect . . .' ": *Ibid.*

page 70 " 'Max's was the place . . .' ": See Andy Warhol and Pat Hackett, *POPism,* page 186. For further background on Max's, I relied, in part, on Ronald Sukenick's *Down and In.*

page 71 ". . .'leather version of Sigmunde and Sieglinde.' ": Danny Fields to PM, June 8, 1990.

page 71 " 'One of the essential ingredients of Max's . . .' ": See Sukenick, *Down and In,* page 212.

page 72 " 'Everybody wanted to know . . .' ": Danny Fields to PM, June 8, 1990.

page 72 "To stretch Smith's salary . . .": PS to PM.

page 72 ". . . he began searching through Times Square bookstores for old copies of gay magazines . . .": For background on George Quaintance and Tom of Finland, I relied, in part, on Emmanuel Cooper's *The Sexual Perspective.*

page 73 "He was too nervous . . .": Sandy Daley to PM, December 29, 1988.

page 76 ". . . a series of blood-curdling screams . . .": Sylvia Miles to PM, July 11, 1991.

page 76 " 'Robert and Patti played off each other . . .' ": Sam Green to PM, November 7, 1989.

page 76 " 'I presume I said a lot of stupid things . . .' ": Fredericka Hunter to PM, November 1, 1989.

page 77 " 'I came from a prep school background . . .' ": Charles Cowles to PM, July 12, 1989.

page 78 " 'An assistant at the front desk . . .' ": Sandy Daley to PM, December 29, 1988.

page 78 " 'The nakedness of St. Sebastian . . .' ": See Cooper, *The Sexual Perspective*, page xvi.

page 79 " 'I was having dinner with Charlie Cowles and Klaus Kertess . . .' ": Fredericka Hunter to PM, November 1, 1989.

page 79 " 'There was no doubt that Patti was much smarter . . .' ": Ann Powell to PM, November 20, 1990.

page 80 " 'Patti always looked bizarre and emaciated.' ": Andreas Brown to PM, April 1, 1989.

page 80 " 'I'd sit at the typewriter . . .' ": See Tony Hiss and David McClelland, "Gonna Be So Big, Gonna Be a Star, Watch Me Now!" *The New York Times Magazine*, December 21, 1975.

pages 80–81 See Patti Smith, *Seventh Heaven*, "jeanne d'arc."

page 81 See Jim Carroll, *The Basketball Diaries*.

pages 81–82 " 'Patti was one of the few women I met . . .' ": Jim Carroll to PM, August 9, 1989.

page 82 " 'Robert was living in the weirdest . . .' ": *Ibid.*

page 82 " 'The stout man . . .' ": See Jim Carroll, *Forced Entries: The Downtown Diaries, 1971–1973*, page 8.

page 83 Hollywood's depiction of gays: See Vito Russo, *The Celluloid Closet*.

page 83 " 'I knew how to make class transitions . . .' ": Jim Carroll to PM, August 9, 1989.

Chapter Seven

page 84 " 'Robert and Patti had gone through a lot . . .' ": Jim Carroll to PM, August 9, 1989.

page 85 " 'David was completely image conscious.' ": Richard Bernstein to PM, April 6, 1989.

page 86 " 'Robert was a real Cocteau beauty.' ": David Croland to PM, November 9, 1988.

page 86 " 'The relationship just took off like a rocket.' ": *Ibid.*

page 86 " 'It was an unusual request . . .' ": Herb Krohn to PM, November 13, 1989.

page 87 " 'When Robert took pictures . . .' ": David Croland to PM, May 30, 1990.

page 88 "Carroll then wrote a thinly veiled account . . .": See Carroll, *Forced Entries,* page 5.

page 89 ". . . he came to regard him as a 'truly caring person . . .' ": Jesse Turner to PM, November 17, 1989.

page 89 "Mapplethorpe had been taking LSD . . .": *Ibid.*

page 89 " 'How can I be the devil?' ": David Croland to PM, May 30, 1990.

page 90 " 'I wish I could be elegant . . .' ": David Croland to PM, November 9, 1988.

page 90 ". . .'intuitively knew how to move . . .' ": Arnon Vered to PM, August 28, 1989.

page 90 " 'I thought Robert was just divine.' ": Berry Berenson Perkins to PM, May 23, 1990.

page 91 " 'At the time we didn't have any big plans . . .' ": Lenny Kaye to PM, June 13, 1990.

page 93 " 'She wasn't known at all . . .' ": Gerard Malanga to PM, June 18, 1989.

page 94 " 'I think Sam was terribly jealous . . .' ": Ann Powell to PM, November 20, 1990.

page 94 " 'You're twisting me up.' ": See Sam Shepard and Patti Smith, *Cowboy Mouth,* in *Angel City, Curse of the Starving Class and Other Plays.*

page 95 " 'It didn't work out . . .' ": See Don Shewey, *Sam Shepard.*

page 95 " 'Patti was devastated . . .' ": Ann Powell to PM, November 20, 1990.

page 95 ". . . a drunken Smith was carried out of Max's . . .": Helen Marden to PM, June 5, 1990.

page 95 "One day she became so exasperated . . .": PS to PM.

Chapter Eight

page 98 " 'My father believes in Labour . . .' ": See Robert Colaciello, "It's a Family Affair," *Interview,* March 1973.

page 99 " 'John turned blue . . .' ": Allen Rosenbaum to PM, July 24, 1990.

page 99 " 'I married the Met . . .' ": Maxime de La Falaise to PM, April 11, 1989.

page 99 " 'It was too bizarre for words.' ": Andrea Stillman to PM, October 31, 1989.

page 100 " 'John was playing a game of Russian roulette . . .' ": Maxime de La Falaise to PM, April 11, 1989.

page 100 " 'John was fascinated by the forbidden.' ": Allen Rosenbaum to PM, July 24, 1990.

page 101 " 'I think people were rather horrified . . .' ": Maxime de La Falaise to PM, April 11, 1989.

page 101 " 'I thought Robert was rather weird.' ": Boaz Mazor to PM, June 12, 1989.

page 102 " 'I'm meeting John in Europe at the end of the week.' ": David Croland to PM, May 30, 1990.

page 103 " 'I think Robert felt very at home in England . . .' ": Maxime de La Falaise to PM, April 11, 1989.

page 103 "He had recently begun sporting a swastika pin . . .": Sandy Daley to PM, December 29, 1988.

page 104 ". . . Mapplethorpe made the mistake of having sex with McKendry . . .": RM to PM.

page 104 " 'Robert was one of those people . . .' ": Fernando Sanchez to PM, April 25, 1989.

page 106 " 'John believed Robert was a divine creature.' ": Gary Farmer to PM, July 26, 1990.

page 106 " 'highly talented verbal and visual originals'. . .": See Bob Colaciello, "Some Might Call It Degeneracy," *The Village Voice*, December 30, 1971.

pages 106–7 " 'I helped launch . . .' ": Sandy Daley to PM, December 29, 1988.

page 107 "Mapplethorpe woke up one morning . . .": Allen Lanier to PM, July 23, 1991.

page 107 " 'She was like a creature . . .' ": Maxime de La Falaise to PM, June 8, 1989.

page 108 " 'John taught Robert about photography . . .' ": Henry Geldzahler to PM, July 6, 1990.

page 109 " 'John was trying to hold it together . . .' ": Allen Rosenbaum to PM, July 24, 1990.

Chapter Nine

page 111 "[Beauty] makes princes . . .' ": See Oscar Wilde, *The Picture of Dorian Gray*, Penguin Classics, 1985, page 45.

page 111 " 'Sam was remarkable-looking.' ": Klaus Kertess to PM, November 27, 1989.

page 112 " 'It was like I gave them to each other.' " David Croland to PM, May 30, 1990.

page 112 "Wagstaff immediately telephoned Mapplethorpe . . .": RM to PM.

page 115 " 'Every girl would swoon . . .' ": Dominick Dunne to PM, June 29, 1990.

page 116 ". . .'I've always been visually acclimatized . . .' ": See Margarett Loke, "Collecting's Big Thrill Is the Chase."

page 116 " 'Sam could be unbearable.' ": Sam Green to PM, November 7, 1989.

page 116 " 'Hartford was consumed . . .' ": Jim Elliott to PM, November 14, 1990.

page 117 " 'What Sam did for Robert . . .' ": Mary Palmer to PM, August 7, 1990.

page 118 " 'The important thing Sam did in Detroit . . .' ": Ellen Phelan to PM, November 30, 1989.

page 118 " 'Sam was a visionary . . .' ": Susanne Hilberry to PM, January 30, 1990.

page 118 " 'Detroit was in the dark ages . . .' ": Anne (Manoogian) Mac-Donald to PM, May 22, 1989.

page 119 ". . .'a victory for manicured grass . . .' ": See "Parties and Dedication Mark Curator's Good-by," *Detroit News,* October 10, 1971.

page 120 " 'I looked at this young man . . .' ": Susanne Hilberry to PM, January 30, 1990.

page 121 " 'It was the first time . . .' ": See Penny Green, "Patti Smith," *Interview,* October 1973.

page 121 " 'He wanted me to be . . .' ": See Dave Marsh, "Her Horses Got Wings, They Can Fly."

page 121 " 'A lot of people had those kinds of offers . . .' ": Fran Lebowitz to PM, June 12, 1990.

page 122 " 'Robert had worked hard . . .' ": Kenny Tisa to PM, March 30, 1989.

PART THREE: SEX AND MAGIC

Chapter Ten

page 126 " 'The whole point is to . . .' ": See Martin Filler, "Robert Mapplethorpe."

page 127 " 'Once Sam needed ten dollars . . .' ": Anne (Manoogian) Mac-Donald to PM, May 22, 1989.

page 127 "A few weeks after Robert moved to Bond Street . . .": RM to PM.

page 128 ". . . his erotic tastes ran to private parties . . .": RM to PM.

page 128 "Mapplethorpe's Polaroids impressed Jones as different . . .": Harold Jones to PM, May 11, 1989.

page 129 " 'What the hell is going on here?' ": Tennyson Shad to PM, August 10, 1989.

page 131 " 'Such distinction . . .' ": See Barbara Rose, "The Triumph of Photography."

page 131 ". . . celebrate 'the essential oneness of mankind . . .' ": See Edward Steichen, in his introduction to the "Family of Man" catalogue, Museum of Modern Art, 1955.

page 131 " 'The kiss of death . . .' ": See *The New York Times Magazine*, March 17, 1985.

page 132 ". . . Saul of Tarsus blinded . . .": *Ibid*.

page 132 " 'I thought this photograph . . .' ": See "An Irreverent Eye," *Newsweek*, April 8, 1985.

page 133 " 'I think Sam had always felt his life . . .' ": Paul Walter to PM, July 23, 1990.

page 133 " 'It [photography] was the perfect medium . . .' ": RM to Janet Kardon, "The Perfect Moment" catalogue, Institute of Contemporary Art, University of Pennsylvania, 1988.

page 134 " 'Aside from that . . . he had mostly chicken porn.' ": Gerrit Henry, "Robert Mapplethorpe—Collecting Quality."

page 134 " 'If you had a classical column . . .' ": Allen Ellenzweig to PM, August 10, 1990.

page 134 " 'I took a taxi down to this terrible street . . .' ": George Rinhart to PM, July 16, 1990.

page 135 "He attempted to set up a photo session with Patti Smith . . .": PS to PM.

page 137 " 'I don't think any collector . . .' ": See Susan Colgan, "Sam Wagstaff, Collector of 19th- and 20th-Century Photographs."

page 137 " 'I did learn a lot . . .' ": RM to Janet Kardon, "The Perfect Moment" catalogue.

page 138 "Wagstaff had given him fifty thousand dollars . . .": RM to PM.

page 138 " 'It was a very exciting time for Robert . . .' ": Robert Fosdick to PM, November 17, 1989.

page 139 ". . .'visionaries who stumble . . .' ": See Michael Andre, "Recent Religious and Ritual Art."

page 139 " 'Here was this skinny little thing . . .' ": Jane Friedman to PM, May 24, 1990.

page 140 " 'Maybe a little filth'll . . .' ": See *The Village Voice,* May 3, 1973.

page 140 ". . . Mapplethorpe and Warhol showed up to photograph Rudolf Nureyev . . .": See Bob Colacello, *Holy Terror: Andy Warhol Close Up.*

page 140 " 'You don't have a crush . . .' ": Bob Colacello to PM, October 2, 1989.

page 141 " 'They must have been good . . .' ": Andreas Brown to PM, April 1, 1989.

page 141 "It was like no other artist . . .": Sam Green to PM, November 7, 1989.

page 141 " 'You should know his work . . .' ": See foreword by Tom Armstrong in catalogue to the Mapplethorpe retrospective, Whitney Museum of American Art, 1988.

Chapter Eleven

page 144 ". . .'doped-up, sexed-out Marlboro man.' ": See Martin P. Levine, "The Life and Death of Gay Clones," in Gilbert Herdt, ed., *Gay Culture in America,* page 69.

page 146 ". . .'the only image . . .' ": See Susan Sontag, "Fascinating Fascism," in *Under the Sign of Saturn,* paperback ed., The Noonday Press, 1989, page 101.

page 146 " 'The billboard showed a woman . . .' ": See Karen Durbin, "Pretty Poison: The Selling of Sexual Warfare."

page 147 " 'Robert and Sam had come to London . . .' ": Philippe Garner to PM, June 18, 1994.

page 148 ". . .'become almost a cliché for sexual ardor . . .' ": Allen Ellenzweig to PM, August 10, 1990.

page 148 "; . . .'more like one of Michelangelo's slave sculptures . . .' ": See Allen Ellenzweig, *The Homoerotic Photograph,* page 51.

page 148 " 'Robert was very insistent . . .' ": Klaus Kertess to PM, November 27, 1989.

page 148 " 'Robert and Patti were so intertwined . . .' ": Jane Friedman to PM, May 24, 1990.

page 149 ". . .'absorption with demonic, romantic excess.' ": See John Rockwell, "Imagery by Patti Smith, Poet Turned Performer," *The New York Times,* July 12, 1974.

page 149 " 'At the Whiskey . . .' ": Lenny Kaye to PM, July 13, 1990.

page 149 " 'John was in his hotel room . . .' ": Gary Farmer to PM, July 26, 1990.

page 150 ". . .'rather bad Italian.' ": Maxime de La Falaise to PM, June 8, 1989.

page 150 " 'The Met would never think . . .' ": Andrea Stillman to PM, October 31, 1989.

page 151 ". . .'a kind of blissful eroticism . . .' ": See Roland Barthes, *Camera Lucida,* paperback ed., The Noonday Press, 1988, page 59.

page 151 " 'This is crazy! . . .' ": Allen Rosenbaum to PM, July 24, 1990.

page 151 " 'John had read somewhere . . .' ": Gary Farmer to PM, July 26, 1990.

page 152 " 'It's just so stupid.' ": PS to PM.

page 152 " 'I was shattered . . .' ": Maxime de La Falaise to PM, April 11, 1989.

page 154 " 'Robert had much more of a society success . . .' ": Bob Colacello to PM, October 2, 1989.

page 154 ". . .'otherworldly version of amphetaminized beefcake . . .' ": See Craig Bromberg, *The Wicked Ways of Malcolm McLaren,* page 430.

page 155 " 'We're totally committed . . .' ": See interview with Vivienne Westwood, *Forum,* June 1976.

page 156 ". . .'she seems destined . . .' ": Stephen Holden, *Rolling Stone,* August 14, 1975.

Chapter Twelve

page 157 " 'terminal violence'. . .": See Greil Marcus, "Patti Smith Exposes Herself," *The Village Voice,* November 24, 1975.

page 158 ". . .'phenomenal anomaly.' " See James Wolcott, "A Punk with Charm," *New York,* September 15, 1975.

page 158 " 'Robert and Patti talked about the cover endlessly.' ": Janet Hamill to PM, March 24, 1989.

page 158 "On the day of the shoot . . .": PS to PM.

page 159 "Clive Davis did not share Mapplethorpe's enthusiasm . . .": PS to PM.

page 160 ". . .'The 100 Greatest Album Covers . . .' ": See *Rolling Stone,* November 14, 1991.

page 160 " 'I saw *Horses* . . .' ": Paul Taylor to PM, November 1, 1989.

page 160 ". . . an 'extraordinary disc . . .' ": See John Rockwell, *The New York Times,* November 7, 1975.

page 161 ". . .' "performance" terrifying in its intensity . . .' ": John Rockwell, "Patti Smith Battles to a Singing Victory."

page 161 ". . .'eyes like pinwheels . . .' ": See "pinwheels," *Babel,* Berkley ed., 1979, page 187.

page 162 " 'He's very beautiful . . .' ": Reinaldo Herrera to PM, January 19, 1988.

page 164 " 'The brilliant aspect of Robert's career . . .' ": George Stambolian to PM, July 23, 1990.

page 164 " 'Robert figured if he could get a cover . . .' ": Jack Fritscher to PM, August 4, 1989.

page 165 ". . .'I remember my father . . .' ": See Steven M.L. Aronson, *Interview,* December 1985.

page 166 ". . .'Honey is roughly 6 years old . . .' ": See Judith Reisman, "Promoting Child Abuse as Art."

page 166 " 'I am not certain . . .' ": See Arthur C. Danto, "Playing with the Edge," *Mapplethorpe,* Random House, 1992.

page 167 " 'You can't control them.' ": Gilles Larrain to PM, January 23, 1994.

page 167 " 'It was all done in a spirit . . .' ": Clarissa Dalrymple to PM, May 23, 1990.

page 167 " 'Children are sexual beings . . .' ": See William Ruehlmann, Norfolk *Ledger-Star*, January 25, 1978.

pages 167–68 ". . .'[It] makes me think of sex . . .' ": See Victor Bockris, "Robert Mapplethorpe."

page 168 " 'In the mid-seventies . . .' ": Caterine Milinaire to PM, July 20, 1990.

page 171 " 'I never thought the "dirty pictures". . .' ": Holly Solomon to PM, March 3, 1989.

page 172 ". . .'an interminable Sixties freak-out.' ": See Charles M. Young, "Patti Smith Catches Fire."

page 173 "Arista executives implored her . . .": PS to PM.

pages 173–74 " 'Physically I have to be like . . .' ": See Caroline Coon, "Punk Queen of Sheba."

page 174 " 'I remember each show . . .' ": Lenny Kaye to PM, June 13, 1990.

Chapter Thirteen

page 177 ". . . Mapplethorpe persisted in trying to convince her . . .": PS to PM.

page 178 " 'Sam was a very sweet . . .' ": Holly Solomon to PM, March 3, 1989.

page 178 ". . .'Vermeer-type sidelighting.' ": See David Bourdon, "Robert Mapplethorpe."

page 179 ". . .'fag decorator'. . .": Maria Morris Hambourg to PM, October 3, 1989.

page 179 " 'When you discuss frames . . .' ": Jared Bark to PM, March 1, 1990.

page 180 "He was so excited . . .": PS to PM.

page 180 " '. . . our boy is finally the belle of the ball.' ": PS to PM.

page 181 " 'I played around with the flowers . . .' ": Inge Bondi, "The Yin and Yang of Robert Mapplethorpe."

page 182 ". . .'bourgeois blooms'. . .": See Joris-Karl Huysmans, *Against Nature,* page 96.

page 182 " 'I hate flowers . . .' ": Holly Solomon to PM, March 3, 1989.

page 182 " 'I am obsessed with beauty.' ": See Anne Horton interview, "Robert Mapplethorpe 1986," Raab Galerie, Berlin; Kicken-Pauseback, Cologne.

page 183 " 'You lucky bastard!' ": William Targ to PM, May 21, 1990.

page 183 "Smith's mind had become even more . . .": PS to PM.

page 183 " 'i haven't fucked w/the past . . .' ": See "babelogue," *Babel,* page 193.

page 184 " 'What am I going to say to them?' ": PS to PM.

page 184 ". . . Joan had taken her friend Pat Farre . . .": Joan Mapplethorpe to PM, November 19, 1988.

page 184 ". . . complained of feeling down all the time . . .": Nancy Rooney to PM, December 10, 1988.

page 185 "Afterward he took his parents to lunch . . .": RM to PM.

page 185 " 'You know, *I'm* one of the best . . .' ": Harry Mapplethorpe to PM, October 20, 1989.

page 186 ". . . he later boasted about his son's exhibit . . .": *Ibid.*

Chapter Fourteen

page 188 " 'All the great libertines who live . . .' ": See Georges Bataille, *Eroticism: Death and Sensuality,* page 173.

page 190 " 'The scene at the Mineshaft . . .' ": Peter Reed to PM, December 2, 1988.

page 192 ". . .'a perfect picture . . .' ": RM to Janet Kardon, "The Perfect Moment" catalogue.

page 192 " 'Robert was really interested . . .' ": Scott Facon to PM, February 2, 1990.

page 192 ". . . Pasolini's *Salo,* which was loosely based on . . .": See Barth David Schwartz, *Pasolini Requiem,* Pantheon, 1992.

page 193 "He even gave a party . . .": RM to PM.

page 193 ". . .'cold-blooded angel figure . . .' ": John Richardson to PM, June 3, 1989.

page 193 " 'The images don't register . . .' ": George Stambolian to PM, July 23, 1990.

page 194 " 'Robert complained a lot about Holly . . .' ": Klaus Kertess to PM, November 27, 1989.

page 195 " 'I found the work amazingly thrilling.' ": Robert Miller to PM, June 16, 1989.

page 195 " 'Hey, please don't come to my gallery . . .' ": Holly Solomon to PM, March 3, 1989.

page 195 " 'My mother had recently died . . .' ": *Ibid.*

page 197 " 'Sam loved drugs.' ": Daniel Wolf to PM, April 18, 1989.

page 197 " 'The common thread throughout . . .' ": See Colgan, "Sam Wagstaff, Collector of 19th- and 20th-Century Photographs."

page 198 " 'Here was this tall, slender . . .' ": Jane Livingston to PM, October 27, 1989.

page 199 " 'Sam needed a muse.' ": Norman Rosenthal to PM, April 18, 1989.

page 199 " 'I was a little nervous . . .' ": Gérald Incandela to PM, March 7, 1989.

page 199 " 'I once wrote a piece . . .' ": Klaus Kertess to PM, November 27, 1989.

page 199 ". . .'the finest show of photographs . . .' ": See Paul Richard, "Sam Wagstaff, the Collector the Establishment Trusts."

page 200 " 'Sam had an arrogant confidence . . .' ": Jane Livingston to PM, October 27, 1989.

page 200 " 'Everyone was speechless.' ": Anne Horton to PM, December 29, 1988.

page 200 ". . .'You naïve bastard! . . .' ": Ben Lifson to PM, February 6, 1990.

page 201 " 'This book is about pleasure . . .' ": See Sam Wagstaff, *A Book of Photographs.*

page 201 " 'Joy takes many aspects . . .' ": See Ben Lifson, "Sam Wagstaff's Pleasures."

page 202 " 'I had kind of exhausted the S&M thing.' ": RM to PM.

Chapter Fifteen

page 203 " 'The pictures were remarkably strong . . .' ": Simon Lowinsky to PM, May 19, 1989.

page 204 "He accused Lowinsky of censoring his work and complained to . . .": See Mark McDonald, "Censored."

page 205 " 'Jim brought Robert . . .' ": Edward de Celle to PM, August 8, 1989.

page 205 " 'No way!' ": *Ibid.*

page 206 ". . .'as pedestrianly conventional' and 'somewhat melodramatically . . .' ": See Thomas Albright, "Realism, Romanticism and Leather."

page 206 ". . .'a very young artist . . .' ": See Joan Murray, "Weegee the Famous."

page 206 ". . . compared the bloody 'Richard' to a Willem de Kooning . . .": See Mark McDonald, "Censored."

page 207 " 'It was pretty much a disaster.' ": Edward de Celle to PM, August 8, 1989.

page 207 "He was completely starstruck . . .": Art Nelson to PM, August 22, 1989.

page 207 "Nelson's fantasies . . .": *Ibid.*

page 208 " 'The persistent rumor . . .' ": Sam Green to PM, November 7, 1989.

page 208 ". . .'alternately dazzling, uneven, arousing . . .' ": See Jonathan Cott, "Rock and Rimbaud," *The New York Times Book Review,* February 19, 1978.

page 208 "*Rolling Stone* featured Smith . . .": See Charles M. Young, "Patti Smith Catches Fire."

page 209 " 'Their friendship is their masterpiece.' ": See René Ricard, "Patti Smith and Robert Mapplethorpe at Miller."

page 211 "He constantly teased Leatherdale . . .": Marcus Leatherdale to PM, September 29, 1989.

page 211 " 'Whenever you make love . . .' ": *Ibid.*

page 211 " 'I had never seen a black leather bedspread . . .' ": Robert Sherman to PM, July 5, 1990.

page 212 " 'Robert was one of the most tortured . . .' ": Marcus Leatherdale to PM, September 29, 1989.

page 213 "Davis met Mapplethorpe in late 1976 . . .": Lynn Davis to PM, May 31, 1990.

page 213 " 'I remember being at a cocktail party . . .' ": Ben Lifson to PM, February 6, 1990.

page 214 " 'Robert got crazy . . .' ": Marcus Leatherdale to PM, September 29, 1989.

page 214 " 'Mapplethorpe's skill overwhelms . . .' ": See Ben Lifson, "Games Photographers Play."

page 214 " 'I was so devastated . . .' ": Lynn Davis to PM, May 31, 1990.

page 215 " 'Robert was working very hard . . .' ": Carol Squiers to PM, February 13, 1990.

page 215 ". . .'the homosexualization of America.' ": See Frank Rich, "The Gay Decades."

page 215 ". . .'the sex that looks . . .' ": See Margaret Walters, *The Nude Male.*

page 215 " 'For years the male nude . . .' ": George Stambolian to PM, July 23, 1990.

page 217 " 'Everybody showed up.' ": *Ibid.*

page 217 " 'Robert always walked the line . . .' ": John Cheim to PM, July 25, 1989.

page 218 ". . .'turn a brown paper wrapper blue . . .' ": See Vicki Goldberg, "Robert Mapplethorpe."

page 218 " '[The] very real interest of this show . . .' ": See Hilton Kramer, "Robert Mapplethorpe," *The New York Times,* April 6, 1979.

page 219 " 'Everything about this show is hostile. . . .' ": See Ben Lifson, "The Philistine Photographer: Reassessing Mapplethorpe."

page 219 " 'a street kid who figures he can make a lot of money . . .' ": See Richard Whelan, "Robert Mapplethorpe: Hard Sell, Slick Image."

pages 219–20 " 'It was a tough-minded . . .' ": Ben Lifson to PM, February 6, 1990.

page 220 ". . . celebrated her good fortune by purchasing a mink coat.": Andi Ostrowe to PM, November 26, 1991.

page 221 ". . . a group of women who . . . provided the 'domestic energies'. . .": See Eric Ehrmann, "MC5."

page 221 " 'It was an astonishing thing . . .' ": Danny Fields to PM, June 8, 1990.

page 221 ". . .'pure pop pap sheep-dipped in transparent raiments . . .' ": See Julie Burchill and Tony Parsons, *The Boy Looked at Johnny,* Pluto Press, London, 1978, page 5.

page 222 " 'It wasn't like we hadn't seen her naked . . .' ": Jim Carroll to PM, August 9, 1989.

page 223 ". . . a 'transitional album in the most transient sense . . .' ": See Tom Carson, "Patti Smith: Under the Double Ego."

page 223 " 'Patti was absolutely brutal . . .' ": Andi Ostrowe to PM, November 26, 1991.

page 223 ". . .'dispirited'. . .": See Michael Anthony, "Concert Proves Patti Smith Can Be Bad."

page 223 ". . .'stream-of-conscious . . .' ": See Steve Morse, "Lackluster Patti Smith."

page 223 ". . .'like a crazy woman'. . .": See Michael Goldberg, "Whatever Happened to Gracious Patti Smith?"

page 223 ". . .'prattled on in a stoned manner . . .' ": See Joel Selvin, "Patti Puts Her Fans to the Test."

page 223 ". . .'closer to demagoguery . . .' ": See *Newsday,* May 25, 1979.

page 224 " 'We were sitting in the hotel . . .' ": Ivan Kral to PM, October 10, 1991.

page 225 " 'She zeroes in on this Italian lumberjack . . .' ": See Caroline Coon, "Punk Queen of Sheba."

page 225 ". . . she missed New York so much . . .": Janet Hamill to PM, March 24, 1989.

PART FOUR: BLACKS AND WHITES

Chapter Sixteen

page 229 " 'Robert worried that Patti hadn't been strong enough . . .' ": Kathy Acker to PM, 1989.

page 230 " 'Jim was a trick . . .' ": Klaus Kertess to PM, November 27, 1989.

page 230 " 'Sam once told me the only reason . . .' ": Paul Walter to PM, July 23, 1990.

page 231 "Ultimately she would be diagnosed as having manic-depression . . .": Lisa Lyon to PM, February 7, 1989.

page 231 ". . .'ancient warriors . . .' ": *Ibid*.

page 232 " 'I was using LSD . . .' ": *Ibid*.

page 232 "Mapplethorpe worried that he wouldn't be able to contribute . . .": Jim Clyne to PM, June 6, 1991.

page 233 " 'I never thought of it as an issue.' ": Lisa Lyon to PM, February 7, 1989.

page 233 ". . . process of 'carding' nonwhites for admission . . .": See John L. Peterson, "Black Men and Their Same-Sex Desires and Behaviors," in Herdt, *Gay Culture in America*.

page 234 " 'For one thing, the texture . . .' ": Kelly Edey to PM, May 16, 1990.

page 234 " 'Robert had drawn a picture . . .' ": George Stambolian to PM, July 23, 1990.

page 235 " 'When the ancients did a painting . . .' ": Kelly Edey to PM, May 16, 1990.

page 235 " 'Robert's eyes just blazed . . .' ": *Ibid*.

page 236 " 'It has to be racist. . . .' ": See David Hershkovits, "Shock of the Black and the Blue."

page 236 ". . .'free enough'. . .": John Abbott to PM, December 7, 1988.

page 236 ". . .'they weren't black anymore.' ": *Ibid.*

page 236 " 'Robert's leitmotif . . .' ": Kelly Edey to PM, May 21, 1990.

page 237 " 'I like to look at pictures, all kinds . . .' ": See Kelly Wise, ed., *Portrait: Theory,* page 132.

page 237 ". . .'one of the first photographic embodiments . . .' ": See Estelle Jussim, *Slave to Beauty,* page 107.

page 237 " 'Certainly Day proferred the black male . . .' ": See Ellenzweig, *The Homoerotic Photograph,* page 51.

page 238 " 'The magazine wasn't going to be . . .' ": Kelly Edey to PM, May 21, 1990.

page 238 ". . . he eventually began to photograph his black models . . .": Miles Everett to PM, May 31, 1990.

page 238 " 'I ran a little kingdom . . .' ": George Dureau to PM, June 18, 1990.

page 239 " 'My lifestyle is bizarre . . .' ": Tom Baril to PM, June 6, 1988.

page 239 " 'All Robert wanted to do . . .' ": *Ibid.*

page 240 " 'During the reception . . .' ": Edward de Celle to PM, August 8, 1989.

page 241 " 'I do wonder if he has something . . .' ": *Ibid.*

page 242 "He began climbing the rocks . . .": Lisa Lyon to PM, February 7, 1989.

page 242 " 'I looked in the mirror . . .' ": *Ibid.*

page 242 "That night they celebrated . . .": *Ibid.*

page 242 " 'If Robert spent the night with someone . . .' ": Tom Baril to PM, December 6, 1988.

page 243 " 'Don't you care about getting diseases?' ": Bobby Miller to PM, June 12, 1990.

page 243 " 'I was having a conversation . . .' ": Kelly Edey to PM, May 21, 1990.

Chapter Seventeen

page 244 "He looked in the window . . .": RM to PM.

page 244 "Milton Moore had just finished . . .": Milton Moore to PM, August 15, 1989.

page 245 ". . . invited him to dinner . . .": *Ibid.*

page 245 "Bond Street's eerie atmosphere . . .": *Ibid.*

page 245 "Moore later claimed . . .": *Ibid.*

page 245 ". . . embarrassed by his generous proportions . . .": RM to PM.

page 246 "Having already served . . .": RM to PM.

pages 246–47 "No sooner had they arrived . . .": Lia Fernandez to PM, January 11, 1989.

page 247 "He would lapse into a trancelike state . . .": RM to PM.

page 248 "He encouraged Moore . . .": *Ibid.*

page 248 " 'Wouldn't a nigger . . .' ": John Abbott to PM, December 7, 1988.

page 248 " 'Mapplethorpe's eye pays special attention to the penis . . .' ": See Essex Hemphill, "Does Your Mama Know About Me? Does She Know Just Who I Am?"

page 249 " 'When Robert Mapplethorpe looks at black men . . .' ": See Edmund White, Introduction, *Black Males,* Galerie Jurka, Amsterdam, 1980.

page 249 " 'Now you know . . .' ": Edmund White to PM, August 7, 1990.

page 250 " 'Wouldn't it be great . . .' ": Bobby Miller to PM, June 12, 1990.

page 251 " 'Robert didn't have to be there.' ": Diego Cortez to PM, July 17, 1990.

page 252 " 'Robert was a fluke in a sense.' ": Howard Read to PM, July 25, 1989.

page 252 " 'The grain of each photograph looks . . .' ": See Kay Larson, "Robert Mapplethorpe at Robert Miller," *New York,* June 7, 1981.

page 252 " 'Mapplethorpe signals unambiguously . . .' ": See Allen Ellenzweig, "Robert Mapplethorpe at Robert Miller," *Art in America,* November 1981.

page 253 " 'Main picture here is a big black dude . . .' ": See Fred McDarrah, *The Village Voice,* May 27, 1981.

page 253 "He suggested Moore apply . . .": RM to PM.

page 253 ". . .'dangerous and totally paranoid'. . .": Lia Fernandez to PM, January 11, 1989.

page 254 " 'Robert kept complaining . . .' ": *Ibid.*

page 254 " 'We drove directly to the beach . . .' ": Klaus Kertess to PM, November 27, 1989.

page 255 "Mapplethorpe seemed incapable . . .": Betsy Evans to PM, September 21, 1989.

page 255 " 'Robert kept very bad records . . .' ": *Ibid.*

page 256 " 'He'd come in around five P.M. . . .' ": Mark Isaacson to PM, January 27, 1989.

page 257 " 'I'm doing everything for you.' ": RM to PM.

page 257 "Moore grabbed a kitchen knife . . .": *Ibid.*

page 257 " 'Robert had this poor black kid . . .' ": Bruce Mailman to PM, March 8, 1989.

page 257 " 'I thought he was very sweet . . .' ": Edmund White to PM, August 7, 1990.

page 257 "A few weeks later . . .": RM to PM.

page 257 " 'My God, where have you been?' ": *Ibid.*

page 258 " 'I was stunned . . .' ": Ingrid Sischy to PM, July 26, 1989.

page 259 " 'I'm having a lot of problems.' ": Michael Stout to PM, March 4, 1989.

page 259 " 'Milton was jumping out the window . . .' ": *Ibid.*

page 260 "Mapplethorpe made one last effort . . .": RM to PM.

page 261 " 'We never really had . . .' ": Milton Moore to PM, August 15, 1989.

Chapter Eighteen

page 262 " 'Robert was absolutely grief-stricken . . .' ": John Abbott to PM, December 7, 1988.

page 263 " 'I'm not interested in being . . .' ": Jack Walls to PM, October 25, 1988.

page 263 " 'I also dealt drugs . . .' ": *Ibid*.

page 264 " 'Robert not only chose . . .' ": Michael Stout to PM, March 4, 1989.

page 264 " 'Jack suddenly disappeared . . .' ": Amy Sullivan to PM, August 2, 1989.

page 264 " 'We had to have sex . . .' ": Jack Walls to PM, October 25, 1988.

page 264 " 'I think I'm in love.' ": Jack Walls to PM, October 25, 1988.

page 265 " 'I don't particularly care . . .' ": Ed Maxey to PM, October 18, 1988.

page 265 " 'Robert didn't say a word . . .' ": *Ibid*.

page 266 " 'The last thing I need . . .' ": *Ibid*.

page 267 ". . . 'light effects that are the visual equivalents . . .' ": *ARTnews*, April 1977.

page 268 " 'I don't know why my pictures . . .' ": Ed Maxey to PM, September 22, 1989.

page 268 " 'Robert was really afraid . . .' ": Gilles Larrain to PM, January 23, 1994.

page 269 " 'I get sick to my stomach . . .' ": See Dorothy S. Gelatt, "Mapplethorpe's Photography Collection Sold," *Maine Antique Digest*, August 1982.

page 269 " 'With the money he made . . .'": Amy Schiffman, "Through the Loupe."

page 269 Frequency of enteric disorders: See Randy Shilts, *And the Band Played On*, Penguin ed., 1988, page 18.

page 270 " 'I don't use recreational drugs . . .' ": Brobson Lutz to PM, February 24, 1992.

page 270 " 'Robert was in a panic . . .' ": *Ibid.*

page 270 " 'You know, faggots are . . .' ": Jim Clyne to PM, June 6, 1991.

page 270 " 'You could not ride the subway . . .' ": Howard Read to PM, July 25, 1989.

page 271 ". . .'the best vulva'. . .": Veronica Vera to PM, July 10, 1990.

page 271 " 'The shoot was a little . . .' ": Marty Gibson to PM, July 13, 1990.

page 271 " 'What should I do . . .' ": *Ibid.*

page 271 ". . .'continued fascination with pornography. . .' ": See Andy Grundberg, "Is Mapplethorpe Only Out to Shock?"

page 271 : " 'Maplethorpe's [*sic*] strategy is . . .' ": See Gil Reavill, "Review of Sex in the News," *Screw,* April 18, 1983.

page 272 " 'Basically, it had to do . . .' ": Howard Read to PM, July 25, 1989.

page 272 ". . . some 'kind of sick joke . . .' ": See *People,* March 21, 1983.

page 272 " 'How new is it for a woman . . .' ": See Carol Squiers, "Undressing the Issues."

page 273 " 'It was like I'd humiliated . . .' ": Carol Squiers to PM, February 13, 1990.

page 273 " 'I know I disappointed . . .' ": Lisa Lyon to PM, February 7, 1989.

page 273 " 'He tortured . . .' ": Howard Read to PM, July 25, 1989.

page 274 " 'Except for *Man in Polyester Suit* . . .' ": Peter MacGill to PM, July 11, 1990.

page 274 " 'Robert would hang up the phone . . .' ": Betsy Evans to PM, September 21, 1989.

page 274 " 'I thought Jack was the perfect . . .' ": Lisa Lyon to PM, February 7, 1989.

page 274 " 'Robert said he wanted . . .' ": Jack Walls to PM, June 22, 1989.

page 275 " 'How could you do this to me?' ": *Ibid.*

page 275 "...'to a silly but perverse ...' ": See C. S. Manegold, "Robert Mapplethorpe, 1970–1983."

pages 275–76 " 'I was a great fan ...' ": Sandy Nairne to PM, June 21, 1990.

page 276 " 'The selection didn't reflect ...' ": *Ibid.*

page 277 " 'I was struck ...' ": *Ibid.*

page 278 " 'I was suddenly part of the process ...' ": *Ibid.*

page 278 " 'I'm not going to have my kid brother ...' ": Ed Maxey to PM, October 18, 1988.

page 279 " 'Robert was terrified ...' ": *Ibid.*

page 280 " 'How dare you?' ": *Ibid.*

page 280 " 'I can't just have anybody ...' ": *Ibid.*

page 280 " 'He doesn't speak English ...' ": *Ibid.*

page 281 " 'I was happy to get away ...' ": Jack Walls to PM, June 22, 1989.

Chapter Nineteen

page 282 " 'Sam told me ...' ": George Rinhart to PM, July 16, 1990.

page 283 " 'Sam had a lifelong ...' ": Jane Livingston to PM, October 27, 1990.

page 283 " 'I used to think of Sam and Robert ...' ": Howard Read to PM, July 25, 1989.

page 284 " 'Despite the chicness ...' ": See Ingrid Sischy, "Sam Wagstaff's Silver."

page 284 " 'The Venini glass ...' ": Mark Isaacson to PM, January 27, 1989.

page 285 "...'blue-chip bohemia where ...' ": See Maureen Dowd, "A Different Bohemia."

page 286 " 'I find the work ...' ": Allen Ellenzweig to PM, August 10, 1990.

page 286 " 'In the beginning we would ...' ": Anne Kennedy to PM, February 4, 1989.

page 287 " 'Robert was very Catholic . . .' ": Paul Schmidt to PM, November 16, 1988.

page 288 " 'It was a nightmare . . .' ": Mark Isaacson to PM, January 27, 1989.

page 288 " 'I wanted one . . .' ": Fern Logan to PM, November 23, 1988.

page 288 " 'They're black . . .' ": *Ibid.*

pages 289–90 " 'I was really intent . . .' ": Dimitri Levas to PM, January 24, 1989.

page 290 ". . .'the black body graphic. . .' ": See Stephen Koch, "Guilt, Grace and Robert Mapplethorpe."

page 291 " 'Considering the technical . . .' ": See John Tavenner, "Safe Art."

page 292 " 'The place was more like a beach shack.' ": Sam Green to PM, November 7, 1989.

page 293 " 'I shouldn't have subjected . . .' ": Kelly Edey to PM, May 21, 1990.

page 293 " 'You're like a kamikaze. . . .' ": Fran Lebowitz to PM, June 12, 1990.

page 294 " 'I know where you're going.' ": Barbara Gladstone to PM, November 21, 1988.

page 294 " 'We were leaving the party . . .' ": Steven Aronson to PM, June 7, 1989.

Chapter Twenty

page 295 ". . .'the best portrait photographer . . .' ": See Andy Grundberg, "Certain People."

page 296 ". . .'blow everyone's minds away'. . .": Jack Woody to PM, July 11, 1990.

page 296 " 'I wanted to include . . .' ": *Ibid.*

page 296 " 'The message that Mapplethorpe . . .' ": See David Joselit, "Robert Mapplethorpe's Poses," *The Perfect Moment*, Institute of Contemporary Art, University of Pennsylvania, 1988.

page 297 " 'New York squalor . . .' ": See Stephen Koch, "Guilt, Grace and Robert Mapplethorpe."

page 297 ". . .'aesthetic genealogy'. . .": See Martin Filler, "Robert Mapplethorpe."

page 297 " 'Don't get any big ideas . . .' ": Jack Walls to PM, September 18, 1989.

page 298 " 'It wasn't like I had anything . . .' ": *Ibid.*

page 298 " 'He really enjoyed . . .' ": Suzie Frankfurt to PM, July 30, 1990.

page 299 " 'Suzie was passionately . . .' ": Michael Stout to PM, March 4, 1989.

page 299 " '. . ."You've got to hire Robert Mapplethorpe." ' ": Suzie Frankfurt to PM, July 30, 1990.

pages 299–300 " 'The whole thing was just hideous.' ": Anne Kennedy to PM, February 4, 1989.

page 301 " 'God forbid a banker . . .' ": See Michael Daly, "The Comeback Kids."

page 301 " 'There were the names . . .' ": Michael Stout to PM, March 4, 1989.

page 302 " 'Robert was like a drug.' ": Suzie Frankfurt to PM, July 30, 1990.

page 302 " 'They are really what it's all about.' ": Paul Schmidt to PM, November 16, 1988.

page 302 " 'Well, you know, as you get older . . .' ": See Anne Horton interview, "Robert Mapplethorpe 1986," Raab Galerie, Berlin; Kicken-Pauseback, Cologne.

page 303 " 'I remember being so frightened . . .' ": Amy Sullivan to PM, August 2, 1989.

page 304 " 'When we all walked . . .' ": Nancy Rooney to PM, December 10, 1988.

page 304 " 'I'm not going.' ": Ed Maxey to PM, October 18, 1988.

page 305 " 'My sister saw Richard . . .' ": Nancy Rooney to PM, December 10, 1988.

page 305 " 'Instead of thinking . . .' ": *Ibid.*

page 305 " 'Robert was just getting sicker . . .' ": Dimitri Levas to PM, January 24, 1989.

page 306 " 'You heard me.' ": *Ibid.*

page 306 " 'Well . . . I've got it.' ": Amy Sullivan to PM, August 2, 1989.

PART FIVE: THE PERFECT MOMENT
Chapter Twenty-one

page 309 "Patti Smith was in the kitchen . . .": PS to PM.

page 310 " 'How's Robert doing? . . .' ": *Ibid.*

page 310 "When she heard about Mapplethorpe . . .": Lisa Lyon to PM, February 7, 1989.

page 311 "She then disappeared into the bathroom . . .": RM to PM

page 311 "That relationship had ended . . .": Gilles Larrain to PM, January 23, 1994.

page 311 " 'I was in love with him.' ": Alexandra Knaust to PM, December 6, 1988.

page 312 " 'I'm so lucky . . .' ": Lia Fernandez to PM, January 11, 1989.

page 312 ". . . Mapplethorpe took a cab . . .": RM to PM.

page 313 " 'We didn't talk about photography . . .' ": Brian English to PM, December 1, 1988.

page 313 "Mapplethorpe's eye immediately noticed . . .": PS to PM.

page 313 "He had always admired . . .": *Ibid.*

page 313 " 'Oh, Robert.' ": *Ibid.*

page 315 " 'I had three great loves . . .' ": *Ibid.*

page 315 "He reached out to take his hand . . .": *Ibid.*

page 315 " 'This is going to happen . . .' ": *Ibid.*

page 316 " 'He was too weak . . .' ": Ron Hoffman to PM, August 22, 1989.

page 317 " 'Sam's dead.' ": PS to PM.

page 317 ". . .'he's sick.' ": See Pat Hackett, ed., *The Andy Warhol Diaries,* page 793.

page 317 " 'How could you do such a thing?' ": Suzanne Donaldson to PM, November 22, 1988.

page 317 " 'We stayed at this funky little motel . . .' ": Lynn Davis to PM, January 15, 1995.

page 318 " 'Robert was really running away . . .' ": Mike Myers to PM, July 18, 1990.

page 318 "One man screamed at him . . .": RM to PM.

page 318 " 'I asked myself several times . . .' ": George Dureau to PM, June 18, 1990.

page 318 " 'You had a hairdresser . . .' ": Michael Stout to PM, March 4, 1989.

page 319 " 'Some of what Sam saw . . .' ": Leonard Bloom to PM, July 11, 1989.

page 319 " 'If you give him too much . . .' ": *Ibid.*

page 320 " 'How can you give a dinner . . .' ": Anne Horton to PM, December 29, 1988.

page 320 ". . . his hands suddenly began to tremble . . .": PS to PM.

page 320 " 'It's not what I wanted . . .' ": *Ibid.*

Chapter Twenty-two

page 322 " 'I don't think it's impossible . . .' ": Peter MacGill to PM, July 11, 1990.

page 323 " 'AIDS had a *terrific* influence.' ": Howard Read to PM, April 13, 1994.

page 323 " 'The dealer said . . .' ": Lisa Lyon to PM, February 7, 1989.

page 323 " 'The weird part about it . . .' ": Suzanne Donaldson to PM, November 22, 1988.

page 323 ". . .'Mr. Mapplethorpe's longterm devotion . . .' ": See Andy Grundberg, "Prints That Go Beyond the Border of the Medium."

page 323 " 'By this point you could presell . . .' ": Howard Read to PM, July 25, 1989.

page 324 "... he toyed with the idea of making them as large ...": Martin Axon to PM, August 7, 1993.

page 325 "... he never bothered to tell him ...": Thomas Williams to PM, March 17, 1989.

page 325 " 'A lot of people yelled ...' ": Mark Isaacson to PM, January 27, 1989.

pages 325–26 Peter Hujar: See Stephen Koch, "Peter Hujar and His Secret Fame," in *Peter Hujar*.

page 326 " 'I just hope I can live ...' ": Kenny Tisa to PM, March 30, 1989.

page 326 " 'I can't believe you've done ...' ": Carol Squiers to PM, February 13, 1990.

page 326 " 'It was just this barrage ...' ": *Ibid*.

page 326 "... Taylor ... had managed to alienate ...": Paul Taylor to PM, November 1, 1989.

page 327 "He was upset by a caption ...": Carol Squiers to PM, February 13, 1990.

page 327 "... he convinced Ed to take part ...": Ed Maxey to PM, October 18, 1988.

page 327 " 'Ed really adored ...' ": Brian English to PM, December 1, 1988.

page 328 "Danielson had worked as a dominatrix ...": Melody Danielson to PM, December 7, 1988.

page 328 " 'Ed was really dedicated ...' ": *Ibid*.

page 329 "Mapplethorpe hated going to Sloan-Kettering ...": Lia Fernandez to PM, January 11, 1989.

page 330 " 'It's got me.' ": *Ibid*.

page 330 " 'I couldn't take a bloody penis ...' ": Maria Morris Hambourg to PM, October 3, 1989.

page 331 " 'Robert had always loved Amsterdam ...' ": Lynn Davis to PM, January 15, 1995.

page 331 " 'I wasn't really thinking along the lines ...' ": Robin Gibson to PM, April 11, 1994.

page 332 " 'He was like a rock star.' ": Sandy Nairne to PM, June 21, 1990.

page 332 " 'Certainly no photographer of recent times . . .' ": See John Russell Taylor, "Images Without a Vision," *The Times* (London), April 5, 1988.

page 332 " 'I suppose a certain percentage . . .' ": Tim Jefferies to PM.

page 333 " 'Alex destroyed the film.' ": Nigel Finch to PM.

page 333 " 'We did them in editions . . .' ": Howard Read to PM, July 25, 1989.

page 334 " 'I'm over that phase.' ": RM to Janet Kardon, *The Perfect Moment* catalogue.

page 334 ". . .'chilly white icons of desire'. . .": See Kay Larson, "Robert Mapplethorpe," *The Perfect Moment* catalogue.

page 334 " 'This is ridiculous.' ": Dimitri Levas to PM, January 24, 1989.

page 336 " 'After a while it got to be . . .' ": *Ibid.*

page 336 " 'It was really kind of neurotic . . .' " Brian English to PM, December 1, 1988.

page 336 " 'Who wouldn't need . . .' ": Jack Walls to PM, October 25, 1988.

page 336 " 'Robert would never have . . .' ": Lynn Davis to PM, May 31, 1990.

page 337 " 'I thought Robert handled his illness with such dignity.' ": Lynn Davis to PM, January 15, 1995.

page 337 " 'Robert knew he had the power . . .' ": Melody Danielson to PM, December 7, 1988.

page 338 " 'It was one of the worst times . . .' ": Brian English to PM, December 1, 1988.

page 338 " 'Robert set up the foundation . . .' ": Lynn Davis to PM, January 15, 1995.

page 339 ". . . a 'pathological liar'. . .": James Bell to PM, April 6, 1994.

page 339 ". . . Mapplethorpe had discussed the lawsuit . . .": See Ellen Hopkins, "Silver Rush," *New York*.

page 340 " 'Well, I guess Mom and Dad . . .' ": Ed Maxey to PM, October 18, 1988.

page 340 " 'It's AIDS, isn't it?' ": Nancy Rooney to PM, October 10, 1988.

page 341 " 'Listen, Ma . . .' ": *Ibid.*

page 342 " 'I went from being with Robert . . .' ": Jack Walls to PM, October 25, 1988.

page 342 " 'I was never so uncomfortable . . .' ": Steven Aronson to PM, June 7, 1989.

page 343 " 'He won't leave me alone.' ": *Ibid.*

page 343 " 'All through Robert's illness . . .' ": Dimitri Levas to PM, January 24, 1989.

Chapter Twenty-three

page 344 "Mapplethorpe captures . . .": See Janet Kardon, *The Perfect Moment* catalogue.

page 344 " 'You know what they say . . .' ": Sam Green to PM, November 7, 1989.

page 345 " 'I want to thank you . . .' ": Tom Armstrong to PM, August 3, 1989.

page 345 " 'I found the whole experience . . .' ": Dimitri Levas to PM, January 24, 1989.

page 346 " 'Mapplethorpe mania has arrived . . .' ": See Andy Grundberg, "The Allure of Mapplethorpe's Photographs."

page 346 ". . . a 'lightning rod . . .' ": See Cathleen McGuigan, "Walk on the Wild Side."

page 346 ". . .'with the era of sexual extremity . . .' ": See Richard Lacayo, "Leatherboy and Angel in One."

page 346 ". . .'a show of Mapplethorpe . . .' ": See Arthur C. Danto, "Robert Mapplethorpe."

page 347 ". . . Mapplethorpe had 'ridden a cultural curve . . .' ": See Kay Larson, "Getting Graphic."

page 347 " 'It doesn't take a genius . . .' ": Jane Livingston to PM, October 27, 1989.

page 347 " 'Ultimately one doesn't know . . .' ": Philippe Garner to PM, June 18, 1994.

page 348 " 'Can you imagine . . .' ": Anne Kennedy to PM, February 4, 1989.

page 349 " 'Robert was lyrically selfish . . .' ": Steven Aronson to PM, June 7, 1989.

page 349 "When Robert Rauschenberg . . .": *Ibid.*

page 350 " 'I don't care if I die . . .' ": Leonard Bloom to PM, July 11, 1989.

page 350 " 'I can't face them now.' ": *Ibid.*

page 350 " 'Didn't you hear? . . .' ": Art Nelson to PM, August 22, 1989.

page 350 " 'Do you think it would be . . .' ": Steven Aronson to PM, June 7, 1989.

page 351 ". . .'the really offensive ones'. . .": Harry Mapplethorpe to PM, October 20, 1989.

page 351 " 'No big deal.' ": *Ibid.*

page 352 " 'It was like the human spirit . . .' ": John Shea to PM, February 24, 1989.

page 354 "A few days after Thanksgiving . . .": Father George Stack to PM, December 8, 1988.

page 355 " 'We had a huge run-up . . .' ": Howard Read to PM, July 25, 1989.

page 355 " 'It had become an assembly-line process . . .' ": Tom Baril to PM, December 6, 1988.

page 355 " 'You are a fine art photographer . . .' ": Suzanne Donaldson to PM, November 22, 1988.

page 356 " 'In two years we did three . . .' ": Howard Read to PM, July 25, 1989.

page 356 " 'The pictures were really just . . .' ": Brian English to PM, December 1, 1988.

page 356 " 'It was not a good show . . .' ": Dimitri Levas to PM, January 24, 1989.

page 357 " 'I'm going to die.' ": Tom Peterman to PM, April 19, 1989.

page 357 " 'That's the one thing . . .' ": Dimitri Levas to PM, January 24, 1989.

page 358 ". . . *Vanity Fair* article . . . confirmed his worst fears.": See Dominick Dunne, "Robert Mapplethorpe's Proud Finale."

page 358 " 'To allude to such a link . . .' ": Mathilde Krim, letter to the editor, *Vanity Fair*, September 1989.

page 360 " 'You'd go from rooting . . .' ": Brian English to PM, December 1, 1988.

page 363 " 'You're nothing but a hustler.' ": Tom Peterman to PM, April 19, 1989.

page 363 "One afternoon a nurse presented him . . .": Alexandra Knaust to PM, July 18, 1989.

page 363 " 'Please . . . don't let them hurt me . . .' ": *Ibid*.

page 363 " 'His body was being . . .' ": *Ibid*.

page 364 " 'He had the same look . . .' ": Nancy Rooney to PM.

Epilogue

page 367 " 'Where's your ticket?' ": Danny Fields to PM, June 8, 1990.

page 369 " 'Robert was in this little bag . . .' ": Lynn Davis to PM, January 15, 1995.

page 369 " 'Lynn didn't want to . . .' ": Ed Maxey to PM, May 12, 1994.

page 369 ". . .'for private reasons'. . .": Harry Mapplethorpe to PM, May 11, 1994.

CHRONOLOGY

page 373 " 'Whoa! We funded that? . . .' ": See "Mean for Jesus," *Vanity Fair*, September 1990.

page 374 " 'The people of this community . . .' ": See Isabel Wilkerson, "Trouble Right Here in Cincinnati: Furor Over Mapplethorpe Exhibit," *The New York Times*, March 29, 1990.

page 375 ". . .'a search for understanding . . .' ": See Milo Geyelin, "Cincinnati Sends a Warning to Censors."

page 375 "I'm not an expert . . .": *Ibid*.

Bibliography

BOOKS

Barthes, Roland. *Camera Lucida*. New York: The Noonday Press, 1981.

Bataille, Georges. *Eroticism: Death and Sensuality*. San Francisco: City Lights Books, 1986.

———. *The Tears of Eros*. San Francisco: City Lights Books, 1989.

Billeter, Erika, ed. *Self-Portrait in the Age of Photography*. Lausanne: Musee cantonal des Beaux-Arts, 1985.

Bockris, Victor. *The Life and Death of Andy Warhol*. New York: Bantam Books, 1989.

Bogdan, Robert. *Freak Show*. Chicago: University of Chicago Press, 1988.

Bromberg, Craig. *The Wicked Ways of Malcolm McLaren*. New York: Harper & Row, 1989.

Browning, Frank. *The Culture of Desire*. New York: Crown, 1993.

Burchill, Julie, and Tony Parsons. *The Boy Looked at Johnny*. Winchester, MA: Faber and Faber, 1987.

Carroll, Jim. *The Basketball Diaries*. New York: Viking Penguin, 1987.

———. *Forced Entries: The Downtown Diaries, 1971–1973*. New York: Viking Penguin, 1987.

Colacello, Bob. *Holy Terror: Andy Warhol Close Up*. New York: HarperCollins, 1990.

Coleman, A. D. *Light Readings*. New York: Oxford University Press, 1979.

Cooper, Emmanuel. *The Sexual Perspective*. London: Routledge & Kegan Paul, 1986.

Crane, Diana. *The Transformation of the Avant-Garde*. Chicago: University of Chicago Press, 1987.

D'Emilio, John, and Estelle B. Freedman. *Intimate Matters*. New York: Harper & Row, 1988.

Downing, Christine. *Myths and Mysteries of Same-Sex Love*. New York: The Continuum Publishing Co., 1989.

Ellenzweig, Allen. *The Homoerotic Photograph*. New York: Columbia University Press, 1992.

Feinberg, David B. *Eighty-Sixed*. New York: Viking, 1989.

Finkelstein, Nat. *Andy Warhol: The Factory Years, 1964–1967*. New York: St. Martin's Press, 1989.

Frank, Peter, and Michael McKenzie. *New, Used & Improved: Art for the 80's*. New York: Abbeville Press, 1987.

Garber, Marjorie. *Vested Interests: Cross-Dressing & Cultural Anxiety*. New York: Routledge, 1992.

Gill, Michael. *Image of the Body*. New York: Doubleday, 1989.

Gitlin, Todd. *The Sixties: Years of Hope, Days of Rage*. New York: Bantam, 1987.

Gonzalez-Crussi, F. *On the Nature of Things Erotic*. New York: Vintage, 1989.

Green, Jonathan. *American Photography*. New York: Harry N. Abrams, 1984.

Grundberg, Andy, and Kathleen McCarthy Gauss. *Photography and Art*. New York: Abbeville Press, 1987.

Hackett, Pat, ed. *The Andy Warhol Diaries*. New York: Warner Books, 1989.

Hager, Steven. *Art After Midnight*. New York: St. Martin's Press, 1986.

Herdt, Gilbert, ed. *Gay Culture in America*. Boston: Beacon Press, 1992.

Hess, John L. *The Grand Acquisitors*. Boston: Houghton Mifflin, 1974.

Holleran, Andrew. *Dancer from the Dance*. New York: William Morrow, 1978.

Hughes, Robert. *Nothing If Not Critical*. New York: Alfred A. Knopf, 1991.

Hujar, Peter. *Peter Hujar*. New York: Grey Art Gallery & Study Center, 1990.

Huysmans, J.-K., *Against Nature,* New York: Viking Penguin, 1959.

Jussim, Estelle. *Slave to Beauty*. Boston: David R. Godine, 1981.

Koch, Stephen. *Stargazer: Andy Warhol's World and His Films*. New York: Marion Boyars, 1973.

Kramer, Hilton. *The Revenge of the Philistines*. New York: The Free Press, 1985.

Kramer, Larry. *Faggots*. New York: Random House, 1978.

Levin, Kim. *Beyond Modernism*. New York: Harper & Row, 1988.

Lippard, Lucy R. *Pop*. London: Thames and Hudson, 1966.

Malcolm, Janet. *Diana & Nikon*. Boston: David R. Godine, 1980.

McShine, Kynaston. *Andy Warhol: A Retrospective*. New York: Museum of Modern Art, 1989.

Monette, Paul. *Borrowed Time*. New York: Harcourt Brace Jovanovich, 1988.

Newhall, Beaumont, ed. *Photography: Essays & Images*. New York: Museum of Modern Art, 1980.

Newton, Helmut. *Sleepless Nights*. New York: Congreve, 1978.

Paglia, Camille. *Sex, Art, and American Culture*. New York: Vintage Books, 1992.

———. *Sexual Personae*. New Haven: Yale University Press, 1990.

Perl, Jed. *Gallery Going*. New York: Harcourt Brace Jovanovich, 1991.

A Personal View: Photography in the Collection of Paul F. Walter. New York: Museum of Modern Art, 1985.

Phillips, Donna-Lee, ed. *Eros & Photography*. San Francisco: Camerawork/NFS Press, 1977.

Pincus-Witten, Robert. *Postminimalism into Maximalism*. Ann Arbor: UMI Research Press, 1987.

Pronger, Brian. *The Arena of Masculinity*. New York: St. Martin's Press, 1990.

Rachleff, Owen S. *The Occult in Art*. London: Cromwell Editions, 1990.

Ratcliff, Carter. *Warhol*. New York: Abbeville Press, 1983.

Rosenblum, Naomi. *A World History of Photography*. New York: Abbeville Press, 1984.

Russo, Vito. *The Celluloid Closet*, rev. ed. New York: Harper & Row, 1987.

Sandler, Irving. *American Art of the 1960s*. New York: Harper & Row, 1988.

Saunders, Gill. *The Nude*. New York: Harper & Row, 1989.

Sayre, Henry M. *The Object of Performance*. Chicago: University of Chicago Press, 1989.

Shepard, Sam. *Angel City, Curse of the Starving Class and Other Plays*. New York: Urizen Books, 1976.

Shewey, Don. *Sam Shepard*. New York: Dell, 1985.

Shilts, Randy. *And the Band Played On*. New York: St. Martin's Press, 1987.

———. *The Mayor of Castro Street*. New York: St. Martin's Press, 1982.

Singer, June. *Androgyny*. New York: Anchor Press/Doubleday, 1976.

Smith, Joshua P. *The Photography of Invention*. Washington, D.C.: National Museum of American Art, Smithsonian Institution, 1989.

Smith, Patti. *Babel*. New York: G. P. Putnam's Sons, 1978.

———. *Early Work 1970–1979*. New York: W. W. Norton, 1994.

———. *Seventh Heaven*. New York: Telegraph Books, 1972.

———. *Wītt*. New York: Gotham Book Mart, 1973.

Sobieszek, Robert A. *Masterpieces of Photography*. New York: Abbeville Press, 1984.

Sontag, Susan. *AIDS and Its Metaphors*. New York: Farrar, Straus and Giroux, 1988.

———. *On Photography*. New York: Farrar, Straus and Giroux, 1980.

———. *Under the Sign of Saturn*. New York: Farrar, Straus and Giroux, 1980.

Stambolian, George. *Male Fantasies/Gay Realities*. New York: SeaHorse Press, 1984.

Stein, Jean. *Edie: An American Biography*. New York: Alfred A. Knopf, 1982.

Stich, Sidra. *Made in USA*. Berkeley: University of California Press, 1987.

Sukenick, Ronald. *Down and In: Life in the Underground*. New York: Beech Tree Books, 1987.

Sullivan, Constance. *Nude: Photographs 1850–1980*. New York: Harper & Row, 1980.

Szarkowski, John. *Looking at Photographs*. New York: Museum of Modern Art, 1973.

———. *Photography Until Now*. New York: Museum of Modern Art, 1989.

Taylor, Paul, ed. *Impresario: Malcolm McLaren and the British New Wave*. Cambridge: The MIT Press, 1988.

———. *Post-Pop Art*. Cambridge: The MIT Press, 1989.

Thorn, Dr. Mark. *Taboo No More*. New York: Shapolsky Publishers, 1990.

Tompkins, Calvin. *Post- to Neo- New York*. New York: Henry Holt, 1988.

———. *The Scene: Reports on Post-Modern Art*. New York: Viking, 1976.

Turner, Florence. *At the Chelsea*. New York: Harcourt Brace Jovanovich, 1987.

Ultra Violet. *Famous for 15 Minutes*. New York: Harcourt Brace Jovanovich, 1988.

Wagstaff, Sam. *A Book of Photographs*. New York: Gray Press, 1978.

Walters, Margaret. *The Nude Male*. London: Paddington Press, 1978.

Warhol, Andy, and Pat Hackett. *POPism*. New York: Harcourt Brace Jovanovich, 1980.

Weaver, Mike, ed. *The Art of Photography, 1839–1989*. London: Royal Academy of Arts, 1989.

Webb, Peter. *The Erotic Arts*. London: Secker & Warburg, 1983.

Wise, Kelly, ed. *Portrait: Theory*. New York: Lustrum Press, 1981.

Woody, Jack, ed. *George Platt Lynes: Photographs 1931–1955*. Pasadena: Twelvetrees Press, 1981.

PERIODICALS AND NEWSPAPERS

Albright, Thomas. "Realism, Romanticism and Leather." *San Francisco Chronicle*, February 24, 1978.

———. "The World of Decadent Chic." *San Francisco Chronicle*, May 1, 1980.

Alfred, William. "The Roller Coaster History of Coney Island." *New York*, September 9, 1968.

Altman, Billy. "Lenny Kaye Speaks His Mind." *Creem*, September 1979.

Anderson, Alexandra. "The Collectors." *Vogue*, March 1985.

Andre, Michael. "Recent Religious and Ritual Art (Buecker and Harpsichords)." *ARTnews*, March 1974.

Anthony, Michael. "Concert Proves Patti Smith Can Be Bad." *Minneapolis Tribune*, June 29, 1979.

Aronson, Steven M. L. "The Art of Living." *Vanity Fair*, April 1987.

Artner, Alan G. "The Eye of the Storm." *Chicago Tribune*, March 5, 1989.

———. "Going for a Gut Reaction." *Chicago Tribune*, March 5, 1989.

———. "Mapplethorpe Photographs Seek More Than Arousal." *Chicago Tribune*, February 29, 1980.

———. "The 1989 Artist of the Year: Photographer Robert Mapplethorpe." *Chicago Tribune*, December 31, 1989.

———. " 'Sex Specific' Exhibit Is Tiring in Its Unoriginality." *Chicago Tribune*, November 16, 1984.

Bannon, Anthony. "Show Is Echo of College Art." *Buffalo Evening News*, August 16, 1979.

Barker, Paul. "Vulgar Factions." *Evening Standard*, March 24, 1988.

Black, Cindy. "Patti Smith in 78." *New Wave*, November 1978.

Bloom, Michael. "Dancing Critic: The Patti Smith Band." *Boston Phoenix*, December 21, 1976.

Bockris, Victor. "Robert Mapplethorpe." *New York Rocker,* 1976.

Boettger, Suzaan. "Black and White Leather." *Daily Californian,* April 11, 1980.

Bohdan, Carol Lorrain, and Todd Mitchell Volpe. "Collecting Arts & Crafts." *Nineteenth Century,* Autumn 1978.

Bondi, Inge. "The Yin and the Yang of Robert Mapplethorpe." *Print Letter,* January–February 1979.

Bourdon, David. "The Artist As Sex Object." *New York,* September 16, 1974.

———. "Not Good Ain't Necessarily Bad." *The Village Voice,* December 8, 1975.

———. "Robert Mapplethorpe." *Arts Magazine,* April 1977.

Brazier, Chris. "The Resurrection of Patti Smith." *Melody Maker,* March 18, 1978.

Broe, Dennis. "Patti Smith and Other Artists 'Draw.' " *Good Times,* February 12, 1979.

Brown, Susan Rand. "Sam Wagstaff: Photography Collecting's Howard Hughes Brings An Exhibit to Hartford." *Hartford Courant Magazine,* April 26, 1981.

Bulgari, Elsa. "Robert Mapplethorpe." *Fire Island Newsmagazine,* July 3, 1978.

Bultman, Janis. "Bad Boy Makes Good." *Darkroom Photography,* July 1988.

Burn, Gordon. "Will Patti Smith Ever Get to You?" *Honey,* February 1977.

Burnett, W. C. "Ex-Painter Gets in Focus with Camera." *Atlanta Journal,* April 2, 1982.

Burnham, Sophy. "The Manhattan Arrangement of Art and Money." *New York,* December 8, 1969.

Burroughs, William. "When Patti Rocked." *Spin,* April 1987.

Carlson, Margaret. "Whose Art Is It, Anyway?" *Time,* July 3, 1989.

Carson, Tom. "Patti Smith: Under the Double Ego." *Rolling Stone,* June 28, 1979.

Castro, Janice. "Calvin Meets the Marlboro Man." *Time,* October 21, 1985.

Certain People review. *Photo Design,* December 1985.

———. *The Print Collector's Newsletter,* March–April 1986.

Christgau, Robert. "Save This Rock & Roll Hero." *The Village Voice,* January 17, 1976.

Christy, Duncan. "Howard Read's Photo Opportunities." *M,* April 1988.

Cohen, Scott. "Radioactive." *Circus Magazine,* December 14, 1976.

Colgan, Susan. "Sam Wagstaff, Collector of 19th- and 20th-Century Photographs." *Art & Antiques,* November–December 1982.

Coon, Caroline. "Punk Queen of Sheba." *Melody Maker,* January 15, 1977.

Cooper, Dennis. "At the Mapplethorpe Opening." *7 Days,* August 10, 1988.

Corbeil, Carole. "For Wagstaff, the Image Is Everything." *The Globe and Mail,* January 24, 1981.

Cott, Jonathan. "Rock and Rimbaud." *The New York Times Book Review,* February 19, 1978.

Dadoma, Giovanni, "This Girl's Got a Lotta Neck." *Sounds,* April 23, 1977.

Daly, Michael. "The Comeback Kids." *New York,* July 22, 1985.

Danto, Arthur C. "Robert Mapplethorpe." *The Nation,* September 26, 1988.

Danziger, James. "Miller Time." *New York,* January 11, 1988.

Davila, Albert. "On Borderline, It's a Victory." *Daily News,* October 13, 1988.

Davis, Douglas. "An Irreverent Eye." *Newsweek,* April 8, 1985.

———. "The Return of the Nude." *Newsweek,* September 1, 1986.

———, with Mary Rourke. "Doctored Images." *Newsweek,* August 15, 1977.

———. "The Romance of Old Photos." *Newsweek,* February 21, 1977.

Davis, Peter. "The Man Who Undressed Men." *Esquire,* June 1986.

Davis, Stephen. "They Speak for Their Generation." *The New York Times,* December 21, 1975.

Demorest, Stephen. "Patti vs. the Devil—the Artist Wins!" New York *Daily News,* April 10, 1977.

Donovan, Mark. "You Don't Have to Be an Expert." *People,* April 17, 1978.

Dowd, Maureen. "A Different Bohemia." *The New York Times Magazine,* November 17, 1985.

Dricks, Sally. "Poet for Good Fortune, in a Brand New Army." *Aquarian Weekly,* May 18, 1977.

Duka, John. "For the Fine Art of Collecting Photography, a Newfound Status." *The New York Times,* November 19, 1980.

Dundy, Elaine. "Crane, Masters, Wolfe, etc., Slept Here." *Esquire,* October 1964.

Dunne, Dominick. "Grandiosity: The Fall of Roberto Polo." *Vanity Fair,* October 1988.

———. "Robert Mapplethorpe's Proud Finale." *Vanity Fair,* February 1989.

Durbin, Karen. "Pretty Poison: The Selling of Sexual Warfare." *The Village Voice,* May 9, 1977.

Edwards, Owen. "Blow-Out: The Decline and Fall of the Fashion Photographer." *New York,* May 28, 1973.

Ehrmann, Eric. "MC5." *Rolling Stone,* January 4, 1969.

Ellenzweig, Allen. "The Homosexual Aesthetic." *American Photography,* August 1980.

———. "Picturing the Homoerotic." *Out/Look: National Lesbian and Gay Quarterly,* no. 7, Winter 1990.

———. "Robert Mapplethorpe at Robert Miller." *Art in America,* November 1981.

Everly, Bart. "Robert Mapplethorpe." *Splash,* April 1988.

Ferguson, Scottie. "Erotica: An Old Pro Gets a Grand New Show." *The Advocate,* February 1980.

Ferretti, Fred. "A Very Fine Line Divides Floral Park from Floral Park." *The New York Times,* November 2, 1977.

Filler, Martin. "Robert Mapplethorpe." *House & Garden,* June 1988.

Fischer, Hal. "Calculated Opulence." *Artweek,* November 21, 1981.

———. "An Eye for Photographic Expression." *Artweek,* December 9, 1978.

———. "The New Commercialism." *Camera Arts,* January 1981.

Forgey, Benjamin. "A Photo Exhibit Combines Technical and Historic Import." *Washington Star,* February 3, 1978.

Frith, Simon. "Patti: Love Conquers All." *Melody Maker,* May 5, 1979.

Fritscher, Jack. "Fetishes, Faces, and Flowers of Evil." *Drummer* 133.

Gaines, Steven. "Sometimes a Somebody." *Vanity Fair,* January 1987.

Gamarekian, Barbara. "Crowd at Corcoran Protests Mapplethorpe Cancellation." *The New York Times,* July 1, 1989.

———. "Hundreds in the Arts Rally for Grants Without Strings." *The New York Times,* March 21, 1990.

———. " 'Tragedy of Errors' Engulfs the Corcoran." *The New York Times,* September 18, 1989.

Gelatt, Dorothy S. "Mapplethorpe's Photography Collection Sold." *Maine Antique Digest,* August 1982.

Geyelin, Milo. "Cincinnati Sends a Warning to Censors." *The Wall Street Journal,* October 8, 1990.

Gleason, Kathryn. "Photographs: The Whole Truth." *Metro Herald,* September 14, 1988.

Glueck, Grace. "Images of Blacks Refracted in a White Mirror." *The New York Times,* January 7, 1990.

Goldberg, Michael. "Whatever Happened to Gracious Patti Smith?" *San Francisco Examiner,* July 22, 1979.

Goldberg, Vicki. "The Art of Salesmanship." *American Photography,* February 1987.

———. "Robert Mapplethorpe." *New York,* April 13, 1979.

Goldstein, Patrick. "Patti the Rock Poet, Screaming and Loving It." *Chicago News,* December 4, 1976.

————. "Patti Smith: Rock 'n' Roll Pandora Unleashes Violence and May-hem." *Creem*, March 1977.

Gooch, Brad. "Club Culture." *Vanity Fair*, May 1987.

Green, Roger. "Dureau and Mapplethorpe." *The New Orleans Times-Picayune*, January 3, 1982.

————. "Softening a Sexy Image with Flowers." *Lagniappe*, January 30, 1987.

Grimes, William. "The Charge? Depraved. The Verdict. Out of the Show." *The New York Times*, March 8, 1992.

Gross, Kenneth. "Stepchild of Queens Fights City's Neglect." *Newsday*, February 13, 1978.

Gruen, John. "The Best Thing in Life Is Me." *New York*, October 18, 1971.

Grundberg, Andy. "The Allure of Mapplethorpe's Photographs." *The New York Times*, July 31, 1988.

————. "Certain People." *The New York Times Book Review*, December 8, 1985.

————. "Is Mapplethorpe Only Out to Shock?" *The New York Times*, March 13, 1983.

————. "The Mix of Art and Commerce." *The New York Times*, September 28, 1986.

————. "Prints That Go Beyond the Border of the Medium." *The New York Times*, May 3, 1987.

Haden-Guest, Anthony. "The Macabre Case of the Man in the Mask." *New York*, June 24, 1985.

————. "Steve Rubell: From the Big House to His House." *New York*, October 8, 1984.

Hagen, Charles. "Robert Mapplethorpe: Black-and-White Polaroids, 1971–1975." *The New York Times*, May 28, 1993.

Hanson, Bernard. "Compelling Contrasts of Images." *Hartford Courant*, August 12, 1984.

Hawkins, Margaret. "Pictures Sharpen into Focus." *Chicago Sun-Times*, November 29, 1985.

Hayes, Robert. "Robert Mapplethorpe." *Interview*, March 1983.

Hellman, Peter. "Soho: Artists' Bohemia Imperiled." *New York*, August 21, 1970.

Hemphill, Essex. "Does Your Mama Know About Me? Does She Know Just Who I Am?" *Gay Community News*, March 25–31, 1990.

Henry, Gerrit. "Robert Mapplethorpe—Collecting Quality." *The Print Collector's Newsletter*, September–October 1982.

Hershkovits, David. "Shock of the Black and the Blue." *The Soho Weekly News*, May 20, 1981.

———. "Sight Unseen." *Paper*, May 1985.

Hilburn, Robert. "Patti Smith on a Hot Streak." *Los Angeles Times*, May 15, 1978.

———. "The Return of Rock's High Priestess." *Los Angeles Times*, July 24, 1988.

Hodges, Parker. "Robert Mapplethorpe, Photographer." *Manhattan Gaze*, December 10, 1979.

Hoelterhoff, Manuela. "New Values in Vintage Photographs." *The Wall Street Journal*, July 17, 1974.

Holleran, Andrew. "Dicks and Daffodils." *Christopher Street*, June 1983.

Holmes, Jon. "Black Leather in Black and White." *Boston Phoenix*, November 11, 1980.

Honan, William H. "Senators Reject Curb on U.S. Fund for the Arts." *The New York Times*, September 29, 1989.

Hopkins, Ellen. "Silver Rush." *New York*, July 11, 1988.

Hughes, Robert. "Art, Morality and Mapplethorpe." *The New York Review of Books*, April 23, 1992.

Hume, Martha. "A Surprise Pop Hit for Punk Rocker Patti Smith." *US*, June 13, 1978.

Huntington, Richard. "Kenan Center Offers Collection of Winners." *Buffalo Courier-Express*, April 17, 1979.

Indiana, Gary. "Mapplethorpe." *The Village Voice*, May 14, 1985.

———. "Robert Mapplethorpe." *Bomb*, Winter 1988.

Jarman, Derek. "In Art, As Life." *The Independent,* November 8, 1992.

Jentz, Terri. "Robert Mapplethorpe: Restless Talent." *New York Photo District News,* April 1983.

Jones, Allan. "Meet the Press." *Melody Maker,* October 30, 1976.

Jones, Gwen. "My Style: Lisa Lyon in Conversation with Gwen Jones." *Los Angeles Herald Examiner.* July 11, 1983.

Kemnitz, Robert. "Patti Smith in Combat." *Los Angeles Herald-Examiner,* November 12, 1976.

Kimmelman, Michael. "Bitter Harvest: AIDS and the Arts." *The New York Times,* March 19, 1989.

King, Nicholas. "Familiar Thrills: Coney Island Revisited." *The Wall Street Journal,* June 30, 1988.

Kissel, Howard. "A Focus on Unsettling Images." *Women's Wear Daily,* July 8, 1986.

Kisselgoff, Anna. "Dance: Lucinda Childs Offers World Premiere." *The New York Times,* January 29, 1986.

Koch, Stephen. "Guilt, Grace and Robert Mapplethorpe." *Art in America,* November 1986.

Kogan, Rick. "Puzzling Patti Smith—Interesting to Hear and See." *Chicago Sun-Times,* June 11, 1979.

Kohn, Michael. "Robert Mapplethorpe." *Arts Magazine,* September 1982.

Kolbowski, Silvia. "Covering Mapplethorpe's 'Lady.' " *Art in America,* Summer 1983.

Kozak, Roman. "Patti Smith Group—*Wave*." *Billboard,* June 9, 1979.

Kramer, Hilton. "Mapplethorpe Show at the Whitney: A Big, Glossy, Offensive Exhibit." *New York Observer,* August 22, 1988.

———. "Robert Mapplethorpe." *The New York Times,* June 5, 1981.

Kron, Joan. "Copping a Feel at *Vogue*." *New York,* May 26, 1975.

Lacayo, Richard. "Leatherboy and Angel in One." *Time,* August 22, 1988.

"Lady: Lisa Lyon" (review). *People,* March 21, 1983.

Lafferty, Elizabeth. "The Cool Elegance of Robert Mapplethorpe." *San Francisco Focus,* April 1980.

Larson, Kay. "Between a Rock and a Soft Place." *New York,* June 1, 1981.

———. "Getting Graphic." *New York,* August 15, 1988.

———. "How Should Artists Be Educated." *ARTnews,* November 1983.

———. "Plundering the Past: The Decline of the New-York Historical Society." *New York,* July 25, 1988.

Leland, John. "The New Voyeurism: Madonna and the Selling of Sex." *Newsweek,* November 2, 1992.

Lemon, Brendan. "Aftershocks." *Aperture,* Spring 1989.

Leonhart, Mark Michael. "Photographer Evokes Precise Portrait Statements." *Gay Life,* February 29, 1980.

Lewis, Jo Ann. "Mapplethorpe's Transformations." *The Washington Post,* July 21, 1989.

Lifson, Ben. "Games Photographers Play." *The Village Voice,* April 2, 1979.

———. "The Philistine Photographer: Reassessing Mapplethorpe." *The Village Voice,* April 9, 1979.

———. "Sam Wagstaff's Pleasures." *The Village Voice,* July 17, 1978.

———. "The Simple Art of Persuasion." *The Village Voice,* October 8, 1980.

Lingeman, Richard. "Where Home Is Where It Is." *The New York Times Book Review,* December 24, 1967.

Lipson, Karin. "Celebration and Crisis." *Newsday,* August 1, 1988.

"Lisa Lyon: Body Beautiful." *Playboy,* October 1980.

"Lisa Lyon by Robert Mapplethorpe." *Artforum,* November 1980.

Loder, Kurt. "The Resurrection of Patti Smith." *Good Times of South Florida,* July 11, 1978.

Loke, Margarett. "Collecting's Big Thrill Is the Chase." *The New York Times Magazine,* March 17, 1985.

Lucie-Smith, Edward. "The Gay Seventies?" *Art and Artists,* December 1979.

————. "Mapplethorpe Gets His Revenge." *The Independent,* November 18, 1989.

Manegold, C. S. "Robert Mapplethorpe, 1970–1983; On the 1983–1984 Retrospective." *Arts Magazine,* February 1984.

"Mapplethorpe's Art: a Sensual Symphony in Black and White." *Milwaukee Journal,* June 30, 1985.

"Mapplethorpe: Split Vision." *The New York Times,* January 10, 1986.

"Mapplethorpe at the Whitney." *W,* August 22, 1988.

Marsh, Dave. "Can Patti Smith Walk on Water?" *Rolling Stone,* April 20, 1978.

————. "Her Horses Got Wings, They Can Fly." *Rolling Stone,* January 1, 1976.

Marzorati, Gerald. "Just a Bunch of Photographs." *Soho Weekly News,* July 13, 1978.

Masters, Kim. "Cincinnati Gallery Indicted for Mapplethorpe Show." *The Washington Post,* April 8, 1990.

McDarrah, Fred. "In Print—Reviews of the Black Book, 50 New York Artists." *Photo District News,* April 1987.

McDonald, Mark. "Censored." *The Advocate,* June 28, 1978.

McGuigan, Cathleen. "A Garden of Disco Delights." *Newsweek,* May 20, 1985.

————. "New Art, New Money." *The New York Times Magazine,* February 10, 1985.

————. "The Pleasure of the Chase." *Newsweek,* January 30, 1989.

————. "Walk on the Wild Side." *Newsweek,* July 25, 1988.

McKendry, Maxime de La Falaise. "Patti Smith." *Interview,* February 1976.

McKenna, Kristine. "Patti Smith's 'Wave': For Those Who Think Jung." *Los Angeles Times,* June 3, 1979.

Morgan, Stuart. "Something Magic." *Artforum,* May 1987.

Morse, Steve. "Lackluster Patti Smith." *Boston Globe,* May 14, 1979.

Mortifoglio, Richard. "Patti Smith's Leaps of Faith." *The Village Voice,* June 4, 1979.

Murray, Joan. "Weegee the Famous." *Artweek*, March 11, 1978.

" 'New York/New Wave' at P.S. 1." *Artforum*, Summer 1981.

O'Brien, Glenn. "In Memory of Max's." *The Village Voice*, January 6, 1975.

Oreskes, Michael. "Senate Votes to Bar U.S. Support of 'Obscene or Indecent' Artwork." *The New York Times*, July 27, 1989.

Panicelli, Ida. "Robert Mapplethorpe, Palazzo delle Centro Finestre, Galleria Lucio Amelio." *Artforum*, October 1984.

Papale, Richard S. "Mapplethorpe's Forgotten Art." *Bostonia*, January–February 1980.

Parsons, Tony. "Seventh Vertebra During the Seventh Number." *New Musical Express*, February 5, 1977.

Post, Henry. "Mapplethorpe's Camera Lusts for Exposing Sex Objects." *GQ*, February 1982.

Pousner, Howard. "Shoot First, Ask Questions Later." *Atlanta Constitution*. April 17, 1982.

Puzo, Mario. "Meet Me Tonight in Dreamland." *New York*, September 3, 1979.

Raedeke, Paul. "Interview with Sam Wagstaff." *Photo Metro*, December 1985.

Ratcliff, Carter. "The Art Establishment: Rising Stars vs. the Machine." *New York*, November 27, 1978.

Rathbone, Belinda. "The Photography Market: Image or Object?" *The Print Collector's Newsletter*, March–April 1989.

Raynor, Vivien. "Photographic 'Feast' Ending 3-Year Tour." *The New York Times*, June 7, 1981.

Reif, Rita. "Silver Spoons for Victorian Yuppies." *The New York Times*, January 8, 1989.

Reilly, Peter. "Patti Smith's 'Radio Ethiopia.' " *Stereo Review*, February 1977.

Reisman, Judith. "Promoting Child Abuse as Art." *Washington Times*, July 7, 1989.

Reynolds, Charles. "From the Wagstaff Collection." *Popular Photography*, May 1985.

Ricard, René. "Patti Smith and Robert Mapplethorpe at Miller." *Art in America,* September–October 1978.

Rich, Frank. "The Gay Decades." *Esquire,* November 1987.

Richard, Paul. "Sam Wagstaff, the Collector the Establishment Trusts." *The Washington Post,* February 3, 1978.

"Robert Mapplethorpe." *Artforum,* February 1978.

"Robert Mapplethorpe." *Photo/Design,* August 1985.

"Robert Mapplethorpe: Blacks and Whites." *San Francisco Guardian,* April 3, 1980.

"Robert Mapplethorpe," review of "Contact." *Arts Magazine,* June 1979.

Robinson, Lisa. "Patti Smith: Songs from a Marriage." *Vogue,* March 19, 1988.

Rockwell, John. "Patti Smith Battles to a Singing Victory." *The New York Times,* December 28, 1975.

———. "Patti Smith Personalizes Rock Art." *The New York Times,* November 25, 1976.

———. "The Pop Life." *The New York Times,* November 25, 1977.

Rodriguez, Richard. "Late Victorians." *Harper's,* October 1990.

Rose, Barbara. "The Triumph of Photography, or: Farewell to Status in the Arts." *New York,* March 6, 1972.

———. "Vaginal Iconology." *New York,* February 11, 1974.

Ruehlmann, William. "It May Be Kinky but He Says It's Art." Norfolk *Ledger-Star,* January 25, 1978.

Russell Taylor, John. "Images Without a Vision." *The Times* (London), April 5, 1988.

Ryan, Robert. "The Lost Community." *Herald-Tribune,* May 29, 1964.

"Sam Hardison." *Provincetown Arts,* 1990.

Schiffman, Amy. "Through the Loupe." *American Photography,* August 1982.

Schjeldahl, Peter. "The Mainstreaming of Mapplethorpe." *7 Days,* August 10, 1988.

———. "New Wave No Fun." *The Village Voice,* March 4, 1981.

———. "Photo Synthesis." *7 Days,* March 14, 1990.

Schruers, Fred. "Patti Smith Riding Crest of New Wave." *Circus,* June 22, 1978.

Schwartz, Andy. "Patti Smith." *New York Rocker,* October 1980.

Scobie, W. I. "Mad for Each Other." *The Advocate,* June 9, 1983.

Selcraig, Bruce. "Reverend Wildmon's War on the Arts." *The New York Times Magazine,* September 2, 1990.

Selvin, Joel. "Patti Puts Her Fans to the Test." *San Francisco Chronicle,* July 28, 1979.

Shafter, Richard A. "Investing in Photos Spreads, but It Has Its Negative Aspects." *The Wall Street Journal,* July 7, 1977.

Simels, Steve. "Patti Smith." *Stereo Review,* August 1978.

———. "Patti Smith Has Not (Yet) Gone Disco." *Stereo Review,* July 1979.

Simson, Emily. "Portraits of a Lady." *ARTnews,* November 1983.

Sischy, Ingrid. "Sam Wagstaff's Silver." *HG,* January 1989.

Smith, Paul. "Bruce Weber at Robert Miller." *Art in America,* November 1986.

Smith, Roberta. "It May Be Good But Is It Art?" *The New York Times,* September 4, 1988.

———. Review of "Book of Photographs from the Collection of Sam Wagstaff." *Art in America,* September–October 1978.

Somer, Jack. "Gurus of the Visual Generation." *New York,* May 28, 1973.

Sozanski, Edward J. "Distinctive Artistry in Photographs." *Philadelphia Inquirer,* December 18, 1988.

Spina, James. "Patti Smith: Rock 'n' Roll Renegade." *Women's Wear Daily,* June 20, 1978.

Spritz, Kenneth. "Will Coney Island Go the Way of Fun City?" *The Village Voice,* July 18, 1974.

Squiers, Carol. "Mapplethorpe off the Wall." *Vanity Fair,* January 1975.

———. "Undressing the Issues." *The Village Voice,* April 5, 1983.

Squiers, Carol, Allan Ripp, and Stephen Koch. "Mapplethorpe." *American Photography,* January 1988.

Stambolian, George. "Sleaze." *New York Native,* February 15, 1982.

Stambolian, George, and Sam Hardison. "The Art and Politics of the Male Image." *Christopher Street,* March 1980.

Steinbach, Alice C. "Photography Comes Out of the Closet." *Baltimore Sun,* November 9, 1975.

Stevens, Mark. "Direct Male." *The New Republic,* September 26, 1988.

Szegedy-Maszak, Andrew. "A Distinctive Vision: The Classical Photography of Robert Mapplethorpe." *Archaeology,* January–February 1991.

Tamblyn, Christine. "Poses and Positions." *Artweek,* June 27, 1987.

Tavenner, John. "Safe Art." *New York Native,* October 7, 1985.

Taylor, Paul. "Mad Max's." *Fame,* May 1989.

Thompson, Mark. "Mapplethorpe." *The Advocate,* July 24, 1980.

Thornton, Gene. "Portraits Reflecting a Certain Sensibility." *The New York Times,* November 21, 1982.

———. "This Show Is a Walk Down Memory Lane." *The New York Times,* September 18, 1983.

———. "The Wagstaff Collection." *The New York Times,* July 2, 1978.

Tobias, Tobi. "Mixed Blessings." *New York,* February 17, 1986.

Tolchin, Martin. "Congress Passes Bill Curbing Art Financing." *The New York Times,* October 8, 1989.

Tompkins, Calvin. "Disco." *The New Yorker,* July 22, 1985.

Tosches, Nick. "Patti Smith, Straight, No Chaser." *Creem,* September 1978.

"Twelve on 20-by-24." *Boston Globe,* November 16, 1984.

Von Lehmden, Mark. "Patti Smith, CBGB." *Rolling Stone,* July 28, 1977.

Walker, Barry. "Subversive Classicism." *New York Native,* March 28, 1983.

Weaver, Mike. "Mapplethorpe's Human Geometry: A Whole Other Realm." *Aperture,* Winter 1985.

Weber, Nicholas Fox. "Silver Futures." *House & Garden,* March 1987.

Welch, Marguerite. "Mapplethorpe Garden: Manhattan 'Fleurs du Mal.' " *New Art Examiner,* January 1982.

Whelan, Richard. "Robert Mapplethorpe: Hard Sell, Slick Image." *Christopher Street,* June 1979.

White, Edmund. "The Irresponsible Art of Robert Mapplethorpe." *The Sentinel,* September 5, 1980.

Wilkerson, Isabel. "Cincinnati Jury Acquits Museum in Mapplethorpe Obscenity Case." *The New York Times,* October 6, 1990.

———. "Clashes at Obscenity Trial on What an Eye Really Sees." *The New York Times,* October 3, 1990.

———. "A Nervous Cincinnati Awaits Exhibit Today." *The New York Times,* April 7, 1990.

———. "Obscenity Jurors Were Pulled 2 Ways." *The New York Times,* October 10, 1990.

———. "Profiles from Cincinnati: Cutting Edge of Art Scrapes Deeply Held Beliefs." *The New York Times,* April 14, 1990.

———. "Test Case for Obscenity Standards Begins Today in an Ohio Courtroom." *The New York Times,* September 24, 1990.

Wilson, William. "Upstaged by Its Own Notoriety." *Los Angeles Times,* January 21, 1990.

Woodward, Richard B. "It's Art, but Is It Photography?" *The New York Times Magazine,* October 9, 1988.

Young, Charles M. "Patti Smith Catches Fire." *Rolling Stone,* July 27, 1978.

———. "Patti Smith Whirls into Hospital." *Rolling Stone,* February 10, 1977.

Zurlinden, Jeff. "Robert Mapplethorpe: Art on the Edge." *Outlines,* March 1989.

Acknowledgments

In six years of work on this book, I have been helped by many people who shared their thoughts and recollections of Robert Mapplethorpe with me. I'm particularly grateful to Patti Smith for her guidance and cooperation; Edward Maxey for his generous insights and help in organizing the picture section; and Michael Stout for allowing me to reproduce Mapplethorpe's art photographs in the book. Above all, I'm indebted to Robert Mapplethorpe for trusting me with his story.

My thanks to the following: John Abbott, Kathy Acker, Michael Alago, Russ Albright, Sam Alexander, Claude Alverson, Stanley Amos, Pierre Apraxine, Tom Armstrong, Steven M.L. Aronson, Susan Arthur, Martin Axon, Linda Bahr, Stanley Bard, Tom Baril, Jared Bark, Bob Barrett, James Bell, Richard Bernstein, Stan Bernstein, Marieluise Black, Leonard Bloom, Victor Bockris, William Burke, Jim Carroll, Bill Cassidy, Dorothy Cassidy, Jim Cassidy, John Cheim, Lydia Cheng, Lucinda Childs, Jim Clyne, David Cochrane, Bob Colacello, Diego Cortez, Charles Cowles, David Croland, Rosita and Violetta Cruz, Sandy Daley, Clarissa Dalrymple, Melody Danielson, Lynn Davis, Ingeborg Day, Edward de Celle, Loulou de La Falaise, Maxime de La Falaise, Joe Dolce, Suzanne Donaldson, Dovanna, Bill and Nancy Dugan, Dominick Dunne, George Dureau, Phillip Earnshaw, Kelly Edey, Linda Lee Egendorf, Allen Ellenzweig, Jim Elliott, Brian English, Betsy Evans, Miles Everett, Scott Facon, Gary Farmer, Pat Farre, Tom Farre, Agustin and Lia Fernandez, Danny Fields, Nigel Finch, Fred Folsom, Robert Fosdick, Jeffrey Fraenkel, Suzie Frankfurt, Andrew Freireich, Jane Friedman, Jack Fritscher, Julie Gallant, Philippe Garner, Henry Geldzahler, Monah Gettner, Marty Gibson, Robin Gibson, Barbara Gladstone, Fay Gold, Brad Gooch, Dotty Gray, Terry Gray, Sam Green, Dr. Jerome Groopman, Claudia Gropper, Andy Grundberg, Catherine Guinness, Agnes Gund, Maria Morris Hambourg, Janet Hamill, Sam Hardison, Reinaldo Herrera, Peter Hetzel, Susanne Hilberry, Charles Hill, Ron Hoffman, Bob Hogrefe, Anne Horton, Fredericka Hunter, Gérald Incandela, Mark Isaacson, Colta Ives, Bob Jacob, Barbara Jakobson, Tony Jannetti, Tim Jefferies, Harold Jones, Rob Jurka, Janet Kardon, Lenny Kaye, Anne Kennedy, Margaret Kennedy, Patrick Kennedy, Klaus Kertess, Alexandra Knaust, Stephen Koch, Herb Krohn, Allen Lanier, Gilles Larrain, Kay Larson, Marcus Leatherdale, Fran Lebowitz, Carol Judy Leslie, Bonnie Lester, Dimitri Levas, Gerard Levy, Ben Lifson, Judy Linn, Ann Livet, Jane Livingston, Fern Logan, Tom Logan, Simon Lowinsky, Harry Lunn, Lisa Lyon, Anne MacDonald, Peter MacGill, Bruce Mailman, Gerard Malanga, Harry Mapplethorpe, James Mapplethorpe, Joan Mapplethorpe, Helen Marden, Richard Marshall, Jim Maxey, Elaine Mayes, Boaz Mazor, Harry McCue, Howie Michels, Sylvia Miles, Caterine Milinaire, Bobby Miller, Robert Miller, Stan Mitchell, Ken Moody, Milton Moore, Mike Myers, Sandy Nairne, Marjorie Neikrug, Art Nelson, Nancy Nemeth, Guy Nevill, Jeremiah Newton, Nick and Ray, Andi Ostrowe, Rande Ouchi, David Palladini, Mary Palmer, Tom Peterman, Berry Perkins, Ken Perkins, Ellen Phelan, Lisa Phillips, Victor Pope, Ann Powell, Nicholas Quennell, Howard Read, Peter Reed, John Reinhold, Dan Renuss, John Richardson, George Rinhart, Lisa Rinzler, Nancy Mapplethorpe Rooney, Allen Rosenbaum, Howard Rosenman, Norman Rosenthal, Fernando Sanchez, Susan Sarandon, Francesco Scavullo, Peter Schjeldahl, Helmut Schmidt, Paul Schmidt, Susan Mapplethorpe Schneider, Peter Schub, Marylynn Celano Serrafin, Tennyson Shad, John Shea, Robert Sherman, Laurie Simmons, Ingrid Sischy, Jane Smith, Linda Smith, Todd Smith, Holly Solomon, Carol Squiers, Father George Stack, George Stambolian, Dr. Barbara Starrett, Carol Steen, Andrea Stillman, Amy Sullivan, Tina Summerlin, William Targ, Paul Taylor, Kenny Tisa, Jesse Turner, Veronica Vera, Arnon Vered, Jack Walls, Paul Walter, Shelley Wanger, Beth Gates Warren, Thomas Williams, Daniel Wolf, and Jack Woody.

I owe a large debt to my first editor, Susan Kamil, for nurturing both the book and me during the early years of the project. Her energy and enthusiasm never wavered, and I regret she couldn't have seen me to the end.

My agent, Kathy Robbins, deftly guided me through the twists and turns of the publishing business. She offered encouragement and expert counsel, and for that—and more—I am especially grateful. My thanks as well to Elizabeth Mackey for her sound advice and efficiency.

At Random House, I was lucky to meet Kate Medina, who assumed the editing responsibilities during my last year of writing. Her sensitivity and professionalism helped bring the book to the finish line. I'd also like to thank Ned Rosenthal, at Frankfurt, Garbus, Klein & Selz, for giving the manuscript a careful legal reading, and Vincent Virga for his skillful and creative picture editing.

A number of articles I wrote for *New York* in the 1980s helped inspire this book, and I'd like to thank Ed Kosner for giving me the confidence to tackle any subject. Peter Herbst was unfailingly generous with his time and advice, and I am grateful to him for being my editor and friend.

James Danziger deserves special thanks for introducing me to Robert Mapplethorpe, and for his thoughtful comments on the manuscript.

Writing about someone else's life invariably takes a toll on the writer's, and I'd like to thank my friends and support team. I am indebted to Dr. Clarice Kestenbaum for her wisdom and insight; Ira Resnick for being the funniest and most kind-hearted man in New York; and Jamie Delson for staging my first writing offensive and remaining a loyal friend.

Thanks as well to David Blum, Jennifer Delson, Glynnis O'Connor and Doug Stern, Elaine Spivak, and Dorothy Stern. Stephanie Fogel was a true friend and gifted listener. I regret that her own story ended too soon.

Thanks to my parents for years of love and care, and to my sisters and closest allies, Marise and Nancy, for making me realize it is not better to be an only child.

Last and most important, I am eternally grateful to my husband, Lee Stern, whose love, strength, and serenity have sustained me for over a decade.

Index